Real World Instructional Design

Katherine Cennamo
Virginia Tech

Debby Kalk
Cortex Learning

THOMSON
™
WADSWORTH

Australia • Canada • Mexico • Singapore • Spain
United Kingdom • United States

THOMSON

WADSWORTH

Publisher: *Vicki Knight*
Education Acquisitions Editor: *Dan Alpert*
Development Editor: *Tangelique Williams*
Assistant Editor: *Dan Moneypenny*
Editorial Assistant: *Erin Worley*
Technology Project Manager: *Barry Connolly*
Marketing Manager: *Dory Schaeffer*
Marketing Assistant: *Andrew Keay*
Advertising Project Manager: *Tami Strang*
Project Manager, Editorial Production: *Emily Smith*
Art Director: *Carolyn Deacy*

Print/Media Buyer: *Judy Inouye*
Permissions Editor: *Stephanie Lee*
Production Service: *Melanie Field, Strawberry Field Publishing*
Text Designer: *Kathleen Cunningham*
Copy Editor: *Tom Briggs*
Illustrator: *Shepherd, Inc.*
Compositor: *Shepherd, Inc.*
Cover Designer: *Ross Carron*
Cover Image: *EyeWire Images*
Text and Cover Printer: *Webcom*

Printed in Canada
1 2 3 4 5 6 7 08 07 06 05 04

For more information about our products, contact us at:
Thomson Learning Academic Resource Center
1-800-423-0563
For permission to use material from this text or product, submit a request online at
http://www.thomsonrights.com
Any additional questions about permissions can be submitted by email to thomsonrights@thomson.com

Library of Congress Control Number: 2004102456

ISBN 0-534-64267-5

Thomson Wadsworth
10 Davis Drive
Belmont, CA 94002–3098
USA

Asia
Thomson Learning
5 Shenton Way #01-01
UIC Building
Singapore 068808

Australia/New Zealand
Thomson Learning
102 Dodds Street
Southbank, Victoria 3006
Australia

Canada
Nelson
1120 Birchmount Road
Toronto, Ontario M1K 5G4
Canada

Europe/Middle East/Africa
Thomson Learning
High Holborn House
50/51 Bedford Row
London WC1R 4LR
United Kingdom

Latin America
Thomson Learning
Seneca, 53
Colonia Polanco
11560 Mexico D.F.
Mexico

Spain/Portugal
Paraninfo
Calle/Magallanes, 25
28015 Madrid, Spain

To Pat Smith, a master teacher and practitioner whose meticulous feedback made instructional designers out of us both.

Brief Contents

Contents

 # Foreword

Kent L. Gustafson

What do we really know about instructional design (ID)? Skeptics point out how little we know about how people learn and how to design effective instruction, while others point out how much more we know now than we did when instructional design was just emerging as a design methodology. Both sides are right! There is so much more to be learned, but we do possess some valuable guidance on designing instruction that Katherine Cennamo and Debby Kalk have captured in this very useful text.

Developments in learning theory and learner assessment, demands for more individualized learning, and new technologies for design and delivery, along with many other social and economic factors, are driving the future of the field. All this interest and excitement is bringing into the field many individuals from nontraditional backgrounds who have much to contribute. However, the risk is that these individuals will ignore or be unaware of the solid base of knowledge already available and upon which they can build, and instead reinvent it at great cost and time. This very readable and practical book by Cennamo and Kalk makes a valuable contribution to "spreading the word" to those unfamiliar with what is already known and how it can be intelligently applied. It contains a strong synthesis of the intellectual and practical sides of ID.

This book represents not only a basic resource for those just entering the field but also a reference and reminder to more experienced instructional designers. The extensive documentation and lists of additional readings provide a cornucopia of resources for further exploration of all major topics—for novices and experts alike. This book will serve as a valuable reference for years to come. The "extras," including examples, case studies, design aids, and electronic support, also ensure that this text will continue to be valuable to its readers.

The authors' spiral ID model is worthy of particular note. It captures the dynamic and evolving nature of the ID process while emphasizing that all of the components of the process are essential to its successful application. The model provides the necessary structure for teaching and learning about ID without reducing it to a mechanistic and purely technical process. All the richness and creativity of designers and other team members can be comfortably incorporated when following this model.

I agree wholeheartedly with the authors that this is an exciting time to be in the field of ID. The journey has just begun, there is much to be learned and applied, and the future promises to be exciting, challenging, and rewarding. Bon voyage!

Preface

There is a growing demand for skilled instructional designers. The demand is partly the result of increased implementation of computer-based learning systems that require sophisticated course development. In the corporate world, trainers and content experts are being asked to develop instructional materials, but many lack formal education and experience in instructional design. *Real World Instructional Design* is a basic instructional design textbook targeted at novices entering the field and professionals seeking to increase their knowledge and skills in this area.

As authors, we bring a complementary set of instructional design perspectives. For the past 10 years, one co-author has been involved in training instructional designers as a college professor; the other co-author presided over a nationally recognized e-learning company that created award-winning programs for corporate training, customer education, and secondary and college education. Drawing on our extensive experience designing instruction in multiple settings and our understanding of research and theory, we have created an introductory instructional design textbook that provides students with the basic skills and knowledge they need to succeed as practitioners.

Overview

Building from previous models and direct experiences, this textbook presents instructional design as an iterative, knowledge-building cycle that can be represented as a spiral with *five distinct phases*. Starting at the center of the spiral with the Define phase, and moving out through the Design, Demonstrate, Develop, and Deliver phases, we teach students to continuously question, communicate, collaborate, and refine. Running through the five phases are *five essential elements* that form the building blocks of systematically designed instruction: learner needs and characteristics, goals and objectives, instructional activities, assessments, and formative evaluation. As designers cycle through the stages of Define, Design, Demonstrate, Develop, and Deliver, they continually revisit these five foundation elements, revising their understanding as necessary, adding details, and building knowledge. The collaborative nature of instructional design practice is emphasized throughout. This focus on interpersonal skills acknowledges the reality that designers work on teams with co-workers, clients, subject matter experts, and representatives of the target audience.

The textbook begins with an introduction to this model. The next five chapters introduce students to the critical elements of instructional design. Students learn to conduct an audience analysis, consider needs, identify learning outcomes, develop assessments, design instructional activities, and do formative evaluations. Following an examination of these essential elements, students learn to work with other design team members collaboratively and to consider each of the design elements at varying levels of precision as they cycle through the stages of Define, Design, Demonstrate, Develop, and Deliver.

We incorporate current developments in the field in our treatment of the model. Along with traditional cognitive and behavioral methods, we present constructivist beliefs and instructional strategies as potential tools for instruction. We include rapid prototyping, scenario-based design methods, and other visioning tools throughout the recommended design and development sequence. Students can explore case studies and design artifacts that illustrate the development of e-learning and knowledge resources, as well as traditional instructional materials. Numerous complex examples derived from our experiences illuminate the concepts and processes of instructional design.

Whether the book is incorporated into a degree program, read for self-study, or used as a professional reference, our goal is to help instructional design students and professionals learn the skills they need to be successful practitioners. We've aimed for a book that's highly readable and useful, providing many illustrations, exercises, job aids, and examples. Our expectation is that practitioners will keep this book on their shelves as they move from academia into job settings.

Features

The following pedagogical features appear throughout the book:

- *Chapter overviews.* Each chapter begins with a "chapter map" that diagrams the relationship among the topics presented in the chapter, a list of learning outcomes, an orientation to where the chapter fits in the design process, and, when appropriate, a table of the tasks that should be performed in each phase relative to each essential element of design.

- *Voice of experience.* Throughout the text, brief scenarios, vignettes, and narrative case studies illustrate the complexities and iterative nature of instructional design.

- *Designers' toolkits.* Specific "how to" guides, checklists, and helpful hints are included throughout the text to support learners as they engage in the design process.

- *Examples, figures, and tables.* Numerous examples from actual projects show what and to whom various design and production documents need to communicate. They provide concrete models from which students can develop their own project materials. Figures and tables further illustrate and organize the concepts.

- *House analogy.* Each chapter features a recurring analogy linking the building of a house to the process of instructional design and compares phases and elements in instructional design and development to the process of designing and constructing a house.

- *Chapter summaries.* Each chapter concludes with a brief summary of the chapter contents.

- *Application activities.* Open-ended activities include the following recurring prompts, as well as unique exercises for each chapter. Reflective assignments encourage students to articulate, clarify, and reconsider their initial understandings. A comprehensive assignment continues from chapter to chapter, providing students with realistic and complex design tasks.

- *Ideas in Action.* Extensive examples that continue from chapter to chapter demonstrate the evolving nature of design projects.

- *Design aids.* Most chapters include design aids to support students in applying the chapter content. Design aids include forms, templates, and questionnaires.

Ancillary Web Site

The interactive components of the Web site extend and enhance the textbook experience and provide substantial support for the large number of instructors who teach the course online. Instructors and their students will find the following information on the Web site:

- Forms, checklists, and job aids that provide learners with a printable version of materials presented in the book. They can use these tools to complete their class projects and to design products in the workplace.

- Online versions of the application activities that students can complete and save, print, or send to the instructor.

- Text and audio case studies that present the actual "real world" experiences of various designers and clients. These provide depth and detail not possible in the context of the book, and model how to do design, and, possibly, how not to do design. The cases are organized by topic, for students to analyze online, through written assignments, and/or during class discussions.

- Testimonials from practicing instructional designers that provide realism as students explore possible career paths. In these testimonials, designers from educational, corporate, and other work contexts describe what they do and how they do it.

- Examples of multimedia products that illustrate how instructional designers meet actual instructional requirements using interactive technologies.
- Threaded discussion features that allow students and instructors to explore concepts together. For online courses, this feature can serve as an equivalent to classroom discussion.
- Resources that provide Web links to professional organizations, journals of interest, publishers in the area, shareware programs or trial versions of useful software, and other resources on specific and general topics of interest to instructional designers.

The Web site also includes material exclusively for instructors. An *Instructor's Guide* includes sample syllabi, schedules, suggested teaching strategies, and grading guides. A threaded discussion board for instructors provides a forum for discussing ideas and issues related to teaching instructional design.

Acknowledgements

In striving for readability, we've resisted the tendency to include many citations throughout the text, but this isn't to imply we haven't been influenced by other authors. We were taught to design instruction by Pat Smith, co-author of *Instructional Design* (Smith & Ragan, 1999), using the second edition of *The Systematic Design of Instruction* by Dick and Carey (1985). Throughout our professional practice, we've used a variety of instructional design textbooks as course texts and reference materials. Our ideas have been influenced by numerous conversations with colleagues, conference presentations, and journal articles. All these ideas have become part of how we design instruction in a way that is no longer distinguishable by source. We have provided references at the end of most chapters, and a list of resources for additional information at the end of the book, but we apologize if we have neglected to cite a particular source. We hope this approach provides a good balance between keeping the textbook readable and making it useful for finding additional information.

We gratefully acknowledge the direct contributions of the following individuals: Dr. Ireta Ekstrom, for her flexibility and willingness to test an earlier version of this text in her courses, and her instructional design students, for sharing their reactions and suggestions; the many graduate students at Virginia Tech who contributed in some way to documents and products used as examples; Pat Sinnott, Jim Bruno, Mack Thomas, Michael Sieben, Stephanie Johnson, Lisa Jordan, Martin Burke, and Cindy Yates, and the many other talented Cortex employees who, along with John Wilson and Chris Burr, created programs used as examples in this book and on the Web site; Miriam Larson, for compiling the extensive lists of additional readings that appear at the end of the book; the instructional designers who contributed cases to the Web site, including June Wilson, Julie Minors, Alan Buller, Gary Worobec, Marc Miller, Christine Fish, and Dee Seligman. Elota Patton and Mary S. Black, for reviewing early drafts; the reviewers who provided helpful comments at various points in the development of this manuscript, including Shelly Bibeau, Saint Paul College; J. Michael Blocher, Northern Arizona University; Robert E. Gillan, Northwestern State University; Teresa H. Delgadillo Harrison, Boise State University; Anne Hird, Bridgewater State College; Keith B. Hopper, Southern Polytechnic State University; Badrul H. Khan, George Washington University; Brenda Litchfield, University of South Alabama; Art A. Lichtenstein, University of Central Arkansas; Joanne Newcombe, Bridgewater State College; and Ryan Watkins, George Washington University. We also want to thank Herbert C. Kalk, Joan Ellis Lowrence, Michael Kalk, Terry Arzola, Brenda Fondren, and Cody Brady, for support and encouragement; and David Orshalick, for believing in the need for this book. A special thanks to our copy editor, Tom Briggs, for his unwavering patience and deft improvements to our text. Most importantly, we are grateful for the encouragement, steady guidance, and enthusiasm provided by our editor, Dan Alpert.

And finally, a heartfelt note of appreciation to our families—Stella Arzola, and Alice, Elliott, and Arthur Cennamo—for their continual support and tolerance.

⟳ To the Instructor[1]

Instructional design (ID) courses traditionally present students with the "tools" necessary to identify and solve instructional problems. In recent years, the practice of teaching instructional design by showing students how to carry out a set of technical and rational procedures using a few straightforward examples has been criticized by several authors. Experts in a domain possess more than knowledge of specific facts, concepts, and procedures (Collins, Brown, & Holum, 1991). They also possess heuristic strategies that include general techniques and "tricks of the trade," control strategies that direct the process of carrying out tasks, and learning strategies that guide them in obtaining new concepts, facts, and procedures. Research in the development of expertise suggests that these additional skills may develop in situations that involve solving complex, ill-defined problems under the guidance of someone with greater skills (Brown, Collins, & Duguid, 1989).

But students may leave school without ever having experienced the "complex and dynamic forces" (Rowland, Fixl, & Yung, 1992) that operate within an actual design environment. And even when students do gain "real world" experience during their education, they often can't generalize beyond their limited experiences to derive principles applicable to other instructional design efforts (Cennamo & Holmes, 2001; Quinn, 1994). Methods that have been suggested to involve students more extensively in the entire design and development enterprise include examining case studies and design artifacts, analyzing examples of expert work, working on real projects in the class, and participating in cognitive apprenticeships (Quinn, 1994, 1995; Rowland, 1993; Rowland et al., 1992; Tripp, 1994). We have incorporated each of these proposed methods into this textbook.

Case Studies

Each chapter includes narrative case studies, presented as short scenarios, examples in text, or extended incidents from design practice. Students also have the opportunity to analyze cases via the course Web site. These examples and case studies, all adapted from actual practice, illustrate a variety of situations so that students can learn to generalize their knowledge to multiple settings.

Analysis of Design Artifacts and Examples of Expert Work

Each chapter also includes design artifacts and examples of expert work. Short excerpts from design documents and data collection instruments illustrate the ideas presented in the chapters. Full-length design artifacts are provided at the end of each chapter and on the course Web site. These concrete examples of expert work and design artifacts contribute to a vicarious experience base that novice designers can draw on as they move into professional practice.

Class Work on Real Projects

Throughout the book, students are encouraged to work with a client to define, and subsequently solve, a real world instructional design problem. We recommend that initial experiences take place in a situated learning environment, where students can observe, implement, and evaluate their own design behaviors. As they develop their skills, they can progress to designing instructional materials independently. Students are encouraged to reflect on their own design decisions and articulate their thought processes. Through reading and responding to students' reflections, instructors are able to monitor their students' evolving skills as designers and provide additional modeling and coaching when needed.

Cognitive Apprenticeship

Although instructors are free to use this textbook in any way they desire, we have included several pedagogical features based on the Collins-Brown-Newman (1989) model of cognitive apprenticeship. The chapter application activities begin with an "orientation stage" in Chapter 1; followed by "situated learning" experiences involving coaching, modeling, reflection, and articulation in Chapters 2–6; and gradually move into an "exploration stage" in Chapters 7–11.

- Just as new employees begin their tenure with an orientation to the job, the introductory assignment in Chapter 1 begins with a general orientation to the "job" of instructional design. Through written reflections, students are encouraged to articulate their preconceived ideas about the instructional design process and to compare their descriptions with those verbalized by practicing instructional designers in interviews on the Web site that supports this book.

- Students then enter a training stage in which they gradually acquire the tools of the trade in a situated learning environment. As they complete the assignments in Chapters 2–6, they progress through two stages of skill development:

  - In the first stage, students define a class problem and build a shared vocabulary in order to articulate and reflect on the instructional design process. In the assignments at the end of the chapters, they are asked to summarize what they judge to be the key points and to consider how the content is meaningful in terms of their own experiences. After students summarize their individual conceptualizations of a specific design element, they are encouraged to engage in small- and whole-group discussions that require them to articulate, clarify, and perhaps reconsider their initial understandings.

  - In the second stage, instructors are encouraged to actively coach their students and model problem-solving processes as the whole class creates design specifications for an instructional module. During this stage, we suggest that the class members function as instructional design teams of four to five members. The instructor can serve as an instructional design manager, leading the design team meetings, checking on the progress of the working groups, and facilitating discussions. Through this group work, students can see that there often are several effective ways to accomplish any one design task. They become aware of multiple perspectives in tackling any given problem.

- The exploration phase of a cognitive apprenticeship involves pushing students into a mode of trying to solve problems on their own; encouraging them to try out different hypotheses, methods, and strategies; and then having them observe the effects. Following guided exploration of the tools of instructional design in Chapters 2–6, students are encouraged to design and develop a project for a real client in Chapters 7–11. As students submit their assignments, we suggest that they include reflective paragraphs that explain why they selected specific actions, how their ideas changed over time, and what they judge to be the next steps in the process. These activities allow instructors to witness students' evolving skills as designers. They also provide an opportunity for a written dialog about the process of instructional design between the design manager-as-coach (instructor) and the apprentice (student).

The ancillary Web site provides additional instructional support. The instructor's area includes sample syllabi, schedules, guidelines for using these activities in classrooms and online, and a threaded discussion board where instructors can exchange ideas and discuss issues relevant to teaching instructional design. Online versions of the application activities provide support for the large number of instructors who teach the course via the Web.

Please feel free to contact us through the course Web site with ideas and suggestions as to how we can enhance the course experience for you and your students. As you engage in the difficult but incredibly important task of preparing future instructional designers, we hope you find this textbook useful!

Note

[1]Adapted from "Teaching instructional design: An apprenticeship model," by P. A. Ertmer and K. S. Cennamo, 1995, *Performance Improvement Quarterly,* 8(4), 43–58. Copyright 1995 by the Learning Systems Institute. Adapted with permission of *Performance Improvement Quarterly.*

References

Brown, J. S., Collins, A., & Duguid, P. (1989). Situated cognition and the culture of learning. *Educational Researcher, 18*(1), 32–42.

Cennamo, K., & Holmes, G. (2001). Developing awareness of client relations through immersion in practice. *Educational Technology, 41*(6), 44–49.

Collins, A., Brown, J. S., & Holum, A. (1991). Cognitive apprenticeship: Making thinking visible. *American Educator, 15*(3), 38–46.

Collins, A., Brown, J. S., & Newman, S. E. (1989). Cognitive apprenticeship: Teaching the craft of reading, writing, and mathematics. In L. B. Resnick (Ed.), *Knowing, learning, and instruction: Essays in honor of Robert Glaser.* Hillsdale, NJ: Lawrence Erlbaum.

Quinn, J. (1994). Connecting education and practice in an instructional design graduate program. *Educational Technology Research and Development, 42*(3), 71–82.

Quinn, J. (1995). The education of instructional designers: Reflections on the Tripp paper. *Performance Improvement Quarterly, 8*(3), 111–117.

Rowland, G. (1993). Designing and instructional design. *Educational Technology Research and Development, 41*(1), 79–91.

Rowland, G., Fixl, A., & Yung, K.(1992). Educating the reflective designer. *Educational Technology, 32*(12), 36–44.

Rowland, G., Parra, M. L., & Basnet, K. (1994, July/August). Educating instructional designers: Different methods for different outcomes. *Educational Technology,* 5–11.

Tripp, S. D. (1994). How should instructional designers be educated? *Performance Improvement Quarterly, 7*(3), 116–126.

About the Authors

Katherine Cennamo has over 20 years of experience in the design and development of instructional materials in the corporate, educational, and nonprofit sectors. She has developed materials on topics ranging from the production of transmission parts for the automotive industry to common health concerns of the elderly. Diverse audiences have included K-12 teachers, university students, factory workers, and visitors to museum Web sites. For the past 12 years, she has been training instructional designers as a professor at Purdue University and Virginia Tech. She has a bachelor's degree in elementary education from Virginia Tech, a master's in educational media from the University of Arizona, and a Ph.D. in instructional technology from the University of Texas at Austin. As the author of more than 20 articles and book chapters, she is interested in the application of learning theories to the design and development of instructional materials.

Debby Kalk, principal of Cortex Learning, is a learning development specialist with more than 20 years of instructional experience. She serves as an instructional designer and e-learning project manager for corporate training and marketing, as well as for secondary, higher education, and workforce development applications. As CEO of a pioneering e-learning company, her clients have included Motorola, National Instruments, Thomson Learning, Harcourt, Delta Air Lines, McGraw-Hill, Pearson Learning, and Dell Computer. Her company's work has been recognized by competitions including InVision, the Cindys, Texas Interactive Media, New York Festivals, *ID* magazine, and ITVA. She speaks frequently on instructional design topics at conferences and has served on many professional boards. She has a BA in history, a BS in radio-television-film, and an MA in instructional technology, all from the University of Texas at Austin.

Chapter 1
Introduction to Instructional Design

Chapter Overview

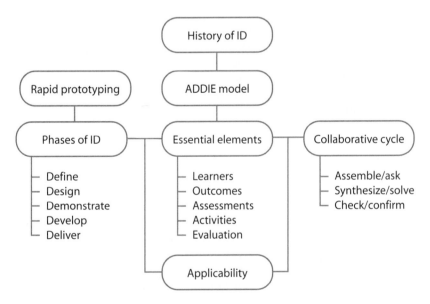

Learning Outcomes

- Briefly discuss the history and evolution of the field of instructional design.

- List the key elements of instructional design and describe their interactions.

- Describe the phases of the instructional design process.

- Describe the collaboration cycle of an instructional design project.

- Identify situations in which instructional design would not be appropriate.

- Identify how the spiral model in this text compares with the ADDIE and rapid prototyping instructional design models.

Orientation within the Design Process

This chapter introduces you to the field of instructional design and to the themes that pervade this book. We begin with a brief overview of the evolution of the field, the elements of instructional design, the phases of an instructional design project, and the need for collaboration and communication. These ideas are illustrated through a list of the activities and deliverables for each phase of design. We also describe common environments in which instructional designers are employed and provide an overview of following chapters.

Introduction to Instructional Design

Imagine that you have contracted with a builder to construct your ideal house. Will the builder simply start digging and nailing? Of course not! How will he know what you want in a house? Perhaps you'll show him photographs of houses you like. You may have a blueprint that you'd like modified to meet your specific needs. You may have enlisted an architect to custom-design your dream house. No matter how you initiate the building process, you begin with conversations and planning. You think through what you need, imagine what you'd like, and work with your architect and builder to explore how you can turn those needs and dreams into reality.

Instructional design involves a similar process. Your client wants a dream product—whether it's a Web site, a workbook, a video, or some other form of instruction. Often, your clients have no experience in creating these kinds of products. One client might propose revamping a university course for Web-based delivery but have no experience with similar courseware. Another client might propose creating a video to promote scientific inquiry but not know what it should include, how it should be designed or produced, or even if video is the best strategy for meeting her goals. As an instructional designer, you work with clients to translate their needs and desires into the design specifications that will yield a successful product.

Design is at the heart of many occupations: architectural design, industrial design, and graphic design, to name a few. Design implies that there is careful planning prior to development. The instructional design process is similar to processes used in other design disciplines. The planning tools are similar to those used in the software development process. The storyboards are much like the blueprints an architect produces to communicate specific instructions to the builder. A learner analysis has a lot in common with the work marketers do to identify a target audience. Like these other designers, instructional designers engage in systematic planning and produce specifications documents before "breaking ground."

Where instructional design diverges from these disciplines is in its focus on learning. But the emphasis on planning, evaluating, and revising is common to all design-based disciplines.

Instructional designers use processes and tools that comprise a soft technology developed and refined over almost 60 years. There are many instructional design models,[1] each presenting variations in the sequencing and individual steps in the process. But the premise of every one of the models is the same: They all begin by figuring out the end. In other words, what does the instruction need to accomplish? What will a successful learning outcome look like? Once the instructional designer has determined this, he or she is ready to go back and figure out how to achieve that goal.

As a discipline, instructional design has its roots in World War II.[2] Tens of thousands of soldiers and civilian workers had to be trained quickly. Many psychologists joined the military initiative to develop effective training materials. After the war, several of these psychologists, including Robert Gagné and Leslie Briggs, continued to work on improving the instructional process by considering instruction as a system. One development was programmed instruction. Mager's classic *Preparing Objectives for Programmed Instruction* (1962) and Bloom and colleagues' *Taxonomy of Educational Objectives* (1956) popularized the use of behavioral objectives. Criterion-referenced testing gained acceptance. In the mid-sixties, Gagné published one of the most influential books in the field of instructional design, *The Conditions of Learning* (1965). His ideas about various domains of learning outcomes, instructional conditions for different domains of learning outcomes, and specific events needed for instruction to be effective remain influential today. When the former Soviet Union launched the *Sputnik* satellite in the late 1950s, the U.S. government responded by providing extensive funding to develop math and science materials. Unfortunately, many of these materials were developed by subject matter experts, not teachers or instructional designers, and were not particularly effective. This highlighted the need for effective evaluation, so formative evaluation tools and methods were refined during this period.

These ideas, worked on throughout the 1950s and 1960s, were solidified in instructional design models during the 1970s. The influential models of Dick and Carey (1978), Gagné and Briggs (1974), Kemp (1971), and others were published during this period. Interest in instructional design flourished as the military, business, and industry embraced instructional design methods to enhance training. Instructional design models expanded to include needs assessment. The introduction of personal computers in the 1980s further spurred the demand for instructional design skills. These new computers were adopted in educational and training environments, spawning the need for instructional designers and developers who could create effective, replicable instruction for computer-based delivery. As computers became more powerful, they were able to support color, graphics, audio, and video, allowing the creation of multimedia-based instructional products. Developments in cognitive psychology began to supplement and supplant the behaviorist underpinnings of earlier instructional design strategies and practices.

During the 1990s, the field was challenged by several new developments (Gustafson & Branch, 1997a; Reiser, 2001). The performance technology movement led corporate training departments to address performance problems with noninstructional interventions such as online help and job restructuring. Individuals who ascribed to a constructivist view of learning harshly criticized the use of behavioral objectives and other methods and strategies that served as foundations for the field. Despite these challenges, the demand for instructional design and development skills continued to grow. Distance education became prevalent, and the use of the Internet for knowledge dissemination exploded. The Web created new demand for specialists with systematic design skills who also could understand users. Instructional designers, in response to corporate interest in electronic performance support systems, began to provide "just in time" information instead of training.

As a relatively new discipline that seeks to apply principles of educational psychology and communications theory to improve instruction, instructional design continues to evolve in response to new developments in instructional theory and practices. Several developments in particular are shaping the way instructional design is practiced today (Gustafson & Branch, 1997; Tessmer & Wedman, 1995):

1. Instructional design continues to be influenced by the collection of theories, beliefs, and practices that can be roughly classified as constructivism (see Chapter 4). Situated learning, cognitive apprenticeship, constructivism, postmodernism, and other concepts continue to push designers to refine instructional strategies and practices to incorporate new ideas from educational psychology.

2. The nature of instruction itself is changing. The public has free or low-cost access to extensive knowledge resources through the Web, CD-ROMs, television, and other technologies. Teachers and instructional designers often have no control over what learners access and when; learners are in control of their own knowledge acquisition.

3. The demand for "anytime, anywhere" instruction has fueled the need for instructional designers and developers who can quickly translate ideas into effective instructional materials. Designers are as likely to create online courses as individual classroom lessons and as likely to create organized knowledge banks and resources as specific "instruction."

4. The expense of creating e-learning and other multimedia materials requires that instructional solutions be imagined and tested early in the design and development process, before extensive time and resources are committed to a final design.

All of these developments have exciting implications for the practice of instructional design and development. Just as methods and techniques were enhanced in response to the need for formative evaluation during the 1960s, they are now being enhanced in response to the current need for rapid prototyping. And just as the field expanded to incorporate the ideas of cognitive psychology during the 1980s, it is now expanding to incorporate the ideas of constructivism. With technology playing an increasingly important role in all areas of education and training, the field must keep up with rapid changes in developing and delivering that instruction. As the practice of instructional design evolves to meet these changing needs, it continues to serve a responsive, influential, and valuable role in society.

It is an exciting time to be working in the field of instructional design and development. Researchers have begun to investigate what instructional designers actually do in practice (for example, Rowland, 1992). The studies conducted to date have determined that instructional designers seldom perform all the steps prescribed by classic models (Wedman & Tessmer, 1993; Wiener & Vazquez-Abad, 1995). As research studies continue to yield information about how professional instructional designers actually practice their craft, instructional design models should adapt to reflect that reality. Some authors have called for the development of a "practitioner's model" that reflects current practices (Tessmer & Wedman, 1990, 1995).

In this book, we present instructional design as we practice it and as we see our peers practicing it. Our model has evolved from the literature on instructional design and an extensive examination of design artifacts accumulated during more than 30 years of combined experience in academic and corporate settings. We stepped out of the trenches for a while to actively reflect on and debate about *what* we do as designers, *when* we perform specific tasks, and *why* we do these tasks. As we engaged

Table 1.1 The ADDIE model

Stage	Task	Deliverables
Analysis	Needs assessment Learner analysis Task, context, goal, and subordinate skill analysis	Problem statement Behavioral tasks Learner entry skills
Design	Framing of objectives Development of test items Instructional strategy	Objectives Tests Design specifications
Development	Media production Content development Management strategies	Storyboard Script Instructional materials
Implementation	Planning and management of instructional delivery	Teacher's guide and other support materials
Evaluation	Formative evaluation Summative evaluation	Recommendations Project report

SOURCE: Based on Lohr (2003) and Seels and Glasgow (1998).

in active reflection and analysis, we attempted to incorporate emerging ideas from the literature. The resulting model is consistent with literature (Gustafson & Branch, 1997; Tessmer & Wedman, 1995) that calls for instructional design models to represent four things:

1. The concurrent nature of instructional design, whereby multiple tasks may be performed simultaneously rather than sequentially.

2. A layered approach that takes the design context into account.

3. Holistic processes, whereby designers constantly seek to align key components.

4. Early synthesis processes, whereby imagining solutions serves to further develop an understanding of the problem.

Like many instructional designers, we were trained to use classic instructional design models. But we've found that, in practice, instructional design is not merely about following a model. It's about using a systematic, collaborative planning process to convert ideas into effective instructional products. Three key ideas permeate this book and our view of instructional design:

1. Design involves planning around critical issues (represented as *five elements* of design).

2. Design is an iterative knowledge-building cycle (represented as *five phases* of design).

3. Design is a collaborative activity among individuals who offer differing perspectives and expertise (represented as the *ASC cycle*).

In this chapter, we briefly introduce these three ideas.

Critical Issues: The Elements of Instructional Design

Almost all classic instructional design models are a variation of the **ADDIE model**, which stands for *A*nalysis, *D*esign, *D*evelopment, *I*mplementation, and *E*valuation (see Table 1.1). As you'll notice in Table 1.1, the Analysis stage of the ADDIE model includes needs assessment, identification of the goal, and learner, task, context, goal, and subordinate skill analysis; the Design stage includes the development of objectives, test items, and an instructional strategy; the Development stage includes preparation of instructional materials; Implementation includes activities in support of the delivery of instruction; and Evaluation includes formative and summative evaluations. Although classic models such as ADDIE are presented in a linear sequence, instructional design is rarely practiced that way (see, for example, Gustafson & Branch, 2002; Rowland, 1992; Tessmer & Wedman, 1990).

Expert designers often use a mental "template" to provide a framework for collecting the information necessary to perform these tasks. As they collect information throughout the design process, they fill in the "slots" in their mental template (Rowland, 1992, 1993). Throughout the instructional design process, designers must consider key factors that impact the success of the instruction. These factors, or elements, are the component parts of instructional design and can be thought of as a set of questions (Rowland, 1992). The answers to

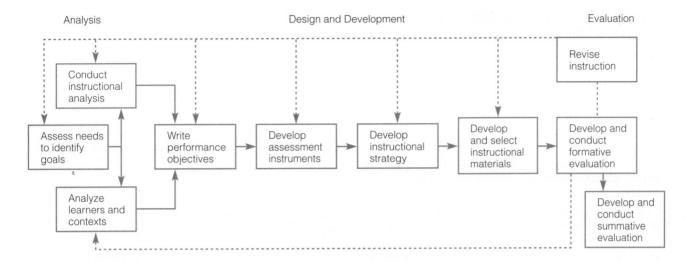

Figure 1.1 *Dick, Carey, and Carey model.* This model has been modified to illustrate the major stages in instructional design.

SOURCE: From Walter Dick, Lou Carey, James O. Carey, *The Systematic Design of Education,* 5th ed. (Boston, MA: Allyn and Bacon, 2001). Copyright © 2001 by Pearson Education. Adapted by permission of the publisher.

these critical questions guide the instructional design and development process:

- What are the learners' information needs, prior experiences, beliefs, and values relative to the topic of instruction? Instructional decisions should be based on what we know about the *learners'* characteristics and informational needs.

- What changes in thinking or performance do we want to occur? How will we know if these changes have occurred? How will we provide opportunities for learners to engage in activities that may stimulate changes in thinking or performance? The designer examines these questions, determining the *outcomes, assessments,* and *activities* of the instructional intervention, and recognizing that to be effective instruction requires alignment among the outcomes, goals, assessments, and activities.

- How do learners respond to the materials? Are they effective? Instruction should be tested with a group of learners prior to distribution and modified based on the results of a pilot test or formative *evaluation.*

These three areas of concern parallel the stages of Analysis, Design and Development, and Evaluation that are common to most instructional design models (Gustafson & Branch, 1997). (For an example of one popular model, see Figure 1.1.) Where traditional instructional design models include discrete stages for Analysis, Design, Development, and Evaluation activities, we find that most projects do not unfold in a linear fashion. Instead, instructional designers refine their understanding of learners, outcomes, assessments, activities, and evaluation throughout the design process.

The relationship among these essential elements of instructional design can be illustrated as an equilateral triangle (see Figure 1.2). Outcomes, Activities, and Assessments are placed in each of the three corners to illustrate that they must be in balance, or alignment, for the instruction to be effective. These elements support the key element, the Learners, which is why Learners are at the center of the triangle. Evaluation is wrapped around the others elements in the triangle. Throughout the instructional design and development process, formal and

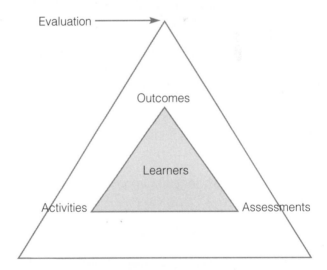

Figure 1.2 *Essential triangle of instructional design.* The elements of Outcomes, Activities, and Assessment form an equilateral triangle with the Learner in the center. Evaluation wraps around all of the elements.

informal Evaluation provides feedback on the program's effectiveness and helps the designer determine what, if any, adjustments are necessary.

These five elements interact to create systematically designed instruction. A **system** is a "set of interrelated parts, all of which work together toward a defined goal" (Dick, Carey, & Carey, 1996, p. 3). As a set of interrelated parts working toward a common goal, the outcomes, assessments, and activities all interact to fulfill the needs of the learners. Learners provide the input to the instructional system; the nature of the input affects the components of the system. For example, if you are creating a lesson on the Maya for second-grade students, your outcomes, assessments, and instructional activities will be different than if the material is aimed at college students. Instructional design systems, as is true of all systems, have built-in feedback loops. Within an instructional design system, evaluations determine whether it is working as intended. By pilot testing the program with learners, you verify that the program will deliver effective instruction to the learners. If a subsequent evaluation indicates that the system is no longer meeting the needs of learners, then, as with any system, it is adjusted until, once again, the instruction meets the goals.

Most traditional instructional design models require that you determine needs before objectives, objectives before assessments, and assessments before instructional strategies. That's a fine tactic, but you can actually start at any place on the essential triangle—you simply have to ensure that all parts are in alignment. Sometimes, your client or team will have some components in place when you join the project. For example, your client may have an assessment test that's required for certification to operate a piece of equipment in a manufacturing facility. In this case, the goal is to train employees so that they have the knowledge and skills to pass the assessment and use the equipment. You'll start with the assessment but will complete work on the other elements before delivering the training program. You can develop the objectives from the assessment and then develop the activities from them. Regardless of where you start on the triangle, you have to complete work on each of the elements, and all five must eventually be in alignment.

Knowledge-Building Cycles: The Phases of Instructional Design

Unlike the crisply delineated, step-by-step instructions that you typically find in cookbooks or owner's manuals, instructional design resists tidy, easily replicated solutions. Each instructional design project, by definition, involves creating new work. You can't follow the same instructions in the same way each time and get equally positive results. Instructional design requires problem-solving skills (Rowland, 1993). As you work on a project, you collect in-

formation and make tentative hypotheses about solutions. You build your understanding of learners, goals, delivery environments, and the contexts in which skills will be applied. At some point, you decide that there's nothing more to add, either because experts and resources have yielded all the information that's needed or because of time or budget constraints. Throughout the process, you make tentative decisions based on the information available at that time; develop design documents and other products; present them to the client, subject matter expert, or learners for feedback; and then revise them based on that feedback.

In this book, we've divided this knowledge-building cycle into five phases of instructional design: Define, Design, Demonstrate, Develop, and Deliver (see Figure 1.3). This model merges the elements of traditional instructional design models with the iterative cycles found in rapid prototyping models.

We and all practicing designers are indebted to those who dedicated their professional lives to developing those earlier, classic instructional design models, even as we acknowledge that the practice has evolved. In an article discussing the development of a performance support system, Gustafson (2000) called for a blending of traditional instructional design models and rapid prototyping models. The **rapid prototyping model,** as described by Dorsey, Goodrum, and Schwen (1997), emphasizes collaboration with "end users" to create a series of progressively more developed prototypes, from low-fidelity paper sketches to high-fidelity working models. Gustafson went on to say that "interestingly, this blending of approaches is what has been found in how much instructional design is

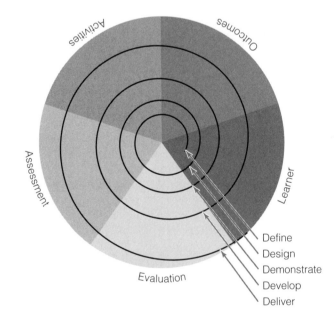

Figure 1.3 *Five phases of instructional design.* In this spiral model, the designer begins in the center, the Define phase, and moves out through the phases, acquiring a deeper understanding of each element in each phase.

actually practiced, although it is not how practitioners are taught or how the process is typically described in the literature"(Gustafson, 2000, p. 43).

We believe that this blended approach, represented in our spiral model, is appropriate for all instructional design projects. Like rapid prototyping models (Dorsey, Goodrum, & Schwen, 1997), our spiral model calls for designers to proceed through a series of steps that lead to progressively more complete versions of the product (see Table 1.2). The end users with whom designers collaborate to create a learning system should encompass clients, subject matter experts (SMEs), team members, and instructors, as well as learners. As designers move through the phases of Define, Design, Demonstrate, Develop, and Deliver, all of these stakeholders should be involved in the ongoing conceptualization and testing of the product. As designers collaborate with those who have an interest in the product, they progressively refine the essential elements of systematically designed instruction.

As in the rapid prototyping process (Dorsey, Goodrum, & Schwen, 1997), we recommend that you move in iterative cycles from a vaguely defined vision to a concrete product of proven effectiveness. Into each phase of design, we incorporate the essential elements of systematically designed instruction: learners' needs and characteristics, desired learning outcomes, assessments, instructional activities, and evaluation. As the designer cycles through the phases of Define, Design, Demonstrate, Develop, and Deliver, he or she revisits each of the essential elements of instructional design.

In the **Define phase**, you begin to determine the project scope, outcomes, schedule, and deliverables:

- Identify learners' characteristics and needs.
- Specify overall outcomes.
- Establish potential benchmarks of success (assessments).
- Determine the product.
- Plan a strategy for determining the program's effectiveness (evaluation).

This stage results in a project proposal.

The **Design phase** involves the major planning effort:

- Confirm and fully define instructional needs and learner characteristics.
- Clarify outcomes and identify subskills.
- Convert benchmarks to an assessment plan.
- Identify instructional strategies and implications for activities.
- Determine the general scope and sequence of content.
- Plan for acquiring all content.
- Plan for prototype testing and formative evaluation.

This stage results in instructional design documents.

In the **Demonstrate phase**, you continue to develop design specifications and ensure quality as the preliminary media production begins:

- Monitor development to ensure that materials are appropriate for learners' characteristics and needs.
- Ensure that activities are appropriate for the intended learning outcomes.
- Ensure that assessments are included as planned.
- Ensure that materials match the instructional strategy as designed.
- Develop and test a prototype with a few learners to get feedback on the prototype prior to large-scale development.
- Make changes to the design based on the testing or evaluation.

This stage results in detailed production documents such as storyboards and templates, and a prototype consisting of a "slice" of the instructional materials.

As the team moves into the **Develop phase**, you continue to serve as an advocate for the learner:

- Work with team members to ensure that materials are appropriate for the audience characteristics and needs.
- Make sure activities are appropriate for the intended learning outcomes.
- Ensure that assessments are included as planned.
- Ensure that materials match the instructional strategy as designed.
- Continue to evaluate materials until acceptable, revising as needed.

This phase results in a complete set of instructional materials.

Finally, you reach the **Deliver phase**, when you deliver the materials to your client and make recommendations for future development. When you present the product to your client you also:

- Provide source materials, documentation, users' guides, licenses, release forms, and any other materials that support the product.
- Provide client training if requested.
- Conduct a postproject review to determine whether the team worked as effectively as possible, materials were appropriate for the learners, learning objectives and assessments were clear and appropriate for the materials, and materials were implemented as planned.
- Determine whether to conduct additional evaluations or a field trial with large numbers of learners.

This phase results in the successful conclusion of this instructional design project—and, we hope, the beginning

Table 1.2 Comparison of rapid prototyping model with spiral model

Rapid prototyping model	Spiral model
Level 1: Create a vision	**Define**
• Briefly describe problem as currently understood. • Briefly describe users' requirements based on problem understanding. • Identify resources for and constraints on project. • Estimate scope and complexity. • Brainstorm solution ideas. • For each solution, estimate impact to organization and individuals including cost and amount of change. • Prioritize solution visions for next level of prototyping.	• Develop initial understanding of instructional problem or opportunity, project goals, audience description, delivery environment, and project timeline. • Brainstorm potential solutions. • Write project proposal that describes initial understanding of instructional problem or opportunity, goals, audience, product, timeline, costs, assumptions, and risks to completion. • Present project proposal to client for feedback and revision of concepts.
Level 2: Explore with conceptual prototypes	**Design**
• Use low-fidelity tools to create idea sketches. • Show/demonstrate existing products to illustrate vision. • Use conceptual prototypes as catalyst to elicit new ideas, test understanding of problem and user needs, and compare alternative solutions. • Brainstorm new solution ideas and/or make real-time modifications. • Estimate impact of solutions. • Prioritize solution visions for next level of prototyping.	• Meet with SME to define outcomes and assessments. • Demonstrate examples and/or mock-ups. • Create possible product scenarios. • Write design document that includes goals, delivery environment, audience definition, outcomes, assessment strategies, content organization and sources, instructional strategies, and evaluation plans. • Present design documents to client representatives for review and revision.
Level 3: Experiment with hands-on mock-up prototypes	**Demonstrate**
• Create alternative mock-ups that appear to work. • Conduct hands-on sessions in lab with users trying out prototypes. • Implement modifications of mock-ups for repeated user tryouts. • Give mock-ups to users to "play" with but not to incorporate. • Brainstorm new solution ideas and/or modifications to existing ones. • Estimate the impact of solutions. • Prioritize solution visions for next level of prototyping.	• Develop "paper prototypes" such as treatments and storyboards. • Develop mock-ups/prototypes with limited functionality and content to further refine ideas. • Develop production documents such as template guides, requirement specs, and media assets for proof-of-concept prototype. • Conduct on-going review of paper prototypes, mock-ups, and production documents, and incorporate suggested revisions.
Level 4: Pilot testing with working prototypes	**Demonstrate**
• Construct high-fidelity prototypes, employing materials to be used in formal implementation. • Conduct observations and evaluative sessions with users during and after use of prototypes. • Brainstorm new solution ideas and/or modifications to existing ones. • Modify prototype according to feedback results.	• Develop proof-of-concept prototype of "slice" of product. • Conduct user tryouts of prototype. • Modify design as needed based on user tryouts. • Develop production documents such as template guides, requirement specs, and media assets for remaining materials.
Level 5: Evolutionary development	**Develop**
• Limit population initially served. • Let users determine when change is necessary. • Proactively seek user feedback on regular basis. • Modify prototype according to feedback.	• Conduct small-group evaluations and/or field trials of materials. • Modify materials if evaluations indicate need. **Deliver** • Continue to collect feedback from users. • Begin redevelopment cycle when ongoing evaluations indicate materials are no longer effective.

SOURCE: Column 1 from "Rapid Collaborative Prototyping as an Instructional Development Paradigm," by L. T. Dorsey, D. A., Goodrum, and T. M. Schwen, in C. R. Dills and A. J. Romiszowski (eds.), *Instructional Development Paradigms* (Englewood Cliffs, NJ: Educational Technology Publications). Copyright © 1997 by Educational Technology Publications. Adapted with permission.

of a long and fruitful relationship with your client and design team.

During each phase, you visit each "element" of design, spiraling back and adding details as information becomes apparent or relevant. As you revisit the same questions, at different times, for different purposes, you build on ideas generated in previous phases in iterative, knowledge-building cycles (Rowland, 1992). As in Tessmer and Wedman's layers-of-necessity instructional design model, phases "are not distinguished by the type of task *per se,* but by the level of complexity associated with the tasks in that layer" (Tessmer & Wedman, 1990, p. 81):

> *While [traditional] models may have iterative features that allow for a reconsideration of earlier design activity outputs, they emphasize closure of each component in the process to serve as input to the next component. . . . A layered approach assumes that components of the ID process will be repeated to a greater degree of precision and sophistication in subsequent layers of the process. This repetition is not for the purpose of revising earlier components (as iterative models suppose) . . . but of adding onto the work that was done earlier.*
> *(Tessmer & Wedman, 1990, p. 80)*

You don't revisit a decision in order to stall progress; on the contrary, you revisit a decision in order to move onward. In the instructional design process, you often have to make decisions quickly, before all the relevant factors are known. You generate hypotheses and make "best guess" decisions in order to move forward, then confirm or revise those decisions as your understanding grows. Think in terms of a spiral: In the initial phase, your understanding of the material is minimal, like the tight inner coils of the spiral. As you move through subsequent phases, you often revisit the same issues, but you bring greater understanding each time, moving into outer layers of the spiral.

Design as Collaborative Practice

Instructional designers must create instruction *with* as well as *for* others. At a minimum, a project is likely to involve a client, an SME, and media production specialists, in addition to the instructional designer. In some situations, one individual may play several of these roles. For example, if you are developing a Web-based course for a university professor, your client may also be the SME. On the same project, you may serve as both the instructional designer and the media producer. On the contrary, your team might include graphic designers, programmers, video and audio producers, an evaluator, and a project manager. You may need to interact with members of the target audience or other individuals who are familiar with the learners' needs and characteristics.

Various team members come from different professional cultures, each with his or her own set of

---

Training Instructional Designers

by Katherine Cennamo

I have been a practicing instructional designer for more than 20 years. For the past 10 years, I've been involved in training instructional designers in my role as a college professor. But recently, I had a unique experience for me: I was the client—and what a shock it was! In the role of client, I became aware of how little formal preparation our students receive in the interpersonal aspects of designing instruction. I realized that instructional design books and models emphasize the tasks the designer performs, with little regard for how to interact with the client. Some students intuitively understand how to interact with clients. Some learn through the school of hard knocks. Others never learn, constantly complaining about difficult clients. Thinking back to research I had conducted and literature I had read, I realized that my experience was not unusual. Several authors have called for more effective preparation of instructional designers.[3] Few academic programs adequately prepare students for their interactions with clients.

To enhance the education of instructional designers, my colleagues and I developed a course in which students worked on "real world" projects under the guidance of course instructors. The students clearly were frustrated as they tried to apply skills in client interactions, skills that are not addressed by typical coursework in instructional technology. Most students assumed that the problems they had were *unique to that particular client.* Semester after semester, working with different clients, under the direction of different faculty, students bemoaned their "difficult" clients. But from our perspective as faculty members with extensive experience in design and development, our interactions with the clients were not atypical.

Supervising Instructional Designers

by Debby Kalk

As the owner of an e-learning development company, I've been hiring instructional designers for more than 10 years, most of them graduates from the country's most highly regarded programs. Most of these new designers arrived well equipped to perform tasks such as writing objectives and correlating them to assessments. But they were stumped by SMEs who never seemed to provide the right information or by clients who reviewed and revised endlessly. After many hours of one-on-one coaching and training, I started collecting my thoughts on paper. Here are some thoughts:

- Instructional development is a team sport—you don't work in a vacuum; you work with clients, SMEs, team members, and learners.
- Instructional design is really difficult! As a designer, you start with a blank page and have to fill it in. Other team members use and react to materials you generate, such as storyboards.

- Communication takes work. You want to work proactively to keep everyone aware of what you are doing, to get their feedback, and to incorporate it in your work. This gives them validation for their contributions. Make your communications clear, brief, and timely. Many difficulties with clients and team members can be avoided through strong communication.
- Comments and criticism are inevitable—don't take it personally. When you've poured your heart and soul into a deliverable, it's hard to hear criticism. Some criticism will seem personal even if that wasn't the intent. You need to develop a thick skin and look at the content of the feedback. Keep your focus on the objective and ignore the subjective. Sometimes, reviewers don't have enough experience to articulate what's bothering them. Help your reviewers by educating them about your needs for and expectations of them.

expectations, vocabulary, timelines, rewards, and consequences. Expert instructional designers have learned to expect these conflicts of culture and techniques, and they know how to overcome barriers to progress. They also have learned how and when to communicate with team members to allow them to be a part of the collaborative problem solving that is a key component in the instructional design process.

Just as learners come to an instructional experience with understandings, beliefs, and values shaped by their prior experiences, members of the instructional design team begin the process of designing instruction with their own sets of understandings, values, and beliefs. The instructional design process should involve the sharing of "cultural knowledge" possessed by the designer, client, learners, and other members of the project team. As you move through the various phases in the instructional design process, considering each of the essential elements of design, keep the ASC cycle in mind:

- *Assemble* information and *Ask* questions.
- *Synthesize* information and *Solve* problems.
- *Check* your understanding and *Confirm* work.

(See Figure 1.4.)

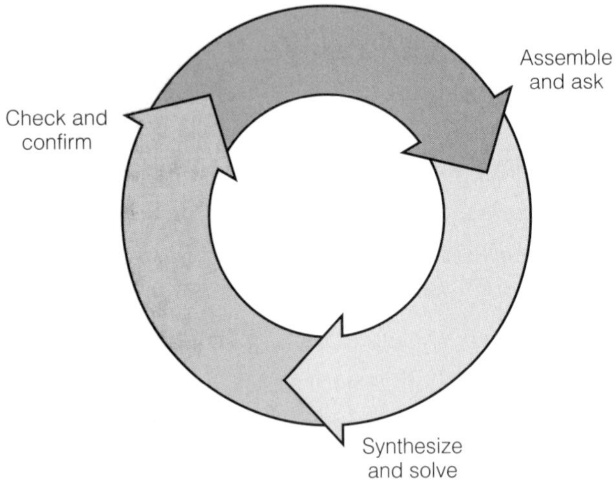

Figure 1.4 *Collaborative ASC cycle.* Throughout the instructional design process, you Assemble information and Ask questions, Synthesize material and Solve problems, Check your understanding and Confirm your work.

In the Define phase, you:

- *Assemble* information from communications with clients, including Request for Proposal, Request for Information, or Request for Quote.
- Generate tentative *solutions* and *synthesize* them in the project proposal.
- *Check* the validity of proposed solutions with clients, as presented in the project proposal.
- Repeat this cycle until the project proposal is approved.

In the Design phase, you:

- *Assemble* information on learner characteristics, instructional needs, content, intended outcomes, and delivery method from communications with clients, SMEs, learners, and the project team.
- Generate tentative *solutions* and *synthesize* them in the design documents.
- *Check* the validity of your proposed solutions as you review design documents with clients, SMEs, and the project team.
- Repeat this cycle until the design documents are approved.

In the Demonstrate phase, you:

- *Assemble* content from SMEs and media assets from available sources.
- *Synthesize* information into production documents, and prototypes.
- *Check* the validity of production specifications and various prototypes with clients, SMEs, the project team, and learners.
- Repeat this cycle until an acceptable prototype is approved.

In the Develop phase, you:

- *Assemble* the final set of production specifications and media assets.
- *Synthesize* the various parts into a complete set of instructional materials.
- *Check* the effectiveness and efficiency of the complete set of materials with learners.
- Repeat this cycle until instructional materials are acceptable to learners and clients.

And in the Deliver phase, you:

- *Assemble* project documentation and recommendations for the next version.
- *Synthesize* information into a project report and guidelines for use.
- Present materials to clients for final *confirmation* and approval.

Throughout the entire instructional design process, you collaborate with a variety of "stakeholders," or individuals who have a vested interest in the finished product. Stakeholders include learners, clients who fund the product, SMEs, production team members, and instructors who may eventually use the materials. The collaborative ASC cycle[4] ensures that you constantly seek information from others in order to design, develop, and revise the materials. Getting feedback on your instructional decisions from these multiple stakeholders enhances the product that results from the design process.

Applicability of Model and Processes

As an instructional designer, you may be employed in a variety of settings. The most common environments in which designers work include educational institutions, corporations and organizations, and companies that specialize in design and development.

Educational institutions have a primary responsibility to develop and deliver instruction, but many also create instructional products and services to share with or sell to other schools and individual students. With the current emphasis on distance learning and distributed education, institutes of higher learning often employ instructional designers in faculty support roles to convert courses offered on-campus to a form suitable for distance delivery. Book and software publishing companies, government agencies, and regional educational laboratories also create instructional materials that support educational institutions.

Corporations and organizations that produce instructional materials do so for a variety of reasons such as to train staff to perform their jobs or enhance their job skills, to train customers to use products, or to create instructional products that the company will sell. A company might even do all these things, like the publisher of this textbook. It is worth noting that many corporations are shifting the focus of their training departments to encompass performance improvement as well as training. An expert in performance improvement, often called a "performance technologist," examines multiple facets of an organization to identify opportunities for improvement. By focusing on improving the "bottom line," the performance expert conducts extensive analysis to determine barriers to maximum human performance within the organization. He or she examines the potential causes of those barriers and develops viable solutions. Solutions might involve restructuring organizations, revising job descriptions, physically altering work spaces, creating performance support or job aides, or training employees. The design and development of instructional solutions will be addressed in this book.

Table 1.3 Instructional designer's roles in various work settings

Work setting	Delivered by others	Delivered by self
Educational institutions	Designers for faculty support services	Teachers
Corporations and organizations	Designers within staff development, marketing, and product support departments	Trainers
Independent design and development companies	Instructional designers of software and training	Consultants or trainers

In addition to corporations, many organizations in the public and nonprofit sectors produce instructional materials. These organizations include hospitals, government agencies, religious institutions, associations, and social service agencies. Patient education, certification and licensing programs, and defensive driving programs are all examples of instructional programs developed by organizations for specific constituencies. The military services also have enormous and critical training requirements that have been the impetus for much of the innovation in instructional technology since World War II.

Large companies and organizations may have instructional designers on staff, but in smaller institutions, it might not be feasible to employ a dedicated team of designers and developers. Many companies and organizations choose to outsource projects to an independent company or to individual freelancers. Outsourcing complex design and development projects to external vendors helps these institutions control their costs.

For each project in each of these sectors, either a team or an individual has to think through the project's requirements in order to design and develop it. In each of these settings, the instruction can be developed to be delivered by the instructional designer or by other people or products (see Table 1.3). In an educational setting, teachers design and deliver their own instruction. In corporations and government agencies, trainers may design and deliver their own instruction. Although teachers and trainers should practice a form of instructional design as they prepare materials for their courses, the limited audience for their products often doesn't warrant full-scale design and development efforts. However, teachers and trainers should engage in a limited form of instructional design. Teachers often follow prescribed curriculums; trainers often use prepared materials to deliver their training. These materials, of course, have been designed and developed by others.

Even when instruction is designed and delivered by the same person, as is often the case with teachers and trainers, systematically designed instruction is still instruction that meets three criteria:

1. Reflects an alignment among the outcomes, activities, and assessments of instruction.
2. Has been designed with the characteristics and needs of the learners in mind.

3. Undergoes continuous evaluation and revision based on the learners' responses to the instruction.

The essential elements of instructional design—learners, outcomes, assessments, activities, and evaluation—reflect factors of concern to *all* instructional design efforts. They should be of concern to teachers designing materials for use in their own classroom and to designers employed by software development companies. These are the essential elements of systematically designed instruction in any situation.

The phases of instructional design (Define, Design, Demonstrate, Develop, and Deliver) and the ASC cycle (Assemble/Ask, Synthesize/Solve, and Check/Confirm) work differently when you are designing instruction you will deliver. As a teacher or trainer, you are your own client, though you'll probably find it helpful to review ideas with colleagues whenever possible. Table 1.4 outlines how the instructional design model presented in this book can be applied in situations in which the designer also delivers the instruction. For teachers, it may be years between phases such as Demonstrate, Develop, and Deliver, but teachers and trainers still go through these phases in designing and developing instruction. Instead of working on one project for months, teachers and trainers may work on many projects over several years.

So when do you engage in formal systematic instructional design? Full-scale, systematic instructional design and development efforts are in order in at least four situations:

1. When the content is stable enough to warrant the time and costs.
2. When the potential audience is large enough to warrant the time and costs.
3. When communication among a team of designers and developers is required.
4. When it is important to make sure that the instruction works before it's used.

Imagine you've been asked to design a CD-ROM to teach digital video skills. Consider the skills needed to develop digital video materials. Certain information, such as principles of lighting and visual composition skills, is stable and doesn't depend on the equipment or software used

Table 1.4 Model as applied by teachers and trainers

Define	• Begin with awareness of need or opportunity and set of learners in mind. *Assemble* resources and come up with tentative *solutions* appropriate to instructional situation. • Consider various outcomes, assessments, and activities to meet needs and characteristics of learners. • Consider costs, time, and potential benefits—personal cost-benefit analysis, or form of "*checking*" ideas. • Perhaps discuss ideas with colleagues, even if designing instruction for your own classroom.
Design	• *Assemble* additional content information such as learners' knowledge of topic, their preferences, and learning environment. • Begin to *synthesize* ideas into instructional plan. • Present ideas to others for discussion. • *Check* instruction yourself: Are outcomes, assessments, and activities in alignment? Will instruction meet needs of learners? Is it appropriate based on your knowledge of learners' characteristics?
Demonstrate	• Move from tentative ideas to limited product to use with learners in demonstration phase. • *Assemble* additional resources and convert ideas to form usable by learners. • Develop draft materials *(synthesis)* and try them with learners *(checking)*. • Refine ideas before committing extensive time and resources to full-scale development.
Develop	• Make modifications based on learners' responses. • *Assemble* learners' responses—what they understood, what they didn't—and develop improved instructional *solution*. • Continue trying modified instruction with learners until confirming as best way to convey content.
Deliver	• Deem instruction as effective as possible, and adopt in its finished state. • Constantly collect data on effectiveness of instruction—observe students, monitor performance on assessments, and ask for opinions of instruction. • Engage in process all over again if instruction is no longer effective or new developments require modifications.

to develop the video. Other information, such as the particular software package used to edit video, might change as frequently as every few months. It's not cost-effective to engage in an extensive design and development effort to prepare instruction on the latest software package for one course. But if the instruction is distributed to all adopters of the software, the size of the target audience may justify the design and development costs. For smaller audiences, you may want to use a systematic instructional design process to develop instruction on a stable topic such as principles of visual composition while using simple step-by-step handouts, or "job aids," to support learners in using a particular software package. Another option when teaching content that quickly becomes outdated is to teach learners "how to learn" about the content. For example, instead of providing instruction on the latest digital video compression process, you might teach learners how to search for and find up-to-date information on the topic.

In this book, you'll learn to create learning and instructional systems using the collaborative, spiral model of instructional design. We illustrate the instructional design process as it applies to designing and developing electronic learning materials. Most of our experience has been in e-

learning environments, and there's a strong probability that most of yours will be, too. We've designed numerous Web sites, videotapes, CD-ROMS, and interactive videodiscs, but we've also designed simple workbooks, instructor-led training, and a variety of other materials. The process we describe is applicable to *all* instructional design efforts. However, much of our discussion focuses on the complex collaboration required to design and develop instruction to be delivered by someone other than the designer.

Book Overview

In Chapters 2–6, you'll learn about the five elements of systematically designed instruction. In Chapter 2, you'll learn how to gather information on learners' needs and characteristics, and the implications of these for instructional materials. In Chapter 3, you'll learn to identify outcomes and write assessment items. We introduce task, content, and instructional analysis techniques, as well as multiple techniques for assessing learning outcomes. Chapters 4 and 5 are devoted to the design and development of instructional activities. In Chapter 4, you'll learn to chunk and sequence content and to create an instructional strategy. You'll also be introduced to the relationship between learning theories and instructional events. In Chapter 5, you'll learn to select from a variety of instructional delivery options, allocate learning events to various components of an instructional package, and choose appropriate media for various learning events. Chapter 6 focuses on the process of evaluation. You'll learn how to conduct expert reviews, test your materials with learners, and handle the revisions that result from the evaluation cycle.

Although we emphasize the importance of effective communication and collaboration skills throughout the book, Chapter 7 focuses on these skills applicable across all phases of an instructional design project. You'll learn techniques for working with clients, SMEs, and other team members; the importance of a communications plan; techniques to manage documents and meetings; and ways to handle out-of-scope requests. You'll also learn to develop scenarios, treatments, prototypes, and other visioning tools to communicate with clients, SMEs, and project team members. As we discuss the review and revision process that is so critical for instructional design, you'll learn to present various design documents and materials to others in order to solicit the feedback needed for refining subsequent iterations of the materials.

Chapters 8–11 introduce each of the five phases of instructional design. In Chapter 8, you'll learn to respond to a Request for Proposal (RFP) and write a project proposal. You'll also learn to determine tentative solutions, create a project schedule and budget, and identify factors that may threaten completion of the project on time and within budget. We conclude the Define phase with information on presenting the proposal to the client and accepting feedback. As you move into the Design phase in Chapter 9, you'll learn to conduct a project kickoff meeting, collect the information needed to write the design documents, and organize the information into a set of instructional design documents. In the Demonstrate phase, presented in Chapter 10, you'll learn to develop production specifications, test a prototype, and identify what needs to be revised. With the product designed and tested, you can move into the Develop phase, during which the actual instructional materials are completed. In Chapter 11, you'll learn to monitor the development of the materials to ensure that they are developed as specified. The Develop phase includes continuous evaluation of the instructional materials. You'll also learn to manage the Delivery phase, providing materials to the client, as well as any accompanying activities, such as holding postproject debriefing meetings, providing support after the instruction is deployed, or summarizing project accomplishments. Finally, in Chapter 12, we prepare you for work in a variety of settings. We conclude with an overview of career paths for instructional designers and discuss ways to promote the instructional design process in the workplace.

Although Chapter 9 is titled "Design Phase," you won't need to wait until Chapter 9 to begin "designing"!

In fact, you're encouraged to start designing instruction in the very next chapter. Chapter 9 simply discusses the Design *phase* within the instructional design *process*. Chapters 2–5 will teach you to prepare the *products* of instructional design: Learner and needs descriptions, outcomes, assessments, instructional strategies, instructional materials, and evaluations. The topics addressed in Chapter 7—collaboration and communication—include critical skills for working with other people such as clients, SMEs, team members, and learners. In Chapters 8–11, you learn to work collaboratively with clients and other team members to design instruction.

Summary

Instructional design as a discipline has evolved over almost 60 years. Designers continually adapt the tools and techniques of practice to new methods of delivering instruction and new developments in educational psychology. Recent trends suggest that instructional design models should reflect the way instructional design practitioners implement design and remain responsive to the needs and constraints of the workplace. Consistent with these trends, the model you will learn in this book presents instructional design as a holistic, collaborative process; acknowledges the concurrent nature of design practice; and supports the creation of scenarios, rapid prototypes, and other concrete means to move the design team forward. Using this model, you will design instruction in a "layered" fashion, spiraling through the essential questions of design—the elements—at increasing levels of specificity as you move through the phases of Define, Design, Demonstrate, Develop, and Deliver.

It's an exciting time to be working in the field of instructional design. Come with us on the journey!

Notes

[1]For an excellent overview of a variety of instructional design models, see Kent L. Gustafson and Robert Branch, *Survey of Instructional Design Models,* 4th ed. (Syracuse, NY: ERIC Clearinghouse on Information and Technology, 2002).

[2]For an excellent overview of the history of the field, see Robert A. Reiser, "A History of Instructional Design and Technology: Part II: A History of Instructional Design," *Educational Technology Research and Development,* Spring 2001: 57–67; see also S. A. Shrock, "A Brief History of Instructional Development," in G. A. Anglin (Ed.), *Instructional Technology: Past, Present, and Future,* 2nd ed. (Englewood, CO: Libraries Unlimited, 1995, pp. 11–19).

[3]See, for example, G. Rowland, A. Fixl, and K. Yung, "Educating the Reflective Designer," *Educational Technology,* *32*(12) (1992): 36–44; G. Rowland, M. L. Parra, and K. Basnet, "Educating Instructional Designers: Different Methods for Different Outcomes," *Educational Technology* (1994, July/August): 5–11; J. Quinn, "Connecting Education and Practice in an Instructional Design Graduate Program,"

Educational Technology Research and Development, 42(3) (1994): 71–82; J. Quinn, "The Education of Instructional Designers: Reflections on the Tripp Paper," *Performance Improvement Quarterly, 8*(3) (1995): 111–117; and S. D. Tripp, "How Should Instructional Designers Be Educated?" *Performance Improvement Quarterly, 7*(3) (1994): 116–126.

[4]The ASC cycle is similar to Lohr's ACE (Analyze, Create, and Evaluate) cycle and Reigeluth and Nelson's ASEC (Analyze, Synthesize, Evaluate, and Change) process of instructional design. Although there are differences among the three processes, each of these models reflects the cyclical nature of progressive decision making: collecting information, generating hypotheses, and testing ideas until a satisfactory solution is achieved. For more information about the ACE and ASEC models, see L. L. Lohr, *Creating Graphics for Learning and Performance* (Upper Saddle River, NJ: Prentice-Hall, 2003); and C. Reigeluth and L. Nelson, "A New Paradigm of ISD?" *Educational Media and Technology Yearbook, 22* (1997): 24–35.

References

Bloom, B. S., Engelhart, E. M., Furst, D. J., Hill, W. H., & Krathwohl, D. R. (1956). *Taxonomy of educational objectives: The classification of educational goals. Handbook 1: Cognitive domain.* New York: David McKay.

Dick, W., & Carey, L. (1978). *The systematic design of instruction.* Glenview, IL: Scott Foresman.

Dick, W., Carey, L., & Carey, J. O. (2001). *The systematic design of instruction* (5th ed.). New York: Longman.

Dorsey, L. T., Goodrum, D. A., & Schwen, T. M. (1997). Rapid collaborative prototyping as an instructional development paradigm. In C. R. Dills & A. J. Romiszowski (Eds.), *Instructional development paradigms.* Englewood Cliffs, NJ: Educational Technology.

Gagné, R. M. (1965). *Conditions of learning.* New York: Holt, Rinehart & Winston.

Gagné, R. M., & Briggs, L. J. (1974). *Principles of instructional design.* New York: Holt, Rinehart & Winston.

Gustafson, K. L. (2000). Designing technology-based performance support. *Educational Technology, 40*(1), 38–44.

Gustafson, K. L., & Branch, R. M. (1997). Revisioning models of instructional development. *Educational Technology Research and Development, 45*(3), 73–89.

Gustafson, K. L., & Branch, R. M. (2002). *Survey of instructional design models* (4th ed.). Syracuse, NY: ERIC.

Kemp, J. E. (1971). *Instructional design: A plan for unit and course development.* Belmont, CA: Fearon.

Lohr, L. L. (2003). *Creating graphics for learning and performance.* Upper Saddle River, NJ: Prentice-Hall.

Mager, R. F. (1962). *Preparing objectives for programmed instruction.* Belmont, CA: Fearon.

Reiser, R. A. (2001). A history of instructional design and technology: Part II: A history of instructional design. *Educational Technology Research and Development, 49*(2), 57–67.

Rowland, G. (1992). What do instructional designers actually do? An initial investigation of expert practice. *Performance Improvement Quarterly, 5*(2), 65–86.

Rowland, G. (1993). Designing and instructional design. *Educational Technology Research and Development, 41*(1), 79–91.

Seels, B., & Glasgow, Z. (1998). *Making instructional design decisions* (2nd ed.). Upper Saddle River, NJ: Prentice-Hall.

Shrock, S. A. (1995). A brief history of instructional development. In G. A. Anglin (Ed.), *Instructional technology: Past, present, and future* (2nd ed.). Englewood, CO: Libraries Unlimited.

Tessmer, M., & Wedman, J. F. (1990). A layers-of-necessity instructional development model. *Educational Technology Research and Development, 38*(2), 77–85.

———. (1995). Context-sensitive instructional design models: A response to design research, studies, and criticism. *Performance Improvement Quarterly, 8*(3), 38–54.

Wedman, J., & Tessmer, M. (1993). Instructional designers' decisions and priorities: A survey of design practice. *Performance Improvement Quarterly, 6*(2), 43–57.

Wiener, L. R., & Vazquez-Abad, J. (1995). The present and future of ID practice. *Performance Improvement Quarterly, 8*(3), 55–67.

Application

1. The RealWorldID Web site includes a case study of the design and development of a museum Web site. Visit RealWorldID Web site to analyze the case online or to print for use during class discussions. Try to identify each of the essential elements within the case. Look for evidence that the elements were revisited at increasingly more elaborate levels of detail.

2. Throughout this book, we encourage you to keep a reflective journal of your instructional design decisions. We also urge you to continuously think about what you are doing and why. Begin your reflective journal by writing your thoughts on what instructional designers do. What is the nature of their day-to-day work? What skills are most beneficial?

3. After you have completed your reflections, interview practicing instructional designers or review the interviews with experienced designers on the RealWorldID Web site that supplements this book. In your reflective journal, make note of your reactions to these interviews. How were the perspectives conveyed in the interviews similar to and different from your perceptions? What skills do you think you need to develop as you progress through this book?

4. As we explore the essential elements of instructional design in Chapters 2–6, the entire class is encouraged to function as an ID team to create the design specifications for an instructional module. The class should be divided into working groups of four to five class members. Your course instructor will serve as an instructional design manager, leading design team meetings, checking on the progress of the working groups, and facilitating discussions.

   a. In this chapter, your working group should develop a list of topics that would be good candidates for a class instructional design and development project. Justify your classifications.

   b. After each group has spent time brainstorming a topic, the class should decide on one topic that will be used for the class activities. Select a topic that will be familiar to all members of the class.

5. Think about the conditions under which the use of systematic instructional design processes are in order. Consider the following situations:

   a. You have been asked to develop a Web site and three-day workshop to meet the goal of promoting "girl-friendly" science teaching. You are given a list of topics and asked to organize a series of lectures on those topics for the workshop. The function of the Web site is to make the presentations available after the workshop. Would this project be a good candidate for the systematic instructional design process? Why or why not?

   b. You've been asked to develop a CD-ROM to promote "girl-friendly" science teaching that will include interactive simulations where the teachers make choices and see the results of their choices. Would this project be a good candidate for the systematic instructional design process? Why or why not?

   c. How about developing a Web site in support of a class that contains teachers' handouts and announcements? What about developing or modifying the entire course package of handouts, assessments, lecture notes, and presentations?

6. Throughout this book, you are encouraged to develop instruction for an actual client. In subsequent chapters, you will be asked to complete the following tasks:

   a. Create a project proposal, present it to your client, and get sign-off (Chapter 8, "Define Phase").

   b. Prepare design documents, present them to your client, and get sign-off (Chapter 9, "Design Phase").

   c. Prepare additional design specifications and prototype instructional materials. Conduct formative evaluation of the prototype, collect data on its effectiveness, and develop a report on the results of the prototype and suggested revisions. Review the prototype report and revisions with your client (Chapter 10, "Demonstrate Phase").

   d. Prepare a complete set of instructional materials that are acceptable to your client. Conduct a formative evaluation of materials, collect data on their effectiveness, and prepare a report of the formative evaluation results and suggested revisions. Present completed materials and the results of the formative evaluation to your client (Chapter 11, "Develop and Deliver Phases").

Begin thinking about a client for whom to design instruction. You may want to consider a peer in the class. A peer will understand your time constraints and should be willing to provide you with the information you need when you need it.

| DESIGN AID |

Instructional Design Tasks Arranged by Phase

Define Phase

Learners

- Determine needs that led to project. Gather informal data to confirm or alter needs statement as time allows.
- Determine whom client perceives as learners. Gather informal data to confirm characteristics of learners as time allows.
- Include statement of needs, as defined by client, in project proposal.
- Describe audience and implications for instructional materials in project proposal.

Outcomes

- Determine client's perception of goals during initial correspondence (meetings, phone conversations, written correspondence).
- Write preliminary goal statements.
- Include goals in proposal document. Present to clients.

Activities

- Discuss content scope and possible instructional activities with client in initial correspondence.
- Determine delivery environment and implications for activities.

(continued on page 17)

(continued)

- Conduct limited initial brainstorming with team to develop ideas for activities to pitch to client.
- Draft description of instructional activities and content. Present to client in proposal.

Assessments

- Determine what client would like learners to be able to do after instruction.
- Draft tentative ideas for assessments. Present to client in proposal.

Evaluation

- Determine plan for prototype development and learner tryouts.
- Draft preliminary formative evaluation plan. Budget for it in proposal.
- Educate client as to importance of this stage.

Design Phase

Learners

- Gain clarity on client's and SME's perception of needs.
- Attempt to obtain permission to contact learners.
- Fully define audience through conversations with client, learners, SME, learner expert, and project team. Conduct research and review of literature as needed.
- If permitted, contact learners to confirm or modify statement of needs.
- Present description of needs and learner characteristics as part of design documents. Gain approval or change as needed.

Outcomes

- Fully develop goals.
- Discuss possible outcomes with client, SME, and learners.
- Write and sequence high-level outcomes.
- Determine prerequisite skills.
- Present goals and outcomes to members of design team, client, and SME. Gain approval or change as needed.

Activities

- Work extensively with SME to define content.
- Brainstorm potential instructional activities with project team.
- Develop instructional strategy based on audience characteristics and needs and instructional outcomes.
- Develop description of materials, including media and navigation, as needed.
- Present instructional strategy and concrete description of materials to client for approval or suggested modifications.

Assessments

- Gather suggestions for assessments.
- Develop concrete description of assessment instruments and/or specifications.
- Present assessment ideas for client approval with design documents.

Evaluation

- Prepare or modify formative evaluation plan.
- Get suggestions for tryout learners.
- Present evaluation plan to client for approval.

(continued on page 18)

(continued)

Demonstrate Phase

Learners

- Monitor development of production documents and prototype to ensure they are appropriate for audience.
- Explain to client how materials will be appropriate for needs and characteristics of audience.
- Monitor ability of materials to meet needs and characteristics of learners during prototype tryout.

Outcomes

- Monitor development of production documents and prototype to ensure consistency with outcomes and sequence.
- Present prototype to client, explaining how developed to teach outcomes.
- Monitor learners' obtainment of outcomes during prototype tryout.

Activities

- Develop production documents including page templates, storyboards, media requirements, and technical specifications. Gain approval and make suggested modifications.
- Develop prototype of materials. Present to learners. Collect data on learners' response to prototype.
- Present prototype and results of learner tryout to clients and SME. Present suggested modifications resulting from prototype testing.

Assessments

- Develop specifications for assessments.
- Develop prototype assessment instruments. Administer assessment instruments during prototype testing. Alter assessments as indicated by prototype tryout.
- Present assessment instruments and/or specifications to client for approval.

Evaluation

- Gain access to learners for prototype testing.
- Develop instruments and procedures needed for prototype testing.
- Compile and analyze evaluation data. Develop proposed changes to product based on data.

Develop Phase

Learners

- Continue to monitor materials development to ensure that they are appropriate for audience.
- Seek data on ability of materials to meet learners' needs during formative evaluation testing.

Outcomes

- Continue to monitor materials development to ensure consistency with goals and outcomes.
- Seek data on learners' obtainment of outcomes during formative evaluation testing.

Activities

- Determine needed modifications to materials based on client's and learners' response to prototype.
- Monitor materials development to ensure consistency with instructional strategy.
- Create instructor's guide, training guide, and other supporting materials requested by client.
- Use materials with learners during formative evaluation.

(continued on page 19)

(continued)

Assessments

- Monitor development of assessment instruments to ensure consistency with specifications.
- Use assessment instruments during formative evaluation. Seek information to determine clarity and usefulness of assessments.

Evaluation

- Gain access to learners for additional formative evaluations.
- Schedule and conduct additional evaluation.
- Analyze data and develop recommendations for modifications.

Deliver Phase

Learners

- Present learners' responses to evaluation.
- Discuss suggested modifications. Determine whether modifications will occur during this development cycle or will form basis of recommendations for version 2.

Outcomes

- Present data on degree to which learners achieve outcomes during formative evaluation.
- Discuss suggested modifications. Determine whether modifications will occur during this development cycle or will form basis of recommendations for version 2.

Activities

- Present materials to client.
- Present results of formative evaluation. Discuss suggested revisions. Determine if changes will be made to current materials or future versions.
- Compile project documentation.
- Conduct training on use of materials if requested by client.

Assessments

- Discuss suggested modifications to assessment instruments resulting from formative evaluation. Determine whether modifications will occur during this development cycle or will form basis of recommendations for version 2.

Evaluation

- Conduct summative evaluation if requested.

Chapter 2
Learner Needs and Characteristics

Learning Outcomes

- Justify a learner analysis to a client or employer.

- Conduct a confirmation of needs.

- Conduct a learner analysis.

- Outline implications of the learners' needs for the instructional outcomes.

- Outline implications of the learners' characteristics for the instructional materials.

Chapter Overview

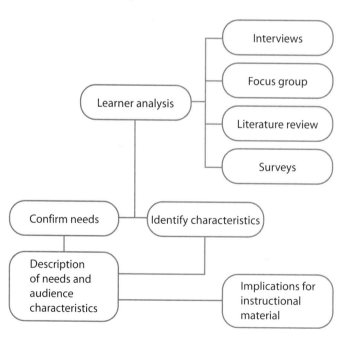

Orientation within the Design Process

Recall that there are five phases in the instructional design process and that in each phase we visit each of the essential elements of instructional design, adding details and performing tasks as required by the deliverables of each phase. In this chapter, we examine Learners. Learners are the first element we consider because they will experience the outcomes, activities, and assessments. While evaluation doesn't directly touch the learner, the evaluation examines the success of the instruction and, ultimately, effects future learners (see Figure 2.1).

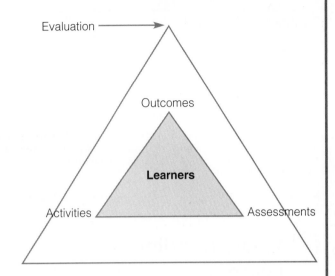

Figure 2.1 *Elements considered.* The learner is at the center of all of the elements.

Tasks at Each Phase

The tasks at each phase are summarized in Table 2.1. As we discuss each of the phases in later chapters, you'll learn more about performing these tasks. But for now, the table provides an overview of where the tasks discussed in this chapter fit into the five phases of design.

Table 2.1 Learner-related tasks within each phase

Define	• Determine needs that led to project. Gather informal data to confirm or alter needs statement as time allows.
	• Determine whom client perceives as learners. Gather informal data to confirm characteristics of learners as time allows.
	• Include statement of needs, as defined by client, in project proposal.
	• Describe audience and implications for instructional materials in project proposal.
Design	• Gain clarity on client's and SME's perception of needs.
	• Attempt to obtain permission to contact learners.
	• Fully define audience through conversations with client, learners, SME, learner expert, and project team. Conduct research and review of literature as needed.
	• If permitted, contact learners to confirm or modify statement of needs.
	• Present description of needs and learner characteristics as part of design documents. Gain approval or change as needed.
Demonstrate	• Monitor development of production documents and prototype to ensure they are appropriate for audience.
	• Explain to client how materials will be appropriate for needs and characteristics of audience.
	• Monitor ability of materials to meet needs and characteristics of learners during prototype tryout.

(continued)

Table 2.1 *(continued)*	
Develop	• Continue to monitor materials development to ensure that they are appropriate for audience.
	• Seek data on ability of materials to meet learners' needs during formative evaluation testing.
Deliver	• Present learners' responses to evaluation.
	• Discuss suggested modifications. Determine whether modifications will occur during this development cycle or will form basis of recommendations for version 2.

Understanding Learners

The most significant element in developing instruction is to understand the learners. Learning activities are designed differently depending on the audience, even if the content is the same. Visualize a room full of seventh-graders in a Spanish I class. Now think of a group of businesspeople enrolled in an evening Spanish program prior to leaving for assignments in Latin America. What are the implications of the learners' needs and characteristics for the design of an introductory course for each of these groups? Although the *content* would be similar for both groups, the actual instruction would be very different. The amount of material covered in each lesson, the pace of the lesson, the amount of practice provided, and the organization of the lessons would differ greatly.

Through your experience as a student, you know that you learn some subjects more easily than others. Perhaps you're an ace in the sciences but struggle to pick up foreign languages. Or perhaps you've always been successful in history courses but have to work very hard in mathematics simply to get a passing grade. In addition to being better in some disciplines than others, you probably have found some classes compelling—perhaps because of a great teacher—and others hard to get excited about for reasons having nothing to do with the subject. Meanwhile, other students in the same classes probably had opposite feelings. From these personal experiences, you intuitively know that each of us learns in our own unique way. Individuals learn different subject areas differently, and they learn differently at different times in their lives. This has implications for each of you as learners—and as instructional designers.

As an instructional designer, one of your most critical tasks is to serve as the learners' advocate throughout the design and development process. You need to speak up when you realize that some learners might lack prerequisite skills or when the artist selects a 10-point font size for a program designed for older people. Others on the team may be concerned with production values or bandwidth or budgets. You should be concerned about those things, but your priority is to ensure that the program will be effective *for its audience*. The learners' information needs will impact the goals and outcomes of instruction. And the learners' characteristics will, in turn, impact the instructional strategy and activities.

How do you begin to understand your learners? The first step is to determine what they already know about the topic and what they need to know. This results in a **needs description**. The next step is to ask representative learners to tell you about themselves, their preferences, their values, and their jobs or school experiences. As you develop a picture of who the learners are as people, you can create a **description of learner characteristics**. You won't always have an opportunity to speak directly with the learners, but you must get this information from your client and others who have insights into the audience. For example, if you are developing a program to improve number skills for second-graders, the children probably can't tell you much about their values or knowledge. Teachers and parents can provide some of this information, and you can review the results of tests and research reports. In this chapter, we discuss the importance of determining learners' needs and characteristics, as well as how to collect and report the necessary data.

Needs Description

In many instructional design models, the design process starts with a needs assessment. In the needs assessment, the instructional designer identifies the gap between the current state of affairs and the ideal situation, with the resulting gap representing the need. In Rossett's (1987) classic model of needs assessment, information is collected on the current situation (the "actuals"), the way the situation should be (the "optimals"), the way people feel about it ("feelings"), potential "causes" of the discrepancy between actuals and optimals, and possible "solutions" to the problem. Sometimes, needs can be addressed through instruction, but that's not always the case. For example, if the needs assessment shows that employees are having trouble understanding when to use capitalization in writing, adding a lesson on this topic is likely to close the gap. How-

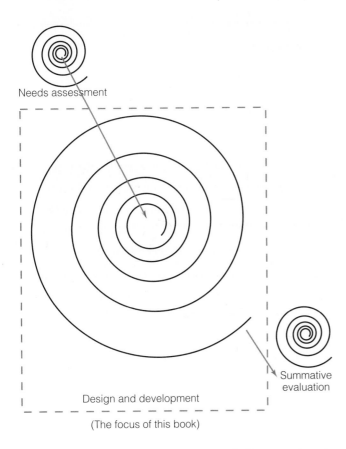

Needs assessment

Design and development

(The focus of this book)

Summative evaluation

Figure 2.2 *Different processes.* In a full instructional development sequence, the process begins with needs assessment and concludes with summative evaluation. In this book, we focus on the design and development that occurs between those activities.

ever, if a needs assessment indicates that employees are misfiling reports because the rules for the filing system are ambiguous, the problem won't be resolved by instruction—it requires writing better rules. If you determine a gap between optimals and actuals for which instruction is the best solution, you have identified the instructional need.

In many cases, the client believes there is a need *before* hiring an instructional designer. In fact, clients often have decided beforehand *exactly* what is needed. That doesn't mean you shouldn't learn about needs assessment or advocate for the appropriate solution. Sometimes, the client will hire a third party—another instructional designer—to conduct the needs assessment. This often is true of evaluation as well—both for formative evaluation, conducted during the development of the product, and summative evaluation, conducted once the product is in use in the field. So it's possible that one entity will conduct a needs assessment, another will design and produce the product, and a third will conduct the evaluation (see Figure 2.2). As an instructional designer, you need to be ready to assume the design role in any of these stages. You also need to prepare your final reports and materials so that designers who follow can do their work. Because this

book focuses on the design and development process, we don't cover needs assessment and program evaluation in great detail. However, many excellent resources are available including those listed in the Additional Readings.

Traditionally, a need is defined as "a discrepancy or gap between the way things 'ought to be' and the way they 'are'" (Burton & Merrill, 1991, p. 21). However, instructional materials often are developed to take advantage of an opportunity instead of in response to a problem. For example, a manufacturer of aquatic products may decide to develop a program to inform prospective customers on how to set up and maintain an aquarium. Although the customers have no expressed "need," the manufacturer sees an opportunity to provide potential customers with valuable information. Or perhaps a university has a resident expert on labor law and sees an opportunity to generate additional revenue by offering an online course through its continuing education division. In these cases, the "need" is anticipated because the learners don't know that they need something yet.

Sometimes, clients will approach you with some *activity* in mind. For example, they may want to create a distance learning course that teaches digital video to alumni, or create a Web site that encourages girls to pursue careers in math and science, or develop a foreign language curriculum for high school students on CD-ROM. Within each of these three requests, a possible need is implied: Alumni may have an interest in learning digital video, or girls may need encouragement to pursue careers in math and science; or a high school foreign language curriculum may be needed. It's up to you to confirm whether these needs actually exist—clients may be incorrect in their assumptions concerning the needs of learners. You confirm needs through informal means in the Define phase and more formally in the Design phase. Once you've defined an area of need (or opportunity), you can determine exactly what information within the broad topic area will be of value to learners. Consistent with the spiral approach to instructional design, you:

- Identify a general area of need or opportunity through conversations with your client and design team.
- Refine your needs statement through conversations, interviews, observations, surveys, and reviews of documents and other artifacts.
- Add details and specifics to your statement of need based on your expanded knowledge of the learners.

The project proposal, created during the Define phase, and the design document, created during the Design phase, should include a narrative statement of the instructional need or the opportunity that the instruction will fill. The needs statement may arise out of discussions with your client, the research literature, a consultant's report, observations, focus groups (perhaps conducted by the marketing department), interviews with learners,

Confirmation of Needs

Sometimes, your client may think there is one need, but when you talk with your learners, you discover that the need isn't quite accurate. Consider the following example:

Polly was an instructional designer. She worked for a production company that was hired to design and develop a series of 14 interactive CD-ROMs to educate potential clients on electronic technologies. The client, a manufacturer of heavy machinery, decided that the first program in the series should focus on large electric motors capable of powering water treatment facilities. Electric motors were considered cleaner than the smoky, noisy, gas-powered engines most treatment facilities used. The client believed that water treatment companies would choose electric motors if they understood that they were available and could do the job. Polly's supervisors wanted her to get the programmers started right away, but she was able to hold them off. She obtained permission to contact a few customer service representatives from the client's company. She talked with those who worked directly with water treatment operators and asked them about their information needs and the needs of their customers. She tried to find out as much as she could about her learners and their needs, and she even got the names and phone numbers of several customers who worked in water treatment plants. In all, she spoke with 16 employees in her client's organization who had direct contact with water treatment operators and 4 employees at water treatment plants.

Excerpts from her description of the learners' needs follow:

The primary audience for the Electric Motor CD-ROM will consist of (1) water-pumping customers and (2) customer service employees who serve water-pumping customers. Information concerning the characteristics and information needs of the customers and employees has been collected through extensive interviews with several customers and employees who have direct contact with the customers. Four water customers, 4 customer service supervisors, and 12 customer contact associates were contacted.

The emphasis of the program will be on the placement of electric motors at sites that currently have internal combustion (IC) engines in order to establish a dual source of power at the

customer's site. The audience for the electric motor instructional program is unique in that many of the customers already have a good understanding of electric motor technology. Many customers currently have electric motors in addition to IC engines. Other customers are well aware of the advantages of electric motors and would like to convert from IC engines to electric motors; however, they are unable to justify the additional expense. The primary purpose of the instructional program will be to reinforce and clarify the customers' existing knowledge of electric motors. The customers' prior knowledge of electric motors has implications for the design of both the customer track and the employee track of the CD-ROM.

CUSTOMERS

Although most of the customers are aware of the benefits of using electric motors, they are interested in a cost-benefit analysis of electric motors and IC engines. They are especially concerned with the length of time that will be required to recoup their investment in electric motors. The instructional program should present the total financial picture. For example, IC engine maintenance costs may be a substantial portion of their operating cost, but these costs may be buried in their general operating budget; consequently, many customers may not be aware of the costs of maintaining an IC engine. In addition, the customers need to be made aware of ways to increase the cost-effectiveness of their pumps and motors. Information on time-of-use rates and pump efficiency tests will be provided.

Although the majority of customers are aware of the benefits of electric motors, some bias may exist against electric motors. This bias may be based on the fact that (1) customers are already very familiar with IC engines, (2) they believe that electric motors do not operate at variable speeds, (3) electric motors are dependent on the availability of electric power, and (4) IC engine mechanics already have a thorough knowledge of maintenance and servicing.

(continued on page 25)

(continued)

The customer service personnel indicated that there is quite a bit of misinformation on the need for variable speed drives. Customers are confused as to when a variable speed drive is necessary and need to be made aware of the advantages and disadvantages of variable speed drives. The program should inform them of the current state of variable speed drive technology and provide the information necessary for the customer to evaluate whether variable speed drives are necessary at their facility.

The customer service personnel also indicated that the customers need detailed information on the air quality standards that affect their businesses.

EMPLOYEES

The customer service personnel have indicated that they need to be able to talk to the customer in terms that are familiar to the customer. In order to do so, they need to understand the customers' business. They also need information on the operation of IC engines, the alternatives for modifying IC engines to meet air quality standards, and the maintenance requirements for IC engines. However, the information concerning the customers' business and IC engines does not need to be very detailed. In general, the customer service personnel indicated that they need to be able to talk to the customers in their own terms, but they do not need in-depth technical information. The customer contact personnel have expressed a need for information on many of the same issues that are of interest to the customers; therefore, the information that is presented to the customer will also be made available to the customer service employees.

What did Polly discover in her confirmation of learner needs? Were the clients correct in their assumption that the water treatment operators would buy electric motors if they knew more about them? If Polly had followed the advice of her client (and her employer), she would have spent several months developing a product that did not meet the needs of her learners! Her analysis revealed that the learners were highly aware of electric motors and knew they could be used to power water treatment plants, but they simply had other concerns. Armed with an awareness of these concerns, Polly could develop instructional goals and create a program that truly would meet learners' needs.

and other sources. The needs statement reflects your best understanding of your learners' needs when you draft the document. Your understanding may deepen and change as you gain additional experience with the audience and the material, but this is where you start.

Learner Characteristics

Learner needs are only part of the story. You also must develop an awareness of what the learners are like and consider implications of the learners' characteristics for the instructional materials. Just as knowledge of the learners' needs provides focus for the goals and outcomes of the instruction, knowledge of their characteristics allows you to create materials to which the learners will be receptive.

Several authors offer extensive lists of learner characteristics on which instructional designers should collect data (see, for example, Morrison, Ross, & Kemp, 2004; Rothwell & Kazanas, 1998; Smith & Ragan, 1999); but there's no need to collect data that won't make any difference in the design of the product. Remember why you want information on the learners in the first place! In order to develop instructional activities, you need to know several things about the learners:

Prior knowledge, which includes factors such as:

- Previous and current employment
- Education and training
- Reading level
- Specific knowledge about the topic
- Vocabulary and language skills
- Visual literacy
- Computer skills

Motivation, which includes factors such as:

- Values
- Interests
- Short- and long-term goals and aspirations
- Attitudes toward the subject matter and learning in general

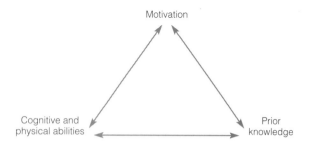

Figure 2.3 *Relationship of learner characteristics.* The learner's motivation, prior knowledge, and abilities all factor into your understanding of that individual.

- Self-concept
- Anxiety regarding the topic, school, testing, or the job environment
- Confidence in self, learning, and the topic, and with peers
- Tendency toward cooperation or competition
- Preferences

Physical and cognitive characteristics, which include factors such as:

- Cognitive developmental level
- Level of language development
- Preferred learning styles
- General learning abilities
- Specific aptitudes for a topic
- Ability to decipher graphics and distinguish among items in a visual field
- Manual dexterity
- Mobility and physical limitations

Of course, each of these areas influences the others (see Figure 2.3). For example, learners with low manual dexterity (physical characteristic) may lack confidence (motivation) in their ability to learn computer-aided drafting skills based on their prior experiences in learning similar topics. Or learners' computer skills (prior knowledge) and preference for visual learning (physical and cognitive ability) may influence their desire to learn about computer-aided drafting to meet future career goals (motivation).

It's often easy to collect demographic information such as age, gender, and marital status. However, demographic information, in and of itself, doesn't influence the design of instruction. Instead, demographic characteristics provide you with data on which to make assumptions about the learners' prior experiences, motivation, and cognitive and physical abilities. For example, if you know that your learners are 3–5 years old, you can assume they probably won't be able to read (prior experience), may not be able to sit still for long periods (cognitive and physical

ability), and like bright colors (motivation). However, you need to be careful not to make assumptions that reinforce stereotypes. In general, it's best to collect information that allows you to answer specific questions of relevance to the design of instruction rather than make assumptions based on demographic data.

To better understand your learners, you also want to determine under what conditions they'll be learning the new information and under what conditions they hope to apply it.[1] The **learning context** influences the nature of the instructional activities and delivery media, while an awareness of the **application context** allows you to develop relevant goals, instructional activities, and assessments. By collecting the following information, you gain insight into the contexts in which the learners will be learning and applying their new knowledge:

- How much time will they have available for study? At what time of day will they be working on the course materials?
- What equipment is available for self-study? For example, if the instructional materials are going to be used in individual homes, you need to know what equipment is available. Do they have VCRs? Computers with CD-ROM drives? Internet access?
- How often will learners have an opportunity to apply these skills? Certain skills that aren't used very often, such as cardiopulmonary resuscitation (CPR), require that learners undergo regular retraining or recertification.
- Will the learners receive social support for the application of these skills? Consider the learners in a program designed to reduce drunk driving. If all of their friends drink (and drive), they'll be less likely to resist alcohol consumption than those who return to an alcohol-free environment.
- What are the rewards for learning new skills? Increased pay? Increased prestige? Increased self-esteem? Will learners receive social support as they learn new skills?

Implications for Instructional Materials

Your knowledge of learner characteristics should influence the design of instructional activities. For example, some children arrive at kindergarten already reading while others have not yet learned the alphabet. If you are developing instructional materials for this group, you need to accommodate both sets of learners. One strategy might be to provide both text and auditory instruction so that both groups can succeed. Table 2.2 illustrates some of the implications learner characteristics can have on the design of instructional materials, but the list is by no means comprehensive.

Table 2.2 Implications of learner characteristics for instruction

Characteristic	Implications for instruction
Prior knowledge and experience	• Speed of presentation (pace)
	• Context of examples and practice items
	• Amount of structure and organization
	• Size of instructional chunks
	• Media used to convey information
	• Number and difficulty of examples and practice items
	• Type of feedback given after practice items
	• Level of learner control
	• Vocabulary and terminology used
	• Amount of time allowed for instruction
	• Redundancy of information
	• Level of detail provided
Motivation	• Number of successful experiences learners should have in practice
	• Types of statements to convince students of relevancy of instruction
	• Techniques for gaining and focusing attention, and frequency of use of techniques
	• Context of examples and practice items
	• Type of feedback given after practice items
	• Amount of time allowed for instruction
	• Level of learner control
	• Amount and types of reinforcement
	• Style of writing
	• Need for rewards and reinforcement
	• User options to access information, repetition, and visual and auditory cues
Cognitive and physical abilities	• Speed of presentation (pace)
	• Amount of structure and organization
	• Level of concreteness or abstraction
	• Collaborative versus individualistic learning
	• Role of peers in instruction
	• Size of instructional chunks
	• Response mode (written, oral, and so on)
	• Number and difficulty of examples and practice
	• Amount of time allowed for instruction
	• Colors and font size
	• Media used to convey information
Learning context	• Media used to convey information
	• Size of instructional chunks
	• Amount of time allowed for instruction
	• Level of learner control
	• Collaborative versus individualistic learning
	• Role of peers in instruction

(*continued*)

Table 2.2 *(continued)*

Characteristic	Implications for instruction
	• Response mode (written, oral, and so on)
	• Types of statements to convince students of relevancy of instruction
Application context	• Reference materials and support tools provided
	• Types of examples
	• Context of practice items
	• Vocabulary and terminology used
	• Redundancy of information
	• Level of detail provided
	• Level of concreteness or abstraction
	• Number of successful experiences learners should have in practice
	• Types of statements to convince students of relevancy of instruction
	• Techniques for gaining and focusing attention, and frequency of use of techniques
	• Style of writing
	• Need for rewards and reinforcement

SOURCE: From *Instructional Design,* 2nd ed., by Patricia Smith and Tillman J. Ragan, p. 56. Copyright 1999 by John Wiley & Sons, Inc. This material is used by permission of John Wiley & Sons, Inc.

Consider the implications of one of the many learner characteristics of which you need to be aware. Each learner has preferred methods of learning and communicating—and these preferences can change depending on the subject, the delivery environment, and the level of motivation. Auditory learners prefer to hear information. They may need to read text aloud in order to comprehend and retain it. Visual learners find it easier to retain information presented as written text or images than information presented orally. If you design materials to appeal to all learning modalities, you are better able to reach each learner in your audience. If you present a lecture (auditory), supplement the lecture with visual aids to appeal to both auditory and visual learners. Then introduce tasks that allow the learners to take action using the material, such as building a model or performing a role play. Many learners have secondary modalities, so presenting the content in a variety of modes will reinforce learning across the spectrum of preferences. Preferred learning modalities are just one of the many learner characteristics of which instructional designers should be aware.

Conducting Learner Analysis of Needs and Characteristics

While some clients understand the value of a learner analysis, others may require some convincing. They might not have budgeted for the cost of a learner analysis, or they might not have time, and/or they may believe that they understand the issues sufficiently. Your goal is to convince them that a learner analysis is part of a high-quality design effort. To convince your client to accept the idea of learner analysis, try to present the concept using examples close to his or her experience. If your client values learning, discuss your need to conduct a learner analysis in terms of learning gains. If your client values efficiency, discuss it in terms of how a learner analysis will save development time. If your client values cost savings, discuss the benefits of a learner analysis in terms of saving development, and redevelopment, costs. And if your client values all of these, include them all!

Business executives are familiar with the purpose and value of market analysis. Learner analysis is similar except that it focuses on the needs of learners instead of consumers and on instructional applications instead of product opportunities. As Rothwell and Kazanas (1998, p. 83) remind us:

Assessing learner characteristics resembles segmentation, the process used to categorize consumers by similar features. A well-known technique in the marketing field, segmentation gives advertisers the ability to target measures to the unique needs and concerns of their audiences. In a similar fashion, learners are consumers of services provided by instructional designers. Consequently, many fundamental marketing principles apply to the process of assessing learner characteristics. Much as an organization competes against other organizations in the marketplace, so instruction must compete with other priorities for the attention of learners and their supervisors.

Analogy

House

Let's return to our home-building analogy from Chapter 1. An architect needs to understand a family well in order to design a home that will meet their needs. A family with young children has different needs from a retired couple, even if the square footage and number of rooms they require is the same. A young couple may want to design the home so that they can add bedrooms later while another couple may want to add a separate apartment for an elderly parent.

Most families can't afford a custom home, but builders try to meet the varying needs of homeowners by building a variety of homes. Builders pay close attention to their customers, noting what customers are looking for in a home and investing in market research to get feedback on new ideas. Some people prefer formal living spaces while others prefer casual, open spaces. Some families see the kitchen as the center of their home while others prefer to gather in the backyard or family room. A family that does a lot of entertaining at home needs a different floor plan from a family of do-it-yourselfers who need a large workshop. Builders respond to these different families by designing products (homes) to appeal to each of them.

The learners in this chapter are analogous to the homeowners. Just as builders need to understand their customers, instructional designers need to understand their learners. Learners' needs and preferences have implications for how you design an instructional product.

Learner analyses can be constructed in one of two ways: contrived or derived. A derived learner analysis is constructed from data *derived* from the learner. A contrived analysis is a best guess based on what you or others know about the target audience. If you or others on your development team have prior experience with the target audience group, the contrived approach is the simplest and least time-consuming method.[2]

A **contrived learner analysis** is often constructed by brainstorming. Consider who will be your primary and secondary audiences: Think about their information needs, their characteristics, and the implications of those needs and characteristics for the development of instructional materials. If you are developing a Web-based course and the primary audience is college freshmen, what are the implications for the course? How would the Web site differ if it were developed for alumni? Work with your team, subject matter expert (SME), and client to develop a profile of your target audience. Although your client might not be an instructional designer, don't underestimate her or his understanding of the audience or the issues! The client often has tremendous knowledge of the audience, perhaps not as learners, but as employees or customers. If the client lacks the training to articulate the instructional needs—you may be able to work with your client to supply the missing vocabulary.

Another way of creating a learner profile is through a **derived analysis**. Collect data from the learners themselves, and then develop a description of the target audience. You can use interviews, focus groups, questionnaires, surveys, and observations. It's best to collect information from several sources to avoid incorrectly stereotyping the audience based on limited information.

Frequently, these methods are used *in combination*. You might begin with a contrived analysis, then proceed to a derived analysis, perhaps to confirm or alter your original analysis, once you have the opportunity to talk with members of the target group. Other times, you may be satisfied with a contrived analysis initially but through the design process find yourself confronting questions that require talking with actual audience members. Your contrived analysis may be right on target—or it may not be. Sometimes only the learners themselves can tell you for sure.

Gathering Information from Learners

Even if you have a description of your learners' needs from your client, and you have brainstormed a list of their characteristics, try to get permission to contact a few representative members of your target audience. Select a sample and contact them to confirm or modify your assumptions. Find out what they already know about the topic, and ask them what else they would like to know. Solicit their help in designing the materials. Once you've collected data, you can analyze them and report your findings. Don't fret over how precise your methods are—even a small sample is likely to give you significant insights into your learners.

Selecting a Sample   Your goal in contacting your learners is to obtain a complete and accurate view of their needs and characteristics. How many people should you contact? You want enough of a sample so that you are confident about representing their interests as you work with your client, SMEs, and other members of the

---

Example 2.1 Excerpt from Questionnaire Using Likert Scale

A Likert scale measures the level to which someone agrees or disagrees with a statement or, in this case, the level to which a student believes he or she can perform the objectives. This scale, from 1 to 5, is the one most commonly used.

Instructions: Please rate your ability to perform the following objectives (circle the appropriate value).

Video Production Objectives	Low				High
List factors that must be considered when correctly using a microphone.	1	2	3	4	5
Describe the type of information included in preproduction planning documents.	1	2	3	4	5
Describe and diagram three-point lighting.	1	2	3	4	5

---

design and development team. Usually, 10–12 people are enough of a sample—if they reflect the diversity of the group. Often there are several sub-categories of potential users. For example, a Web site detailing science experiments that can be conducted on school property may be of value to colleges, as well as secondary school students, teachers, and parents. As you contact representative learners, make sure you include members of each potential audience group. Even within a relatively homogenous audience—for example, sixth-grade teachers—be aware that various cultures and disabilities may be represented. Although designers most often choose learners by convenience sampling, sometimes a more formal method is necessary. You may want to use a simple random sample, in which each member of your target audience has an equal chance of being selected. Or you might use a stratified random sample, in which members of each of the subgroups that compose the population are represented in the proportion comparable to their percentage in the entire population of audience members.

In addition, you should be aware of the needs and characteristics of those who will decide whether to let students participate in the instruction. In a public school setting, the opinions of teachers are of value. In a corporate training context, managers may decide who actually par-

ticipates in the training. They may also make purchasing decisions about whether your project becomes a product sold to this audience. Do not disregard these gatekeepers as you assess the needs and characteristics of your target audience. Even if they won't actually participate in the instruction, these individuals are an important part of your audience!

Collecting Data Of all the data collection methods, interviews are the most time consuming, yet they often yield the most beneficial data, especially in the early stages of your learner analysis. Interviews may be more or less structured but are typically a synchronous conversation by phone, in person, or online. Before the interview, prepare a list of questions or specific topics for discussion. You shouldn't limit your questioning to the prepared list, but it will give the interview structure and purpose. If possible, make the list available to interviewees before the interview so that they can prepare their thoughts. The benefit of a "live" interview is that you can follow up with comments or additional questions. Take notes during the conversation, and make additional notes immediately afterward to capture all that was said while it is still fresh in your mind. You may want to consider tape-recording either a phone or an in-person conversation, but be sure to get the interviewee's permission beforehand.

Like interviews, focus group meetings are semistructured conversations with members of the target audience. Where interviews typically consist of one-on-one conversations, however, focus groups involve small groups who meet to provide feedback on specific products or to generate ideas for a product. A focus group may be led by an instructional designer, a marketing specialist, or a professional facilitator. Plan the focus group questions and topics carefully, providing time for participants to ask follow-up questions and discuss topics of particular interest to them. Group dynamics often can generate levels of creative thinking that might not be possible with one-on-one discussions. However, some individuals might dominate the conversation while others hesitate to suggest ideas that differ from those presented by dominant group members.

DESIGNER'S TOOLKIT

Professional Etiquette

If you have scheduled a meeting with participants in advance, it's a good idea to send them a reminder of the meeting time and place. And don't forget to send them a thank-you note following their participation! Many times, a simple e-mail will do. But if your participants have contributed a large amount of time during their workday, you may want to send a formal letter of appreciation to their supervisors.

Example 2.2 Excerpt from Questionnaire Using Checklist and Open-Ended Questions

Monroe Elementary School—Technology Needs Assessment

If adequate training and equipment were available, would you like to be able to:	Check all that apply
Use the computer for word processing.	
Use e-mail to communicate with colleagues locally and worldwide.	
Use the automatic card catalog.	
Use Monroe's computer network.	
Use the Internet to access worldwide resources.	
Preview instructional programs for students.	
Use the computer to manage classroom records.	
Create multimedia demonstrations.	
Create computer-based presentations.	

Are there other ways that you would like to use computers and other technologies in your classroom?

Other than training and equipment needs, are there other barriers to integrating technology into your classroom practices?

If you have the opportunity to contact a large number of learners, or if they are distributed in many locations, consider developing a questionnaire or survey. A questionnaire presents participants with questions that they answer either in a paper-based form or online. These questions can include scaled responses (see Example 2.1), checklists, and open-ended surveys (see Example 2.2). Open-ended surveys allow for free-form answers and are easier to create but are usually more difficult or time consuming to score than scaled items.

Another strategy to derive the needs and characteristics of the learners is through direct observations, or through indirect observation such as by examining work samples or other artifacts (Rothwell & Kazanas, 1998). You can structure these observations and record the results on checklists, or they can be unstructured, as when you simply make notes of your observations.

Perhaps you can gain access to market analysis data that can be used to develop a learner profile. If your client has conducted focus groups or studies for marketing purposes, ask if you can examine the original transcripts or tapes. They are likely to yield important insights into your audience.

Research literature is another valuable source of information on common characteristics of the target learners. Different age groups have different characteristics, and knowledge of those characteristics is useful when designing instructional materials. For example, middle school students hate to be treated like children, but their behavior typically indicates that they aren't quite ready to accept adult responsibilities. This has implications for reaching learners effectively. Sometimes, the content challenges learners' preconceived notions. For example, the germ theory of disease has been well understood by doctors for decades, but many, if not most, adults persist in believing that we catch common colds by exposure to cold weather. If you are preparing patient education materials, you must identify and address these strongly held beliefs.

Ideally, you should use a *combination* of data collection methods. For example, it is useful to conduct a few interviews before creating a questionnaire. As the designer, you probably aren't a member of the target audience and can't anticipate all of the learners' needs and concerns. These initial conversations with learners can help you refine your ideas for the survey. And a questionnaire pro-

---

Example 2.3 Narrative Learner Analysis

A portion of the learner analysis for this book is included below. Notice how we consider the implications of each target group for the design of the instructional materials (this book). There are three groups of target learners for this textbook: students enrolled in instructional design degree programs, novice instructional designers, and practitioners who want more training in instructional design.

Students Who Want to Become Instructional Designers

Students enrolled in a class will be assigned to read the book and most likely will have to design and develop a project that the instructor will evaluate. Professors and their students are familiar with textbooks such as this one, where each chapter corresponds roughly to a week's worth of class work and lecture. Students will have had a variety of prior experiences but are probably novices with no knowledge of designing and developing instruction in a real world or collaborative setting. Some students may be K-12 teachers seeking to change careers; others may be professionals who work in training-related jobs and seek an advanced degree. The implications for the book are that examples must be realistic.

Instructional Design Graduates Who Are New to the Field

Newly minted graduates with a degree in instructional technology or a related field may have little experience in or knowledge of how to design in the real world for real clients. This book could be assigned through a train-the-trainer program, or the designer might choose it on her or his own. The implications for this busy professional are that he or she doesn't have a lot of time to read, so the presentation needs to be concise and useful. Examples, checklists, and content on collaboration and communication are likely to be the most useful components for this audience.

Practitioners Who Want More Training in Instructional Design

Corporate trainers and SMEs may need to develop instructional materials but lack formal education or experience with the process. Even when familiar with an instructional design model, they may not completely understand the concepts that underpin each step. Some practitioners may desire more education and so seek books and resources on their own. Others might be employed by companies that send staff to workshops or conferences or online programs. This audience needs concise and useful materials so they can get up to speed quickly. They need an introduction to the basic concepts and procedures, and they also need examples to help them link knowledge to their experience.

---

vides a useful tool to confirm trends suggested by interviews or focus groups (Rothwell & Kazanas, 1998, p. 65).

Data Analysis and Reporting

Once you've collected information on your learners, what do you do with it? First, make sure that you have collected information from several sources. Are there common themes in your data? Note both the data that support your themes and the data that appear inconsistent with the majority view. Then present your learner analysis descriptively. You can present the data qualitatively, as a narrative (see Example 2.3), or quantitatively through simple frequencies, means, and percentage (see Example 2.4).

To further understand their audience, some designers find it useful to create imaginary learners, even giving them distinct personalities. They might create several

"sample students" representing multiple segments of the target audience. Some instructional design teams post these descriptions throughout the design project to serve as a constant reminder of just who will receive the instruction. The description of "one college freshman" (see Example 2.5) was created to help instructional designers and developers imagine their audience for a course on study skills. The course was targeted for university freshmen at a small state college in a rural area.

Putting It All Together

Imagine that we called you as part of the learner analysis for this book. First, we'd explain that we're working on a book about how instructional design is practiced. We'd tell you that your instructor gave us your name as some-

Example 2.4 Audience Analysis Reported as Simple Frequencies

Monroe Elementary School—Technology Questionnaire Results

Of the 17 teachers who responded, these are the percentages for using technology to complete tasks.	%
Use the computer for word processing.	70
Use e-mail to communicate with colleagues locally and worldwide.	100
Use the automatic card catalog.	76
Use Monroe's computer network.	100
Use the Internet to access worldwide resources.	88
Preview instructional programs for students.	65
Use the computer to manage classroom records.	65
Create multimedia demonstrations.	82
Create computer-based presentations.	70

Example 2.5 Description of Fictitious Learner

One College Freshman

Jen is a college freshman, living in a dorm. Before this semester, she had never spent much time away from home. Her small, rural high school had computers that were seven years old. Although many of her courses have an online component, she isn't comfortable with her new computer just yet. Besides, there are so many other things to do! Her roommate never wants to study and constantly has people visiting. She knows she could go to the library to study, but it seems so overwhelming.

one with good communication skills who may be able to help us make the book more useful. We'd ask if you have a few minutes to answer some questions. In this introduction, we've informed you of the purpose of the call, told you where we got your name, appealed to your good nature to help out, and asked for your help. Next, we'd ask about your current job and your future aspirations. Then we'd ask what you already know about instructional design and what you would like to learn. We'd take careful notes. After the conversation, we'd write you a note thanking you for your time.

If we asked you what you needed to learn about instructional design, you might have a clear idea, or you might not have any idea. Some of you may want to gain specific skills, such as developing test items for e-learning; others may simply want to learn about instructional design in general. Even when pressed for details, you may not be aware of your information needs or have enough knowledge to construct a response.

One strategy to use with learners who might be shy about revealing much about themselves is to have them talk about "other learners." Sometimes, it's easier for people to talk about someone else. They also may respond more readily to you if they perceive that you're "one of them." Some research indicates that interviewees are more honest with interviewers whom they perceive to be close to their own age range and demographic group (Gall, Gall, & Borg, 2002). For example, an injured coal miner may be more honest with a casually dressed man than with a woman wearing a business suit.

Just as SMEs like to be recognized as "expert" and usually want to help you develop your product, representative learners usually are glad to participate. Once you make connections with a set of learners, they can help you throughout the development process. Let's say you're developing a patient education program for teens who have been diagnosed with diabetes. You've cultivated a group of patients to serve as your representative learners. At several points in the design process, you find yourself bogged down about how to proceed. Should you review diet prior to the section on medications? How much detail should you provide on podiatry (a prime concern for diabetics)?

You can review these issues with your client and SME, but it also would be insightful to contact your learners to discuss these options and solicit their recommendations. If you get a few learners on your team early in the process, they can be invaluable during your design and development efforts.

Summary

In this chapter, we examined the purpose and methods of conducting a learner analysis. As illustrated by the essential triangle of instructional design, the learner is at the center of everything you do as an instructional designer. A learner analysis seeks to confirm learners' needs and identify their characteristics. As you collect information about learners' characteristics and needs, you will want to seek answers to the questions presented in the design aids at the end of this chapter.

Learner Analysis throughout the Phases

Recall that there are five phases to instructional design and that at each phase you visit each of the essential elements of instructional design, adding details as you spiral outward. As you develop your project proposal in the Define phase, you ask your client for information about the audience and their information needs. Next, you can synthesize that information into a contrived audience description within the project proposal. As you present the project proposal to the client, you check to confirm that your understanding of the learners is consistent with that of your client.

Once you've defined the project and received approval to move ahead to design the learning experience, you assemble additional information to elaborate upon your original understanding of the audience. During the Design phase, you may conduct interviews or focus groups with potential learners, read literature that provides insight into your audience's needs and characteristics, observe potential learners, conduct surveys, and engage in other activities that help you develop a clear and consistent picture of the target audience. Then you synthesize this information into a description of your audience and their needs. In addition, you describe the implications of these characteristics for the design of the instructional materials. As you present this information to your client in the design documents, you check to confirm your understanding of the learners.

During the Demonstration phase, you continue to serve as an advocate for the learners as the production document and prototype are developed. As you test a prototype with learners, you determine if your initial assumptions about how the materials should be designed to meet their needs and characteristics were correct. You may gain additional information about their prior experiences, motivation, and physical and cognitive characteristics as you observe how they respond to the instruction. Based on their responses and your refined view of the au-

dience, you develop a list of suggested modifications for the learning materials.

During the Develop phase, you monitor the production process to ensure that the materials meet the needs and characteristics of the learners. You also conduct a pilot test, field trial, or both, in which members of the target audience try out the materials to determine whether they are effective for learning. As you conduct field trials, you gain increased clarity about the learning context as you observe the materials in use in their intended setting.

Finally, the materials are presented to the learners during the Deliver phase.

Learner Analysis and the ASC Cycle

As you develop your learner analysis, you first *assemble* information from your learners and client and from individuals and resources that provide insight into the needs and characteristics of the learners. Next, you *synthesize* your knowledge into a description of the learners' needs and characteristics and the implications for the instructional materials. Finally, you *check* your understanding of the learners by sharing the audience description with the client and monitoring the learners' reactions to the instructional materials.

Notes

[1] Tessmer and Richey call for a separate phase in the instructional design process focused on context analysis. We have chosen to include context analysis with needs assessment and audience analysis. For more information on context analysis, see Martin Tessmer and Rita C. Richey, "The Role of Context in Learning and Instructional Design," *Educational Technology Research and Development, 45*(2): 85–115.

[2] Rothwell and Kazanas use "derived" and "contrived" differently.

[3] Documents prepared by David Halpin, Colleen Kerr, Peter Macedo, and Sandra Schneider, 1998. Used with permission.

References

Burton, J. K., & Merrill, P. F. (1991). Needs assessment: Goals, needs and priorities. In L. J. Briggs, K. L. Gustafson, & M. H. Tillman (Eds.), *Instructional design: Principles and applications* (2nd ed., pp. 17–43). Englewood Cliffs, NJ: Educational Technology.

Gall, M. D., Gall, J. P., & Borg, W. R. (2002). *Educational research: An introduction* (7th ed.). Needham Heights, MA: Allyn & Bacon.

Morrison, G. R. , Ross, S. M., & Kemp, J. E. (2004). *Designing effective instruction* (4th ed.). Hoboken, NJ: John Wiley.

Rossett, A. (1987). *Training needs assessment.* Englewood Cliffs, NJ: Educational Technology.

Rothwell, W., & Kazanas, H. C. (1998). *Mastering the instructional design process* (2nd ed.). San Francisco: Jossey-Bass.

Smith, P. L., & Ragan, T. J. (1999). *Instructional design* (2nd ed.). Upper Saddle River, NJ: Merrill/Prentice-Hall.

Application www

1. The RealWorldID Web site includes a case study of the design and development of a CD-ROM for an audience of furniture manufacturers. You are asked to identify the steps that the instructional designer should take next, develop a contrived audience analysis and a list of suggestions as to how the materials should be designed, and create a plan to collect data on the audience's needs and characteristics. Visit the RealWorldID Web site to analyze the case online or to print for use during class discussions.

2. In your reflective journal, summarize the key points of this chapter. How are the ideas presented consistent or inconsistent with your beliefs and prior knowledge? Compare your perceptions of the chapter with those of your classmates in group discussions.

3. As we explore the essential elements of instructional design in Chapters 2–6, the entire class is encouraged to function as an ID team to create the design specifications for an instructional module. The class should be divided into working groups of four to five members. Your course instructor should serve as an instructional design manager, leading design team meetings, checking on the progress of the working groups, and facilitating discussions. In this chapter, your working group should:
   a. Develop a learner profile for the assigned topic. Consider learners' needs and characteristics.
   b. Describe the implications of your analysis for the instructional materials and the goals of instruction.
   c. Make note of any decisions you'd like to check out in your formative evaluation.

4. Create a contrived analysis of a group of learners. Interview a few representatives of the group. Modify your analysis based on your interviews. Describe how your analysis changed or was confirmed by your interviews.

5. Create a written justification for conducting a learner analysis. Remember to keep the values of your clients in mind as you prepare your justification.

Ideas in Action

In Chapters 2–6, we follow the design of a videotape on food safety. In this chapter, we include a segment from the meeting notes in which the client describes the need for this project and the actual audience analysis created for it.[3] The audience analysis was created through brainstorming a list of learner characteristics and reviewing relevant literature. Can you see how the audience analysis expands on the ideas introduced by the client in the meeting notes? What implications do the learner characteristics have for the instructional materials?

Meeting Notes

The client wants to teach, via film, safe food handling and storage to the elderly who are independent—that is, who do not require assisted care. In the film, he wants to use motivational strategies to show the elderly why they need to be concerned about food safety and how they can protect themselves and others from food-borne illnesses. The issues he wants to focus on include refrigerated, frozen, canned, and dry goods handling, storage, and preparation. A "store to fork" scenario is what he has in mind for the film; from how to pick out food at the store (for example, expiration dates, correct wrappings), to how to prepare the food, to how to store the food as a safe leftover. Currently, no available films address these needs.

He wants the film to be 8–12 minutes in length, preferably 10 minutes. For role models, he wants to use middle-class elderly as actors. The film will be shown in senior centers and retirement communities, and at retiree groups functions such as the Kiwanis Club. Because there are no films like this presently, the film will also be used for evaluation purposes, to see if this kind of instruction, as well as the content itself, produced the desired effects.

Audience Analysis

1. Learner characteristics
   (a) Are over 55.
   (b) Are at-risk group due to weaker immunity against disease.
   (c) May not get to the store as often, so may have to keep food around longer.
   (d) May be on a limited income, and as a result may feel pressured to save food more.
   (e) May have grown up during the Depression and have learned the importance of saving and not wasting.
   (f) May have grown up in a time when there was less awareness of food-borne illnesses.
   (g) Will have a great deal of experience in food preparation.
   (h) May be coping with learning issues including retirement, loss of a spouse, health issues, and keeping up to date.

2. Value systems—Because the audience is made up of senior citizens, their value systems may be more conservative, and as such the instructional design of the video should take this into account to avoid offending anyone. At the same time, they should not be patronized by assuming that they are "out of touch" with today's society and values.

3. Physical traits

   (a) May have impaired sight and hearing.

   (b) May have impaired mobility.

   (c) If there are enough members of the audience with vision problems, then arrangements should be made to use a large-screen TV for showing the video. Make graphics large enough for them to see. Perhaps keep shots on screen a little longer. Volume may need to be louder.

4. Prerequisite skills and attitudes

   (a) Ability to work a TV and a VCR.

   (b) Basic food preparation skills—i.e., cutting, rolling, cooking, use of kitchen appliances.

   (c) Desire for a healthier lifestyle.

5. Findings from literature review

   • Studies show that most senior citizens are aware of food-borne illnesses and are concerned about safety issues, yet many of them fail to practice safe food handling procedures. They may not be aware that they have an increased risk. As a result, they should be agreeable to an education program that points out some of the major concerns.

   • With the exception of adequate cooking of meat items, seniors did not score any lower on food handling practices than any other groups. Adults 18–29 scored lowest. The trouble is, their reduced immunity may cause them more problems than other age groups. Seniors scored lowest on the topic of adequate cooking of meat items. This may be a food preference issue rather than a safety issue. They may prefer rarer cooked meat and not be aware of the dangers of poorly cooked meat. Education could help here.

   • Ability to correctly identify food sources of bacterial contamination is associated with knowing that thorough cooking makes food safe and with knowing and applying rules for prevention of cross-contamination.

   • Most people think that food-borne illness occurs after eating at a restaurant, but most illness originates from foods prepared at home.

   • Many people think that food-borne disease is a minor illness and underestimate the frequency of serious consequences. Education about the dangers of food-borne illness could help here.

6. Decision-related characteristics

   • Decisions about learner participation will be made by the staff at Extension Services, the directors of senior centers, senior groups, retiree functions, and the seniors themselves.

   • It is likely that few seniors will choose not to participate because this will be a passive activity that requires their attention for only about 10 minutes.

   • Because the food safety video will be viewed mainly in an organizational setting (senior centers, retiree functions), participation will be voluntary, and seniors' attitudes about the organization should be positive.

| DESIGN AID |

Learner Characteristics Worksheet

Learner Characteristics	Implications for Instructional Materials
Describe relevant prior experiences.	
Describe motivations.	
Describe relevant physical and cognitive characteristics.	
Describe the learning context.	
Describe the application context.	
Note any decisions you've made that you'd like to check out in your formative evaluation.	

| DESIGN AID |

Learner Needs and Characteristics Questionnaire

Who are the learners?	
What do they already know about the proposed topic?	
What should they know?	
Do they think the information will be useful? When and how? Under what conditions?	
How will instruction solve the problem that led to this need?	
What prior knowledge do they have related to the design of instruction (for example, previous and current employment, education and training, reading level, knowledge about the topic, vocabulary and language skills, visual literacy, computer skills)? Have they ever learned this way before?	
What are their motivational characteristics (for example, values, interests, short- and long-term goals, attitudes toward the subject matter and learning in general, self-concept, anxieties, confidence, competitive tendencies, preferences)? What factors could derail their success?	
What are their cognitive and physiological characteristics (for example, cognitive developmental level, language development, preferred learning styles, general learning abilities, specific aptitudes, manual dexterity, mobility)?	
Under what circumstances will they be learning? What sort of time, social support, resources, and equipment will be available?	
Under what conditions will they apply the skills? How often?	
Who will make the decisions to participate in instruction? What are their characteristics?	

Chapter 3
Outcomes and Assessments

Learning Outcomes

- Identify goals.

- Classify learning outcomes as verbal, intellectual, motor, affective, or attitude cognitive strategy.

- Refine goals and outcomes using content, task, and instructional analyses.

- Determine prerequisite skills.

- Write performance objectives.

- Create assessment instruments for a variety of learning outcomes.

- Develop scoring guides.

- List techniques to determine the validity and reliability of tests.

Chapter Overview

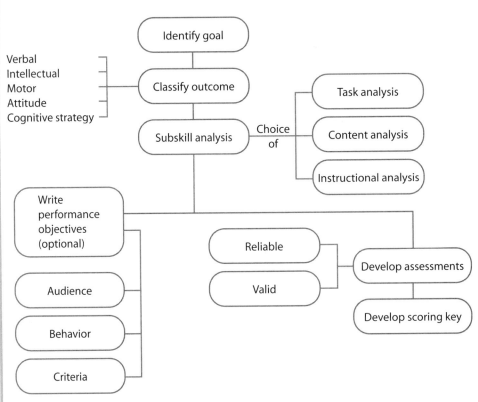

Orientation within the Design Process

Recall that there are five phases in the instructional design process and that in each phase we visit each of the essential elements of instructional design, adding details and performing tasks as required by the deliverables of each phase. In this chapter, we examine the elements of Outcomes and Assessments. Outcomes and assessments are closely related. Outcomes detail the results that are desired from the instruction. Assessments measure whether those results occurred. Outcomes and assessments must be aligned with the activities. This alignment is illustrated as a triangle (see Figure 3.1).

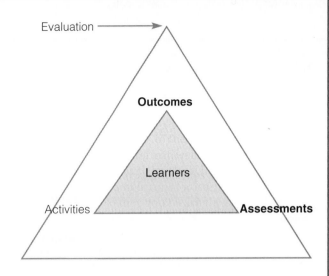

Figure 3.1 *Elements considered.* In this chapter, we consider the elements of outcomes and assessments.

Tasks at Each Phase

The tasks at each phase related to outcomes and assessments are summarized in Tables 3.1 and 3.2. As we discuss each of the phases in later chapters, you'll learn more about performing these tasks.

But for now, the two tables provide an overview of where the tasks discussed in this chapter fit into the five phases of design.

Table 3.1 Outcome-related tasks at each phase

Define	• Determine client's perception of goals during initial correspondence (meetings, phone conversations, written correspondence).
	• Write preliminary goal statements.
	• Include goals in proposal document. Present to client.
Design	• Fully develop goals.
	• Discuss possible outcomes with client, SME, and learners.
	• Write and sequence outcomes.
	• Determine prerequisite skills.
	• Present goals and outcomes to members of design team, client, and SME. Gain approval or change as needed.
Demonstrate	• Monitor development of production documents and prototype to ensure consistency with outcomes and sequence.
	• Present prototype to client, explaining how developed to teach outcomes.
	• Monitor learners' obtainment of outcomes during prototype tryout.
Develop	• Continue to monitor materials development to ensure consistency with goals and outcomes.
	• Seek data on learners' obtainment of outcomes during formative evaluation testing.
Deliver	• Present data on degree to which learners meet outcomes during formative evaluation.
	• Discuss suggested modifications. Determine whether modifications will occur during this development cycle or will form basis of recommendations for version 2.

Table 3.2 Assessment-related tasks at each phase

Define	• Determine what client would like learners to be able to do after this instruction.
	• Draft tentative ideas for assessments. Present to client in proposal.
Design	• Gather suggestions for assessments.
	• Develop concrete description of assessment instruments and/or specifications.
	• Present assessment ideas for client approval with design documents.
Demonstrate	• Develop specifications for assessments.
	• Develop prototype assessment instruments. Administer assessment instruments during prototype testing. Alter assessments as indicated by prototype tryout.
	• Present assessment instruments and/or specifications to client for approval.
Develop	• Monitor development of assessment instruments to ensure consistency with specifications.
	• Use assessment instruments during formative evaluation. Seek information to determine clarity and usefulness of assessments.
Deliver	• Discuss suggested modifications to assessment instruments resulting from formative evaluation. Determine whether modifications will occur during this development cycle or will form basis of recommendations for version 2.

Outcomes and Assessments

In the previous chapter, you learned techniques for determining the needs and characteristics of learners. Learners are the focus of everything you do as an instructional designer. We've represented this relationship as a triangle with learners in the center. The three corners correspond to these critical questions of instructional design:

- What changes in thinking or performance should occur?
- How will you know these changes have occurred?
- What activities will help facilitate these changes in thinking or performance?

As you answer these three questions, you define the outcomes, assessments, and instructional activities—the components that, if implemented appropriately, make a given learning experience effective. These three components, as corners of the equiangular triangle, must be aligned. That is, the outcomes must correspond to the assessment, and the activities must enhance learners' ability to achieve the outcomes and perform successfully on the assessment. Although this chapter focuses on outcomes and assessments, you frequently need to de-velop each of these three elements simultaneously. You might find it easiest to talk with your client about activities first. Or the starting point could be assessment, especially if the training is for a certification program designed to assist learners in mastering the test. The reason you can start at any point is that you eventually have to align each element of the triangle, regardless of where you begin.

Although outcomes and assessments are represented by two distinct points on the essential triangle, we discuss them together in this chapter because their relationship is critical. Outcomes and assessments can be thought of as two sides of the same coin. The **outcomes** refer to what we hope will result from the learning experiences; the **assessments** are designed to determine if the intended outcomes occurred. They measure what the learners actually gained from the instruction. There are four parts to developing outcomes and assessments:

- Identify learning goals and outcomes.
- Classify outcomes by type of learning represented.
- Determine the subskills required to obtain the desired outcomes.
- Develop assessments for each outcome and subskill.

We list these parts in a sequence, but the process is rarely this linear.

⟳ Identifying Learning Goals and Outcomes

What will success look like? That's the question you really need answered when you begin talking with a client about an instructional design project. In other words, what is the expected outcome? Once your client explains what success will look like, your next question should be, "How will you know it's successful?" The answer to this question tells you how you can verify that success using an assessment. Most clients can answer these questions—perhaps not with the detail or precision you'd like—but they can provide you with enough information to get you started in understanding the task ahead.

All instruction is designed and developed with some purpose in mind—it wouldn't be instruction if it didn't have a purpose. Clients often will express the purpose in terms of the product instead of the learning outcomes. For example, your client may say, "We want to create a powerful antismoking video program. We want it to really pack a wallop—the kind of program that can win awards." This goal statement tells you quite a bit about the client's vision of the product's success, but not much about whom it's for and what it will accomplish. Who is the target audience, and what should they do or think after viewing the program? What does "powerful" mean to the client? What is the purpose of creating an award-winning program? If it's simply to win awards, the intended audience will be jurors who select award winners. In that case, you could conduct an audience analysis on the preferences of awards panels. You'd review programs that won awards in the past and research the organizations that sponsor awards to determine their criteria and values. But if the program is to be instructional, it's your job as the instructional designer to help the client define the learning outcome more specifically.

To determine the learning outcome, you have to know something about the target audience, the content, and the context in which the skills should be applied. Perhaps, after discussions with your client, you are able to identify these details about the antismoking program they desire:

1. The audience is middle school students ranging in age from 10 to 14.

2. "Powerful" means it will catch and hold the audience's attention. It may need to have an edginess to work for this audience.

3. "Award-winning" means that the quality is superb.

4. The learners will be able to list some of the hazards of smoking.

5. The learners will be more motivated to not start smoking or to quit if they've started.

Based on these answers, you determine that the client's real goal is to motivate middle school students to refrain from smoking or to quit if they have started through a high-quality program that catches their attention and identifies some of the hazards of smoking. **Goals** reflect the overall learning target—the "big picture"—while **outcomes** provide the details to translate those goals into measurable learning requirements. An outcome is a statement of what the instruction needs to accomplish. It should be written in terms of what the learners will be able to do after the instruction. In the antismoking example, the outcome for the middle school students would be to "Choose to refrain from smoking." Outcomes focus on the changes in thinking or performance that the instructional activities should facilitate.

A program goal might be to "Teach hikers to read topographical maps." With this goal in mind, you can visualize the students, the content, the context in which the skills will be applied, and the actions they'll be able to perform after the instruction. You have enough information to start asking detailed questions and to delve further into the requirements. After additional questioning, you may determine that the learning outcome is for hikers to "Interpret topographical maps to plan a hike."

Another goal might be to "Teach preschool children to care for their new eyeglasses." You can imagine this group of young learners, you probably have some idea about what the content will include, and you can begin to think about how they will be able to handle their glasses following the lesson. But you need to refine this broad goal statement before developing a specific learning outcome. Remember, you need to determine what changes in thinking or performance are desired and how you can determine if these changes have occurred. After participating in the program, should the youngsters be able to demonstrate the proper way to care for their eyeglasses, choose to care for their glasses properly, or list the steps in the proper care of glasses? Each of these learning outcomes is slightly different and so requires different instructional activities and assessments.

Types of Learning Outcomes

Because different types of learning outcomes have implications for the assessments and activities of instruction (see Table 3.3), it often is useful to classify learning outcomes by type. Educational psychologists generally agree that learning outcomes can be classified into declarative, procedural, motor, affective, and metacognitive (or conditional) knowledge (Driscoll, 2000). These "domains of learning" are similar to Robert Gagné's (1985) categories of verbal information, intellectual skills, motor skills, cognitive skills, and attitudes. For simplicity, we will use Gagné's classification scheme.

Verbal Information Verbal information is **declarative knowledge**—content that you can think of as "just the facts." Facts range from incidental information, such as your childhood friend's middle name, to critical information

Table 3.3 Types of learning outcomes and implications for assessments and activities

Type of learning	Sample outcomes	Assessment	Activity
Verbal information	Recall that Ben Franklin invented bifocal eyeglasses. Recall that Amazon River is just below Equator. Recall that 15 is divisible by 3 and 5.	Recall facts.	Provide framework for linking to prior learning, mnemonic devices (arithmetic = a rat in the house might eat the ice cream).
Intellectual skills	Differentiate bifocals from other eyeglasses. Classify living things as mammals. Recognize that a math problem requires division. Read. Solve quadratic equations.	Apply concept or procedure. Solve problems.	Provide examples and nonexamples, demonstration of steps in process, practice. Give feedback.
Motor skills	Drive car. Swing a golf club. Pronounce rolling "r" sound in Spanish.	Demonstrate the skill.	Model behaviors, repeated physical practice. Provide feedback.
Attitude	Quit smoking. Sell more widgets. Work to save endangered species.	Survey attitudes. Observe behavioral change over time.	Engage learners' emotions. Provide role models.
Cognitive strategies	Select study strategy. Determine when to shift to different sales pitch.	Keep reflective journals. Survey strategy usages.	Set personal goals, self-monitor, reflect on progress. Provide role models, examples, coaching.

such as the phone number to call in an emergency. Think of declarative knowledge as all the discrete bits of information you accumulate, both on purpose and without trying. At the simplest level, your declarative knowledge is like a file drawer filled with folders containing all the facts you know. The more frequently you retrieve and use specific knowledge, the more likely you are to recall it each time you need it. For example, you may have called your childhood friend's phone number so frequently in the past that it is still easy for you to recall. Much of what you know can be classified as verbal information.

Intellectual Skills Intellectual skills require procedural knowledge. If declarative knowledge is "what," then **procedural knowledge** is "how." When you learn and perform a skill at an automatic, or habituated, level, it's procedural knowledge. For example, once you master the tasks, you read in your native language automatically. If you had to stop and think about decoding every word, you wouldn't get very far very fast. If you've ever tried to read street signs in a country where people speak a different language, you probably had to think consciously about each action. You also likely realized how much your reading skills are an automatic process in a familiar language.

Much of what we learn involves intellectual skills. The ability to solve a math problem, converse in your native language, diagnose an illness, and correctly file

a report are all examples of intellectual skills. The ability to perform intellectual skills derives from a base of verbal information. Knowing to call 911 in an emergency is verbal information, but determining that a situation is an emergency is an intellectual skill. Writing an essay draws on the ability to harness facts (verbal information) into a persuasive context (intellectual skill).

Gagné further classified intellectual skills into the subcategories of discriminations, concepts, rules, and problem-solving tasks (Gagné, Briggs, & Wager, 1992). **Discriminations** involve distinguishing objects by their features. For example, determining if two pieces of furniture are similar or different involves a discrimination. Discriminations are prerequisite skills for **concepts**, which involve classifying stimuli on the basis of their concrete features or the extent to which they meet a definition. You know that a chair is a chair and not a table because you have learned the specific attributes of both chairs and tables that help you to distinguish between the two. Because these attributes include physical characteristics as well as the function of each item, you are able to differentiate items that fall somewhere between the two, such as a stool or a coffee table. Like all tables, a coffee table has legs, a flat top, and is used to place items upon, while a stool has legs, a flat top, but is used for sitting. However, a stool becomes a table when items are placed on it. Concepts are prerequisite skills for **rules** and their application. For example, a furniture store employee may need to know the company rules for properly displaying chairs and tables. Rules, in turn, are prerequisite skills for higher-order rules and **problem-solving tasks**, such as developing an advertising plan for a furniture company. The solution to this complex problem draws upon discrimination, concepts, and rules, as well as knowledge acquired from solving problems in other settings.

Motor Skills   Motor skills require moving muscle groups to execute a physical performance. Any physical task is a motor skill, such as tying a shoelace, typing 75 words per minute, or swimming the butterfly stroke. Most complex motor skills involve other types of learning. For example, executing a successful golf swing requires selecting the right club, calculating the power with which to hit the ball, checking the wind and turf conditions, and maintaining proper form while swinging. In addition to the purely physical act of swinging the club, the task requires the golfer to apply rules and solve problems. In addition to athletic and fitness activities, motor skills are involved in many occupational tasks, such as lifting a heavy object without stressing the back, and many everyday tasks, such as pronouncing words, making a flaky piecrust, riding a bicycle, and swiping a credit card through the magnetic reader at a store. These are all examples of motor tasks that we had to perform repeatedly until we got them right. Like intellectual skills, motor skills can become automatic after repeated use, but motor skills involve physical rather than mental process.

Attitudes   Feelings that predispose individuals to behave in certain ways are due to affective knowledge, or **attitudes**. Attitudinal capabilities are those that require a change in behavior, such as choosing to eat more fresh produce, making charitable contributions, or maintaining a high grade point average. Art appreciation, character education, personal coaching techniques, and programs to motivate a sales force are all examples of instruction that seek to change affective knowledge. Affective knowledge goals also play a significant role in religious education and military training.

The formation of attitudes usually requires verbal information and intellectual skills development in support of attitude development. For example, Space Center Houston provides visitors with an experience filled with verbal information, intellectual skills, and even motor skills, but the ultimate goal is to inculcate positive attitudes about manned space flight and exploration. By sharing the details of an astronaut's daily life in space (verbal information), asking visitors to plan an astronaut's daily schedule (intellectual skills), and providing opportunities for visitors to try on space helmets and gloves (motor skills), the program's designers sought to give visitors a vicarious sense of the experience of space flight and accomplish that attitudinal goal. As with many programs with attitudinal goals, the Center's managers felt the attitudinal aims needed to be subtle so that visitors wouldn't feel manipulated.

Cognitive Strategies   Cognitive strategies consist of the metacognitive or conditional knowledge used to learn information and solve problems. "Metacognition" refers to the act of "thinking about thinking." Learners who plan ahead, predict their potential for success, monitor their performance, and evaluate the adequacy of a solution are using metacognitive skills (Gagné & Glasser, 1987). Also known as the "control process" (Gagné, Yekovich, & Yekovich, 1993, p. 43) or "conditional knowledge" (Driscoll, 2000, p. 347), cognitive strategies guide learners in acquiring and applying other types of knowledge. For example, you may want to do well in a course, so you adopt the strategy of repeatedly reading sections of the textbook. If this strategy doesn't yield successful outcomes as measured on the assessments, you'll modify your learning strategy. Perhaps you'll shift to outlining the chapters or creating other study aids.

As another example, you may know that you learn verbal information by using it several times soon after being exposed to it. You've used a cognitive strategy based on your understanding of your own learning strengths. Learning cognitive strategies is dependent on intellectual skills such as discriminating one condition from another. For example, you need to discriminate verbal information from other types of learning outcomes. You also need to apply rules for when to apply a particular strategy and when to recognize another would be more effective.

Within a given instructional episode, you may have one or all types of learning outcomes. For example, if you are preparing a lesson on Kanji, one of the four written versions of the Japanese language, students need to learn what the names of the characters are (verbal information), when to use each character (intellectual skill), and how to write each character (motor skill). Students make judgments as to whether they are successfully learning the language (cognitive strategy). And, because this is very hard for Western students to master, you insert a hefty dose of motivational support (attitude).

As another example, the broad goal of teaching preschool children to care for their new eyeglasses might be translated into several different kinds of learning outcomes, each with implications for the design of instructional activities and assessments. This outcome could be taught and assessed as verbal information ("Preschool children will list the steps to properly care for their eyeglasses"), an intellectual skill ("Preschool children will demonstrate the proper care of their eyeglasses"), an attitude ("Preschool children will choose to care for their eyeglasses properly"), or a motor skill ("Preschool children will clean their eyeglasses by rubbing them gently with a soft cloth"). As you define the learning outcome, it is helpful to classify the learning outcome by domain.

Identifying Subskills

Once you have developed and classified the project's general learning outcomes, you'll want to get a better understanding of the content, the learners, and the kinds of skills involved in mastering the content. You need to delve into the material to identify the subskills and knowledge that will yield the desired learning outcomes. This begins the effort, which will continue through the project, to zero in on the specific content, its structure, and the skills required to master that content.

A **subskill analysis** identifies the skills that contribute to an outcome and maps the relationships among the skills in a visual hierarchy, much like an organizational chart. For people who are visual thinkers, this is a powerful tool in understanding the scope of the material. This visual tool is invaluable in communicating with clients, SMEs, and colleagues. Most importantly, these methods of analysis are tools that help you refine your thinking.

Three methods are used commonly for identifying subskills: instructional analysis, task analysis, and content analysis. As you diagram the content, the tasks, or the instructional subskills, you think through the relationships among key ideas. You should select the method or methods that best fit the information sources you're working with and the intended learning outcomes. With each of these methods, the result allows you to create a skills hierarchy with higher-order skills organized in relation to their subordinate skills and to each other.

Instructional Analysis An instructional analysis examines the conceptual building blocks of a skill. To conduct an instructional analysis, you need to determine what type of learning outcome your goal represents, based on Gagné's hierarchy of learning outcomes. As discussed, outcomes can be classified into the following categories:

Verbal information

Intellectual skills (discriminations, rules, concepts, problem-solving tasks)

Cognitive strategies

Motor skills

Attitudes

Next, you need to identify the subskills that lead to the obtainment of that outcome and classify them according to type of learning outcome. For example, if you're teaching a problem-solving skill, you want to consider which rules are necessary to perform the problem-solving task. Once you identify the subordinate rules, you can consider which concepts are necessary to apply those rules. Finally, you consider which discriminations are needed to learn the requisite concepts.

Many, if not most, instructional episodes include verbal information and intellectual skills. Some lessons include each type of learning outcome. For example, in the following situation, a designer is developing a training program on pipeline repair for oilfield contractors. The training could require these different types of learning outcomes:

Task	Type of Learning Outcome
List possible defects.	Verbal information
Diagnose cause.	Intellectual skill (problem solving)
Determine solution.	Cognitive strategy
Perform the repair.	Motor skill

Or, suppose you want learners to create video segments that maintain visual continuity. This task might require the following:

Problem-solving/higher-order rule: Create video segments that maintain visual continuity and are free of jump cuts.

Concept: Identify a video segment as containing jump cuts.

Verbal information: State that a jump cut refers to a sudden change in screen position by an object on the screen.

Discrimination: Identify a sudden change in screen position.

Rule: To avoid jump cuts when shooting, move the camera at least 45 degrees between shots.

Discrimination: Recognize a 45-degree change in camera angle.

Rule: Use a cutaway, cut-in, dissolve, or wipe between two similar shots.

Concept: Identify a cut-in in a video segment.

Concept: Identify a cutaway in a video segment.

Concept: Identify a transition as a wipe or dissolve.

Figure 3.2 illustrates how these skills can be diagrammed in an instructional analysis.

Task Analysis As an alternative to an instructional analysis, a **task analysis** identifies how people perform physical or mental activities. The techniques of task analysis are well suited for procedural and motor skills—those learning outcomes that can be presented as a sequence of steps. Balancing a checkbook, serving a tennis ball, and using a spreadsheet package are all examples of procedural skills. You can use task analysis methods to break down a complex skill into a series of small steps, or subskills.

If you are working with an SME, you can begin the task analysis by prompting him or her to recall the steps involved in performing the task. One technique is to show the SME a product or an outcome and ask what steps

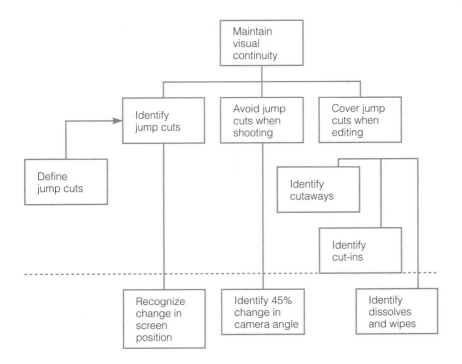

Figure 3.2 *Instructional analysis.* In this example of instructional analysis, the instructional outcome is to create video segments that maintain visual continuity and are free of jump cuts. Note the three prerequisite skills below the dotted line.

were involved in achieving that outcome. For example, show a tennis serve and ask the SME to begin breaking the serve into its component tasks. Continue this questioning as you try to determine what knowledge and skills are needed to perform the steps: How can you determine if the skill is acceptable? What might make it unacceptable? Are certain problems common? Another technique for soliciting the steps involved in performing a task is to describe a challenging event and ask what skills or knowledge are necessary to respond to this event (Tessmer, 1998). For example, ask a golf expert how he would get his ball out of a sand trap, or a video expert how she would shoot in low lighting conditions.

It's not unusual for experts to describe unique or exceptional situations. Often, these are examples that illustrate the expert's great skill in her or his field. However, rare situations are just that: rare. For materials aimed at novices, these unusual cases are sure to be confusing. Explain this delicately to your SME, because this unique situation may represent a career triumph for that individual. Try to present your comments from the perspective of the learner. Explain that in an introductory program you need to focus on basics and that there may be an opportunity to use the additional information in a subsequent program.

Sometimes, experts are unable to state the steps in performing a task. In these cases, you might observe or videotape the expert performing the task in order to docu-

ment the steps that contribute to the performance of the goal. You might also prompt the expert to "think aloud" while he or she performs the task so that you can gain insight into factors that influence performance. You might wonder how an expert could fail to remember the steps in a task in which she or he has expertise, but experts are often so skilled in a task that they don't really think about it anymore. Think about how difficult it is for you to speak a foreign language. You have to think about each word—its meaning, pronunciation, and placement in the sentence—as well as word agreement, verb tenses, and inflection. When you express those same thoughts in your native language, you don't think about any of this. In fact, if you're asked to break down a sentence, you will be hard-pressed to do so. As an expert in speaking your native language, you, like other experts, often function on "autopilot."

Experts can provide too much detail as well as too little. They often are so removed from the novice experience that they don't have the perspective to sort out which tasks are merely "nice to know" and which are essential. On the other hand, if you sense that you don't have enough information, trust your instincts and ask more questions. If you don't understand a sequence or the logic of a task, ask if something else should be included. Anything that is confusing to you is likely to be confusing to learners.

Once you've identified the skills needed to perform the target task, you can create a task analysis diagram. Place the specific tasks in a flowchart, in the order in

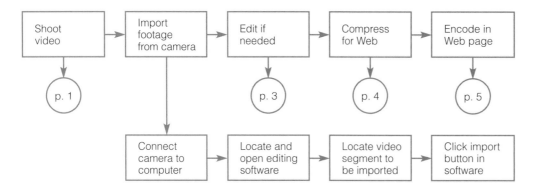

Figure 3.3 *Task analysis.* In this example of a task analysis, the course goal is to create a movie for Web-based delivery.

which they must be performed, and identify which sub-skills need to be performed before other skills. Figure 3.3 illustrates part of the task analysis for a workshop for university alumni on creating an original movie for Web-based delivery. Notice how the skills are diagrammed in the sequence in which they should be performed.

Content Analysis   Whereas the task analysis looks at the performance of a skill, a **content analysis** is similar to an outline of the material to be covered in a lesson, in that you identify the main topics and associated subtopics. However, instead of organizing your content in a list, as in an outline, you place it in a hierarchy, with subcategories of knowledge drawn below higher-level categories. A content analysis is often the best way to organize declarative knowledge—facts that are used in support of concepts, rules, and problem-solving tasks.

In the ideal scenario, the content has been taught before, a good syllabus exists, and the client has a clear understanding of what should be taught and in what sequence. Because this rarely happens, you have to survey the content in any form you can find it: SMEs, clients, books, Web sites, company materials, and so on. As you examine these resources, begin classifying and categorizing key topics in logical groupings.

Figure 3.4 presents part of a content analysis for a program designed to provide water treatment plant operators with the information they needed to select a motor to power their facility. Notice how the broad goal is divided into subtopics, with the subtopics further divided into sub-subtopics. To develop the content analysis featured in Figure 3.4, the designer talked with experts and members of the target audience, reviewed company videotapes, and pored over technical manuals. She assembled information, synthesized it into a content analysis, and then checked her understanding by sharing the content analysis with SMEs, her client, and the design team. In conducting a content analysis, you identify the essential information that should be included in your instructional materials in order for learners to obtain the necessary skills, knowledge, or attitudes. You piece this material together and see if your assumptions are correct by asking for feedback.

Sometimes, you need to determine subskills by examining a set of test items. As you would in organizing any other content, you examine the test items to determine if they cluster into logical groups that can be summarized under a particular heading. Diagram these clusters and try to place them in a hierarchy. Then review your diagram with your client and SMEs. You may find that some test items don't adequately reflect the critical content and

---

Voice of Experience

Videotaping Course for Content Analysis

A software engineer was serving as the SME on a project to produce an online training program on the company's new software product. The SME was busy readying the software product for release into the marketplace and was having a hard time finding time to work with the instructional designer. The SME also had to conduct some training classes on the new product for company staff. The designer asked if she could videotape the SME giving one of the training programs. That

way, the designer could capture the content from the SME, already organized and delivered in an instructional format. An added benefit was that the training would provide screens and examples from the software that would be useful in the online version. The videotape was used for content analysis during the early phases of the instructional design and as a content resource later in the process.

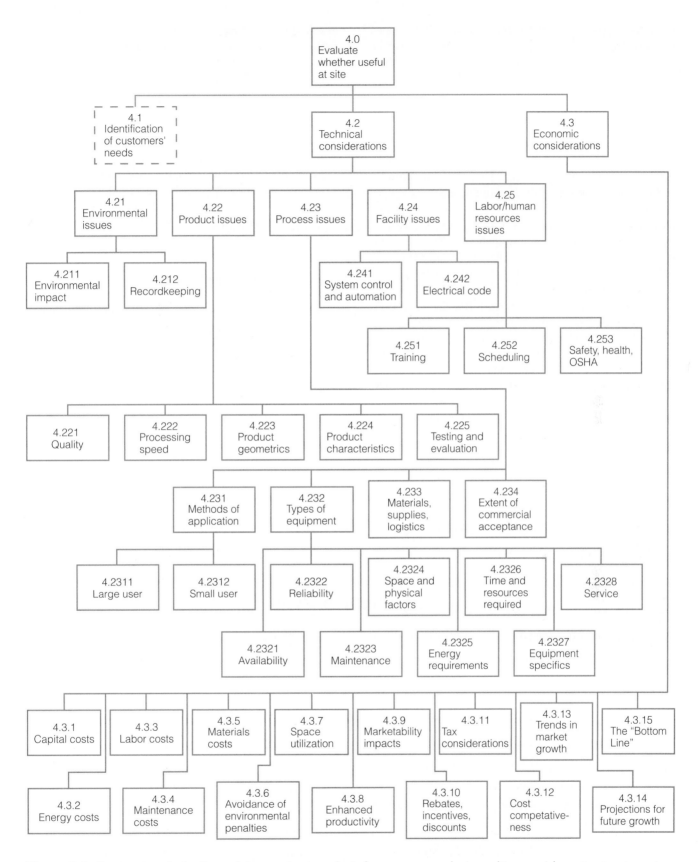

Figure 3.4 *Content analysis.* Part of the content analysis for a program designed to provide water treatment plant operators with the information they needed to select a motor to power their facility.

need to be revised. As with any other document developed in the instructional design process, this analysis is part of an iterative cycle. As you complete tasks throughout the five phases of design, you achieve increasing levels of clarity and precision.

Determining Prerequisite Knowledge

After the earliest stages of infancy, almost everything you learn builds on prior knowledge. When you develop instructional materials, you need to identify the skills and knowledge on which the learning will depend. In some situations, learners must demonstrate that they have these prerequisite skills before being admitted to the instruction. For example, college courses often have prerequisites that must be met prior to enrollment. Other times, the instruction is designed to meet the needs of each learner regardless of prior knowledge. In either case, it's important to identify the prerequisite skills learners need to successfully participate in the instruction.

If you are working with teachers or trainers as your SMEs, they probably can help you identify prerequisite skills fairly easily. These SMEs have direct experience with the target audience and can identify what learners know and what they may need help with. You may hear a teacher or trainer say something along the lines of, "I have to repeat this section over and over before students get it." Pay attention to comments like this, and try especially hard to determine what knowledge or skills are required to understand the problematic content. Perhaps students lack a critical subskill, and the problem can be

resolved by inserting content into the instruction that was assumed to be part of the prerequisite knowledge. If the content has not been taught before, you have to make some educated guesses. In this situation, it's particularly important to question a group of learners to check your assumptions.

On the diagram of subskills that you create, place the prerequisite skills under each of the appropriate subskills. Draw a dotted line separating the subskills from their prerequisite skills. Because of how they appear on the instructional skills diagram, these prerequisite skills are often called "below-the-line" skills. Notice the below-the-line skills in the hierarchy diagram in Figure 3.2.

Creating a Subskill Analysis You've probably noticed that you determine subskills for task, content, and instructional analyses the same way you determine almost anything in instructional design. You:

- Assemble information and ask questions.
- Synthesize information and solve problems.
- Check and confirm your understanding.

As you follow the ASC cycle, ask SMEs what learners need to know to perform the goal. Also ask members of the target audience what they already know about the topic and what they need to know. Examine any available resource materials.

To synthesize this information into a subskill analysis, you have to think carefully about what skills and informa-

---

Voice of Experience

Content Analysis

For a program that aimed to give the general public a sense of what it's like to be an astronaut on the space shuttle, the designer had to decide what topics to include in the program. The shuttle is a complex collection of interrelated functional systems, such as the positioning system, that are too technical for a presentation to the public. The design and development team brainstormed and decided to focus on how astronauts live on the shuttle. This allowed them to limit the content to topics that the public could readily appreciate and still meet the program's goal of helping people better understand life aboard the craft.

After discussions with NASA experts and Space Center Houston project directors, the instructional design team settled on these main sections:

- Propulsion
- Life Support
- Crew Compartment
- Space Navigation
- Communications
- Payload Bay
- Reaction Control

Each of these sections allowed the designer to focus on the astronaut instead of the shuttle. Once she had these subtopics in place, she assembled the material under each topic.

tion depend on learning other skills and information. This isn't an easy process and is likely to require several iterations. Some people like to manipulate index cards or Post-it Notes™ as they explore various ways of organizing the main topics and subtopics. After recording individual ideas on separate pieces of paper, they arrange and rearrange the visual hierarchy until they are satisfied. Others simply jot their ideas down on paper in rough form.

Check your hypothesized subskill analysis with clients and SMEs. If possible, also check your assumptions with representatives of the target audience. If some of your assumptions aren't correct, revise your work and try again.

Think of these tasks, as with most instructional design tasks, the way you think about writing a paper. Drafting, editing, revising, and even completely rewriting are normal steps in the process. So, too, when you develop a subskill analysis hierarchy: Draft, review, revise, and perhaps even start over to get it right. Once you've created the subskill analysis, examine the subtopics to determine if each contributes to the identified outcomes. If not, consider whether you need to modify the outcomes to include the topic or if you should eliminate the extraneous content.

Defining Success

Once you determine the project outcomes and subskills, your next task is to turn them into something more concrete, something that can be measured so that you can verify that the instruction really works. There are two ways to do this: by writing performance objectives and by developing assessments.

Many instructional design models require the designer to write performance objectives before proceeding to the next step, the assessment. However, this rigidity isn't necessary, even in classic instructional design models (see, for example, Dick & Carey, 1996, p. 118). In many situations, you don't even need to write a detailed set of performance objectives. But you do have to define outcomes and subtasks, and you have to align the outcomes, activities, and assessments. If you begin with objectives and aren't getting anywhere, try a different strategy, starting with assessment or activities.

Writing Objectives

Traditionally, objectives describe the assessment and the criteria for acceptable performance. In fact, you can think of objectives as specifications for the assessment. In practice, you usually don't have to create long lists of detailed performance objectives. However, you may be expected to write them, so you should have this skill in your "designer's toolkit" to pull out and use when needed.

Robert F. Mager's classic *Preparing Instructional Objectives* (1997) is one of the best and best-selling books on objectives. Mager recommended that the objective describe three things:

1. The behavior the learner will exhibit

2. The conditions under which the behavior must occur

3. The criteria that must be met for acceptable performance

A classic objective states the performance (what the learner will be able to do), the conditions for the performance, and the criteria for judging how well the learner performed. Here's an example: "Given the names of 20 Mayan sites, identify the time period for each as Formative, Classic, or Post-Classic with 85% accuracy." The performance here is to identify the correct time period for Mayan sites. The condition is that the learner will correctly identify each of 20 sites as Formative, Classic, or Post-Classic. The criterion is to do this with 85 percent accuracy. This objective describes exactly what the learner should be able to do to demonstrate his or her knowledge of the skills.

Heinich, Molenda, Russell, and Smaldino (2001) describe another model for developing objectives, the **ABCD model**, which stands for *Audience, Behavior, Conditions,* and *Degree*. According to this model, a good objective should include the:

- Audience

- Behavior, which is observable and measurable

- Conditions under which the behavior must be performed

- Degree to which proficiency in the behavior will be demonstrated

When defining conditions, avoid the phrase "After instruction, the learner will . . ." What if the learner already has the skill and can perform the task without instruction? Doesn't that count? More precise conditions are needed. For example, the objective "The learner will locate and identify 15 native trees" describes the audience (the learners), the behavior (identify and locate trees), and the criteria for acceptable performance (15 trees). But it doesn't indicate the conditions under which the task should be accomplished. Are learners to locate and identify 15 native trees in the wild? Or from a set of 30 pictures? Can learners use guides to assist in identification, or must they do so from memory? As you define the conditions, keep in mind the context in which the learners eventually will apply their knowledge, and try to make those conditions as realistic as practical. The following objectives include the level of precision needed when writing behavioral objectives:

"Using a guide to identification, the learner will locate and identify 15 native trees in the wild."

"Given a set of 30 pictures, the learner will locate and identify 15 native trees from memory."

Be careful to write objectives in terms of what learners are expected to demonstrate *as a result of* the instruction, not what they will do *during* the instruction. For example, if the goal of instruction is to change the way learners teach science, you don't want to state an objective such as "The learner will view a videotape of science teaching and make notes on the teacher's performance." This might be an acceptable objective if the goal of instruction is to "produce notes about videotapes of teaching," but the goal is to change the way science is taught, so the objective needs to reflect that outcome. A better objective would be "The learner will identify three specific teaching strategies that he or she can implement in his or her science classroom."

Avoid imprecise verbs such as "understand" or "know." Instead, state objectives precisely, using verbs that reflect an observable performance. For example, if your client says that the objective of a training program is to "know about company's policies?" what sort of performance would demonstrate "knowing" the company's policy? Work with your client to develop a measurable objective, such as "Employees will state all company policies related to their specific job duties from memory." Table 3.4 lists verbs that are useful in crafting good performance objectives.

Objectives Issues Some designers and clients are critical of objectives, particularly highly specific behavioral objectives. Some of the "bad press" about objectives in particular, and about instructional design in general, was caused by well-intentioned designers who labored over objectives, halting other productive work and hurting their projects because they couldn't adopt a more flexible strategy. Other critics recall the performance objectives movement that was popular in the 1960s and 1970s. This movement encouraged teachers to write very specific instructional objectives that included observable performances. The idea behind the performance objective movement was good—that teachers should make the intended outcome of instruction explicit. But the reality was that performance objectives often focused on very low-level behaviors that were easily observable and testable, to the exclusion of higher-order thinking skills. Objectives shouldn't have to focus on low-level learning outcomes. In fact, objectives can focus on the process of learning as well as the product.

In this book, we frequently use the term "outcomes" to refer to instructional objectives. The term doesn't carry the baggage of "objectives" and shouldn't prevent your client and team from focusing on the real issue—figuring out the product. For many people, "outcomes" feels less restrictive than "objectives" and seems more focused on the program's success. You'll probably find yourself adopting the terminology and the approach that works for each team. For example, when you are working with a team of seasoned instructional designers, "objectives" will probably work fine. When you meet with a new client and SMEs, it might be more effective to talk about "outcomes."

Table 3.4 The helpful hundred suggested performance terms

Add	Compute	Drill	Label	Predict	State
Alphabetize	Conduct	Estimate	Locate	Prepare	Subtract
Analyze	Construct	Evaluate	Make	Present	Suggest
Apply	Contrast	Explain	Manipulate	Produce	Swing
Arrange	Convert	Extrapolate	Match	Pronounce	Tabulate
Assemble	Correct	Fit	Measure	Read	Throw
Attend	Cut	Generate	Modify	Reconstruct	Time
Bisect	Deduce	Graph	Multiply	Reduce	Translate
Build	Defend	Grasp (hold)	Name	Remove	Type
Carve	Define	Grind	Operate	Revise	Underline
Categorize	Demonstrate	Hit	Order	Select	Verbalize
Choose	Derive	Hold	Organize	Sketch	Verify
Classify	Describe	Identify	Outline	Ski	Weave
Color	Design	Illustrate	Pack	Solve	Weigh
Compare	Designate	Indicate	Paint	Sort	Write
Complete	Diagram	Install	Plot	Specify	
Compose	Distinguish	Kick	Position	Square	

SOURCE: From Instructional Media and Technologies for Learning, 7th ed., by R. Heinich, M. Molenda, J. Russell, and S. Smaldino, © 2002. Reprinted by permission of Pearson Education, Inc., Upper Saddle River, NJ.

As an instructional designer, you create goals and objectives for several reasons. Most importantly, when included within the instruction, they guide learners in allocating their attention. Explicit statements of learning outcomes can benefit learners (Driscoll, 2000; Gagné, Yekovich, & Yekovich, 1993) in several ways:

1. By activating prior knowledge, which helps them connect new learning to material they already know

2. By allowing them to adopt or reject the objectives as their personal goals

3. By helping them set up a cognitive organizational scheme for the new information

4. By providing cues about what to attend to within the instruction

Just as outcomes serve a critical role in guiding learners, they also guide the design and development team. When your team is immersed in a project, the outcomes keep everyone focused. You should revisit them throughout production and review them in discussions with clients, SMEs, learners, and other members of the team. Even if you cover them thoroughly early in the production process, it's important to review them in each phase of design. Each time you work with new content or a new component, consider whether it supports the intended learning outcomes. If it fails to do so, it probably doesn't belong in the product. The outcomes serve as a road map—an instructional mission statement of where you're headed and what you're trying to achieve.

In some situations, you don't need to write a detailed set of performance objectives. But you do have to identify outcomes and supporting subskills, and you have to ensure that the outcomes and subskills are aligned with the assessments. You can do this at almost any point in the early stages of the instructional design process. If you are having trouble identifying the learning outcomes, one strategy is to write the assessment and then go back and write the objectives if necessary. The assessment is where learners demonstrate their knowledge and skills. By working with your client to develop the test items, you answer two key questions: What kinds of changes will

---

Voice of Experience

Writing Assessments First

When working with a construction company to develop training materials for a certification program, the designer found that the SMEs selected to assist her were experienced construction workers who were not accustomed to sitting in an office for days at a time, working on instructional specifications. Although they were selected because of their depth of knowledge of the regulations related to certification, their usual work environment was the construction site. They frequently commented about how difficult it was for them to have to be indoors all day—let alone in a conference room.

They readily identified the training goals that would make the certification program successful. They were able to help define the novice learners who were the target audience for the course. But when the designer tried to enlist their help in developing objectives, the process ground to a halt. The SMEs had trouble understanding how the objectives, or subskills, differed from the high-level goals. They couldn't understand why the objectives had to be stated in a certain format. They weren't trying to be difficult, but the process clearly wasn't working.

The designer knew that the SMEs would be available for only a few more days before they had to return to the field. She didn't have time to teach them how to write good objectives, and they didn't really want to learn something that wasn't directly relevant to their world. So she switched gears, asking them to concentrate on writing assessment questions. She explained that by writing the test they would be able to identify the important chunks of content in the program. Once they had the questions developed, she would be able to backtrack and turn the assessment items into effective objectives.

The SMEs were surprised and wondered if this didn't imply that the course would be "teaching to the test." The designer explained that the training *should* teach to the test. The test should be a valid and reliable measure of a worker's readiness to perform a job. A test item should measure the learner's proficiency on a chunk of knowledge considered essential to performing the job.

The SMEs were relieved by this strategy because they certainly understood what tests look like and how they work. They quickly identified all of the topics that were covered by the regulations. Then they developed questions that they felt would effectively gauge whether a novice really understood the material. They developed all of the assessment items quickly, and the designer was then able to go back and turn the assessment questions into objectives.

occur? and How will we know them when we see them? Clients usually understand assessment—we've all taken tests—so this typically is easier for them than trying to develop objectives. If the goals and objectives state where you're going, the assessment lets you know if you got there. Often, assessment questions are restatements of objectives. Once you write your objectives, you usually can write the test. The reverse is true, too. Whether you write both objectives and assessment items or simply develop assessments, these are the details that turn the goals into a specific instructional agenda.

Notice how the assessment in Example 3.1 is linked to the outcomes and includes all the parts of traditional objectives: the conditions, the criteria, and the desired behavior. This assessment contains the level of specification that is recommended for objectives in many instructional design models.

Developing Assessments

In your years as a student, you've no doubt taken numerous multiple choice tests, essay tests, and performance tests. These different types of tests are designed to measure and evaluate different kinds of skills. To evaluate your knowledge of needs assessment for an instructional design course, your professor might ask you to complete a multiple choice quiz, write a reflective summary of the topic, conduct a needs assessment, or analyze a case

---

Example 3.1 Outcomes and Assessments

It's not always necessary to write detailed performance objectives. In the following example from a video production course, the assessment outlines the conditions, criteria, and behavior required to obtain the desired outcomes.

Outcomes

In this course, students are expected to:

1. Demonstrate correct video camera operation through the production of short video segments.
2. Demonstrate principles of visual continuity through the production of video segments.
3. Correctly use digital editing equipment to create analog and digital video segments.
4. Use digital compression software to create video to be distributed in digital form.

One of Three Course Assessments

Project 2: Brief edited sequence: 100 points (Outcomes 1, 2, and 3)
This activity provides practice in using digital editing software and editing for continuity.

1. Shoot 5–10 shots that present an "event" or action that progresses through time. Edit the sequence to compress time, yet maintain continuity. It should include sound.
2. View and prepare an oral critique of your videotape. Consider things such as:

   • Is each of your shots of high quality?

   • Are the camera moves well executed?

   • How did you control the pacing of your program? Speed of cuts? Movement within scenes?

   • What types of transitions did you use, and why?

   • What did you cut on? Action? Music? Dialogue? Reaction?

   • How did you order the images? Narrative progression? Free association?

   • Did (or would) titles help the presentation?

   • Is the audio clear? What type of sound did you use, and why?

   • What worked well? What did you like about the segment?

   • What would you do differently if you were to redo the segment?

   • How was the segment in general?

   Be honest! You will be evaluated on your correct use of terminology, the accuracy with which you describe the strengths and limitations, and the general quality and thoughtfulness of the critique.

DESIGNER'S TOOLKIT

Sample Assessments for Different Types of Learning Outcomes

Outcome	Assessment
Verbal information	Short-answer, matching, multiple choice, free recall
Intellectual skills	Application in varied situations
Motor skills	Demonstration
Attitudes	Determination of frequency of new attitude
Cognitive strategies	Reflective journal

concerning needs assessment. Each of these assessments will require different behaviors on your part; your performance on the different assessments will reflect slightly different skills.

The type of assessments you choose to develop should depend on the desired learning outcomes and the context in which learners ultimately will apply the skills. For example, the best way to assess psychomotor skills is through demonstration. The best way to assess attitudes is by determining the frequency and resolution with which learners exhibit the desired behavior. When assessing intellectual skills, learners may need several opportunities to apply their skills, each representing different situations, to demonstrate mastery of the skill. If you're testing verbal information that requires memorization or other skills for which there are specific correct answers, then short-answer, matching, or multiple choice tests may be appropriate. Other times, the goal is not to memorize a correct answer, but to engage in a process. Portfolios, case analyses, and reflective journals are examples of assessments that document the process of learning in addition to the product.

There are many kinds of tests and many kinds of test items. Matching the right test item to the right skill isn't effortless. You don't want the format of the test to interfere with learners' ability to demonstrate their mastery. When selecting among potential assessment items, you need to consider factors such as the type of learning outcome to be measured, the number of retrieval cues to provide to learners, the time required to respond, and the ease with which responses can be scored (see Figure 3.5).

Forced-Choice Questions

Test items that require learners to select among a set of response options include multiple choice, matching, and true/false. You are probably familiar with multiple choice questions in this format:

1. Which type of microphone, when positioned correctly, will pick up only within a narrow range, such as one voice?
   a. A wireless microphone
   b. A directional microphone
   c. A voice-activated microphone

Figure 3.6 shows another example of a forced-choice item.

These types of test items usually provide cues to stimulate recall of relevant information. They test learners' ability to recognize, identify, categorize, and differentiate the content. When tests are constructed carefully, the wrong answers selected by students can be very useful in identifying misconceptions common to the audience. Although these types of questions are easy to grade using an answer key, they can be time consuming to develop.

Short-Answer Questions

These items require students to recall the correct answer with few cues and to state their responses in their own words. For example, learners may be asked to respond to the following short-answer item: "What are three strategies employees can use to accommodate employees with vision impairments?" Figure 3.7 shows another example. These items can be easy to construct but it can be difficult to develop a scoring key due to variations in acceptable responses.

Essay Tests

Essay items usually require students to recall information with a minimum of cues and to organize it into a meaningful and persuasive piece of writing. For example, learners may be asked to do the following:

Write an essay describing the major groups of Native Americans of the Southwest. Include details on each tribe, their language and customs, food sources and hunting range, artifacts, and relationships to other native groups. Describe the time ranges when each group first appeared in the Southwest and what happened to the group. Give examples to support your explanations. Your essay will be judged based on accuracy, number of supporting examples and details, clarity of

Figure 3.5 *Time required to complete and score.* Assessments that can be responded to quickly also can be scored quickly. Likewise, assessments that take a longer time to respond to usually take longer to score.

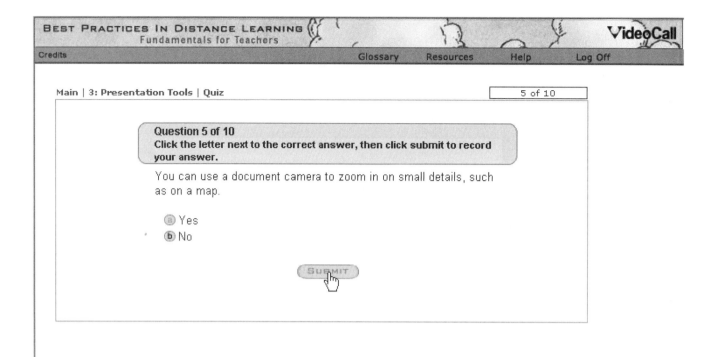

Figure 3.6 *Forced-choice testing.* In this simple example of a forced-choice exercise, the program displays feedback on the answer once the answer is submitted.

SOURCE: From *Best Practices in Distance Learning: Fundamentals for Teachers,* © 2004 by The VideoCall Company. Used with permission.

language, organization, and cohesion of argument. You may not use any notes, books, or other resources. You have three hours to complete this assessment.

Essay responses can be time consuming both to create and to score. Scoring keys typically consist of a checklist of items that should be included, with points assigned to each of the items. Other techniques of scoring include rating scales that indicate quality judgments and rubrics that describe scoring options. Sample essays representing the range of possible scores also can help make scoring consistent among graders.

Reflections and Case Analyses Reflections and case analyses (such as those included in the Application section of this chapter) can be used to assess learners' engagement with and application of new knowledge. In some courses, learners who produce reflections, case analyses, and similar assignments get credit simply for performing the task. Other times, the scorer tries to evaluate students' reasoning skills. In these situations, the designer can develop a rating scale or checklist to determine the level of student understanding. For example, if managers in a workshop on crisis management keep reflective journals based on their readings, the grader can use a checklist to determine if the managers described the key ideas and used the right vocabulary. The checklist might include a frequency count to determine the number of additional con-

nections between key ideas and their own work experience. The information on which students base their reflections and analyses can also be judged. For example, when analyzing a case of science teaching, students can interpret the case based on their readings, their experiences as students, or their perception of themselves as potential teachers. If the goal of the instruction is for students to actively integrate all three sources of knowledge, a checklist might be used to determine which sources of knowledge were used in the students' analyses. The designer also might use a rating scale to rank how strongly the students linked their reflections to the knowledge sources.

Performance-Based Assessments These assessments can provide a realistic context in which students demonstrate their knowledge. Students might be asked to perform a skill, create instruction for others, make a presentation, or develop products as diverse as Web sites and model vehicles. In fact, most of the chapters in this book include a project-based assignment that requires you to demonstrate a skill. Assessments of this type usually require students to engage in sustained work to complete the task. Students' products, presentations, and performances can be scored using checklists, rating scales, or rubrics.

Portfolios A portfolio is simply a collection of a student's work. It can include multimedia products, artwork,

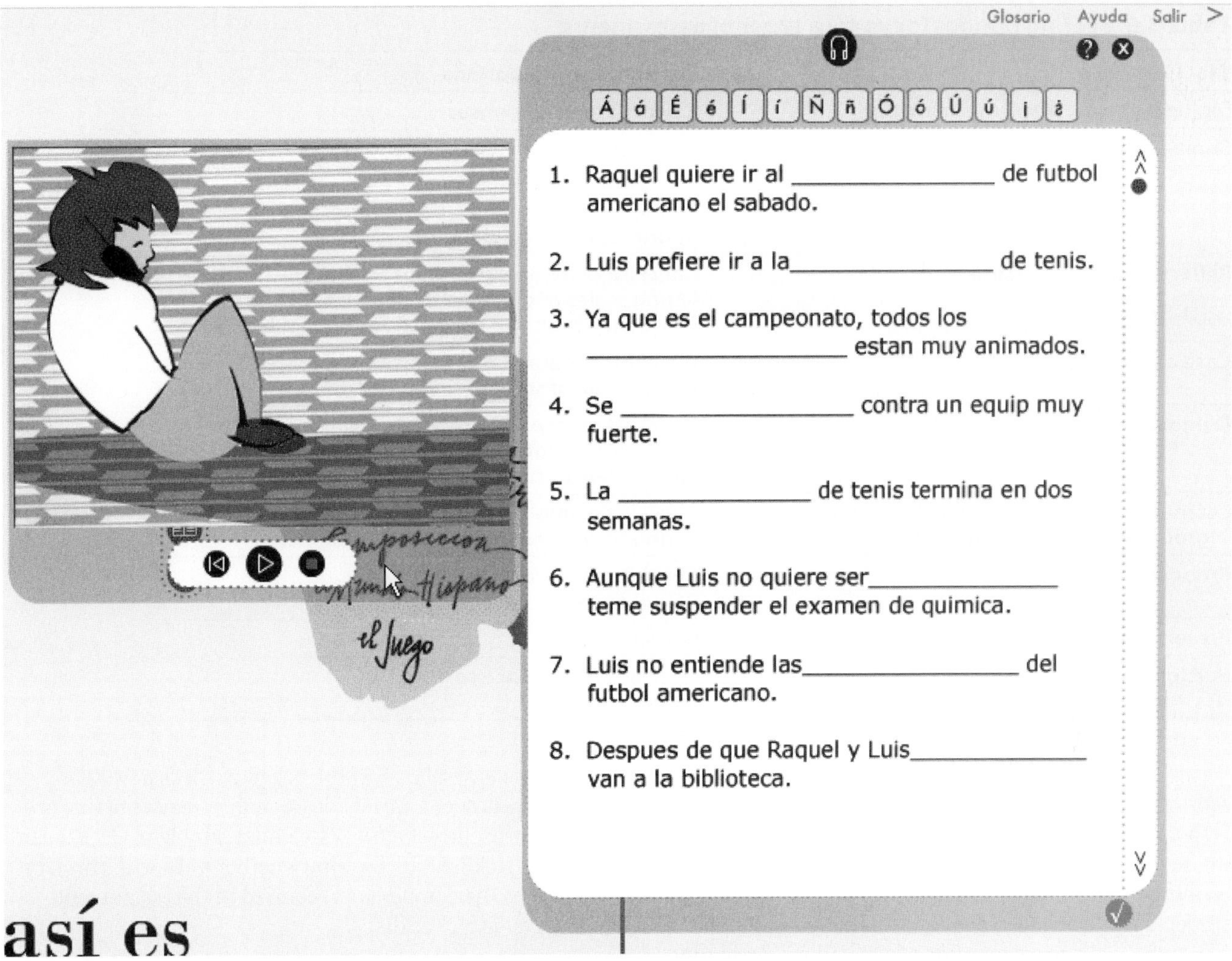

Glosario   Ayuda   Salir >

Á á É é Í í Ñ ñ Ó ó Ú ú ¡ ¿

1. Raquel quiere ir al _____ de futbol americano el sabado.

2. Luis prefiere ir a la_____ de tenis.

3. Ya que es el campeonato, todos los _____ estan muy animados.

4. Se _____ contra un equip muy fuerte.

5. La _____ de tenis termina en dos semanas.

6. Aunque Luis no quiere ser_____ teme suspender el examen de quimica.

7. Luis no entiende las_____ del futbol americano.

8. Despues de que Raquel y Luis_____ van a la biblioteca.

así es

Figure 3.7 *Fill in the blanks.* In this foreign language exercise, the learner types in the correct words, clicking the checkmark graphic for feedback on correct answers.

SOURCE: Así Es CD-ROM, 4th ed., by Levy-Konesky and Daggett. © 2004 by Heinle & Heinle. Reprinted with permission of Heinle, a division of Thomson Learning.

problem solutions, reflections, and self-assessments. As with other project-based assessments, portfolios typically are evaluated using a checklist, rating scale, or rubric for quality judgments.

Developing Scoring Keys

When designing assessment instruments, you also have to develop scoring criteria. On the assessment, the instructions to learners should include the criteria on which learning will be assessed. For example, the directions and criteria for an essay question might read, "Write a 500-word essay exploring Macbeth's state of mind in the final battle scene. Your essay should include specific examples from the play that support your thesis. Your grade will be based on the quality of your argument (40%), supporting examples (30%), organization (10%), completeness (10%), and grammar (10%)." Often, it's easy to develop the assessment item; the difficult part is developing the criteria on which the products will be judged.

Scoring keys should be developed in such a way that different judges would all assign the same score to a given response. Some tests have specific right and wrong answers and can be scored using an answer key. Other assessments are open-ended in nature and can be used to monitor changes over time, as well as specific "right" or "wrong" answers.

As Table 3.5 shows, checklists, frequency counts, rating scales, and rubrics are useful in judging the quality of students' responses to several types of open-ended assessment questions.

If possible, try to develop scoring guides for open-ended items in an iterative cycle. Assemble a collection of student responses and look at the range of responses reflected in the assignment. Synthesize your perceptions of the range in a scoring guide. Check the validity of the

Table 3.5 Scoring options for various types of assessments

Test item type	Possible scoring options
Multiple choice, true/false, matching	Key to correct responses
Short-answer	List of acceptable responses and key phrases needed
Essay	Checklist of key points Rating scale for organization, clarity, and coverage Rubric for quality judgments
Reflection and self-assessment	Checklist of items that should be included Rating scales of quality and organization Frequency counts of connections between ideas
Case analysis	Checklist of data examined Rating scale of student understanding
Demonstration	Checklist of steps Frequency counts Rating scale or rubric for quality judgments
Learner-designed instruction (individual or group presentation, video, etc.)	Checklist of important points Rating scale or rubric for quality judgments
Product development	Checklist of important features Rating scale
Presentation	Rating scale
Portfolio	Checklist of evidence to look for Rating scales

scoring guide by using it to score a variety of students' responses to the assessment. Consider whether the resulting scores seem reasonable. Is the assessment instrument yielding the results you expected? Do the scores show that students are learning? You may find that you need to revise the assessment questions, instructions, or scoring guide. Keep working within the cycle of continuous improvement until the assessments and scoring guides yield reliable results.

Answer Keys Multiple choice, matching, and true/false tests require students to choose among a limited set of possible answers. For this sort of forced-choice test, the answer key consists of a list of correct responses. This objective test format lends itself to computerized test administration and grading. Other types of tests require constructed responses that can still be judged right or wrong. Scoring keys for short-answer questions typically consist of lists of acceptable answers. These lists should include common variations in wording. This type of test can also be administered by computer, though developing a program to score constructed responses is more difficult than developing one to score forced-choice responses.

Checklists Checklists require "yes" or "no" judgments and are useful when you want to observe behaviors or evaluate products. Checklists are appropriate for judging psychomotor skills such as operating a piece of machinery and for determining whether certain behaviors are exhibited. For example, you can use a checklist to rate whether teachers accept a variety of student responses before providing the correct answer to a math problem. Or you can use a checklist to determine whether a student's project contains the components required in the assignment. To develop a checklist:

- Identify components that are important to successful performance.
- Sequence them in the order in which they are likely to occur.

Frequency counts often supplement checklists when the desired behavior is likely to be repeated several times. To add a frequency count to a checklist, simply provide a space to tally the incidents.

Rating Scales Rating scales are appropriate when you need to judge the quality of a product, process, or performance (see Example 3.2). To develop a rating scale:

- Identify the components to include.
- Sequence them in the order in which they are likely to occur.
- Determine negative and positive poles on the scale.

Rubrics Rubrics also include a judgment of quality (see Example 3.3). Typically, **rubrics** include a statement to represent various levels of performance on each component identified as important to successful performance. Word the phrases representing various levels of

Example 3.2 Rating Scale

Presentation Evaluation

Name of presenter:_____

Please rate the presentation on the following criteria. Add comments below each rating if desired.

1. A command of the subject was displayed.

Weak	1	2	3	4	5	6	7	8	9	10	Excellent

2. Ideas were clearly presented.

Weak	1	2	3	4	5	6	7	8	9	10	Excellent

3. Appeared comfortable and self-assured.

Weak	1	2	3	4	5	6	7	8	9	10	Excellent

4. Gestures and stance were natural and not distracting.

Weak	1	2	3	4	5	6	7	8	9	10	Excellent

5. Used vocal variety, adequate volume, and comfortable pacing.

Weak	1	2	3	4	5	6	7	8	9	10	Excellent

6. Visual aids were effective and easy to understand.

Weak	1	2	3	4	5	6	7	8	9	10	Excellent

7. Handouts were coordinated with presentation.

Weak	1	2	3	4	5	6	7	8	9	10	Excellent

8. Used time allocated well.

Weak	1	2	3	4	5	6	7	8	9	10	Excellent

9. Logical organization and sequencing.

Weak	1	2	3	4	5	6	7	8	9	10	Excellent

10. Overall quality:

Weak	1	2	3	4	5	6	7	8	9	10	Excellent

performance so that representative levels of performance are obvious. To develop rubrics:

- Identify the components that are important to successful performance.
- Sequence them in the order in which they are likely to occur.
- Create a statement that represents each level of student performance for each component.

Reliability and Validity

Assessments should be both a valid and reliable measure of the extent to which learners have obtained the desired learning outcomes. *Valid* assessments are those that adequately measure what they are supposed to measure. *Reliable* assessments consistently measure what they are supposed to measure.

Instructional designers make sure their tests are valid by checking for consistency among the outcomes, activities, and assessments of instruction, and by soliciting reviews from SMEs. A test on topics not covered in instruction is not a valid assessment. This doesn't mean that the invalid test items are incorrect; rather, if the content hasn't been part of the instruction, it's inappropriate to include it on the test. Writing multiple choice and true/false test items can be tedious and it's sometimes tempting to write "tricky" questions in order to save time or inject levity into the process. Questions that try to fool learners into answering incorrectly don't gauge their understanding of the material—they gauge the learners' ability to solve tricky word problems or to catch jokes masquerading as something serious. Trick questions aren't valid assessment questions, so try to avoid them.

Ensuring that assessment items are consistent with instructional outcomes and content is one of the instructional designer's primary tasks. You need to consult with your SME to determine if the instruction assesses the appropriate skill set. Ask your client and SME these questions:

- Does this test measure what should be measured?
- Is anything missing—a critical task, skill, fact, concept, or procedure?
- Is the test too hard? Would an experienced person who has mastered this content but not taken this course be able to pass this test?

Example 3.3 Rubric

Computer Applications in Education
Grading Criteria

I. Materials
  - 3 Complete list of necessary materials
  - 2 List of necessary materials missing one item
  - 1 Incomplete list of materials, missing more than one item
  - 0 No list of materials

II. Activities
  - Includes examples of critical questions, statements by teacher
    - 2 Excellent examples, very complete
    - 1 Some examples, not complete
    - 0 No examples, uncertain what teacher would talk about
  - Steps complete and logical, engage students
    - 2 Logical flow of activities, good use of student participation
    - 1 Logical flow of activities, could engage students more
    - 0 Steps confusing, no logical flow
  - Appropriate application of computer within theme unit
    - 3 Excellent application of computer in theme unit
    - 2 Computer used, could have been more appropriate
    - 1 Computer use weakly linked to unit
    - 0 Not very appropriate use of computer relative to unit

III. Evaluation
  - Adequately evaluate relative to objectives and purpose of activities
    - 2 Above-average relation to objectives, purpose, activities
    - 1 Average relation to objectives, purpose, activities
    - 0 Below-average relation to objective, purpose, activities

IV. Overall form
  - Directions stated in adequate detail so others could teach lesson
    - 4 Directions precise, complete, described in excellent detail
    - 3 Above-average directions, complete, could be described in more detail
    - 2 Average directions, with gaps, could be described in more detail
    - 1 Below-average directions, somewhat difficult to follow
    - 0 Directions vague, confusing, lacking in detail
  - Format neat and free from typos
    - 1 Yes
    - 0 No

Extra credit: Some aspect of lesson plan exhibits exceptional qualities over and above those expected (1 or 2 points).

- Does this test adequately delve into the depth of knowledge that learners should have and be able to demonstrate?
- Would those who perform well on this test be able to do the job well?
- Are any of these questions "tricky"? If so, how could they be rewritten?

You also need to determine if the assessment is reliable. Although several statistical tests calculate test reliability, in most circumstances, such calculations aren't necessary and, may even confuse your clients. But you should take every possible step to ensure the reliability of your assessments. Some of the strategies designers use to ensure reliability include:

- *Clarity of instructions.* Strive to make sure all learners will interpret the assignment in the same way. Keep test activities and their directions as simple as possible.
- *Clarity of test items.* Make sure questions are not confusing and do not include unfamiliar vocabulary. If someone else writes the test items, make sure that the test writer understands the vocabulary and kinds of activities that were in the instruction.
- *Consistency with instruction.* Present words, procedures, and concepts in the test just as they were presented in the instructional activities.
- *Sufficient length.* Recognize that too few items won't adequately test learners' knowledge of the topic and that too many items will fatigue learners and distract their attention.

Another factor in ensuring reliability is to develop scoring guides that are precise enough that learners' scores do not depend on who does the scoring. To test the reliability of a scoring key, have two or more graders score the same set of products using the scoring key. If the scores are very similar for each product, then the scoring keys are adequate. If the scores differ, work with the graders to reconcile the differences and adjust the scoring key accordingly.

Assessment Issues

Tests are like medicines: They may be good for us, but few of us can claim to enjoy them. As a result, you'll encounter clients who dislike the idea of assessments and resist including them in a product. And some SMEs may

DESIGNER'S TOOLKIT

Checklist for Developing Outcomes and Assessments

- Develop goals.
- Classify learning outcomes.
  - Verbal information
  - Intellectual skills
  - Motor skills
  - Attitudes
  - Cognitive strategy
- Conduct subskilsl analysis.
- Determine prerequisites.
- Develop statements of outcomes or objectives.
- Develop assessment items or specifications for each "box" in the analysis.
- Identify which outcomes correspond to each assessment item.
- Develop scoring guides.

  Have you made any decisions that you'd like to check out in your formative evaluation? Make note of those areas.

view it as insulting to test learners, especially if the learners are customers or high-level professionals. Regardless of the emotions they evoke, assessments serve two critical purposes in the instructional design process. The most familiar purpose is to determine the degree to which learners have mastered the course content. But another purpose is just as important to the instructional design process: The learner's performance on the assessment tells the designer if the instruction was effective.

Voice of Experience

Designing Fair Tests

A college biology professor thought he had hit on a great idea for his final exam. He modeled the test format on a popular computer game that provided a menu of possible answers instead of the expected multiple choice format. For those who knew the game (which included the majority of students), the test was easy and perhaps even fun. However, students who did not know the game faced a severe limitation. Their poor test scores showed that in trying to learn the game they used too much cognitive capacity, not leaving enough mental "work space" to also produce correct answers. The professor's intent in delivering the test was to measure his students' success in mastering the course content. Unfortunately, the test design obstructed that purpose.

Using Assessments to Monitor Learning Progress A good assessment provides students with a learning opportunity. In preparing for and completing an assessment, learners have to synthesize the content in a new way. For example, when a student reads a horticulture book, she's focused on the content at a micro level. She may read about perennials for shade gardens, for instance. But when she's required to diagram a garden plot on the end-of-course test, she needs to step back from the details of perennial shade gardens and consider multiple factors such as soil type, drainage, and lighting conditions. This activity reinforces her understanding and links it to other knowledge and skills.

Remember, an awareness of the objectives or intended outcomes of instruction informs learners as to what they should attend to within the instruction and guides them in seeking the information necessary for the obtainment of the learning goals. Assessments help learners monitor their own understanding or performance. As an example, consider the assignment that appeared on a Web site developed to teach digital video skills to university alumni (see Example 3.4). The course was strictly for enrichment, no course credit was given, and alumni enrolled for their enjoyment only. At this site, the assignments are accompanied by a list of items that learners should look for in critiquing their own work.

A collection of assessments, or test bank, can be an important asset in diagnosing instructional problems and verifying mastery. In some disciplines, such as foreign languages and mathematics, the availability of many test items is important to fully assess learners' skills. When a test bank is delivered on a computer, it can randomly generate a set of test items so that each learner takes a different test, even when the intended outcomes are identical. A diagnostic test can provide a tool for identifying which outcomes a learner has already mastered and which he or she still needs to master. For computer-based instructional products, the results of a diagnostic test can be used to generate a customized syllabus for each learner. For example, a CD-ROM program on English grammar skills provided learners with a pretest. Each test item was correlated to an outcome and to lesson content. After the learner took the pretest, the program generated a lesson plan for that student. The lessons in the sequence correlated to the items that the learner missed on the diagnostic test.

Example 3.4 Assignment and Checklist for Noncredit Course

The following assignment and "self-check" test is part of a noncredit course on video production offered to university alumni.

Put Your Knowledge to Work

Use what you've learned to shoot some video for distribution over the Web. Capture or import it into your computer.

Compress the video using several different settings in your compression program. For each setting, notice the file size, frame rate, codec used, window size, and other settings provided. View your videos and notice the effects of the various parameters on your finished image. You should begin to notice certain patterns. For example, some codecs work best for outdoor scenes, others for softer images such as children, and still others for shots of buildings.

View your videos and critique them. Be honest! Critiquing your work and the work of others is one of the best ways to improve your skills. Consider the following:

- When shooting, did you keep camera movement to a minimum?
- Is your subject framed carefully to minimize extraneous details in the scene?
- Are your images in focus and well lit?
- Does your subject fill most of the frame?
- Does the video exhibit a minimum of "artifacts"? In other words, does it look good?
- Should you increase the frame rate? Change the codec? Reduce or enlarge your window size?
- Does the video load properly?
- Does the video play smoothly?
- Is the file size reasonable for the length of the video?
- How is your program in general? What worked well? What would you do differently next time?

Assessments can indicate mastery of a specific set of skills, or they can provide dynamic insight into a learner's progress in developing his or her skill set. For example, in a workshop designed to help managers develop a participatory management style, the design team provided the managers with a skills continuum that they could use to rate their developing skills. This type of skill isn't mastered in a day or two—it's an ongoing process—so providing these learners with a meaningful assessment tool that they could use to monitor their progress over time proved invaluable. In this way, success can be reflected by changes over time, rather than specific right or wrong answers on an exam. Whether the classes are on personal finance, home maintenance, or a foreign language, serious students appreciate assessments as tools to monitor their learning progress.

Using Assessments to Determine Instructional Effectiveness

The success of any learning experience depends on both the learners and the materials. If learners aren't motivated, or lack prerequisite skills, or are too tired to attend to the instruction, even the best materials won't be effective. At the same time, even the most motivated and prepared students will have trouble learning a topic if the instruction is disorganized or incomplete. Assessment results can provide you with valuable data as to where the materials are successful and where you still need to make changes to the instruction.

As you'll learn in Chapter 6, you need assessments to use within formative evaluation even if you remove the assessments from the materials after formative evaluation is over. To determine if the instructional material is effective, you need to find out:

- If students obtain the learning outcome, could they do so *before* the instruction?

- Can they demonstrate the desired outcome *within* the instruction?
- Can they demonstrate the desired outcome *after* the instruction?

To answer these questions, there are three types of tests: **pretests** (before instruction), **embedded tests** (within instruction), and **posttests** (after instruction). It also is useful to include an entry skills test to measure whether learners have the necessary prerequisite skills. Items assessing entry skills often are included on the pretest.

The test items on the pretest, embedded test, and posttest must be parallel to ensure that they test identical skills. When assessing declarative knowledge of facts and motor skills, the items may be identical on all three tests. For example, learners may be asked to "list three methods to defrost meat safely" on the pretest, embedded test, and posttest.

When assessing concepts, procedures, attitudes, and metacognitive knowledge, you want to determine learners' ability to apply their knowledge to a variety of problems. Although the skills assessed must be identical on each test, the test items should be different so as to assess learners' ability to generalize their knowledge beyond a single situation. For example, to assess knowledge of two-digit addition, the following items may be used:

> *Pretest:* $23 + 14 =$ ———
>
> *Embedded test:* $67 + 31 =$ ———
>
> *Posttest:* $12 + 85 =$ ———

In Chapter 6, we discuss how to use these tests within evaluations. For now, recognize that you need a pretest, embedded test, and posttest item to measure each of the skills you identified in your subskill analysis. Each "box" in your analysis hierarchy needs to be represented on each test so that if your formative evaluation indicates

Analogy

House

In this chapter, you learned how to identify the outcomes of an instructional program. This is similar to an architect's effort to identify the results a potential homeowner needs, which the architect calls "the program." For your dream house, your architect may ask you to make a list of everything you would love to do and have in your house. You may want lots of windows, a fireplace, plenty of storage, shelves for a collection of old cameras, and sufficient electrical power and outlets for computer and entertainment devices. A family with young children might want to have the parents' and children's bedrooms close to each other. Elderly people desire a one-story home with no stairs. These "programmatic" require-ments shape the home's design much as outcomes do for an instructional product.

Although architects don't prepare assessments, the finished home itself represents the success of the architect's design. You should be able to walk through the finished home with the programmatic list and check off each item as you see it reflected in the home. If every item in the program is represented in the home, the goals and the final product are in alignment. Your final product should also align with the outcomes you devise early in the project. The assessment is like the programmatic checklist—a verification that the final product meets the requirements set at the outset.

that students aren't learning successfully you can identify where the breakdown occurred.

Summary

In this chapter, you learned about the "outcome" and "assessment" elements in the essential triangle of instructional design. As you spiral through the five phases in the instructional design process, you also elaborate and refine the goals and assessments of learning in an iterative fashion.

During the Define phase, you gather information from the client to determine a tentative outcome for the instruction. Your understanding of the outcome typically is limited by the amount of detailed information provided by the client. Often you begin to explore ways to determine if these outcomes are achieved. As you do so, you consider techniques for assessment. You synthesize this information and present a tentative statement of learning outcomes and begin to describe ideas for assessments in the project proposal.

As you move into the Design phase, you examine the learning outcomes to determine the subskills that lead to their obtainment. You assemble information from the client, SMEs, and a variety of resource materials to identify subskills. You might conduct an instructional, task, or content analysis. You may need to negotiate with the client or SMEs to determine exactly what subskills are necessary for learners to obtain the desired outcomes of the instruction. Often a discussion of assessment is necessary to help clients and SMEs identify learning outcomes. This knowledge is synthesized in the design documents, which include statements of learning outcomes and an assessment plan or sample assessment items. You check or confirm your understanding of the outcomes and assessment as you present the design documents for approval.

During the Demonstrate phase, you further refine the outcomes and assessments as you begin to outline the actual instruction—developing storyboards, page templates, and other concrete documents that will guide the production of the instructional materials and accompanying assessments. Sample assessments are developed as part of the prototype and tested with learners during the prototype evaluation. As learners try out the prototype, you check to make sure that they are learning the intended skills and subskills. The results of the prototype evaluation may lead to modifications in the instruction outcomes, assessment items, or scoring keys.

During the Develop phase, you continue to monitor the materials to make sure that, to the best of your judgment, they are designed to facilitate obtainment of the desired learning outcomes. The assessment items are fully developed and tested during pilot tests and field trials. As you conduct pilot tests and field trials, you examine learners' responses on the assessments to determine if the intended outcomes are being achieved and if any additional outcomes or subskills should be taught. These tests also may result in modifications to the assessments.

Finally, in the Deliver phase, you present the instructional materials and assessment items to learners with assurance that, through participation in the instruction, they will indeed achieve the desired learning outcomes.

As you can see from this discussion, the outcomes and assessments are determined primarily during the Define, Design, and Demonstrate phases; thus, the outline of the ASC cycle lists the events that occur during those phases. However, outcomes may be added or deleted and assessment items modified, based on the results of the learner tryouts during the Demonstrate and Deliver phases.

Identifying Outcomes and the ASC Cycle

As you identify outcomes, you first *ask* the client to describe the goals of the instruction and the SMEs to describe the task or job in detail. Work with the SMEs to *assemble* the content. Next, you *synthesize* the content into statements of goals, outcomes or objectives, and a subskill analysis. Finally, you *confirm* that you have correctly identified necessary subskills and outcomes by *checking* your outcomes with the client and SMEs. During pilot testing and field trials, you also *check* to see if all necessary subskills are identified by examining learners' patterns of performance on the assessments of goals and outcomes.

Developing Assessment and the ASC Cycle

As you develop assessments, you first *ask* the client and SMEs to describe tasks indicating that learners have obtained the goals of the instruction. Next, you *synthesize* these tasks into assessment measures. Finally, you present the assessment measures to the client and SMEs to *confirm* that the items accurately access the target skills. You also try out assessment items with learners during prototype testing, pilot tests, and field trials to *check* for item clarity and for the validity and reliability of scoring keys.

Notes

[1]Documents prepared by David Halpin, Colleen Kerr, Peter Macedo, and Sandra Schneider, 1998. Used with permission.

References

Dick, W., & Carey, L. (1996). *The systematic design of instruction* (4th ed.). New York: HarperCollins.

Driscoll, M. P. (2000). *Psychology of learning for instruction* (2nd ed.). Needham Heights, MA: Allyn & Bacon.

Gagné, E. D., Yekovich, C. W., & Yekovich, F. R. (1993). *The cognitive psychology of school learning* (2nd ed.). New York: Longman.

Gagné, R. M., Briggs, L., & Wager, W. (1992). *Principles of instructional design* (4th ed.). New York: Harcourt Brace Jovanovich.

Gagné, R. M., & Glasser, R. (1987). Foundations in learning research. In R. M. Gagné (Ed.), *Instructional technology: foundations.* Hillsdale, NJ: Lawrence Erlbaum.

Heinich, R., Molenda, M., Russell, J., & Smaldino, S. (2001). *Instructional media and technologies for learning* (4th ed.). Englewood Cliffs, NJ: Prentice-Hall.

Mager, R. F. (1997). *Preparing instructional objectives: A critical tool in the development of effective instruction* (3rd ed.). Atlanta: Center for Effective Performance.

Tessmer, M. (1998). Meeting with the SME to design multimedia exploration systems. *Educational Technology Research and Development, 46*(2), 79–95.

Application

1. The RealWorldID Web site includes a case study of the design and development of a workshop for elementary teachers of mathematics. Consistent with the spiral manner in which instructional design projects evolve, instructional activities are developed simultaneously with objectives and assessments. You are asked to notice how the development of tentative activities refines the outcomes and assessments, and to create a subskills analysis, outcome statements, and assessments for the project described in the case. Visit the RealWorldID Web site to analyze the case online or to print for use during class discussions.

2. In your reflective journal, summarize the key points of this chapter. How are the ideas presented consistent or inconsistent with your beliefs and prior knowledge? Compare your perceptions of the chapter with those of your classmates in group discussions.

3. Two of the goals for this textbook are that you'll be able to design instruction and use the vocabulary of instructional design correctly.

   a. We've designed activities and assessments that allow you or your instructor to determine if you've met these objectives. Can you identify some of these assessments?

   b. What other goals do you think we have for this textbook?

   c. Perform a subskill analysis for the goal "design instruction."

4. Look at the project proposal at the end of Chapter 8 and the design documents at the end of Chapter 9. Locate the goals and outcomes in those documents.

5. As we explore the essential elements of instructional design in Chapters 2–6, the entire class is encouraged to function as an ID team to create the design specifications for an instructional module. The class should be divided into working groups of four to five members. Your course instructor should assign a class topic and serve as an instructional design manager—leading design team meetings, checking on the progress of the groups, and facilitating discussions. In this chapter, your working group should:

   a. Develop instructional goals appropriate to the perceived needs of the target audience.

   b. Determine which form of subskills analysis is most appropriate for your goals. Justify your choice.

   c. Perform a subskill analysis.

   d. Identify prerequisite skills and knowledge.

   e. Develop statements of learning outcomes or objectives.

   f. Develop assessment instruments or assessment specifications that match the outcomes.

   g. Develop at least two assessment items for each box in your subskill analysis.

   h. Identify which subskill or entry behavior corresponds with each assessment item.

   i. Develop a scoring key.

Have you made any decisions that you'd like to check out in your formative evaluation? Make note of those areas now.

Ideas in Action

In Chapters 2–6, we follow the design of a videotape on food safety. In this chapter, we include the subskill analysis, outcomes, and assessments created for this project.[1]

Goal

Prevent food-borne illnesses in the elderly by showing them how to purchase, handle, store, and prepare food safely.

Outcome

Elderly individuals will choose to purchase, handle, store, and prepare food safely.

Type of Outcome

Attitude.

Instructional Analysis

The accompanying figure shows the instructional analysis for the food safety video.

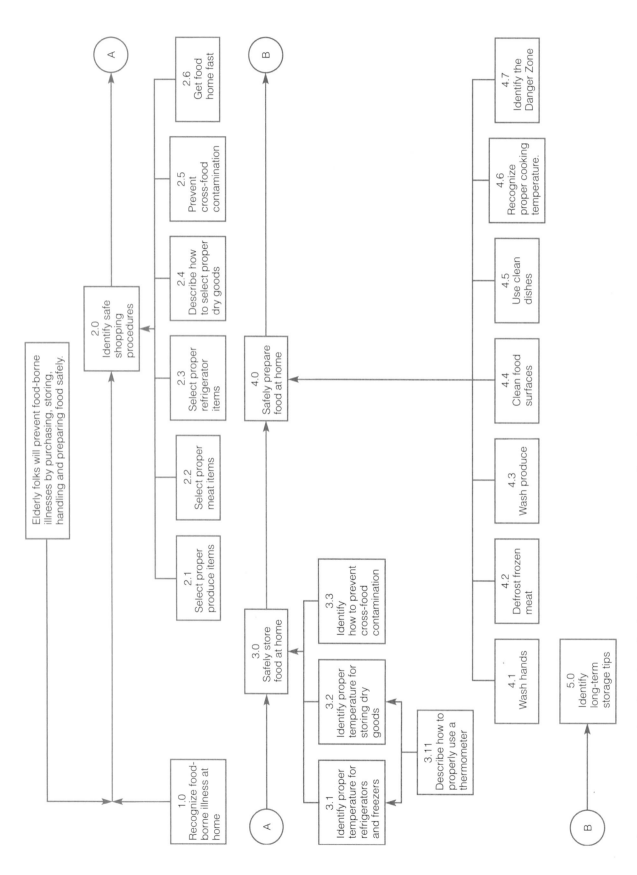

Figure 3.8 *Instructional analysis for food safety video.* Notice how the learning outcomes are arranged in a logical hierarchy, with a "box" that corresponds to each outcome.

Outcomes for Food Safety Video

1.0 Recognize that food-borne illness is a serious problem that often occurs at home.

2.0 Identify safe shopping procedure.

2.1 Select proper produce at the store.

2.2 Select proper meats at the store.

2.3 Select refrigerated items properly.

2.4 Select proper dry goods.

2.5 Prevent cross-food contamination in the store.

2.6 Get cold food home quickly.

3.0 Store food at home to prevent food-borne illnesses.

3.1 Identify the proper temperatures for refrigerator and freezer.

3.2 Identify proper temperatures for storing dry goods.

3.3 Identify ways to prevent cross-food contamination at home.

4.0 Demonstrate knowledge of food safety by properly preparing food products.

4.1 Wash hands when working with raw meat and produce.

4.2 Recognize ways to defrost meat correctly.

4.3 Wash produce before eating.

4.4 Properly clean food surfaces.

4.5 Use clean dishes.

4.6 Recognize proper cooking temperatures.

4.7 Identify "Danger Zone" when storing foods.

5.0 Recognize correct long-term storage procedures.

Pre- and Postvideo Food Safety Questionnaire

Later in the project, the following questionnaires were developed to assess learning. The designers chose a self-report questionnaire, as the learners would view this videotape individually at home or together in senior citizens' centers or at club meetings. The same questionnaire was used as a pre- and postassessment.

Please circle your answer to the following questions.

A = Agree

D = Disagree

U = Undecided

1. Most food-borne illnesses occur in the home.   A   D   U

2. Food-borne illness is a disease that mainly causes upset stomach.   A   D   U

3. Leftovers should not be eaten if kept in the refrigerator for more than 3 days.   A   D   U

4. Raw fish and ground beef should be frozen if it will be longer than 24 hours before you cook it.   A   D   U

5. It is okay to eat ground beef rare.   A   D   U

6. Which of the following are safe methods for defrosting frozen meat? Please check all that apply.

_____ in the refrigerator

_____ on the counter

_____ in still water

_____ in the microwave

_____ in sunlight

7. When grocery shopping, in what order should you purchase the following items? Please number them 1–6, with 1 being what you would pick up first and 6 being what you would pick up last.

_____ canned goods

_____ frozen foods

_____ dairy items

_____ meat and poultry

_____ dry products

_____ fresh produce

8. Refrigerators should be below _____ degrees Fahrenheit.

9. Freezers should be below _____ degrees Fahrenheit.

10. Dry and canned goods should be stored below _____ degrees Fahrenheit.

11. To avoid the "Danger Zone" where bacteria grow rapidly, keep food below _____ degrees and above _____ degrees Fahreheit.

12. Match the foods with the maximum times that they should be stored in the freezer:

Ground meat	12 months
Poultry	9 months
Whole cuts of meat and fish	4 months

Please circle your answer to the following questions.

A = Always

S = Sometimes

R = Rarely

N = Never

13. When shopping, I will check items for damage before selecting them.   A   S   R   N

14. When shopping, I will keep meat separate from other items in my cart.   A   S   R   N

15. At home, I will keep meat separate from other items in my refrigerator.   A   S   R   N

16. When preparing chicken, I will cook it until it is well done.   A   S   R   N

17. I will use bleach to sanitize my food preparation area.   A   S   R   N

18. I will wash fruits and vegetables before eating them.   A   S   R   N

19. I will wash my hands after handling raw meat.   A   S   R   N

20. When shopping, I will check
expiration dates before
placing them in my cart. A S R N

21. When my trip home will be longer
than 30 minutes, I will place frozen
and refrigerated items in a cooler. A S R N

Scoring Guide for Food Safety Questionnaire

1. A
2. D
3. A
4. A
5. D
6. Refrigerator, microwave
7. Meat, poultry, and frozen foods should be last
8. 40
9. 0
10. 85
11. 40, 140
12. Ground meat—4 months; whole cuts of meat
and fish—9 months; poultry—12 months

For the rest of the items, the desired response is A.

| DESIGN AID |

Assessments

Task or Subskill	Assessment	Scoring Criteria

| DESIGN AID |

Objectives

Behavior	Conditions	Criteria

Chapter 4
Activities: Strategies

Chapter Overview

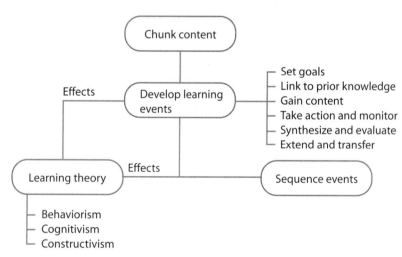

Chunk content

Effects

Develop learning events
- Set goals
- Link to prior knowledge
- Gain content
- Take action and monitor
- Synthesize and evaluate
- Extend and transfer

Learning theory
- Behaviorism
- Cognitivism
- Constructivism

Effects

Sequence events

Learning Outcomes

• Cluster outcomes into logical "chunks."

• Outline a sequence of learning events that includes opportunities for learners to:

   • Focus on goals.

   • Link with prior knowledge.

   • Gain and organize content knowledge.

   • Take action and monitor progress.

   • Synthesize and evaluate learning.

   • Extend and transfer knowledge.

• Align outcomes, assessments, and activities.

Orientation within the Design Process

Recall that there are five phases in the instructional design process and that in each phase we visit each of the essential elements of instructional design, adding details and performing tasks as required by the desired products of each phase. In this chapter, we begin to discuss the essential element of Activities (see Figure 4.1). We examine different theoretical frameworks for developing effective learning activities and ways to structure effective learning experiences, or learning events.

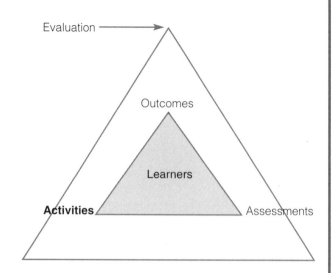

Figure 4.1 *Elements considered.* In this chapter, we examine the element of activities.

Tasks at Each Phase

The tasks at each phase related to activities are summarized in Table 4.1. As we discuss each of the phases in later chapters, you'll learn more about performing these tasks. But for now, the table provides an overview of where the tasks discussed in this chapter fit into the five phases of design.

Table 4.1 Activities-related tasks at each phase

Define	• Discuss content scope and possible instructional activities with client in initial meetings. • Determine delivery environment and implications for activities. • Conduct limited initial brainstorming with team to develop ideas for activities to pitch to client. • Draft description of instructional activities and content. Present to client in proposal.
Design	• Work extensively with SME to define content. • Brainstorm potential instructional activities with project team. • Develop instructional strategy based on audience characteristics and needs and instructional outcomes. • Develop description of materials, including media and navigation as needed. • Present instructional strategy and concrete description of materials to client for approval or suggested modifications.
Demonstrate	• Develop production documents, including page templates, storyboards, media requirements, and technical specifications. Gain approval and make suggested modifications. • Develop prototype of materials. Present to learners. Collect data on learners' response to prototype. • Present prototype and results of learner tryout to clients and SME. Present suggested modifications resulting from prototype tryout.
Develop	• Determine needed modifications to materials based on client's and learners' response to prototype. • Monitor materials development to ensure consistency with instructional strategy. • Create instructor's guide, training guide, and other supporting materials requested by clients. • Use materials with learners during formative evaluation.
Deliver	• Present materials to client. • Present results of formative evaluation. Discuss suggested revisions. Determine if changes will be made to current materials or future versions. • Compile project documentation. • Conduct training on use of materials if requested by client.

⟳ Developing Learning Strategies

Think back to instruction that you found effective or enjoyable. You learned the content, but you probably did so in a way that was meaningful to you. You were actively engaged in learning and probably met some personal learning needs. Good instruction is more than merely a collection of information or facts. To develop effective and enjoyable instruction, you need to consider both *what* will be taught and *how* it will be taught. Your SMEs know the content; it's up to you as the instructional designer to structure that content so as to facilitate learning through well-designed instructional systems.

Online courseware, books, videos, multimedia programs, knowledge management systems, electronic performance support systems (EPSSs), and classroom instruction are just a few of the ways in which you can deliver content in support of learning. We'll look at a variety of formats for delivering instruction in the next

chapter. The focus of this chapter is on developing strategies to facilitate learning.

As you develop strategies for the instructional materials, you should be guided by three considerations:

1. Information needs and characteristics of learners (addressed in Chapter 2)
2. The intended learning outcomes and the context in which the new knowledge will be applied (addressed in Chapter 3)
3. The context of the instruction and the environment in which the learning will take place

We will consider learning environments in more detail in the next chapter. To develop an instructional strategy:

- Chunk the content.
- Plan a sequence of learning events for each chunk of content.
- Align the activities with the outcomes and assessments of instruction.

Voice of Experience

Influence of Learner Characteristics on Activities

As a design team began to plan the redesign of a university course in human development, they recognized that the majority of students who enrolled in this course were freshmen, still accustomed to the more structured environment of high school. A concern was that they may not be able to manage the freedom and responsibility of a course for which the primary content was offered over the Web and class attendance was optional. The team also recognized that distance learning courses have a high attrition rate. They recognized that students would need to be self-directed learners in order to succeed in this type of course.

Seeking Guidance from the Literature
The designers embarked on an extensive review of the literature on self-regulation and metacognition to determine techniques to facilitate self-regulation and support students as they develop the skills of becoming active self-directed learners. The literature outlined three stages in self-directed learning: planning, monitoring, and evaluating one's activities (Ertmer & Newby, 1996). The literature also suggested that the tasks inherent in expert learning could be modeled and demonstrated by teachers and instructional systems and thus provide the scaffolding structures

necessary for students to learn and internalize self-regulating strategies.

Implications for Materials
To foster and promote active self-regulated learning among students, the team incorporated ideas derived from the literature as critical elements in the design for the Web site. The site consisted of a self-assessment inventory of self-regulatory learning skills, a structured arrangement of activities to encourage self-directed learning, and several support tools to assist students in planning, monitoring, and evaluating their learning.

Self-assessment: Students were introduced to self-regulatory strategies during the second week of class. They completed a questionnaire on self-regulation strategy use designed to assess their motivational orientations and their use of different learning strategies for a college course. Based on their responses, students received individualized feedback as to their strengths and weaknesses in the areas of intrinsic motivation, extrinsic motivation, interest in topic, expectancy for success, test anxiety, use of cognitive strategies (such as rehearsal, elaboration, organization, and metacognitive skills), and their time and resource

(continued on page 70)

(continued)

management. Students were referred to supplemental information on increasing their skills in areas in which they showed low scores. These supplemental pages contained an explanation of the term, suggestions for improving or developing skills in that area, and annotated links to other Web sites devoted to developing the target skill.

The GAME plan: The literature indicated that self-regulating individuals engage in the process of constantly planning, monitoring, and evaluating their activities (Ertmer & Newby, 1996). The design team translated these recommendations into an easy to remember acronym: the GAME (*Goal, Action, Monitor,* and *Evaluate*) plan. Course materials and activities associated with goal setting included topic outlines and study guides. The study guides consisted of open-ended outlines to guide students' note taking. Students took action by attending class, reading the book, viewing PowerPoint "lectures" online, completing the

study guides, and participating in lab activities. Students monitored their actions by completing practice quizzes, consisting of 10 questions randomly selected from a test item bank, as often as they liked. Feedback following each response informed students whether the answer was correct, and if incorrect, informed them of the correct response. Finally, students evaluated their actions by completing an online quiz for credit and reviewing their grades. The intent was to provide the necessary structure for fostering the development of self-regulation skills in a new and unique way by providing students with this online protocol for self-regulation.

Other support tools: The Web site also included a "Goals Checklist" feature and "Grades online." The Goals Checklist feature allowed students to create their own time-dependent goals, which were then e-mailed to them via an automated system. Students could check their cumulative grades at any time using the "Grades online" feature.

Chunking and Sequencing Content

In the previous chapter, you acquired several tools to assist you in identifying the knowledge components necessary for obtaining an instructional outcome. Performing subskills analysis, developing assessment items, and writing objectives are all methods of breaking down a general outcome into specific knowledge components that can guide the instructional design and development process. As you organize and sequence your material, you may notice that some of the content falls together in natural units. These small, complete units of content are called "chunks." This may not sound like a technical or official term, but it's widely used in training and instructional development. In addition to using "chunk" as a noun, you'll hear designers use it as a verb, as in "to chunk" the content. It's often easiest to first "chunk the content" and then to grapple with how to treat each chunk.

A chunk is a set of topics that go together logically (see Example 4.1). One useful way of identifying a chunk is to think about what topics could be taught together. How much content can you present before you need to stop and review or summarize? How much content can you present before you provide a practice problem? Each chunk may be a different category of knowledge (verbal, intellectual, and so on), and thus require you to develop a lesson appropriate to each. It also might be appropriate to

use a different assessment strategy for each chunk—some may require simple recall while others require applying concepts to solve a problem.

The Size of Chunks

The size of a chunk depends on the learners and the complexity of the topic. Learners with a great deal of prior knowledge typically can handle a larger or more complex chunk than learners for whom the material is completely new. The developmental level of learners is important, too. You'd certainly include less content in a chunk for kindergartners than for adults. For example, the youngest school-aged children may be able to attend to only 10 minutes of material at a time while college students can remain attentive for a one- or two-hour class period. Students in a high school honors class may comprehend large amounts of novel content within one class period while students in an ESL (English as a second language) class comprehend comparable material at a slower rate because of the additional cognitive demands of understanding the language. Highly complex topics need to be broken into smaller chunks for an audience with little prior knowledge of the topic. Consider a program on the latest treatment options for myocardial infarction (heart attacks). If aimed at elderly patients, the amount of material and the size of the chunks will be very different than if aimed at cardiologists earning continuing education credits.

Example 4.1 Chunking

For a course in which the goal was to create original movies for Web-based delivery, the designer chose to chunk the topics into the following four lessons:

1. Shooting: Art and Science
2. Editing: Art

3. Editing: Science
4. Distribution: Compressing for Web delivery

The accompanying figure shows how these topics might be chunked.

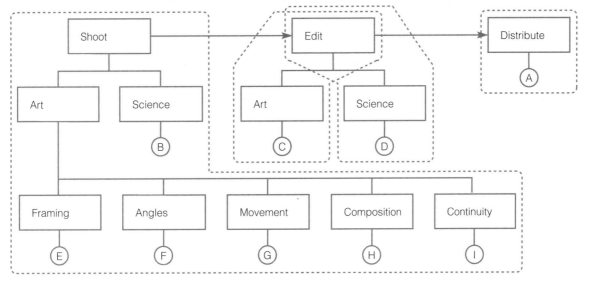

The dotted lines encircle topics that can be chunked together.

Long ago, Miller (1956) established that humans can learn seven, plus or minus two, bits of information in a given instructional episode. This means you can present from five to nine new things in one lesson—perhaps quite a bit less than you'd like to accomplish. The reason for this is that our "working memory"—the area available to learn and recall declarative information such as facts—is limited (Gagné, Yekovich, & Yekovich, 1993).

Because much of what is taught involves declarative knowledge, limiting a lesson to a mere handful of concepts can be hard for clients to accept. This means you have to find creative solutions in order to prioritize, sequence, and organize the material. If you need to present 25 items in a lesson, perhaps you can organize the content into five manageable blocks. The blocks can serve as a structure for presenting, and recalling, the other concepts. Or, instead of trying to cram too much material in a single lesson, you might design lessons that require learners to use other resources to complete the exercises, such as a lesson that asks learners to look something up online or in a users' manual. These lessons give learners practice in learning where to go to find more information on the subject. Your goal is to avoid the common problem of including too much content in each lesson.

Ideally, the amount of time that learners have available to master a set of content should be exactly the amount of time each learner needs. This is somewhat true of self-directed materials such as online courses and self-study print materials. If the material will be delivered in a classroom setting, the amount of class time may be constrained. As you are sequencing and chunking the content, start thinking about how much time it will take to present, practice, and assess learners' mastery of each chunk. Consider how the learners or instructors may allocate their time and how the class schedule might work.

Prioritizing Content

Focus your instruction on what is reasonable for learners to master in a given amount of time. You'll have to work patiently with your client and SME to help them with this reality—because they'll resist! Suppose your client wants to pack a great deal of content into each lesson. Step back and ask why this is important to her or him. Perhaps other strategies are available to accomplish these goals. Ask, "Who are the learners, and what will they do with this material?" Your client may need help in seeing how learners can perform a job, or begin learning to perform a job, even

Example 4.2 Prioritizing Outcomes

SMEs were asked to rate the outcomes of a program intended to educate consumers on the advantages and disadvantages of both electric motors and internal combustion (IC) engines according to "importance" (IM) and "depth of coverage needed" (D).

They rated each outcome on a scale of 1 to 4 where 1 = very important or high depth and 4 = not important or low depth. A small sample of the questionnaire is included here.

Please rate the following topics according to importance and depth of coverage needed:

	Importance				Depth of Coverage Needed			
1. Air quality standards affecting IC engines	1	2	3	4	1	2	1	4
2. Benefits of electric motors in specific applications	1	2	3	4	1	2	1	4
3. Advantages and limitations of IC engines	1	2	3	4	1	2	1	4
4. Pollution control costs for IC engines	1	2	3	4	1	2	1	4

A segment of the results table is included as well. RS, JL, PW, and RF refer to the SMEs who completed the questionnaire. The "All IM" column provides the total score for "importance," and the "All D" column provides the total score for "depth of coverage needed."

	RS		JL		PW		RF		ALL	
Topics	**IM**	**D**	**IM**	**D**	**IM**	**D**	**IM**	**D**	**IM**	**D**
Air quality standards affecting IC engines	1	1	1	1	1	1	2	1	4	4
Benefits of electric motors in specific applications	1	1	1	1	3	1	1	1	6	4
Advantages and limitations of IC engines	1	2	1	1	2	1	2	1	5	6
Pollution control costs for IC engines	1	1	1	1	3	1	2	1	7	7
Methods of retrofitting IC engines to meet air quality standards	1	1	1	1	3	1	2	2	7	5
Servicing of IC engines	1	1	1	3	1	2	1	2	4	8
Maintenance costs for IC engines	1	2	1	4	4	1	2	1	8	8
Pollution control costs for electric motors	1	1	4	2	4	1	2	1	11	5
Costs of electric motors	1	2	4	2	3	2	3	2	11	8
Perspectives of equipment vendors	3	4	3	3	3	3	3	4	12	14

Based on these results, the design team can begin to consider how much instructional time should be allocated to each topic. For example, they now know that it's important to include instruction on air quality standards affecting IC engines and that the standards should be covered in depth. They also know that servicing of IC engines is perceived as important, but it doesn't need to be covered in as much depth as some other topics. The issue of pollution control costs for electric motors isn't viewed as particularly important, but if it is covered at all, it should be addressed in some depth.

---

if they won't know every single thing there is to know about the topic. Try this approach with your client: "Let's say each learner 'gets' only three concepts from each lesson. Which three do you care most about?" Paint the picture that, one year from now, those three things may be all that the learners will recall. Be aware, however, that this may not be easy for your client! It may take several meetings to achieve clarity of learning outcomes, and it might not happen at all. Help clients and SMEs identify the most critical outcomes to keep the content "digestible."

Table 4.2 Differences among learning theories

	Behaviorist	Cognitive	Constructivist
Outcomes	Learning involves strengthening stimulus–response link, requires mastery of prerequisite steps before moving to next step.	Learning involves storing new information with related prior knowledge. Mastery of subskills necessary to understand higher concepts.	Knowledge is acquired through immersion in complex task, with assumption that students gain prerequisite skills through higher-level problem solving and meaningful tasks.
Activities	Present practice with reinforcement. Take small steps with frequent reinforcement, include shaping, chaining, fading, and prompts, and alter reinforcement schedules.	Link to prior knowledge. Use examples and nonexamples. Provide practice with informative feedback to correct misunderstandings. Cover range of skills and outcomes. Arrange from simple to complex.	Focus on meaningful tasks and social negotiation of shared meanings, on self-monitoring strategies, scaffolding, apprenticeship learning. Make relevant data and resources available.
Assessment	Ask to perform target task. Compare to baseline performance of task prior to instruction. Judge performance right or wrong.	Present problems. Arrange from simple to complex so can see when understanding breaks down.	Focus on process, as well as product. Identify where learners are at a particular point in time. Keep ongoing and developmental, not terminal.

Clients and SMEs often misunderstand how instruction works. They assume that everything is equally important and needs to be included in a course. They may be familiar with documentation or users' manuals that make an effort to be comprehensive. Instruction, in contrast, requires editing the comprehensive content and structuring it into a sequence that's appropriate for the target learners. How do you determine which areas are most important to the instruction? How do you eliminate extraneous information? What areas need special treatment, and what areas can be addressed quickly?

One effective technique in prioritizing content is to ask other people (see Example 4.2). You may want to consult with a variety of specialists and representatives of your target audience to rate the degree to which each topic is important and the depth of coverage needed. One topic might warrant coverage, but not necessarily in great depth. Another topic might be less important to include, but if included, would require great depth of coverage. Organize the information as best you can, then ask your SMEs or learners for their comments.

Planning Learning Events

After you chunk the content, you need to develop a plan to facilitate the learning of each chunk. Some learning occurs through reinforcement of actions that are spontaneously generated. For example, humans probably learn to talk by mimicking the sounds in their environment and then receiving reinforcement for those sounds. But as

an instructional designer, you are concerned with the deliberate arrangement of events to facilitate learning. Your chunks contain the "what" of your instructional activities—for example, math concepts, organizational policies, or heart attack prevention; your instructional strategy will describe the "how."

Successful learning experiences typically include a set of predictable events. First popularized by Gagné (1965), and then elaborated upon by various other authors (see, for example, Smith & Ragan, 1999) these events provide guidance in structuring and organizing the learning experience. The learning events presented in this chapter draw upon Gagné's Nine Events of Instruction, expanding on them to accommodate a range of learning and instructional theories.

Learning Theories

Learning and instructional theories fall into the general categories of behaviorism, cognitivism, and constructivism.[1] Historically, instructional design was based on behaviorism and cognitivism, but today, constructivism offers a popular alternative. **Behaviorists** believe that learning occurs through reinforcement of desired responses; in other words, we call a dog a dog because we were reinforced for that behavior. **Cognitivists** believe that learning involves storing new information with related prior knowledge through elaboration, assimilation, and accommodation. According to cognitive theory, we call a dog a dog because we learned the distinguishing characteristics of the concept of "dog." **Constructivists** believe that knowledge is individually constructed as learners attempt to make sense of their world by acting on objects or by deriving meaning through social cues. They recognize that a dog is called a dog within a particular context. We call a dog a dog if doing so is supported in our culture.

Through this simplified differentiation, you should see that each of these theories has implications for the design of instructional activities. Recognize that each theory has its adherents and detractors. Some companies or institutions have adopted one approach and will expect their designers to adhere to it. Other times, you can build programs using the elements of each theory appropriate to your client, the learners, the content, and the context. You may feel more comfortable with one of these approaches and tend to rely on it. Consider your knowledge of learning theories to be part of your designer's toolkit. You can employ one or all of them in any given instructional program. Table 4.2 compares behaviorist, cognitive, and constructivist theories and outlines implications for the design of instructional activities.

Learning Events

Despite differences in perceptions of how learning occurs, most learning and instructional theorists agree that effective learning experiences should:

- Motivate learners to focus on the goals of instruction.

- Provide learners with opportunities to compare new knowledge with existing knowledge in order to make new knowledge their own.

- Provide learners with opportunities to gain content knowledge and integrate it with their prior knowledge to meet their learning goals.

- Provide learners with opportunities to take action, in order to monitor their progress toward obtaining their goals.

- Provide learners with opportunities to synthesize knowledge and evaluate whether personal goals have been met successfully.

- Provide learners with opportunities to extend and transfer their knowledge to new situations.

Table 4.3 lists a variety of activities to support each learning event.

Let's consider a simple example of how these events work together in the context of learning verbal information. When Alexa had to take spelling tests in elementary school, the teacher's goal was for students to learn the spelling words of the week. Alexa wasn't particularly motivated by grades, but she was motivated by the extra free time that she could earn if she spelled all the words correctly. She set a goal of learning to spell the words of the week by Tuesday. She began by examining the list of words in her spelling book to identify those that she already knew how to spell. Then she gained new information by examining the words she still needed to learn. To help her integrate the new words with her prior knowledges, her textbook identified the pattern present in the words of that week. For example, one week, the spelling book pointed out that the word list consisted of pairs of words that sounded the same but were spelled differently and had different meanings. Alexa took action by writing the words several times and rehearsing their spelling in her mind. Sometimes, she would have her mother call out the words while she practiced spelling them from memory. As she checked her spelling against the list of correctly spelled words in her book, she monitored her progress toward meeting her learning goal. Finally, her learning was assessed on the spelling test. Alexa's activities supported her goal, and she earned the free time. And to extend and transfer her learning, she used the words in her everyday writing activities.

As the following discussion illustrates, each learning event can be structured in a variety of ways. Given that learning occurs through means other than direct instruction, these events focus on what learners do rather than on what the instruction should include. However, learning and instructional environments should be designed to provide opportunities for learners to experience each event. As you will see later in the chapter, the order in which the events occur often varies depending on the type of learning outcome desired and the learning theory on which the instruction is based.

Focusing on Goals Visualize a teenager slouched at a desk in a high school classroom dreaming of life after the bell rings. He sends a clear message that he doesn't want to be in that classroom. You might say, "He's not motivated." What if your job required you to reach this student? What would you do to get his attention and hold it? Could you devise a successful learning experience that would engage him and drive him to succeed? It might be a challenge, but it would not be impossible to get that student excited about learning. For learning to be successful, the learner has to want to learn. And as an instructional designer, your job is to create learning materials that will reach your target audience.

As you saw in the example of the bored teenager, learners can allocate their cognitive resources as they please. A teacher can provide the learning objectives, and a computer tutorial can list the outcomes of the program, but unless the learner accepts those goals as his or her own, the statements aren't worth much. Before learning can occur, the individual needs to decide that learning is a worthy endeavor.

Learners choose to engage in a learning experience to meet some need. Sometimes, the need is unrelated to the topic of instruction—for example, to spend time with friends, to graduate from school, to gain a promotion, to get out of the workplace, or to avoid parental disapproval. Other times, learners engage in an instructional event out

Table 4.3 Expanded events of learning and instruction

As this chart shows, a variety of activities support each learning event. Within each event, the techniques and strategies are organized roughly from behaviorist to constructivist.

Event	Possible activities
Focus on goals.	• Explicitly tell students goals of instruction. • Pretest on content to be learned. • Provide example of product to be created or performance to be enacted. • Ask questions about topic to generate curiosity. • Get attention by creating cognitive dissonance. • Place learners in situations in which performance above current level is expected. • Prompt learners to set own goals.
Connect to prior knowledge.	• Pretest on entry skills. • Ask questions to probe what is known about topic. • Explicitly review prior learning related to topic. • Link new information to prior knowledge through use of analogies. • Prompt students to reflect on what they already know about topic.
Gain and integrate content knowledge.	• Present discriminative stimulus that will activate response. • Shape behavior through reinforcements of progressively more specific behaviors. • Signal relationships among ideas through use of relational cues such as "in addition," "because," "in contrast." • Present examples and matched nonexamples of concepts and rules. • Present problems and demonstrate how to solve, explicitly stating strategies used. • Provide memory aids to assist in learning verbal information. • Explain connections between new knowledge and larger context. • Present human models demonstrating desired behavior or attitude. • Use testimonials where appropriate. • Use comparative organizers. • Present concrete or visual models to illustrate ideas. • Help students identify conflict and inconsistencies in their thinking. • Present new information in context in which it will be used. • Present information through multiple modes of representation. • Allow learners to revisit information as needed. • Provide adequate resources.
Take action and monitor learning progress.	• Present discriminative stimulus that will activate response and provide reinforcement for appropriate response. • Ask learners to identify new examples of a concept, apply a rule using new examples, or paraphrase verbal information; provide corrective feedback. • Ask learners to demonstrate skill; provide corrective feedback. • Provide practice in variety of problem types, with informative feedback. • Ask learners to indicate choice of actions in simulated situations and provide feedback on potential consequences of actions. • Test ideas through interactions with and feedback from others. • Provide support and coaching as needed when learners are performing task.
Synthesize and evaluate.	• Posttest on knowledge. • Chain multiple simple skills together into complex skills. • Provide reviews. • Have learners restate verbal information from memory. • Have learners demonstrate procedure or skill. • Have learners develop novel product applying target skills or knowledge. • Have learners generate their own summaries. • Present case studies, role plays, or simulations in which learners demonstrate skills, knowledge, attitudes. • Have students illustrate their mental model of process or procedures. • Have students present portfolios of progress. • Have students self-evaluate. • Self-reflect on information learned.
Extend and transfer.	• Gradually remove prompts and cues. • Alter reinforcement schedule. • Provide practice in variety of situations. • Revisit topic several times at increasing levels of complexity. • Provide opportunity to apply skills to novel situation. • Provide job aids. • Provide access to additional information on the topic. • Provide opportunity to apply skills in realistic contexts until full participants in community of practice.

of a desire to obtain skills they deem valuable. For example, learners may enroll in a course to learn to build Web pages; they may take a course in marketing because they want to work in sales and marketing; or they may take a Web-based course in French because they plan to vacation in France in the near future. Based on their individual needs, learners set personal goals. Then they engage in behaviors to assist themselves in meeting those goals. If their goal is to learn a foreign language in preparation for a vacation abroad, then they will pay particular attention to words they think may be useful in performing day-to-day tasks in a foreign land.

Learning theorists agree that successful learning requires goals (Driscoll, 2000). They disagree, however, on whether goals should be set by the teacher or designer, or left to the individual learners. Even when the goals of instruction are clearly stated, learners are free to pursue their own personal goals. Imagine watching a videotape on Brazil, where the goal of the program is to create awareness of economic initiatives by foreign investors. The program may open with the narrator stating, "By the end of this program, you'll be familiar with the major economic initiatives in Brazil." But you might choose to view the tape for entirely different reasons. Perhaps you want to learn to produce videotapes and are analyzing the editing techniques used. You'd approach the task of viewing the videotape with that goal in mind, and throughout the program, you'd seek information to help you meet that goal.

Depending on the nature of their individual needs, learners are more or less motivated to attend to the content. If they aren't particularly motivated, instructional materials must gain and focus their attention. Techniques to focus learners' attention on the goal of instruction include these:

- Provide a pretest on the content so that learners know what they should pay attention to.
- Provide questions to stimulate curiosity about the content.
- Explicitly state learning objectives. It's a good idea to keep the list short and to use general statements so as not to overload working memory.
- Provide an overview of the content.
- Describe how the content will help learners.
- Pose a problem for learners to solve.
- Use a graphic organizer (such as our triangle of essential elements).
- Appeal to learners' curiosity.
- Purposefully create tension by asking questions that you do not expect learners to be able to answer or asking them to perform a task that they won't be able to perform.
- Create cognitive conflict in the learners through some discrepant event that instigates a "need to know."
- Teach learners to set and monitor their own goals.

Each of these techniques prepares learners for the next steps in the learning sequence.

Recalling Relevant Prior Knowledge

Although theorists differ in their descriptions of how learning occurs, all recognize the role of prior knowledge in the task of learning something new (Driscoll, 2000). By activating prior knowledge, learners can modify their existing knowledge in a way that facilitates the recall of new information.

Think of the human mind as a filing system. Sometimes, you get new information that can be filed in an existing folder because the new information extends upon a category of information that already exists. Other times, you get information that doesn't fit into existing folders. Under those circumstances, you need to think about whether you might want the information at a later date or whether you can simply throw it away. Sometimes, new information requires you to establish a new folder. Perhaps you need a new folder because the information falls in an entirely different category than other information you already have in your filing system. Or perhaps you need a new folder because the information makes your old folders too stuffed to be effective. In that case, you subdivide your folder into smaller categories of information. Occasionally, you may find that information stored in your folders is no longer useful, so you discard the information and collapse the contents of multiple folders into one more-inclusive category. Throughout the process of filing, you look at new information as it comes to you and determine where to file it based on categories of information you already possess. You file the new information with related information so that you can find it easily at a later time.

The mind works in a similar fashion. In fact, as we likened the mind to a filing system, we may have reminded you of prior knowledge that may be useful in understanding how the mind works. We did that to prompt one way in which you may be able to organize your knowledge and to provide a cue for recall. Of course, our mind-as-filing-cabinet analogy may not have "worked" for you. You may have a different mental image of the mind. You may have extensive prior knowledge of how the brain works, and so rejected our analogy as too simple. Or you may have little experience with filing systems, and so lacked the prior knowledge on which our analogy built.

This analogy points out the benefits, and the problems, in attempting to remind learners of prior knowledge. You can make assumptions of prior knowledge based on your knowledge of learner characteristics, but you can never be sure what's in the mind of each individual learner. For example, we assume that learners in college and the workplace have experience with either electronic or paper-based filing systems, but we could be wrong. There are several techniques for reminding learners of their prior knowledge in addition to analogies. You could include a pretest on relevant prior knowledge. You could prompt recall by stating, "As you recall . . . ," or, "In the last lesson, we learned . . ." or you could present a narrative story or examples to provide a familiar context for the new information.

Regardless of how many times you attempt to connect new information to learners' prior knowledge, it's up to the learners to make those mental connections. All you can do is cue them as to what sort of prior knowledge may be related to the new information. As with goal setting, you can remind learners of relevant prior knowledge within the instruction, or you can prompt them to recall their own prior knowledge. One strategy to prompt recall is simply to ask learners what they already know about the topic. Connect it with goal setting by asking, "What do you know? What do you want to know? How will you seek the information you need?" Depending on the learners and the content, you may want them to document their prior knowledge in journals or reflect on how the new information is consistent or inconsistent with their prior knowledge through reflective writing or dialogue with others.

Often, learners begin the instruction with different sets of knowledge and skills. If some learners have the necessary prerequisite skills while others don't, try to design the program so that each group receives the appropriate content. For example, if you are developing an online course on the Mayan archaeological sites, you may have identified "reading and interpreting maps" as part of the necessary prior knowledge. You might create a short, optional tutorial on these skills as part of the course. Or you might design two paths through the material and create an entry exam to advise learners on which path they should pursue. In this case, learners who need help with prerequisite skills receive them in context; others have the option of bypassing the instruction on skills that are part of their prior knowledge.

Gaining and Integrating Content Knowledge
At the heart of most instruction is a set of content for learners to master. (For an example of content presentation, see Figure 4.2.) Whether it's

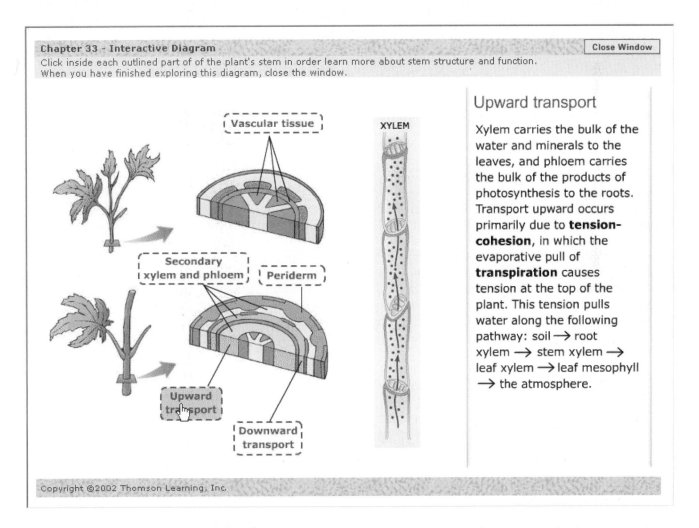

Figure 4.2 *Information presentation.* When the learner clicks on a category, the program displays supporting graphics and text for that category.

SOURCE: From *Biology* CD-ROM, 6th ed., by Solomon. © 2002 by Brooks/Cole. Reprinted with permission of Books/Cole, a division of Thomson Learning.

learning to play guitar, maintain a computer network, or trace the timeline of the Hundred Years War, content forms the basis for mastering the goals. This learning event (acquiring content information) and the next (taking action) go together and can occur in either order. You can present content information and have students solve a problem (take action) in order to practice applying the knowledge. Or you can present a problem (an action) in which students need to seek content information to perform the task. In other words, learners can take action to *practice* content knowledge, or their actions can be the *context* in which they seek content information.

Likewise, content can be structured in a sequential arrangement that leads learners through a set of information or as a set of resources they consult as they take action to achieve their learning goals. For example, this textbook is arranged sequentially within chapters: We lead readers from one point to another and ideas build on one another. However, the individual chapters can be thought of as resources that readers can access in a sequence of their own choosing. As another example, compare a historical narrative with the collection of resources you find on the Web. The narrative is designed to be read from beginning to end, whereas users search the Web in any sequence they choose. Each of these arrangements is effective, depending on the user's goals, needs, and prior knowledge of the content.

In addition to providing content knowledge, this step involves supporting students as they attempt to integrate and make sense of the content. There are many ways to provide support for learners as they are exposed to or explore content. The best ways depend on the individual learner and the desired learning outcome. For instance, mnemonics are useful for learning verbal information. Demonstrations are effective for guiding learners in the obtainment of psychomotor skills such as inserting a catheter and procedures such as reading a topographical map. Examples and matching nonexamples are useful in teaching intellectual skills such as concepts and discriminations. For instance, when learning proper social behavior in a particular culture, examples can be effective means of illustrating ideas in action. Attitude formation is facilitated by observations of models who exhibit the particular actions and attitudes.

When content is provided as a collection of resources, learners should be supported in organizing the content for themselves (Hill & Hannafin, 2001). Comparative organizers are one way to provide structure for learners as they explore open-ended learning environments and assist them in making connections among information more effectively than if they were to explore randomly on their own. For example, in a Web-based course on America's Civil War, students were expected to write an essay explaining the economic and political im-plications of the Civil War. To guide students in collecting information that would contribute to their essays, the instructional designer included forms that students could use to organize the information they found by exploring the many links included on the site (an example is shown in Figure 4.3.) Students were encouraged to determine the who, what, when, where, and how, and the impact of various events that contributed to the economic and political climate of the era. Learners also can be provided with direct cognitive supports such as outlines or concept maps to assist them in making sense of a collection of resources.

Learners who don't have this level of support need metacognitive support to help them assess what they know and what they should do as they learn. Even the most competent learners benefit from gentle reminders to organize and structure information. They need support in using resources such as help functions and site maps. They should be prompted to continually self-evaluate their own learning progress. And finally, they may need strategic support in the form of advice or coaching on how to perform a given task.

In apprenticeship contexts, **modeling** is an effective way of providing content knowledge and guiding learning. In a skill-based apprenticeship, the master demonstrates and explains the steps in the process. In a cognitive apprenticeship, the instructor or instructional materials model behaviors for learners and explain the thought processes that they eventually should adopt. For example, a teacher who was trying to teach students to probe for the reasoning behind classmates' answers noticed that one of her students was not questioning other students. She approached the reluctant pupil and asked, "Jeannette, do you have a question for Roger?" When Jeannette answered "no," the teacher continued, "Well I do," and proceeded to model optimum questioning techniques.

Coaching and scaffolding are preferred methods of providing learners with support for their knowledge acquisition within constructivist learning environments. With **scaffolding**, learners are asked to perform some task and provided with the level of support that is needed based on their performance on the task. When learners initially begin to perform the task, they may have resources (or individuals) readily available to consult when they are unable to complete the task independently. As their competence increases, these resources and supports are gradually removed. **Coaching** is used to prompt the learner to consider ideas that may not have been previously considered. Teachers (or instructional materials) may ask "Have you considered"–type questions to encourage learners to think beyond their current understanding. In these constructivist environments, taking action and gaining content knowledge go hand in hand.

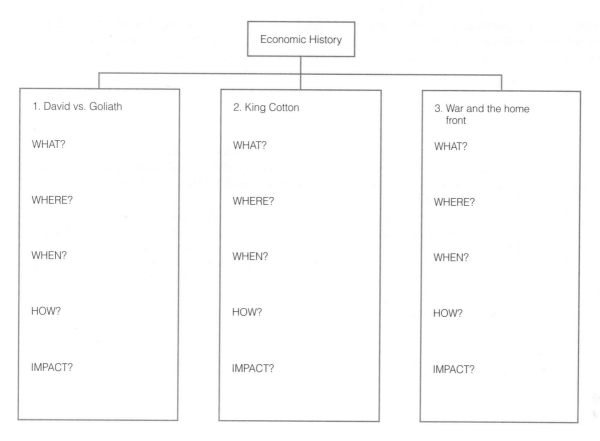

Figure 4.3 *Comparative organizer.* This comparative organizer helps students structure their learning from an open-ended exploration of resources about the Civil War.

SOURCE: Created by Chris Baugh, 1999. Used with permission.

Taking Action and Monitoring Progress

In some circumstances, content information is provided prior to prompting learners to take action. For example, a teacher might demonstrate a new piece of music, review the score with students, point out the critical parts, and then ask the students to perform it. A cooking teacher might talk about a dish by describing the various ingredients, equipment, and preparation, and then demonstrate it. She might break it down, section by section, describing and performing each part, and then ask students to practice what they have seen. Or a mathematics professor might demonstrate solving a type of equation before asking students to tackle practice problems.

An alternative strategy is to have learners perform an activity first, before they are exposed to the content. This creates a "need to know" as learners seek and learn the content within the context of performing the task. Consider the popular high school science project in which students are asked to design packaging for a raw egg so that the egg can be dropped from a height—say, the roof of the school—and survive intact. Students have to solve many science and engineering problems to determine the right design and packaging materials.

They also learn about the scientific process. They receive feedback on their learning progress through the natural consequences of their actions: The egg breaks or it survives.

When learners take action, **feedback** provides them with information as to how their learning is progressing. Feedback can come from a variety of sources and in many different forms, but it consistently provides learners with a means of judging, monitoring, and correcting their learning.

Natural consequences provide one form of feedback. For example, kindergartners who are learning to create the secondary colors of orange, purple, and green by mixing the primary colors of red, blue, and yellow receive feedback through observations of the colors that result from their experimentation. Adults who are learning to make wine receive feedback as to the success or failure of their efforts when they taste the product. In developing instruction, the designer can devise practice exercises, experiments, role plays, and simulations in which learners obtain feedback from observing the natural consequences of their actions. (an example is shown in Figure 4.4).

Direct feedback also informs students whether their response is correct. Consider the following practice test item from a computer-based history lesson:

What relation was President John Quincy Adams to President John Adams?

a. Grandson

b. Son

c. Nephew

d. No relation

If the student selects the answer "a. Grandson," the computer might respond with "Incorrect." This is "knowledge of response" feedback—the student can see that his answer is incorrect but doesn't know why it's incorrect. Using the same test item and student answer, the computer might provide "knowledge of correct response" feedback by stating, "Incorrect. The correct answer is b." Yet more elaborate feedback would yield this response:

"Incorrect. John Quincy Adams, the sixth president of the United States, was the eldest son of John Adams, the second president."

Another type of feedback is reinforcement. If learners are rewarded for their correct actions, they will tend to repeat those responses. The reinforcement can range from the learner's internal satisfaction that an answer is correct to the monetary incentives parents sometimes provide to reward their children for good grades. In corporate settings, employees might receive bonuses or certificates for successfully completing training programs.

Social feedback is critical to many types of learning outcomes. Consider the things we learn simply through paying attention to the responses of others. Most of us probably learned our native language by trying out words and noticing the reactions of others. The unwritten rules of the corporate culture are learned in the same way: Employees observe others' actions, try things themselves, and pay attention to how others respond. Within instruction,

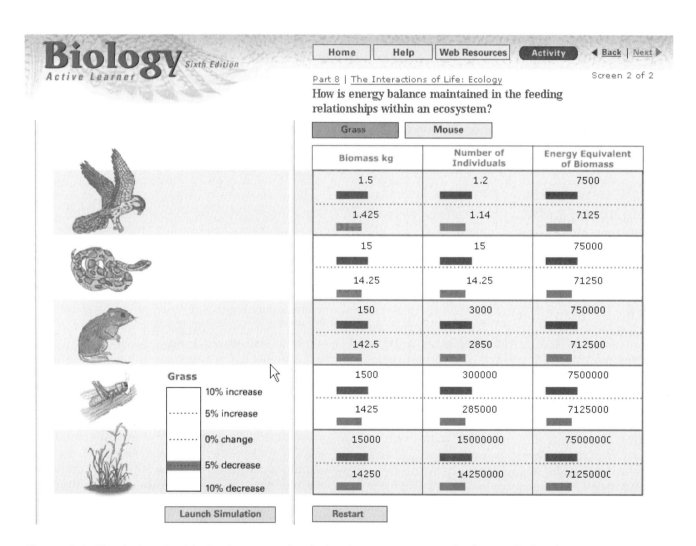

Figure 4.4 *Simulation.* In this single-screen simulation, learners can sample the results by choosing varying increases and decreases in grass and mice. Learners are encouraged to try a range of possible outcomes.

SOURCE: From *Biology* CD-ROM, 7th ed., by Solomon/Berg/Martin. © 2005. Reprinted by permission of Brooks/Cole, a division of Thomson Learning.

designers can provide opportunities for learners to compare their ideas with those of others through chat rooms, online discussion boards, face-to-face discussions, and samples of other students' responses. For instance, when group members are learning conflict management techniques, advice from other participants during a role play can provide information as to the success or failure of an intervention.

An often maligned action strategy is drill and practice—sometimes derisively called "drill and kill." This technique conjures up images of mindless, rote learning of marginally useful facts such as the state capitals. Drill has its place, however. To learn some categories of content, such as a foreign language or math facts, students have to practice repeatedly, until the skill becomes automatic. Motor skills also require repeated practice with corrective feedback in order for learners to master them. As a designer, your goal is to design practice activities that maintain learners' interests while providing the necessary "time on task."

Students can take action and receive feedback in a wide variety of ways other than the traditional drill and practice. A simulation attempts to re-create the "actual" environment so that learners can master the skills without fear that their mistakes could cause harm. For example, pilots train in flight simulators designed to give them feedback that mirrors precisely how an actual plane would respond under the same conditions. Apprenticeships give learners an opportunity to practice in a realistic environment, but one with close supervision. Law clerks, student teachers, and medical interns all learn by applying their professional training in workplace contexts. Learners can be provided with case studies, problems to solve, scenarios to examine, projects to complete, and a variety of other tasks that require them to take action to make knowledge their own. They can take action by teaching others, developing a product, or practicing a skill. But when taking action, learners can be expected to make mistakes and should receive feedback so that they learn to perform correctly. They shouldn't be "graded" on their actions, except perhaps to receive credit for participation. Through taking action and getting feedback, learners make sense of new information and learn to judge the adequacy of their knowledge.

DESIGNER'S TOOLKIT

Computer-Based Interactions

This box presents a few of the many options for creating interactive computer-based programs that are engaging and effective. Strong interactions give learners opportunities to check their understanding in a responsive environment.

Text-Based Multiple Choice

These are the exercise or quiz items that replicate the print-based multiple choice tests that all learners are familiar with. A difference is that in a computer program the learners can get specific feedback on their selections. This strategy is useful for any content that requires knowledge of facts, rules, definitions, and other declarative information. A variation on the multiple choice question is the true/false question. You can use graphical elements such as tables, graphs, and illustrations as "referential" stimuli. In other words, the quiz items can ask about an image. For example, a graph might show a curve. The question might present several possible statements, and the learner selects the one that describes the curve. As a designer, you may be required to write the questions, specify the image, and write the feedback that helps the student understand why his or her choice was incorrect.

Graphical Multiple Choice

This type of activity is similar to a multiple choice activity except that the learners select an image or part of a figure or graph in order to answer the question correctly. This works for any visual content, especially when learners need to differentiate material. For example, for a quiz for apprentice mechanics, the question may ask trainees to select the correct engine for a particular vehicle from several photographs. Another example, for an American history class, is to ask students to click the correct trail for the Pony Express on a map of North America. Each correct selection elicits positive reinforcement. An incorrect selection invokes a targeted response designed to help the student understand why her or his choice was incorrect.

Animated Multiple Choice

A variation on the graphical multiple choice item is the animated version. This is a useful strategy for content such as biological processes that require students to understand sequences and the ways in which structures behave in each segment or in a process.

(continued on page 82)

(continued)

In this type of exercise, the animation "plays" a segment, then presents one or more multiple choice questions. If learners miss a question, the animation replays with an explanation of the correct answer.

Drag-and-Drop

Learners manipulate visual images to complete a graphic or to classify or organize material. For example, a main graphic could serve as a background. Students work through the activity by dragging labels to the appropriate spot on the graphic. The feedback can be visible and audible: Correct answers "stick" with a positive-sounding tone and incorrect answers "float back" with a negative-sounding tone.

Categorizing

Learners drag items into categories or "bins." These items could be words, graphics, equations, or any other content. These exercises work well for tasks requiring classification, discrimination, and identification of examples and nonexamples. For example, trainees might have to classify whether certain chemicals are hazardous. Again, learners can get feedback visually and audibly: Correct answers "stick" with a positive-sounding tone and incorrect answers "float back" with a negative-sounding tone.

Sort Order

This activity requires students to place words or graphics in the proper order, such as on a timeline or in a process. Learners arrange the items in the proper order and then check the answers. One strategy for presenting feedback is to retain learners'

correct answers in their correct portions while incorrect portions "float back" for another try. For example, a photo gallery might require art history students to put famous artworks in the correct historical sequence.

Simulation

A simulation is a contained environment in which learners try their new knowledge and skills without risking any damage to the "real" environment. Simulations allow learners to put their skills into practice, especially in novel situations. For example, simulated chemistry experiments allow high school students to explore the results of mixing chemicals without the risk. A software product might have a simulation mode that allows users to practice the skills without jeopardizing a live installation with other users. Pilots train in complex simulators that even re-create the physical sensations of a plane's movement. If you have an opportunity to design a simulation, keep focused on what your learners need to practice.

Games

Like simulations, games usually have specific goals and strategies that are distinct from the content goals and instructional strategies. For example, a popular program for young learners helps them learn arithmetic via a space adventure. Games often are used to practice and reinforce skills and to reward learners. Because some learners are highly immersed in gaming, this can be an effective device for luring them into a learning setting. However, instructional games need to be sophisticated enough to appeal to learners who may have extensive experience with recreational games.

Devising Effective Activities

For a foreign language CD-ROM product, the developer created a series of games to help students build vocabulary skills. The most effective strategy to learn a language is to practice the language, so these games provided that practice. They were designed very simply but featured fun graphics and zany situations. In one game, students learned parts of the body by clicking on Dr. Frankenstein's creature, who is wired and trying to break free.

In another, about food, a couple sits on an island and watches as their yacht sinks while they dream of all the food they won't be eating that evening. These games are instructionally effective because students enjoy them and so are inclined to return to them many times. Each experience with the game helps build and reinforce vocabulary skills. Additionally, the game templates were designed for reuse in other programs, such as for other languages.

Synthesizing and Evaluating

Synthesizing and Evaluating   Learners need an opportunity to synthesize and evaluate their learning. As they progress through instructional materials, they focus on the details of the content. After learning several chunks of information, they should step back and synthesize the information across chunks. There are several ways of doing so.

You can provide periodic reviews throughout the instruction with summaries that constitute a general overview instead of focusing on specific details. You also can ask students to prepare their own summaries. Because individuals have different learning preferences, some may generate an outline, others may write a narrative, and still others may diagram relationships among topics. Of course, this method is only as effective as the student is in making connections across topics. Because this stage is concerned with both synthesis and evaluation, learners who synthesize information on their own

should check the adequacy of their synthesis. You can provide them with a summary or outline against which they can compare their own summaries, have them submit their summaries to the course instructor for feedback, hold a group discussion (study groups often serve this function), or, as is quite common, test them on their knowledge of the content.

As you will recall from Chapter 3, assessments (or tests) provide learners with an opportunity to synthesize what they've learned and to evaluate their progress in meeting their learning goals. When preparing assessments, you should not limit yourself to easy-to-score, multiple choice formats (see Figure 4.5). End-of-unit projects, portfolios, essay exams, and similar assessments can effectively require learners to synthesize their knowledge in new ways.

No matter what method is used to provide for synthesis and evaluation, most students are interested in monitoring

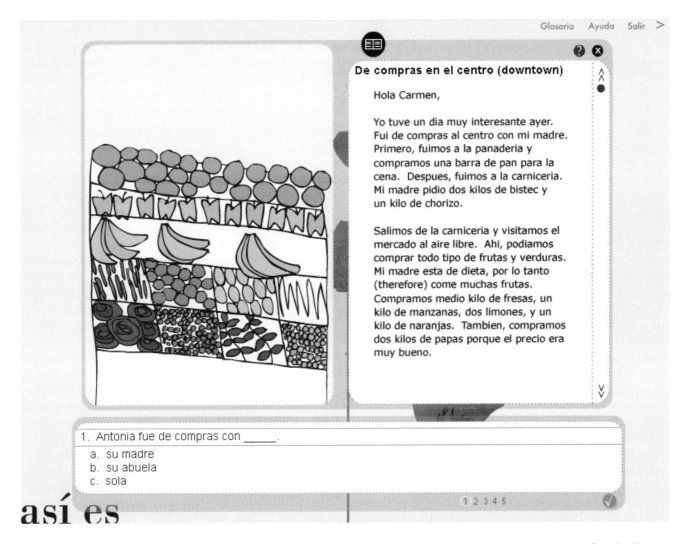

Figure 4.5 *Assessment.* In this language exercise, learners read the passage and answer a series of multiple choice questions.

SOURCE: From *Así Es* CD-ROM, 4th ed., by Levy-Konesky and Daggett. © 2004 by Heinle & Heinle. Reprinted with permission of Heinle, a division of Thomson Learning.

Table 4.4 Common instructional sequences

Learning experiences	Order	
	Direct hierarchy	**Problem-centered**
Convergent experience	*Application model*	*Discovery model*
	• Activate prior knowledge.	• Participate in activities leading toward predetermined end.
	• Acquire skills.	• Acquire skills through activities.
	• Participate in activities to use skills.	• Participate in tasks to enlarge understanding.
	• Reflect on learning.	• Reflect on new learning.
Divergent experience	*Extension model*	*Intervention model*
	• Activate prior knowledge.	• Participate in activity with many possible answers.
	• Acquire skills.	• Acquire skills through working on problem.
	• Participate in activities to increase understanding.	• Coach students to success.
	• Solve problems by applying information in novel ways.	• Reflect.
	• Reflect.	

SOURCE: From *Constructivist Teaching*, by J. A. Zahorik, 1995, Bloomington, IN: Phi Delta Kappa Educational Foundation. Copyright 1995 by Phi Delta Kappa. Adapted with permission.

their own learning progress. In a Web-delivered course, administrators discovered that students checked their grades several times per week even though they were tested weekly (Ross, 1999). In informal learning and training situations, learners should be provided with a self-test, checklist of behaviors, reflective summary, or other means of monitoring their own understanding.

Extending and Transferring Most learning theories recommend that students learn to extend and transfer their newly learned knowledge to other situations (Driscoll, 2000). Students need to reduce their dependence on the cues provided by the instructional environment, learn when and where they should apply knowledge, and explore situations that are both similar to and different from those within which they have been immersed in order to generalize their learning beyond the specific instructional situation. The transfer of new skills is facilitated by practice with a variety of problem types and multiple examples within the instruction. For example, students who participated in a problem-based approach to instructional design believed that the complexities they experienced with their client were unique to that particular client, rather than common to client–designer relationships in general (Cennamo & Holmes, 2001). Exposure to a variety of case studies of client–designer relationships helped these learners to generalize their knowledge beyond their specific experience.

Although most instruction is provided with the hope that learners will apply it outside of the immediate learning environment, learners don't always transfer their

knowledge automatically. To encourage transfer, develop an activity in which students use their knowledge in an authentic setting. For example, participants in a leadership course could be asked to observe and document leadership behaviors exhibited by administrators in their companies. Participants in a nutrition class could be asked to record the food they eat for one week.

It's also useful to create job aids or other performance support tools so that students have a set of tips or reminders to guide them through the tasks after they return to the job site. **Job aids** are quick reference guides to help a user perform some task. Job aids can consist of step-by-step lists, decision aids such as flowcharts or tables, forms, checklists, worksheets, or reference materials that help in locating data. Job aids can be particularly useful for procedural skills. These types of skills typically include facts and sequences of steps that need to become internalized and automatic (Gagné, Yekovich, & Yekovich, 1993). As learners become more proficient in performing the procedure, they won't need to consult the job aid or performance support system. For example, do you remember learning to multiply? When you began to apply your skills, you may have relied on a multiplication table to look up answers to problems. Or if you've tried to learn a foreign language such as Spanish, you may have consulted an English-to-Spanish dictionary on a regular basis. As you used these skills repeatedly, however, they became automatic, and you no longer needed to consult a job aid. At that point, instead of assisting you in performing the task, they slowed you down. Job aids, EPSSs, and other tools provide scaffolding that can be discarded when it becomes unnec-

Example 4.3 Brief Example of Application Model

The application model of direct instruction is used to prepare a sales team to promote a new product.

Event	Examples
Focus on goals.	Tell a joke. Make introductions. Lead icebreaker activity.
Recall relevant prior knowledge.	Review product announcement.
Present and organize content knowledge.	Display series of screen templates that effectively present product information.
Take action and monitor learning progress.	Provide checks for understanding after each chunk of content. Engage learners in sales simulation to apply new content. Give specific feedback to learners based on their performance.
Synthesize and evaluate.	Review main concepts. Provide posttest for certification.
Extend and transfer.	Distribute job aid. Have learners role-play how to make first sales call.

essary. When used to supplement training, they reduce the need to recall steps from memory. That's why we have provided "design aids" at the end of each chapter—to assist you in transferring your knowledge of instructional design to the work environment.

Sequencing Events

The order in which the learning events are sequenced is influenced by the intended outcome of the instruction and the learning theory upon which the instruction is based. Learning experiences can be *convergent,* where the focus is on predetermined ends, or *divergent,* where the focus is on novel or original outcomes. Although instructional methods based on behaviorism consistently focus on predetermined ends, both cognitive and constructivist methods can focus on divergent outcomes. Instruction also can be ordered in a *direct hierarchical* sequence, where learners obtain basic skills before applying them to complex tasks, or a *problem-centered* sequence, where learners obtain basic skills while working on complex tasks. Often, cognitive and behavioral approaches are hierarchical in nature while constructivist approaches are problem-centered. Considering these two dimensions together results in four possible models for learning environments (Zahorik, 1995, see Table 4.4).

In the *application model,* learners proceed through a hierarchical sequence of skills, from simple to complex, toward a predetermined outcome. Using this model, learners activate prior knowledge, acquire new skills, and then participate in activities in which they apply those skills. For example, students may learn to

identify common skin disorders by viewing a variety of examples, then apply these skills in a clinical setting. In this case, there is a correct answer to each problem. This approach is most often associated with cognitive theories of learning.

In the *extension model,* learners also proceed through a hierarchical sequence of skills, from simple to complex, but the outcome is open-ended and focused on the creation of something new. For example, students may be taught to write a three-paragraph theme that includes an opening, a middle, and a closing paragraph, then apply those skills by writing a persuasive essay. This approach is consistent with both cognitive and constructivist theories.

In the *discovery model,* students acquire basic skills by working on a problem, but the activities are arranged to lead them toward a predetermined outcome. For example, students may experiment with the placement of objects on a seesaw to discover the interaction of an object's weight and distance from the fulcrum on lift. This approach usually is associated with constructivist methods.

In the *invention model,* the instruction is problem-centered, and learners are immersed in a complex problem that can yield many possible answers. For example, students may be asked to create a paper airplane that will fly across the room. In researching and experimenting with the plane, students will learn basic principles of flight such as the relationship between lift and weight. This approach also is associated with constructivist theories.

Sample lessons for the application and invention models are illustrated in Examples 4.3 and 4.4.

To plan an instructional strategy, you need to determine how you will provide the learning events for each chunk of instruction. You don't need to include each of the events within a chunk as long as you've accounted for all of them within the lesson. For example, you may want to activate prior knowledge and focus on goals only once, at the beginning of the lesson, instead of including these events at the beginning of each chunk. But each time you present content information and have learners take action, you've taught a chunk. If you arrange the

---

Example 4.4   Brief Example of Invention Model

The invention model of problem-centered instruction is used to prepare a sales team to promote a new product.

Event	Example
Focus on goals.	Introduce problem of selling new product. Have learners set goals on how they will approach task.
Recall relevant prior knowledge.	Ask learners to reflect on what they already know about sales.
Take action and monitor learning progress.	Have learners engage in role-play. Solicit feedback from peers.
Present content knowledge.	Provide product resources so learners can gain information they need to promote product.
Synthesize and evaluate.	Ask learners to summarize what they learned.
Extend and transfer.	Discuss a variety of similar and different scenarios so learners generalize knowledge beyond role play.

Example 4.5   Chunking within an Instructional Sequence

Introduction

• Focus on goals of lesson by gaining attention and presenting overall objectives.

Chunk 1

• Remind of prior knowledge: "Yesterday, we learned about . . ."

• Focus on goals of section: "Today, we'll learn about . . ."

• Present content and provide learning support.

• Take action and monitor learning.

Chunk 2

• Remind of prior knowledge.

• Focus on goals of next two sections.

• Present content and provide learning support.

• Take action and monitor learning.

Chunk 3

• Present content and provide learning support.

• Take action and monitor learning.

Closing

• Synthesize and evaluate (review and test).

• Extend and transfer (provide additional readings on topic).

instruction using a problem-based approach, your sequence of instructional events will differ from the one in Example 4.5, but a chunk will still consist of one problem or action item and the associated opportunities to gain content knowledge.

Aligning the Elements

As you saw in Chapter 3, the type of learning outcome has implications for the assessment of learning. The type of learning outcome also has implications for the instructional activities.[3] Suppose the task is for students to learn the fact that atmospheric pressure changes the temperature at which water boils. Does it make sense to have them boil water and measure the boiling point with thermometers? Unless students can travel to different locations at varying heights above sea level, they won't be able to perform the experiments that illustrate this fact. In this case, students need to recall a fact: Atmospheric pressure affects the boiling point of water. And their knowledge of this fact can be assessed simply by asking them to recall it.

When teaching verbal information, you should link it to other knowledge or help learners create new webs of information. Provide a meaningful context for encoding verbal information and cues to assist in recall. Mnemonics, stories, imagery, and related "memory tricks" help call attention to the information to be learned and can provide cues to assist in its recall.

The key to teaching intellectual skills that consist of specific procedures is to break each skill down into subskills, then allow ample time for learners to practice and to get feedback so they don't learn the skill incorrectly. Provide plenty of cues as to how learners should perform the component skills. You don't want learners to practice a faulty skill repeatedly. For example, it's difficult for children (and adults) to "unlearn" incorrect grammar. To assist in learning concepts, call attention to the distinctive features of the concepts, and use examples as well as nonexamples to illustrate important attributes. When teaching rules, show how they can be applied in a variety of contexts using a variety of examples. Learners also need opportunities to apply the rules or concepts as well as feedback on their performance. Practice in a variety of

---

DESIGNER'S TOOLKIT

Instructional Devices for Verbal Information

This box illustrates several techniques to learn verbal information. Some people dismiss mnemonic, or memory, devices, calling them a type of "cheating," implying that that they are less worthy than other strategies. This is similar to arguing that medicine must taste bad to be good for you. An instructional strategy that works well is an excellent strategy!

Songs and Stories

How do children learn the letters of the alphabet? Most of them can learn the simple, catchy alphabet song in just one lesson. This doesn't teach children what the specific letters are or what they sound like or how to read or write them. But it does suggest a strategy for quickly learning a lot of content, even if the learner is not a sophisticated student.

Flash Cards

An example of a highly sophisticated student is a medical student. If first-year medical students need to learn the name of every bone in the human body, is there a way to create a lesson that allows them to practice this until they master it? For most of us, the names of each bone would constitute declarative knowledge. But a doctor needs to know the names at a procedural

level, so repeated practice and feedback are called for, such as with flash cards. In fact, many medical students create flash cards in order to practice these types of skills, taking advantage of every free minute in the course of a busy day.

Narrative

Before people could read and write, they drew pictures and told stories. The oral tradition allowed societies to transmit their traditions to succeeding generations. Stories as complex as Homer's *Iliad* and *Odyssey* were passed orally from one generation to the next before it became possible to write them down. The sacred texts that form the core of the major religious traditions are told as a series of stories. We seem to be predisposed to remembering stories.

Memory Devices

Many people learned to spell *arithmetic* using the mnemonic device "a rat in the house might eat the ice cream." The first letter of each word in the nonsense phrase forms the correct spelling. There are other popular mnemonics such as "on old Olympus's treeless tops, a Finn and German viewed some hops," which gives students the first letters of each of the twelve cranial nerves.

Voice of Experience

Affective Skills

A nonprofit agency that works with troubled teenagers produced an interactive program on drug abuse and addiction. In addition to providing accurate information on alcohol, drugs, addiction, and treatment, the program aimed to change teens' attitudes toward drug use. The producers grappled with how to accomplish this, because teens can sniff out contrived material immediately. They decided to create provocative, video-based stories. Each sequence of content (which included intellectual knowledge about drug abuse) concluded with a powerful, realistically staged vignette in a teen drug user's life. The raw power of the video sequences, featuring potent performances by young actors and a gritty cinema verité style, provided a highly emotional experience. In pilot testing with the target audience, "tough" teens cried. It achieved the emotional response the producers hoped for, as was documented in survey results from before and after the program.

House

Analogy

Consider our house analogy: You have decided to build a house in an area of town that is undergoing a renaissance. Many of the homes in the area date from the early twentieth century and are considered to have historical value. Some are being extensively renovated according to certain standards. You call several architects to find the one you want to hire. The first explains that his philosophy of architecture is to develop an aesthetic that respects the arts and crafts movement style of the homes but adapts them to the modern lifestyle, with open floor plans and contemporary materials. He attempts to create a house that looks as if it were original to the neighborhood. The next architect specializes in historical preservation. She uses authentic materials and methods to re-create historical homes as closely as possible, although she makes concessions for modern conveniences and safety issues, such as air conditioning and updated fire-proofing. A third architect explains that he is a modernist and that his approach is to "honestly" acknowledge the time period in which a home is constructed. He discourages the idea of attempting to camouflage what is essentially a modern home inside a historical shell. He recommends creating a house that complements the architecture of the neighborhood but does not attempt to mimic it.

Which of these approaches is the right one? The answer will be influenced by building codes, the budget, and the timeline, but mostly it will depend on the homeowner's personal preferences. In fact, each option will be attractive to someone. And it's possible that the homeowner will seek a solution that combines two or all of these options. But the critical issue is to identify each component needed in the home—space needs, electrical needs, lighting and sound considerations, to name just a few. Components are clustered by the needs of certain spaces. For example, a kitchen will need storage space, ample electrical wiring, plumbing, and several forms of lighting. The architect will work with the homeowner to determine how to address each "chunk" of components in a plan that appeals to the homeowner while still meeting identified space and usage needs.

Developing an instructional product also requires a theoretical framework. Some designers strongly support a theory and adhere carefully to it in producing their work. Others find merit in using any portion of a theory that they find beneficial in addressing a specific design problem. But as in building a home, it's critical to cluster the content into reasonable chunks and develop a plan to present those chunks of content in a way that is effective and appealing to the end users.

Example 4.6 Outcome, Assessment, and Strategy Table

This table was created for a Web-based course in digital video. The overall goal of this instructional sequence is for students to create video segments that contain no jump cuts.

Outcome	Type	Learning Events Provided by Instruction	Assessment
Chunk 1			
1.0 Identify segment containing jump cut.	Concept	Define jump cut as sudden change in screen position. Show examples and nonexamples, pointing out changes in screen position. Show several video segments, have students identify those with jump cuts and give feedback as to whether they were correct.	Show several video segments and have students identify those with jump cuts.
Chunk 2			
2.0 Move camera at least 45% between similar shots.	Rule	State rule. Show video example. Have students create video segments applying the rule and critique their work to determine if rule was applied.	Have students develop video segments with no editing allowed. Deduct points for jump cuts.
Chunk 3			
3.0 Cover jump shots with cut-ins, cutaways, dissolves, or wipes.	Rule	State rule. Demonstrate application of rule using video segments. Show several video segments; have students identify technique used to cover potential jump cut and give feedback as to whether they were correct.	Have students edit long action sequence to compress time and identify the technique used to cover jump cuts. Deduct points for jump cuts. Provide points for correctly labeling technique used to cover potential jumps.
3.1 Identify cut-in.	Concept	Define cut-in. Show video example. Show video segments and have students select one with cut-in.	(Assessed in 3.0.)
3.2 Identify cutaways.	Concept	Define cut-in. Show video example. Show video segments and have students select one with cutaway.	(Assessed in 3.0.)
3.3 Identify dissolve.	Concept	Define dissolve. Show video example. Show video segments. Have students select one with dissolve.	(Assessed in 3.0.)
3.4 Identify wipe.	Concept	Define wipe. Show video example. Show video segments. Have students select one with wipe.	(Assessed in 3.0.)

Activities Checklist, Part 1

- Chunk outcomes.
- Create instructional strategy for each chunk. *Provide support for the following learning events:*
- Focus on goals.
  - ○ State objectives OR personal goal setting.
- Compare with existing knowledge.
  - ○ Remind of prior knowledge or have students generate comparisons.
- Gain and integrate content knowledge.
  - ○ Present information OR access to resources.
  - ○ Support and organize learning (examples, modeling, coaching, demonstrations, etc.).
- Take action and monitor progress.
  - ○ Provide opportunity for practice and give feedback OR immerse in problem situation with coaching, peer feedback.
- Synthesize and evaluate knowledge.
  - ○ Review/summarize.
  - ○ Provide assessment.
- Extend and transfer.
- Match activities to outcomes and assessments.

contexts can assist learners in transferring intellectual skills to applicable situations.

Motor skills have to be practiced—knowing how to do something is not the same thing as doing it. Like procedural skills, motor skills should be broken down into subskills, and then learners need plenty of time to practice and get feedback to prevent learning a skill incorrectly. Take a cue from top athletes. When golfer Tiger Woods sought to improve his already formidable game, he and his coach broke his swing into the smallest possible components. For months, he practiced these subskills, perfecting each, before putting them back together into an improved swing.

When teaching attitudes, the instruction needs to connect with learners on an emotional level so that they are motivated to change their behavior. This kind of knowledge can be difficult to measure, but it is possible to do and is often a part of an instructional program. For example, you can measure whether learners are eating healthier foods, making more charitable contributions, or maintaining a high grade point average. To influence attitude changes, design instruction to include personal testi-

monials and opportunities for learners to observe an admired role model performing the desired behaviors. In addition, affective learning goals often require declarative knowledge that provides a rationale for changing behavior.

Finally, you can develop learners' cognitive strategies by giving them opportunities to set personal goals and monitor their own performance. For example, instruction can be designed to prompt learners to set learning goals, outline strategies to achieve those goals, and self-assess the effectiveness of their learning strategies. Learners often need guidance in choosing successful strategies and support in using metacognitive techniques. Explicit instruction in cognitive strategies should be accompanied by examples of their use in a variety of appropriate situations. Learners benefit from observing models who apply cognitive strategies effectively, especially if the techniques they use are identified for the learners. The development of cognitive strategies also is strengthened by practice followed by feedback that informs learners of their progress.

As you plan the instructional strategy, you must make sure that the outcomes, assessments, and activities are in alignment. Learners should participate in activities that prepare them to perform the desired skill on the assessment measure. Notice how the activities and assessments align with the outcomes in Example 4.6. As you read the table from left to right, notice, too, that the tasks learners were asked to perform on the assessment were demonstrated and practiced in the instructional activities.

Summary

In this chapter, you learned several steps leading to the development of specific learning activities, including chunking and prioritizing your learning outcomes, planning learning events for each chunk, and aligning the activities with the outcomes and assessments. Learning experiences should be arranged to support learners as they:

- Focus on the goals of instruction.
- Compare new knowledge with prior knowledge.
- Gain and integrate new content knowledge.
- Take action and monitor learning progress through feedback.
- Synthesize and evaluate their progress in obtaining new knowledge.
- Extend and transfer the new knowledge to novel situations.

All of these learning events should be provided within each lesson, though the sequence will vary depending on the desired outcome of the instruction and the learning theory upon which the instruction is based. In some cases, learning events may be initiated by the learners, however, designers should consider each of the events when developing an instructional program.

This chapter has outlined the steps in creating an instructional strategy. However, the specific instructional strategy is influenced by the context in which the instruction will be delivered and the conditions under which learners will participate. In Chapter 5, you will learn to consider a variety of means to deliver the instruction and to select the media to deliver each learning event. Although we present this material after the chapter on instructional strategies, the information presented in Chapters 4 and 5 must be considered simultaneously in planning for and developing instructional activities.

Notes

[1]For a clear discussion of these three learning theories and their implications for instructional design, see Peggy Ertmer and Timothy Newby, "Behaviorism, Cognitivisim, Constructivism: Comparing Critical Features from an Instructional Design Perspective," *Performance Improvement Quarterly* (Fall 1993): 50–72.

[2]Based on a project designed by the first author, described in more detail in K. S. Cennamo, J. D. Ross, and C. S. Rogers "The evolution of a web-enhanced course incorporating strategies for self regulation," *Educause Quarterly,* 25(1) (2002):28–33.

[3]For an excellent discussion of instructional strategies for different types of learning outcomes, see P. L. Smith and T. J. Ragan, *Instructional Design* (2nd ed.). Upper Saddle River, NJ: Merrill/Prentice-Hall.

[4]Adapted from documents prepared by David Halpin, Colleen Kerr, Peter Macedo, and Sandra Schneider, 1998. Used with permission.

References

Cennamo, K., & Holmes, G. (2001). Developing awareness of client relations through immersion in practice. *Educational Technology, 41*(6), 44–49.

Driscoll, M. P. (2000). *Psychology of learning for instruction,* 2nd ed. Boston: Allyn & Bacon.

Ertmer, P. A., & Newby, T. J. (1996). The expert learner: Strategic, self-regulated, and reflective. *Instructional Science, 24*(1), 1–24.

Gagné, E. D., Yekovich, C. W., & Yekovich, F. R. (1993). *The cognitive psychology of school learning,* 2nd ed. New York: Longman.

Gagné, R. M. (1965). *Conditions of learning,* New York: Holt, Rinehart & Winston.

Hill, J. R., & Hannafin, M. J. (2001). Teaching and learning in digital environments: The resurgence of resource-based learning. *Educational Technology Research and Development, 49*(3): 37–52.

Miller, G. A. (1956). The magical number, seven, plus or minus two: Some limits on our capacity for processing information. In G. A. Miller (1967), *Psychological Review, 63,* 81–91.

Ross, J. D. (1999). Regulating Hypermedia: Self-regulation learning strategies in a hypermedia environment. Unpublished dissertation, Virginia Tech.

Smith, P. L., & Ragan, T. J. (1999). *Instructional design,* 2nd ed. Upper Saddle River, NJ: Merrill/ Prentice-Hall.

Zahorik, J. A. (1995). *Constructivist teaching* Bloomington, IN: Phi Delta Kappa Educational Foundation.

Application

1. The RealWorldID Web site includes a case study of the development of video-based science instruction. Because Chapters 4 and 5 both address the development of activities, the same case is used for analysis in both chapters. As a follow-up to Chapter 4, you should develop an instructional strategy for this case. After reading Chapter 5, you should outline the instructional materials. Although we have posed problems related to the content of each individual chapter at the end of Chapters 4 and 5, you may choose to work on the entire case at the end of Chapter 5. Visit the RealWorldID Web site to analyze the case online or to print for use during class discussions.

2. In your reflective journal, summarize the key points of this chapter. Are the ideas presented consistent or inconsistent with your beliefs and prior knowledge? Compare your perceptions of the chapter with those of your classmates in group discussions.

3. Review a variety of instructional materials. Try to identify each learning event. Notice what techniques are used to address each event and how the events are sequenced. To broaden your knowledge beyond the specific examples you analyze, you and your classmates may want to share your instructional materials and analyses with each other.

4. As we explore the essential elements of instructional design in Chapters 2–6, we encourage your class to function as an ID team to create the design specifications for an instructional module. In this chapter, your working group should develop an instructional strategy for a chunk of content.

    a. Consider the type of learning outcome.

    b. Describe how you will address each of the learning events.

    c. Outline an instructional sequence.

    d. Have you made any decisions that you'd like to check out in your formative evaluation? Make note of those areas now.

Ideas in Action

In Chapters 2–6, we follow the design of a videotape on food safety. In this chapter, we include the instructional strategy table below that outlines how each learning event will be presented in the video and illustrate how the outcomes, assessments, and activities are aligned.[4] Remember, the goal of the program is to "prevent food-borne illnesses in the elderly by showing them how to purchase, handle, store, and prepare food safely."

Instructional Strategy

From Store to Fork: Safe Food Guidelines for Older Adults

Outcome	Learning Event	Contained in Video
Overall	Activate prior knowledge	Newspaper clippings sliding/spinning in?
1.0	Gain and integrate content	Shots of preparing food, eating food, children, elderly, uncooked ground beef, fruits and veggies, food-handling shot, food-eating shot, shot of older woman, family shot.
		Narration states: "Each year millions of people get sick from eating food contaminated with food poisoning bacteria or bacterial toxins, and many die. Most of these illnesses occur from foods prepared and eaten in the home. Infants, children, pregnant women, and the elderly are particularly susceptible to food-borne illness."
Overall	Focus on goals	Title screen:
		From store to fork:
		Safe food guidelines for older adults
		"Disease-causing bacteria may be present in potentially hazardous foods."
		Animated bacteria—dissolve to . . .
		MS meat section
		MS poultry section
		MS fish section
		MS egg section
		MS dairy section
		CU prepared dish
		MS fruits
		MS vegetables
		CU meat sitting on counter—time lapse as bacteria grow on the surface
2.0	Focus on goals	"The first step in preventing food-borne illness begins at the grocery store."
		WS outside grocery store
		WS woman getting cart and entering store
		Title overlay: *Purchasing*
2.0	Gain and integrate content	"When grocery shopping, always plan to pick up refrigerated and frozen foods at the end of your shopping trip, just prior to checkout."
		OTS shot of woman grouping items on her list
2.1	Gain and integrate content	Demonstrate shopping in produce section. Check for damage.
2.4	Gain and integrate content	Demonstrate purchasing of dry and canned goods. Check for damaged cans and expiration dates.
2.2, 2.5	Gain and integrate content	Demonstrate shopping for meat. Check expiration dates. Check for leaking meat.
		Place in separate part of cart.

Instructional Strategy (continued)

Outcome	Learning Event	Contained in Video
2.3	Gain and integrate content	Demonstrate shopping for refrigerated items. Check expiration dates. Check that frozen foods are solid.
2.6	Gain and integrate content	Demonstrate foods being bagged, with frozen and refrigerated foods bagged together. Place cold food in cooler for long drives. Drive home.
3.0	Focus on goals	Unloading groceries at home. Graphic overlay: *Proper food storage*
3.3, 5.0	Gain and integrate content	Demonstrate storing of foods in refrigerator and freezer. Demonstrate storage of meat. Place meat on bottom shelf. Discuss cross-contamination. State storage times. Graphic screen slides in: *Store in the freezer: if not used within: Ground meats/fish 24 hours Other meats 3 days*
3.1	Gain and integrate content	Demonstrate use of thermometer. Point out that refrigerator should be set to stay below 40 degrees and freezer below 0 degrees Fahrenheit. Reinforce with graphic.
3.2	Gain and integrate content	Demonstrate storage of dry goods. Show thermometer dry goods stored below 85 degrees Fahrenheit.
4.0	Focus on goals	Title screen: *Handling and preparing*
4.1	Gain and integrate content	Demonstrate hand washing. State need to wash for 20 seconds.
4.2	Gain and integrate content	Graphic screen: *Listing of the ingredients for meatloaf* Demonstrate woman taking beef out of the fridge. Transition to woman taking beef out of freezer. Demonstrate ways to thaw meat: in fridge, under running water, in microwave. Overlay bacteria animation over image of meat on counter—repeat the bacteria animation.
4.3	Gain and integrate content	Gather ingredients. Rinse produce under water.
4.4, 4.5	Gain and integrate content	Demonstrate mixing ingredients. State and show using clean bowls. Place mixed ground beef and ingredients in a clean pan and transfer to the oven. State and demonstrate cleaning and sanitizing all food contact surfaces, and wash hands again.
4.6, 4.5	Gain and integrate content	Show checking meat. State and demonstrate ways to determine if properly cooked: with meat thermometer (graphic overlay of 160 degrees), no pink. Demonstrate transfer to clean dishes.
4.7	Gain and integrate content	Woman places meat back in oven and adjusts the temperature control. State, if mealtime is delayed, that meatloaf may be held in the oven above 140 degrees Fahrenheit for no longer than four hours. Demonstrate and discuss dividing meatloaf into clean, sanitized shallow containers and cooling in the refrigerator. Identify Danger Zone (between 40 and 140 degrees). Use graphic to reinforce range on thermometer.
4.4	Gain and integrate content	Demonstrate washing counters and dishes with soapy water and a bleach solution containing a teaspoon of bleach per quart of water.
5.0	Focus on goals	Graphic overlay: *Long-term storage*
5.0	Gain and integrate content	Demonstrate cleaning out fridge and cabinets of old food. Graphic overlay: *Outdated food Immediately Leftovers 3 days Poultry 12 months Meat/fish 6–9 months Ground meats 4 months Outdated food Immediately Stale Immediately Show signs of spoilage Immediately*

Instructional Strategy (continued)

Outcome	Learning Event	Contained in Video
Overall	Synthesize and evaluate	Summary accompanied by quick shots from earlier portions of program.
		Narration states: "Remember, the main causes of food-borne illness are improperly cooked beef and poultry, inadequately washed fruits and vegetables, and poor food-handling practices. Most food-borne illnesses occur from foods prepared and eaten in the home. This means that we all play an important role in helping to prevent these outbreaks."
Overall	Extend and transfer	"We've given you some guidelines for purchasing, storing, preparing, and handling food, and by following these steps, you can be assured that you are serving safe food for yourself and your family."

Note: There is no chance to actively take action and monitor progress within videotaped instruction. Learners will receive a print-based self-assessment to use to "test their knowledge."

Alignment of Components

The following table illustrates the alignment of the outcomes and assessments. See the instructional strategy for the activities that correspond to each outcome.

Outcomes	Assessment
1.0 Recognize that food-borne illness is a serious problem that often occurs at home.	T/F Most food-borne illnesses occur in the home. T/F Food-borne illness is a disease that mainly causes upset stomach.
2.0 Identify safe shopping procedure.	When grocery shopping, in what order should you purchase the following items? Please number them 1–6, with 1 being what you would pick up first, and 6 being what you would pick up last. _____ canned goods _____ frozen foods _____ dairy items _____ meat and poultry _____ dry products _____ fresh produce
2.1 Select proper produce at the store (free from damage).	(Rate as always/sometimes/rarely/never)
2.2 Select proper meats at the store (check dates, damage, leaking; store separately).	When shopping, I will check items for damage before selecting them. When shopping, I will check expiration dates before placing them in my cart.
2.3 Select refrigerated items properly (check dates, damage).	
2.4 Select proper dry and canned goods (check dates, damage).	
2.5 Prevent cross-food contamination.	(Rate as always/sometimes/rarely/never) When shopping, I will keep meat separate from other items in my cart.
2.6 Get cold food home fast.	(Rate as always/sometimes/rarely/never) When my trip home will be longer than 30 minutes, I place frozen and refrigerated items in a cooler.
3.0 Store food at home to prevent food-borne illnesses.	(Assessed by items 3.1–3.4)
3.1 State proper temperatures for refrigerators and freezers.	Refrigerators should be below _____ degrees Fahrenheit. Freezers should be below _____ degrees Fahrenheit.

Alignment of Components (continued)

Outcomes	Assessment
3.2 Identify proper temperatures for storing dry goods.	Dry and canned goods should be stored below _____ degrees Fahrenheit.
3.3 Identify ways to prevent cross-food contamination at home.	(Rate as always/ sometimes/ rarely /never) At home, I will keep meat separate from other items in my refrigerator.
4.0 Demonstrate knowledge of food safety by properly preparing food products.	(Assessed by items 4.1–4.7)
4.1 Wash hands when working with raw meat and produce.	(Rate as always/sometimes/rarely/never) I will wash my hands after handling raw meat.
4.2 Recognize ways to defrost meat correctly.	Which of the following are safe methods for defrosting frozen meat? Please check all that apply. _____ in the refrigerator _____ on the counter _____ in still water _____ in the microwave _____ in the sunlight
4.3 Wash produce before eating.	(Rate as always/sometimes/rarely/never) I will wash fruits and vegetables before eating them.
4.4 Clean food surfaces.	(Rate as always /sometimes/rarely/never) I will use bleach to sanitize my food preparation area.
4.5 Use clean dishes.	(Rate as always/sometimes/rarely/never) I will never place cooked food on a dish that has been used for raw food unless I wash it first.
4.6 Recognize proper cooking temperatures.	T/F It is okay to eat ground beef rare. (Rate as always/sometimes/rarely/never) When preparing chicken, I will cook it until it is well done.
4.7 Identify the "Danger Zone" when storing foods.	To avoid the "Danger Zone" where bacteria grow rapidly, keep food below _____ degrees and above _____ degrees Fahrenheit.
5.0 Recognize correct food storage procedures.	T/F Leftovers should not be eaten if kept in the refrigerator for more than 3 days. T/F Ground meat and fish should be stored in the freezer if it will be longer than 24 hours before you cook it. How long can leftovers be stored in the refrigerator? _____ 1 day _____ 3 days _____ 5 days _____ 10 days Match the foods with the maximum times that they should be stored in the freezer: Ground meat 12 months Poultry 9 months Whole cuts of meat and fish 4 months

| DESIGN AID |

Aligning the Components Worksheet

Outcome and Type of Learning	Assessment	Activity

| DESIGN AID |

Instructional Strategy Worksheet

Outcomes addressed: _____

Describe how you will address the following learning events:

Set goals.	
Connect to prior knowledge.	
Present and organize content information.	
Take action and monitor progress.	
Synthesize and evaluate.	
Extend and transfer.	

Chapter 5

Activities: Delivery Systems

Learning Outcomes

- Describe the learning environment and delivery context for instructional activities.

- Select a delivery mode.

- Outline the contents of each component in an instructional package.

- Select media assets for each learning event.

- Describe basic principles of computer screen design and usability.

Chapter Overview

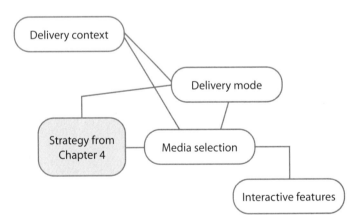

Orientation within the Design Process

Recall that there are five phases in the instructional design process and that in each phase we visit each of the essential elements of instructional design, adding details and performing tasks as required by the deliverables of each phase. In this chapter, we continue to examine the element of Activities (see Figure 5.1). In the previous chapter, we considered the instructional strategy. In this chapter, we look at techniques to deliver the instructional strategy to learners. (See Table 4.1 for a summary of the tasks at each phase related to activities.)

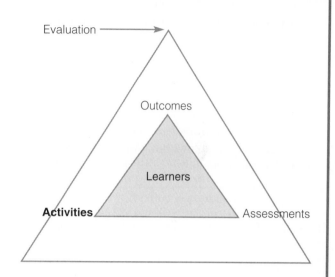

Figure 5.1 *Elements considered.* In this chapter, we continue to examine activities.

Delivering Instructional Activities

In the previous chapter, you learned to classify the learning outcomes by learning domain, to chunk and sequence content, and to develop learning events for each chunk of content. In developing instructional activities for each chunk, you also need to take into account the conditions under which the instruction will be delivered. Although this information is presented after the chapter on instructional strategies, the arrangement of the chapters is not meant to imply that these events occur after those discussed in the previous chapter. Instead, the material presented in both chapters must be considered simultaneously in order to plan for and develop instructional activities. In this chapter, we consider the learning and delivery contexts, delivery mode, and media assets. These factors, in turn, influence the instructional strategy.

Defining the Delivery Context

The delivery mode and media assets are influenced by the context in which learners will receive the instruction and the context in which the client will deliver the content. In classroom instruction, these contexts are one and the same. However, in other situations, there may be conflicts between the desires of the client and the reality of the environment in which the learners will receive the instruction. As you learned in Chapter 2, the instructional designer

needs to serve as an advocate for learners and ensure that the client understands their needs and characteristics.

You should gather information about the delivery and learning contexts from your client and learners in the early stages of defining the project. However, as you begin to develop the material, you may need to seek additional information. Before you can plan the instructional activities, you need answers to questions such as the following: Where will the instruction take place? What training and background will the instructors have? What equipment will be available in the instructional setting? Will instruction occur during the workday or after hours? Should the instruction be designed according to a particular philosophy? Will it fit within an existing curriculum? As you plan activities, consider aspects of the instructional setting such as the following:

Technical skills of the users

Availability of technical support

Group size

Curriculum into which the instruction may need to fit

Formality of the instructional setting

Equipment available in the instructional setting

Software available on the server that will deliver the instruction

Time available for instruction

Location of instruction

Required delivery media

Example 5.1 Scenario Describing Delivery Context

Turkey farms are managed by a central corporation, and representatives from the corporation visit each farm monthly. The corporation wants to certify that each farm manager has basic knowledge of salmonella prevention. Company representatives can deliver instructional materials to the farm managers during their monthly visits. The farm managers can learn the content through self-study after regular work hours. The farm managers probably speak English, but many of their workers will not. They may not be very computer literate and may have older computers. Company reps can administer certification tests on their follow-up visit to the farm.

The answers to these questions will influence the delivery mode, the media used to convey the information, the size of instructional chunks, and instructional strategy variables such as the role of peers in instruction, response mode required, and amount of practice and feedback.

For example, if you're preparing instruction to minimize salmonella contamination at a turkey processing plant, you need to learn about the context in which the instruction will be provided. During the Define or Design phase, you should seek answers to questions such as these: Will the instruction take place in a classroom setting? Does it need to be sent to individual farms for self-study by turkey farm managers? What technical skills do the intended users have? Do they have computers? VCRs? Internet access? Will instruction occur during the workday or after hours? One useful way of summarizing this information is to develop a scenario describing how learners will gain the necessary instruction (see Example 5.1). Scenarios such as these can serve as a constant reminder to the instructional design and development team of the restrictions on and opportunities available to learners within the context in which they will receive the instruction. The influence of the learning and delivery contexts on the design of instructional activities cannot be overstated.

Delivery Options

Instructional delivery modes include the classroom, print, video, computer-based, online, and blended combinations thereof. The timing and delivery of instructional episodes can be **synchronous**, with learners working through the materials in concert, or **asynchronous**, with learners working independently. Learning can occur at a distance or face-to-face. The settings can range from the formal and structured, such as a university course, to the informal and casual, such as activities for pre-K children on a zoo's Web site. When people think of instruction, they usually envision an instructor and a classroom full of students. This traditional model describes what most K-12 and higher education looks like, as well as training and adult education. But there are many other instructional delivery modes, and as an instructional designer, you'll probably be designing for these classroom alternatives. Each mode has unique benefits and challenges for the instructional designer.

Synchronous versus Asynchronous Learning As you know from your classroom experiences, not all learners in a given class master the material at the same pace. Teachers try to address this by creating activities that keep students who finish quickly from getting bored and keep those who work more slowly from falling behind. Classroom learning is widely understood in most cultures. Classrooms are available, instructors and learners understand how the system works, and decision makers are familiar with ways to evaluate the outcomes. Contrast this to an online training course used for self-study. In this asynchronous distance learning environment, each learner proceeds through the material at his or her own pace. If the program is well designed, it will provide each learner with an opportunity to master the material without feeling bored or overwhelmed. The drawback for this type of asynchronous learning is that it can be more expensive to develop and deliver than classroom learning. Additionally, both learners and decision makers may be unfamiliar with this type of instruction.

Learners must be self-directed to successfully complete asynchronous learning activities on their own. To encourage learners to be self-directed, you should emphasize their personal responsibility for learning. Include activities and support materials that help them learn how to learn. Support them in identifying ways in which learning the content will help them meet their long-term goals. Encourage them to set short-term learning goals, and monitor their progress toward achieving those goals. For example, you may want to include a feature in an online program that allows students to enter study activities and deadlines and that sends them e-mail reminders on a certain date and time. You may want to provide access to resources on effective study strategies and time management techniques.

Distance versus Face-to-Face Learning In addition, instruction increasingly is delivered to learners at a distance. Distance learning can be synchronous, as

Voice of Experience

On Context[1]

As they worked on a project to deliver existing instructional materials to a developing African country through distance learning, a design team realized firsthand the importance of considering the delivery environment and other related cultural issues.

They began the analysis of the delivery environment by considering the existing materials' delivery mode and comparing that mode with the options available in the target country. The materials were originally delivered electronically via the Web. However, in the target country, few, if any, of the learners—public school teachers—had computers—even telephones and television were not accessible to many of the learners.

Although the team was not able to visit the targeted delivery environment, they did have several citizens of that country on the design team. With their assistance, the team was able to identify many characteristics of the target delivery environment. They discussed questions such as these: Would the learners be interacting with one another? How would learners communicate with the instructor(s)? How timely would

feedback from instructors be? What media would all learners be able to receive? Would textbooks be available? How would learners submit their assignments?

The team decided that the materials would be delivered via the country's postal system and that most, if not all, of the coursework would be done in the learners' homes. The skills, knowledge, or attitudes obtained from the materials, however, would be applied in the learners' workplaces. At this point, the team had to consider the application environment: What resources would the learners have in their classrooms? Would photocopying be possible? Would students of the target learners be expected to do all of their work at school, or would homework be assigned? Would textbooks be available? Answering these questions helped team members understand how important context is to the design process. They learned that it's crucial to look at the delivery and application environments in detail, visiting the environments or talking with representatives from the environment early in a design project. After all, they wanted to create good instruction, and good instruction is that which can be practically delivered (Tessmer, 1990).

when learners participate in a teleconference, or asynchronous, as when learners participate in a self-instructional course online. There are additional considerations in designing courses in which learners participate at a distance.

To reduce the sense of isolation that many distance learners feel, it's important to provide opportunities for them to communicate with the instructor and with each other. Some instructors like to get to know the students in a distance learning class and provide opportunities for learners to learn more about each other. They may gather information from students about their goals, expectations for the course, and previous experiences so that they can make the instruction more personally relevant to the students. They may establish small collaborative groups responsible for specific activities. They may share class lists and distribute contact information among students to encourage the formation of study groups. They may ask students to post photos of themselves and personal profiles in a section of the course site that is accessible only to those who are enrolled. Some instructors like to have at least one face-to-face meeting during the course so that participants can get to know each other.

As in any course, students should be provided with opportunities to ask questions of the instructor and of each other. At a minimum, distance learning instructors should make it easy for students to contact them outside of class time—through e-mail or during online office hours. As is true in any instructional situation, teachers should answer questions and provide students with feedback in a timely manner.

To engage students, incorporate active learning techniques such as role plays, discussions, and case study analyses. Make sure that each of the activities is linked to one of the learning outcomes, and is not included simply because it seems like a good idea. For example, if you include group discussions, make sure the discussions are related to the desired outcomes of the instruction. Suppose the goal of the instruction is for trainers to learn to incorporate icebreaker activities into their courses. You may have them read articles on icebreaker strategies, then participate in a group discussion. Instead of simply asking them to discuss the articles in an online forum, have them share ways that they could use the strategies described in the articles in their own training course. The learners' understanding of the techniques presented in the lesson will be enhanced by the ideas of others in a way that is directly related to the goals of instruction. Focus group discussions so that the learners can see the benefits to participating.

Although designing distance learning courses requires creativity, most techniques used in the classroom can be adapted for distance learning. In fact, distance learning may open up some opportunities that are not available in classroom-based instruction. For example, students may be less aware of differences in social position or status when they are physically removed from their peers. Students who are typically reluctant to speak up in face-to-face meetings may be more willing to share their ideas online. Students who have difficulty speaking the language have unlimited time to compose their responses within an online discussion forum, unlike in often rapid-paced classroom discussions.

Formal versus Informal Instruction

In some settings, instruction is overt and purposeful, such as in schools and in training programs in which the purpose is for learners to acquire new knowledge and skills. These are the formal settings that we usually think of when we think about instruction. In other settings, instruction is subtle and perhaps even disguised. For example, museums may downplay their educational aims while promoting their efforts to entertain and inspire visitors. Some corporations provide their employees with online resources that give "just-in-time" information instead of formal instruction. These are examples of informal instruction. Throughout this book, we focus primarily on formal instruction, but instructional designers have many opportunities to develop materials for informal settings as well.

There's no clear set of rules that instructional designers can apply to determine when a formal training program is necessary and when other strategies are sufficient. Learners who are encountering new content areas, who aren't particularly motivated to learn, or who lack well-developed learning strategies are most likely to benefit from a formally designed instructional experience. Sometimes, instead of or in addition to instruction, employees and learners benefit from job aids or an electronic performance support system (EPSS). The purpose of job aids, EPSSs, and similar support tools is to provide learners with references they can check when they need the information. By storing information that is not used frequently in an assessable form, these tools decrease demands on users' working memory and support users during the process of learning complex procedures to the extent that they can be performed automatically (Gagné, Yekovich, & Yekovich, 1993). The decision whether to develop formal or informal instruction will depend on the client, learners, content, schedule, costs, and other factors.

The development of EPSSs and other informal learning systems such as knowledge management systems have expanded instruction beyond the classroom walls, literally and figuratively. Even with these shifts beyond direct instruction, instructional design methods and procedures are as applicable as ever. When designing instruction for informal settings, you still need to address the five essential elements and work through the five phases of design. You also need to collaborate and communicate with team members and SMEs. Classroom instruction, Web-based courses, and textbooks all support learning, but so do a variety of other learning materials. Today, instructional designers are in demand to design and develop knowledge management systems, EPSSs, and resource-based learning environments in addition to formal instructional materials.

Delivery Modes

The Classroom

In spite of all the new technologies available for delivering training, classroom instruction remains popular. It is usually the best option for presenting basic skills, orienting learners to new content or a new company, building a team, and teaching communication and social skills. A class is easier to design than other methods and can be delivered more quickly. If a new policy needs to be implemented quickly, and 20 or 30 people need the new policy training, a class will probably be the most time- and cost-effective option.

Most commonly, the classroom instructor delivers a lecture from the front of the room, a model that dates from long before there were formal schools. If the lecturer is a dynamic speaker with dazzling presence, learners may be sufficiently engaged. If you are designing classroom-based courses, build in opportunities for learners to actively "check their understanding" through discussions, worksheets, quizzes, practice and feedback, group projects, and presentations. Consider ways to challenge the advanced learners while helping those who need more time and practice. Be sure to include opportunities for learner interactions in every class session.

Voice of Experience

Just-in-Time Training

A large manufacturer wanted to train its entire telephone support staff on its latest products. However, the products were upgraded frequently, so it wasn't practical to pull staff away from their jobs to provide a formal classroom training session. The solution was to develop brief online lessons on each product. Just before the product was released, the lessons were uploaded to the company's internal Web site. The phone support staff could access and complete each lesson from their workstations. They could also return to the lesson at any time if they needed to review any content. The training was available whenever learners needed it.

Telecourses and Teleconferences A video-based distance learning class, or "telecourse," features an instructor at an originating location and students at one or more remote locations. The originating location may contain students as well. Interactions take place through two-way audio and video (often via satellite) or one-way video and two-way audio (via phone lines). Telecourses work well for rural learners or those who can't attend a campus due to distance or disabilities. For example, a high school student in a small town may be able to take an advanced mathematics course that isn't offered at the local high school through a telecourse offered by a distant university. Corporate training can be provided to multiple sites simultaneously through teleconferencing. These types of distance learning courses work very much like regular classroom-based courses. If you are designing a course for this type of delivery, try to include group projects that involve students at different locations. To discourage cheating, some teachers prefer authentic assessment strategies such as portfolios and student presentations.

Live Web A synchronous technology that is popular with training managers, live Web sessions feature an instructor delivering the content using video, graphics, and audio to learners who are logged onto the course via the Web. These formats are sometimes called "Web-inars." Learners follow along by reading, watching, and listening; they can also take notes and send questions or make comments to the full group, so there is some opportunity for discussion. When you design courses for this type of delivery, provide frequent opportunities for learners to take action. These courses can be tiring for learners because they are synchronous (everyone moves at the same pace) yet lack the dynamic interactions of a live classroom. They also lack the convenience of "anytime, anywhere" learning that asynchronous Web-based delivery offers.

Print Materials A self-paced book, with exercises that learners complete throughout the course, can be used to supplement other media or by itself. This delivery mode is appropriate for material that lends itself well to a print format (see Example 5.2). Chunk the content so that

---

Example 5.2 Self-Study Materials Based on Social Constructivist Theory

The following list outlines the first few lessons from a series of self-study workbooks and accompanying videotapes intended to instruct learners in how to teach mathematics in elementary classrooms (Mathematical Association, 1991). The low-tech materials were designed to be completed by individual students working alone. The designers attempted to provide opportunities for learners to compare their answers with those of other learners, as required by social constructivist theories of learning. Notice the major learning events in the sequence of activities outlined below:

1. Students are asked to begin the self-study courses by writing their expectations for the course in their notebook.
2. This is followed by a few pages of notes about expectations from previous students.
3. The first major section introduces students to the course with an overview of the lesson.
4. Students are asked to describe their earliest memories of mathematics on the left side of their notebook page.
5. Then they read comments from other students about *their* earliest memories and record their reactions to the comments from other students in their notebooks.
6. Students are then asked to use the right side of their notebooks to describe (a) what they think learning mathematics is like, (b) what they enjoy about learning mathematics, and (c) what they dislike about the topic.
7. Then they read what others said about the assignment and react to what others have said with additional comments in their notebooks.
8. Students next read a series of articles. They are asked to make notes in their notebooks on points that seem significant, statements they find problematic or surprising, and points that are consistent with their experiences.
9. These activities are followed by opportunities to read what a few others have written about the articles and to add to their notes based on the reactions of others.

This pattern continued throughout the entire curriculum. Learners examined materials; made notes on their reactions to the readings, videotapes, or audiotapes provided in the instruction; had the opportunity to read what other learners had written in response to the assignments; and were asked to make additional comments comparing their perceptions with those of others.

Which learning events were included? Which events are missing from this incomplete description? What sort of activities could be included to address the missing events?

learners can concentrate on one digestible block at a time, and provide opportunities for practice during or at the end of each chunk. A strategy that often works well is to provide learners with a workbook that they fill in as they move through the material. If possible, design the layout so that learners check their answers by turning the page. If no instructor is right there to answer questions, try to provide the full explanation of each answer.

Other courses feature a set of individual activity sheets that the instructor can distribute at the appropriate times. The benefit of intact books is that the material is produced and distributed at one time, and learners can begin building their understanding of the entire course by previewing upcoming material. Individual activity sheets may work better for younger learners, in peer review activities, and in situations in which learners give completed worksheets to the instructor for grading. A logistical advantage of individual activity sheets is that, if authorized, instructors can make copies and distribute them as needed. A disadvantage of separate sheets is that they aren't physically collected in one place, making it easier for learners to lose track of them.

Videos Video programs are effective in demonstrating procedures, showing rare or hazardous situations, telling stories, presenting cases for analysis, creating an emotional response, and influencing attitude formation through modeling. Video can be delivered on tape or DVD as a self-paced program, often with a workbook. It also can be delivered online in one of several downloadable or streaming video file formats. Thousands of people have taken defensive driving courses that are widely available at video rental stores—an example of a self-paced instructional video program. Of course, video also can be delivered synchronously as a television broadcast or viewed in a classroom setting. Within an instructional setting, video is often most effective when short segments of content are interspersed with opportunities to act on the content by responding to a discussion question, taking notes, or completing a worksheet. Depending on the complexity of the program, video production often requires the services of a team of experts and can be expensive.

Online Delivery Like other self-directed learning options, online learning isn't restricted to a specific time and location. Learners can work on the material anytime and anywhere they have an Internet connection. Web sites can deliver the primary instructional content or extend and enhance other forms of instruction by providing simulations, media databases, exercises, and production tools. An advantage of Web programs is that the material can be updated readily. Web-based courses also provide opportunities for discussions, group work, and other activities that involve interactions among participants.

Most online programs require registration and track learner performance. For example, a learner could complete two of seven modules in one session and return later to complete the others. An advantage of online delivery is that learners, especially trainees in a corporate setting, can access the material when they need it, instead of having to attend a class months before a new product is ready or months after it has come out.

Many companies have invested in complex systems to support online course delivery to their employees and customers. These **learning management systems** (LMSs) and **learning content management systems** (LCMSs) provide unique benefits—and constraints—for the instruction delivered. An LMS might bundle all of the functions of managing students in one software package, tracking information such as course catalogs, learner records, and aggregate data. Or a corporate LMS might include information on the courses required to ascend a career ladder or to qualify for certain positions or pay. Another level of tracking and management is for organizations that sell courses, or any educational product or service, online. In this situation, an LMS needs to have functionality that allows learners to register and pay for the course. Where an LMS handles the infrastructure that makes it possible to present courses online, an LCMS provides the tools to develop the actual course content. To complicate things, some LMS products also include components to develop and deliver courses, and some LCMS products handle management tasks. Some companies purchase both products and integrate them. The most important thing for you to remember about LMSs and LCMSs is that these systems are designed to make it easier to manage course delivery, not to facilitate effective instruction. As is true of other media, some instructional strategies are easier to implement in some systems than in others.

CD-ROMs CD-ROMs can hold a great deal of media-rich content and are a relatively reliable technology compared with the Web. This makes them a popular choice for multimedia projects and for wide distribution to schools and consumers. Many textbooks are bundled with CD-ROMs that provide supplemental content. Other times, CD-ROMs deliver text components, allowing publishers to save on printing and distribution costs. In addition to providing significant cost savings, it's faster and easier to update electronic materials. Some publishers prefer to distribute Web-based programs on CD-ROM (a Web site on a CD-ROM) in order to control access, minimize download time, and overcome Internet accessibility issues. These CD-ROM-based courses can include a server-based database that tracks learner performance. For content such as history, CD-ROMs offer images, video clips, and interactive components like maps (see Figure 5.2) to extend and enhance the learning experience. For foreign languages, CD-ROMs provide extensive audio and video sequences to provide practice in comprehending the spoken language. For science content, a CD-ROM's capacity allows for practice and feedback, labs, and simulations.

If you design a CD-ROM course, you probably will work with a full production team. Typically, costs for

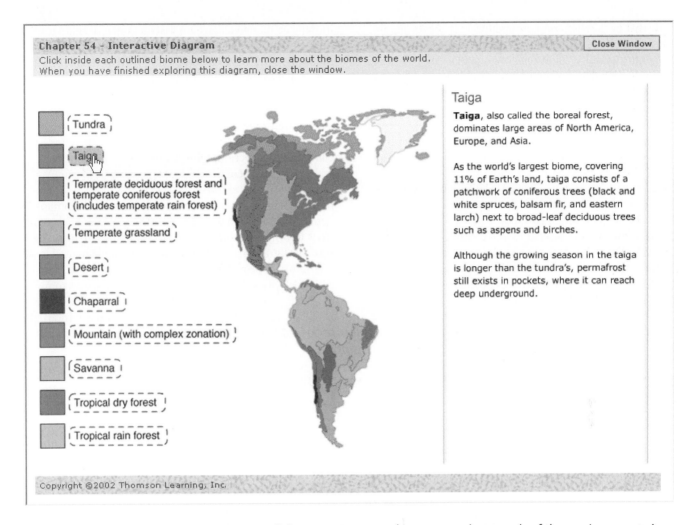

Figure 5.2 *Interactive map.* Learners can click on a category to learn more about each of the environments in the Americas. The text appears in the right-hand column.

SOURCE: From *Biology* CD-ROM, 6th ed., by Solomon. © 2002 by Brooks/Cole. Reprinted with permission of Brooks/Cole, a division of Thomson Learning.

producing a CD-ROM are higher than for other delivery formats, and production schedules are longer. There is more technical and production complexity involved in producing a CD-ROM, but the result can be a highly engaging, content-rich, and instructionally effective product.

Performance Support Systems

Sometimes, the solution to a performance problem isn't an instructional product but a support tool that guides users in performing a task. Well-designed job aids can reduce training time and costs. They are easy to update and revise, and are especially appropriate for tasks in which the methods of performance change quickly, are too complex to remember easily, or are not performed frequently enough to be committed to memory. Job aids are especially useful in easing the transition from training settings to the workplace.

An electronic performance support system (Gustafson, 2000), or EPSS, integrates features of job aids, tutorials, and resource databases into one system so that employees can get training support when they need it. EPSS features include online help, wizards that assist in task performance, templates, and tutorials. Your word processing software probably incorporates many of these features, thus providing a basic form of an EPSS. The purpose of EPSSs and similar support tools is to provide learners with instruction and performance support at the moment they need the information. For example, an insurance company may make policy and procedure updates available through an EPSS, instead of sending employees to a class. The system may include a searchable online manual, tutorials on how to implement the policy and procedures, online forms for common tasks, and printable job aids. An employee could check the online system to quickly learn a procedure right before she needs to perform a task using that procedure.

Several decades ago, when computers first began to appear on desktops in offices, visionary trainers imagined systems such as these that would train, guide, coach, and answer questions as needed. Early EPSS programs were complex to design and implement, and very expensive.

Now that personal computers and Internet access are almost ubiquitous in the workplace, the promise of EPSS is becoming a reality. Additionally, companies are beginning to use hand-held devices including personal digital assistants (PDAs) and mobile phones that support text messaging to deliver EPSS support to the field.

Blended Learning and Other Combinations

Most courses include two or more delivery modes. A classroom-based course may include a self-directed workbook, video, or online component. A Web-based course may include a workbook or a separate video either on tape or DVD. A CD-ROM course may have paper-based study guides or assessment components. Many textbooks and print-based instructional materials include companion Web sites or CD-ROMs.

The use of multiple delivery modes within e-learning is known as **blended learning**. Blended learning programs initially combined classroom instruction with self-paced online materials, but the term has come to mean much more. Blended learning combinations may include real-time collaborative interactions, either online or face-to-face, and self-paced materials. They may combine EPSSs with Web-based courses, face-to-face instruction, and on-the-job training (Singh, 2003). For example, learners may review readings on their own and then participate in classroom instruction, followed by on-the-job practice and an online discussion.

When planning learning experiences that use a combination of delivery modes, you should use each component in an optimum way. For example, this textbook provides information that is stable in printed form; it can be read almost anywhere. The textbook is supplemented by a Web site that provides up-to-date information and interactive activities and forms that allow you to easily compose assignments and submit them to your instructor. However, you need access to a computer and the Internet to take advantage of these resources. As with all effective

Table 5.1 Learning events for combined delivery environments

The following table outlines a training course that uses several types of delivery

Focus on goals.	*Online introduction* • Begin with online "teaser" that serves to motivate. • Follow with series of online questions designed to get learners to set goals. *Classroom* • Ask learners about goals they have for course.
Link to prior knowledge.	*Online* • Give quick quiz of prerequisite content to determine learners' readiness. *Classroom* • Review how new material ties in with previous material.
Gain and organize content knowledge.	*Classroom* • Present primary content. • Tie chunks of learning together with a framework—the big picture. • Demonstrate and review each step.
Take action and monitor progress.	*Classroom* • Provide opportunities for taking action and getting feedback. *Workbook* • Include exercises featuring several different forms of active processing (verbal, visual). *Classroom* • Lead class and peer review of workbook exercises. • Provide feedback on performance to correct errors quickly before they "set in."
Synthesize and evaluate.	*Online* • Review and discuss. *Classroom* • Give final assessment.
Extend and transfer.	*Classroom* • Discuss opportunities to apply new learning. *Online* • Preview next chunk (to extend learning).

combinations of delivery modes, the individual components of the instructional package are designed to complement each other to provide a comprehensive and meaningful learning experience.

If you are designing a course with multiple components, you need to keep track of how the learning events and the content sequence will function seamlessly for learners. In the previous chapter, you learned that effective learning experiences should provide opportunities for learners to focus on goals, link new knowledge to prior knowledge, gain new content and integrate it within their existing knowledge base, take action and monitor their learning progress, synthesize and evaluate their learning, and extend and transfer their new knowledge to the application environment. Table 5.1 outlines the instructional events included in a training course that uses several types of delivery.

Components of an Instructional Package

One of the reasons clients seek an instructional designer is that they require learning materials that will deliver consistent results. They want a workbook that always provides practice opportunities for the target learners, or a video program that always tells the story effectively, or an online program that always delivers the content fully and clearly. For example, the American Red Cross offers a first aid course to the public. Many individuals become certified to teach these courses, but they come from varied backgrounds. Some are health care professionals, scout leaders, parents, caregivers, or simply civic-minded citizens; few

are public health educators. The Red Cross needed to develop a curriculum ensuring that all learners from all backgrounds would have an equal opportunity to master the life-saving skills in the course, regardless of the skills and knowledge of the instructor. The program they developed includes lectures and demonstrations by the instructor, a textbook, workbook assignments, video programs, hands-on exercises with lifelike models, and assessments. Learners who successfully complete the hands-on portion and the assessments receive certification in first aid because Red Cross is confident that the curriculum works.

As in the Red Cross example, many instructional products have more than one primary component to provide support for instructors as well as students. Textbooks frequently are accompanied by an instructor's guide and companion CD-ROMs or Web sites for students. Training courses that will be delivered in a classroom may include the student manual, an instructor's manual, a test bank, and a set of PowerPoint programs for each session. Online and self-directed curriculum products often include additional components too. A CD-ROM product may require an instructor's guide, a Web-based product might include a test bank, and self-paced print materials might be supported by an online discussion forum. All of these components require the instructional designer's attention.

Learners' Materials

Materials for learners serve several purposes. They might provide a format for content delivery, such as a textbook or Web site, or they might supplement a classroom presentation, such as a workbook containing opportunities for practice and feedback. Learners' materials also can be packaged in a variety of ways—for example, as a Web site, CD-ROM, video program, or series of print materials. When developing materials for learners, you may want to include many of the following components:

Table of contents
Schedule
Grading policies
Course contact information
Installation procedures for computer materials
URL for associated Web site
Glossary
Pretest and posttest
Objectives
Overview
Motivational material
Directions on how to use materials
Content presentation

Examples

Performance activities and practice exercises

Feedback

References for remediation and enrichment

Extension and transfer activities

A job aid (also called a cheat sheet) with quick prompts for performing the skill

Instructor's Guides

An instructor's guide usually reflects the complete instructional design for a course. It incorporates the content, learning strategies, instructional events, exercises, feedback, assessment, and resources. It usually includes the entire student guide along with information specifically for instructors. For example, in a teacher's edition of a textbook, the instructor's information often is printed in wide margins, "wrapping around" the student material. The instructor's "wrap" typically includes tips on presenting the content, correct answers for exercises, and other strategies for presentation and feedback. Some companies that deliver training by instructors may require that the instructor's guide include a script that leads the instructor through the

entire course; other companies are comfortable with bullets or an outline for each chunk of material.

Many curriculum products feature presentation materials for instructors to use in their class. These include overhead projector slides, posters, and, increasingly, PowerPoint programs that feature series of bulleted lists and graphics that support the instruction. PowerPoint programs also can be delivered online as part of asynchronous lessons or in blended systems that deliver "live" or synchronous instruction consisting of video, audio, and graphic presentations. Some products provide a database of visual materials relevant to the content so that instructors can build customized presentations. For example, an environmental science program might include an image bank of photographs illustrating rain forests, oceans, estuaries, wetlands, and other regions. An instructor could choose images from any of these areas to punctuate a lecture on urbanization or industrialization or any other topic.

Whether the instruction will be presented in a classroom, online, through video conferencing, or with a blended approach, a good instructor's guide provides the capable instructor with everything he or she needs to conduct a successful class, including how to prepare for the class and how to follow up after the class. For computer-based programs, the instructor's materials can be accessed

---

DESIGNER'S TOOLKIT

Classroom Tips

In all delivery environments, it's important for learners to take breaks. Learning can be exhausting. Whether they find a session exhilarating, stressful, or boring, by the end of the session, learners will be tired. If you are developing materials for a classroom training environment, keep these considerations in mind:

- People can attend to classroom material for only a certain time before their attention begins to wane. Attention spans are limited by the age of the learners, the complexity of the material, the time of day, and many other factors. As a rule, adults should be allowed to take a break after about two hours. In most settings, a 10- to 15-minute break is sufficient.

- A strategy that some training facilities find effective is to schedule a six-hour class with two 20-minute breaks. The three blocks of time can be used, respectively, to present the content, take action and provide feedback, and give assessment and remediation.

- The session immediately after the lunch break may be difficult because people can get sleepy after eating. Try

to plan activities that require physical movement using the large muscle groups—for example, doing role plays, posting materials on the board, writing on flip charts, meeting with classmates, making reports, doing group projects, touring a facility, or practicing a motor task.

- Try to avoid scheduling class sessions that begin on Monday mornings. It is a busy time for most professionals, and they are likely to be distracted by pressing issues back at the office.

- Another difficult time to conduct a class is on Friday afternoons or just before holidays. People are tired and eager to conclude the work week. The level of absenteeism is likely to be high even in professional settings.

- Evening classes usually work well even for trainees who have worked a full day before class. Try to start after the dinner hour and limit the session to two hours. If it will run longer than two hours, you need to schedule a break, and attention is likely to sag in the second half.

Example 5.3 Components of Instructional Package

The following table lists the components of a 15-week university course delivered over the Web. The course materials also include a textbook.

Component	Contents
Learners' materials	Contained on Web site. Includes: • Information on how to use these materials • Syllabus • Schedule • Technical requirements • Links to technical help sites • Course news • Reading assignments • Each of 12 topics presented using PowerPoint accompanied by audio lecture • Study guides for each quiz—students encouraged to print guides and complete them as they examine Web site materials and read text chapters • Database of approximately 100 test items for each of 12 topics—quiz program that randomly generates 10-item practice quizzes on each topic, gives feedback; test program that randomly generates 10-item tests for grading, gives no feedback
Instructor's guide	Provided as password-protected administrative site. Instructors able to: • Modify schedule and syllabus • Add and delete test items • Download student grades into gradebook program • Post course news Easy for novices to use—through use of forms. Instructors supported in using administrative site with downloadable step-by-step handouts.

---

through a password or other security device. Even when instructor's guides are accessible electronically, many instructors prefer to work from a printed guide, so "printer friendly" files will be appreciated.

When you prepare instructor's guides, you want to write for the novice instructor but make it easy for the expert to find the key directions and information. You may want to include the following components:

Overview of the course

Intended outcomes for the instruction

Information about the target population

Suggestions on how to adapt the class in different settings, such as a large class or a very small class

A list of everything the instructor needs for each class session including materials and equipment

A list of learner materials required for each class and exercise

A schedule for each section of the class including time estimates for each lesson or chunk

Suggestions for using the materials

Suggestions for materials management

A test item bank (can include alternative tests)

Test answer keys

Enrichment and remediation activities

Example 5.3 illustrates how each of these components can work together in an instructional package.

Selecting Media Assets

Compared with the days when instructional support consisted of a slate board and a stub of chalk, the range of media available today is breathtaking, even for those who have grown up taking them for granted. Media assets allow you, as a designer, to reach learners more effectively. You can show photographs of the surface of Mars, hear Mark Twain's voice from an early Edison recording, play animation showing DNA replication, build a graph of composite interest, or create a simulation using videos portraying customer support vignettes. Although you may work with production specialists to develop the actual media assets, you may be on your own in coming up with ideas. Often, the instructional designer identifies the media assets needed within the instruction (see Example 5.4).

Example 5.4 Assigning Media Assets

The following table of learning events, activities, and media assets is a small section of a table developed for a Web site designed to teach teachers how to conduct scientific inquiry using objects found in the schoolyard. This table addresses the chunk of content on "planning a lesson."

Event	Instructional Activities	Media Assets
Focus on goals.	Title screen. Welcome message. Outline menu choices and subtopics to preview topics of site.	Need attractive and colorful graphic to capture attention. Include pictures of people to create approachable image. Also include background images of objects and people exploring to attract attention. Try to create feeling that science is for everyone.
Remind of prior knowledge.	Title of section "planning a lesson" should be sufficient prompt because so familiar to teachers.	Menu button. Also explain subtopics in text.
Present and organize content.	Text explanation of steps in object-based inquiry. Demonstrate how others have done it.	Text on Web pages explains steps in object-based inquiry. Video cases demonstrate lessons. Lesson plans used in video lessons should be available to download and to view on the screen. Web page window should have sections for steps in process, lesson plan, and video case so teachers can view each—steps, plan, and demonstration—in close proximity to each other.
Take action and monitor progress.	Provide lesson plans. Encourage teachers to try them and discuss results on discussion forum. Teachers gain feedback on success of lesson through reflecting on the results and comparing their results with others.	Database of lesson plans with option to search based on state standards of learning and by season. Discussion forum for teachers to discuss results of lessons with threads based on lesson plans.
Synthesize and evaluate.	During formative evaluation, teachers will be given paper-based test of cued recall (short-answer and essay). After pilot testing, ongoing synthesis and evaluation will occur informally. Teachers encouraged to post reflections on their ability to plan object-based lessons on discussion board.	Paper-based test for formative evaluation. Threaded discussion board on general topic of planning object-based inquiry.
Extend and transfer.	Database of lesson plans submitted by teachers. Teachers encouraged to try some of these or to develop their own and post to site.	Database of teacher-submitted lesson plans. Forms so teachers can submit own plans.

For example, when designing computer-based products, instructional designers create storyboards that include a description or diagram of each of the media assets required for the program. (For more information on identifying media assets, see Chapter 10.)

To choose the best medium for each chunk of content, think through what the asset needs to accomplish. For example, images can enhance the appeal of the instruction, illustrate steps in a process, detail parts, or provide examples of textual information. Visuals can perform an organizational function by simplifying complex information, as when a map shows the path to some location. They can provide a concrete reference for verbal information or provide visual analogies or mnemonics to help learners recall abstract information. Text and narra-

tion offer clarity, factual information, and explanations. Music and sound effects can add emphasis and emotion. Video can also create emotion, develop characters, show historical perspectives, and create realism. Animation effectively illustrates events that unfold over time and views that aren't feasible in reality, as well as provides many of the advantages of video (see Figure 5.3). In general, the most expensive options are video production and 3-D animation. Table 5.2 outlines guidelines for selecting media assets.

The specific media available for a given project depends on the schedule, budget, and delivery environment. Sometimes, you can license the exact photo you want—for example, Albert Einstein at a blackboard. Other times, you can't afford to create the 3-D animation you want that

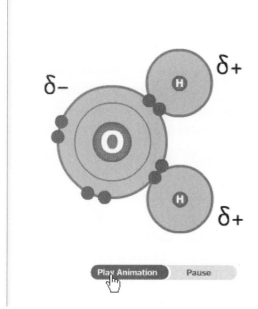

Biology *Sixth Edition*
Active Learner

Part 1 | Chapter 2 Tutorial Home

Screen 3 of 6

How do atoms and molecules interact?

δ−   δ+
H
O
H
δ+

Play Animation   Pause

POLAR COVALENT BONDING
All nuclei of a given type of atom (e.g., all carbon atoms) have equal affinity for electrons. But the nuclei of different types of atoms (e.g., oxygen and hydrogen) have very different affinities for electrons.

The nucleus of oxygen has a much stronger affinity for electrons than does the nucleus of hydrogen. This differential affinity for electrons is demonstrated when a covalent bond forms between an oxygen and a hydrogen atom. Since the oxygen has a higher affinity for electrons than does the hydrogen, the electrons in the covalent bond between the two atoms spend a greater fraction of their time close to the oxygen atom.

This results in diminished density of the electron cloud surrounding the nucleus of the hydrogen atom. The diminished density of the electron cloud lets the positive charge of the hydrogen nucleus "show through" the electron cloud, resulting in a partial positive charge ($\delta+$). Since the elctron spends a greater fraction of time associated with the oxygen atom, there is a partial negative charge ($\delta-$) associated with the oxygen atom.

The partial positive and partial negative charges of polar covalent bonds interact with other partial positive and partial negative charges associated with other molecules that have polar covalent bonds.

Figure 5.3 *Animation.* A simple animation demonstrates a biological process. The learner can pause or replay the animation. Later in the program, learners are quizzed on their understanding using the same animation.

SOURCE: From *Biology* CD-ROM, 6th ed., by Solomon. © 2002 by Brooks/Cole. Reprinted with permission of Brooks/Cole, a division of Thomson Learning.

Table 5.2 Guidelines for choosing media assets

Choose this	To show or do this
Two-dimensional images (2-D)	What something looks like
Photograph	Examples, details, comparisons; historical source material
Illustration	Show object clearly, create characters
Diagram	Process, relationships, sequences, categories
Moving images	Sequence in time, multiple angles
Video	Real situations, sequence in time, historical events
Animation	Sequence of events or actions
3-D animation	Inner workings, views not feasible in real life, cutaways; create characters
Narration	Explain, guide
Sound effects	Highlight, punctuate, guide
Other sounds	Historical source material such as FDR saying, "a day that will live in infamy," or sound of rocket blasting off
Music	Emotion, continuity

will show what vision is like before and after cornea surgery. In the cornea example, you have to find affordable alternatives, such as a series of still images that convey the same information. Because media acquisition can be the most expensive budget item in a multimedia product, work with the specialists on your production team to find cost-effective alternatives. Put your resources where your learners will get the most benefit. One place to concentrate resources is on the content that gives learners the most difficulty. Ask your client, "Where do learners get confused or make the most mistakes?" Also ask how trainers or instructors help learners comprehend the confusing content. Do learners need interactive practice to achieve high levels of performance? Do learners require additional examples or media assets such as a video program? Be prepared to accept changes and find new solutions if there are time or budget constraints.

Media Assets and Licensing

Not all media assets need to be produced from scratch. Many of the materials may already exist and be available through licensing. You may work with a producer who is responsible for acquiring media assets—or the job may fall to you. If your design specifies a particular asset, you should determine whether it's available and if so, whether your project's budget can afford it. For example, if you are designing a program on the U.S. Constitution for middle school students, you can download the text and an image of the actual Constitution at no cost from the Library of Congress. For another American history class, you might want to use a video clip of Martin Luther King, Jr., delivering his "I Have a Dream" speech from the steps of the Lincoln Memorial. For this clip, you will need to get permission from the King family's foundation, which controls these assets.

Be careful not to use any copyrighted material in your work without authorization. You can cite the work of others, even using short quotes if full credit is included. If you want to use longer quotes, graphics, or other media, write to the publisher or copyright holder and request

permission to do so. Consult with a lawyer who has expertise in this area before using any copyrighted materials in a product that will be replicated and sold. You want to make sure that the person or entity that grants you permission is, in fact, authorized to do to. You need to ensure that the release or authorization you receive is a legally valid document. If you do receive permission to use copyrighted work, be sure that the quote is accurate and that your citations are correct and easily located, such as in a picture credit line, a footnote, or an appendix listing all credits.

Fair Use   In the United States, there is a protection available to educators who want to make copies of copyrighted material for teaching purposes. The fair-use doctrine is not a specific law but a body of legal

Analogy

House

When building a house, you select brick, tile, flooring, paint, and all the other building materials. These decisions are influenced by the context in which the home will be situated. If your home is to be built in a historical area or subdivision, there may be stipulations on the building materials and colors that can be used for the home's exterior. In selecting interior materials, you'll consider the way you plan to use each room. The kitchen and bathrooms may need waterproof flooring and wall coverings. You may want relaxing paint colors in the bedroom. Similarly, in instructional design and development, you select media formats, assign media assets to specific activities, and begin to develop draft materials. Both for you as the designer and for your client, this is an exciting task because you start to imagine the finished product. There's still plenty of hard work ahead, but it is satisfying to begin seeing the actual product taking shape.

Voice of Experience

Accessibility

For a middle school social studies program that featured many multimedia components, the design team sought strategies to ensure that the product would be accessible to all learners, including those with sight and hearing disabilities. This is always a worthy goal, and in this case, it was also a requirement for delivery. Like many educational projects, it needed to comply with accessibility standards such as those in the federal government's Section 508 requirements.

Team members initially were concerned that development of a rich multimedia product would not be compatible with accessibility compliance. After consulting with accessibility specialists, however, they learned that they could readily design features which ensured that the product would work with common adaptive devices. These devices are installed on learners' computers and allow disabled students to use the program.

For hearing-impaired students, the team designed a closed-captioning system. The student simply selected "closed captioning" from a menu of audio options. For each audio segment, the team transcribed the narration into a text file.

When a learner used the program, the appropriate text file was displayed in an unobtrusive window at the bottom of the screen. The closed-captioning option could be toggled on or off easily so that the student could see the full screen at any time.

Sight-impaired students often use an adaptive product that reads text files out loud to them. Screen reader products like JAWS use hardware and software to adapt computer displays so that sight-impaired users can navigate and access information on the computer. For these students, the team wrote descriptions of each image in the program. In addition to illustrations and photographs, these images included graphs, diagrams, and tables. Each graphic file had an associated text description file. When a student used the program, the screen reader read the text description to the student that explained what content was presented in the visual.

The design team learned that accommodating all learners does not require any sacrifices in producing a rich, highly interactive product. The key was identifying the accessibility requirements early in the design process so that there wasn't a need to retrofit later on.

---

opinions and, as such, is subject to new interpretation with each lawsuit. Key aspects of fair use in education include the amount of material copied, how it is copied and distributed, and how making such copies deprives the copyright holder of royalties. For example, copying a few pages from a book and distributing the copies to the class may be permissible; copying the entire book, or a significant number of pages, and distributing it online, is not.

Because it is open to interpretation, the fair-use doctrine does not provide clear protection to instructional designers and development teams. Particularly for those creating multimedia or Web-based instructional materials, the legal framework is still very much a work in progress. If you are working for an academic institution, be sure to check and adhere to the school's policies before distributing any copied materials. If you are creating materials for a publisher or corporation, check to see if there are guidelines for you to follow. Your best strategy as an instructional designer is to avoid using copies of any copyright materials unless you have explicit permission from the copyright holder. When in doubt, don't use it. Don't jeopardize your career by making a costly mistake. Guidelines on fair use in educational contexts are available on the Web from the U.S. Copyright Office.

Accessibility

As an instructional designer and advocate for learners, try to make sure that your designs accommodate all learners. Learners with physical disabilities, including hearing and sight impairments, can use adaptive tools that allow them to fully use online and multimedia programs. For example, all audio elements can be transcribed and presented as text in an optional captioning system for hearing-impaired learners. Images can include a hidden tag with text describing the image, much like a caption. This tag is invisible to most learners, but specially equipped computers will "see" the text caption and read it aloud to the sight-impaired learner. However, the programs must be designed with adaptive tools in mind.

Products developed for most public and academic institutions must adhere to accessibility standards. In the United States, these standards are contained in a law referred to by its governmental name, Section 508, administered by the General Services Administration. These requirements do not prevent you from delivering rich interactive materials. However, you may find that you, and your team, need to be inventive in finding instructional solutions that work for *all* learners. Consult with an accessibility specialist to determine how to design features that ensure your products will work with common adaptive devices.

Figure 5.4 *Simple interface.*   Users have options at the global level (Credits, Glossary, Resources, Help, Log Off) and at the screen and module level (Return to Main Menu, Return to Module Menu, Go Back, Go Forward). The Back/Next options appear at the top and bottom of the frame for convenience.

SOURCE: From *Best Practices in Distance Learning: Fundamentals for Teachers,* © 2004 by The VideoCall Company. Used with permission.

Structuring Interactive Programs

When designing interactive computer-based programs, keep in mind that most learners and most programs are best served by a simple structure (see Figure 5.4). The easier it is for learners to use the program, the less they have to think about it, and the more they can attend to learning the content. As a designer, you are particularly concerned that learners don't waste their limited working memory trying to remember how to use the program, leaving little room for content acquisition. Keep interactive programs as simple as possible so that learners never become frustrated by the design.

One strategy for ensuring that learners can use an interactive program effectively is to design a "guided tour" of each of the kinds of interactions expected of them. This can be included in the "help" section so it's always available to users (see Figure 5.5). For example, if there's a "matching" exer-cise, capture the screen and provide specific instructions on how to interact with each of the steps in the exercise.

Here are some general rules for creating interactive programs:

Organization

- List sections on a main menu. List menu options in the order you think users should use them or learn them. In Western culture, we read from left to right and top to bottom. Most people will work through sections "in order."

- Try to limit the program to a maximum of 12 sections, with no more than 12 subsections each. More than that can feel overwhelming. However, if you have a good reason for having more sections or subsections, don't hesitate to break this rule.

- Try to limit the number of levels so that learners never have to delve more than three levels deep before they encounter primary content.

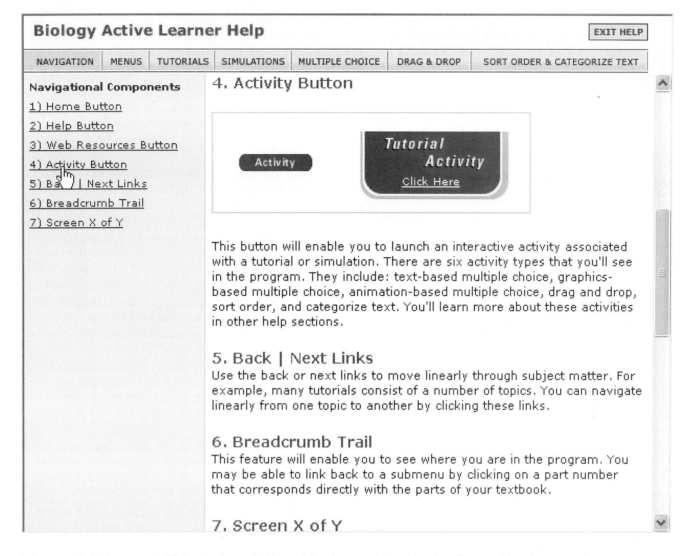

Figure 5.5 *Help screen.* This text-based aid explains how each navigation feature functions and how to use each feature. It is available from every screen in the program.

SOURCE: From *Biology* CD-ROM, 7th ed., by Solomon/Berg/Martin. © 2005. Reprinted by permission of Brooks/Cole, a division of Thomson Learning.

Moving Around

- Allow learners to explore freely. Just as some readers will thumb through this textbook, some users will want to browse or get a feel for what is in each section. Through this strategy, these learners develop a mental model of the content that helps them learn the upcoming material.

- Make sure it is easy for users to move to the next screen, return to the previous one, or return to the main menu.

- Place headings at the top of each screen to show users where they are. A header or title bar works like a street sign to help users understand their location within the program.

- In each sequence of screens, include a counter that lets users know they are on, say, screen 5 of 11.

Individual Screens

- Design screens so that they model natural eye movements, with important information beginning in the upper left corner and moving gradually to the right and down.

- Keep screens uncluttered, with one or two key points per screen.

- Place all critical information and links within the screen space that appears upon loading. You cannot be sure that users will scroll down to find additional information.

- Provide opportunities for learners to take action frequently.

- Use graphics and visuals instead of text whenever possible.

Activities Checklist, Part 2

- Describe the context of instruction.
- Determine a delivery mode.
- Outline the components needed in the instructional package.
  - Learners' materials
  - Instructor's guide
- Assign learning events to each component of the instructional package.
- Determine media assets needed for each learning event.

- Prompt users to help them understand what responses are expected.
- Provide clear directions for each action you require of users.

The task of ensuring that computer-based programs are usable often is the responsibility of usability specialists. Not all usability experts have experience working with educational or training products. For example, they may have worked only on Web sites designed for e-commerce or corporate communication applications. The needs in an instructional product are different. The most important factor on a commercial site might be speed of display and interaction, which isn't as significant in an educational program. If you work with a usability specialist, help her or him understand the educational context for the product.

The usability process involves a complex set of knowledge and skills and is beyond the scope of this book. However, if you will be working in an environment in which you are likely to conduct usability testing, your instructional design training and experience will provide you with a strong foundation for learning usability skills and knowledge.

Summary

Often, novice designers, clients, and SMEs begin designing instruction with an emphasis on the type of learning activities they want to include. The client might say, "I would like a Web site with video" or "a videotape to orient new employees" or "problem-based learning activities." People often envision instruction in these terms. But to be effective, activities should be influenced by learners' needs and characteristics, the learning and application contexts, the desired learning outcomes, and the delivery context. In this chapter, you learned about a range of options for delivering instructional activities. You learned to describe your instructional environment,

determine how you'll deliver each chunk of content, and assign media assets to learning events. You also learned about structuring interactive computer-based programs.

Activities throughout the Phases

Both Chapters 4 and 5 described the "activities" element of instructional design. In the Define phase, you begin to propose activities that should enable learners to obtain the desired goals of the instruction. You propose those activities based on your best guess of what will facilitate learning. You also begin to describe the methods and media through which you will deliver the instruction. In the project proposal, you may suggest activities to enable learners to focus on goals, relate new information to prior knowledge, gain and organize content, take action and monitor their own learning, synthesize and evaluate their learning, and extend and transfer their learning to the application environment.

During the Design phase, you examine the content to be presented and collect information from learners on their prior knowledge, motivation, and cognitive and physical abilities. As you collect information from the learners, you gain insight into learning and application contexts. You also work with your client and SME to examine various ways in which the content may be presented. You may demonstrate similar projects or develop a rapid prototype that contains some of the features desired in the finished product. Ideas developed during these exploratory sessions inform the detailed description of the media and delivery mode that you include in the design documents.

After you receive client and SME approval of your design documents, you continue to elaborate on the instructional activities during the Demonstrate phase. You develop paper prototypes in the form of storyboards, templates, and scripts, and a working prototype with limited functionality in order to continue to fine-tune the activities to be included in the final product. You present these various iterations to the client, SME, and learners to gather suggestions that can help you refine the activities.

During the Develop phase, you monitor the production of the materials to ensure that the activities are structured as planned. Learners use the activities in their prototype form during the Demonstrate phase and in a fully developed form during the Develop phase. Based on feedback from learners and analysis of their performance, the materials may be modified to increase their potential to influence learning.

Finally, in the Deliver phase, you present the completed materials to the client and learners.

Activities and the ASC Cycle

As you develop your materials, you first *assemble* content information and information about the learning and application context. Next, you *synthesize* a description of the product in the Define phase, an outline of learning events and a description of the media and delivery mode in the Design phase, paper prototypes (story boards, wire frames, templates) and working prototypes in the Demonstrate phase, and completed instructional materials in the Develop and Deliver phases. Finally, you *confirm* the accuracy of the materials with the client and SMEs, and the effectiveness of the materials with learners.

Notes

[1]Prepared by Charles B. Hodges, 2003.

[2]Documents prepared by David Halpin, Colleen Kerr, Peter Macedo, and Sandra Schneider, 1998. Used with permission.

References

Gagné, E. D., Yekovich, C. W., & Yekovich, F. R. (1993). *The cognitive psychology of school learning* (2nd ed.). New York: Longman, 1993.

Gustafson, K. L. (2000). Designing technology-based performance support. *Educational Technology, 40*(1), 38–44.

Mathematical Association. (1991). *Develop your teaching.* Cheltenham, UK: Stanley Thornes.

Singh, H. (2003). Building effective blended learning programs. *Educational Technology, 43.*

Tessmer, M. (1990). Environment analysis: A neglected stage of instructional design. *Educational Technology Research & Development, 38*(1), 55–64.

Application

1. The RealWorldID Web site continues the case study that began in Chapter 4. In this chapter, you'll outline the instructional materials, based on the instructional strategy you developed in the case analysis activity for Chapter 4. Although we have posed problems related to the content of each individual chapter at the end of Chapters 4 and 5, you may choose to work on the entire case at the end of this chapter. Visit the RealWorldID Web site to analyze the case online or to print for use during class discussions.

2. In your reflective journal, summarize the key points of this chapter. Are the ideas presented consistent or inconsistent with your beliefs and prior knowledge? Compare your perceptions of the chapter with those of your classmates in group discussions.

3. Examine a variety of instructional materials.

   a. Identify the learning environment for which the materials are appropriate.

   b. Identify the components of the instructional package and the contents of each component.

   c. Notice the media assets used within the instruction. Can you identify why each asset was selected? Would other media assets have been more effective? Why or why not?

4. As we explore the essential elements of instructional design in Chapters 2–6, the entire class is encouraged to function as an ID team to create the design specifications for an instructional module. In this chapter, your working group should:

   a. Describe the learning and delivery contexts for the instructional materials.

   b. Identify the components of your instructional package, and outline the contents of each component.

   c. Identify the media assets needed for each learning event.

Ideas in Action

In Chapters 2–6, we follow the design of a videotape on food safety. In this chapter, we include a description of the context and the actual script that was developed for the video.[2] Remember, the goal of the program is to "prevent food-borne illnesses in the elderly by showing them how to purchase, handle, store, and prepare food safely."

Context and Implications for Delivery Mode and Media Assets

This program will be shown in senior centers, retirement communities, and retiree group functions, such as the Kiwanis Club, in order to reach this audience. It is likely to be shown by volunteers, so a commonly available VHS format will be used. It should be 8–12 minutes in length, preferably 10 minutes. Skills will be applied within the learners' homes, so the video should be filmed in an average home. Middle-class elderly should be used as actors to encourage identification with the role models. As some audience members may have hearing disorders, the narrator should speak clearly, and major points should be reinforced with graphics. Specific media assets are identified in the following video script.

Script for Food Safety Video

From Store to Fork:
Safe Food Guidelines for Older Adults

Video	Audio
Newspaper clippings sliding/spinning in? 2 shots side-by-side. Shot 1 will change after shot 2 comes in, then shot 2 changes after a new shot 1 comes in. This alternating pattern continues throughout the intro and the voice-over. Shots of preparing food, eating food, children, elderly, uncooked ground beef, fruits and veggies, food-handling shot, food-eating shot, shot of older woman, family shot Title screen: *From store to fork:* *Safe food guidelines for older adults*	(1) **VO:** Each year millions of people get sick from eating food contaminated with food poisoning bacteria or bacterial toxins, and many die. Most of these illnesses occur from foods prepared and eaten in the home. Infants, children, pregnant women, and the elderly are particularly susceptible to food-borne illness. Uncooked ground beef and poultry . . . inadequately washed fruits and vegetables . . . and poor food-handling practices will increase your risk of contracting a food-borne illness. How can you, as an older adult, protect yourself and your family from the many diseases that cause food-borne illness? This video program updates you on safe practices for purchasing, storing, preparing, and handling food. Let's get started!

Animated bacteria—dissolve to . . .
     MS meat section
     MS poultry section
     MS fish section
     MS egg section
     MS dairy section
     CU prepared dish
     MS fruits
     MS vegetables
     CU meat sitting on counter—time lapse as bacteria
     grow on the surface
	(2)
	 Disease-causing bacteria may be present in potentially hazardous foods—such as meat, poultry, fish, eggs, and dairy products—or in any dishes that include these foods. These potentially hazardous foods should never be allowed to sit at room temperature, because a few bacteria can grow to millions within four hours. And once this happens, cooking won't kill the toxins that may have been created. In addition, bacteria may be present on the surface of fresh fruits and vegetables.

WS outside grocery store WS woman getting cart and entering store OTS shot of woman grouping items on her list	(3) (Purchasing) The first step in preventing food-borne illness begins at the grocery store. Being a smart grocery shopper will reduce your risk of food-borne illness. When grocery shopping, always plan to pick up refrigerated and frozen foods at the end of your shopping trip, just prior to checkout.
MS woman browsing the produce CU of fruits being picked through (perhaps some bad fruits here, followed by good fruits) CU woman picking up nice veggies MS woman packing veggies in bag and placing them in her cart	(4) In the produce section, select fresh fruits and vegetables that show no signs of surface slime, mold growth, or off-color. Fruits should be colorful and firm to the touch. Vegetables should be crisp and fresh in appearance. In addition, you should package your fresh fruits and vegetables in plastic bags to prevent contamination from other grocery items.
MS woman browsing dry-goods aisle CU dry mixes—CU breadcrumbs CU spices—CU seasonings CU sauces—CU canned goods MS woman checking out torn dry package MS woman checking dented can CU of box being picked up and checked for date	(5) When purchasing dry, staple foods—such as dry mixes, breadcrumbs, spices, seasonings, sauces, and canned goods—make sure the packaging is intact. For instance, dry mix packages should be free of tears, dampness, or mold. Canned goods should not be rusty, leaky, swollen, or badly dented. Damaged cans may be contaminated with harmful microorganisms. Also, look for expiration dates on food packages and cans. The expiration date tells you the date that the food should be bought and used by to ensure product quality and safety.

Script for Food Safety Video (continued)

Video	Audio
WS woman browsing meat section—picks up package of ground beef MS ground beef package CU date WS woman placing good beef in her cart CU of cart as woman places beef item away from other items. Fish and poultry items are already in there	(6) Fresh meats, such as ground beef, should have a bright red color and be free of slime and off-odors. Ground beef and other potentially hazardous foods—such as fish, poultry, and dairy products—have a "sell-by-date" to indicate how long the food can be displayed for sale. For optimal freshness, always purchase food before the "sell-by-date" expires. And remember, keep your meat, poultry, and fish away from produce and other open foods when you place them in the cart.
MS woman on refrigerated aisle—picks up eggs and checks them MS woman in frozen section reaching in to pull out a gallon of ice cream CU gallon of ice cream WS woman placing ice cream in cart	(7) In the cold foods section, refrigerated foods should be cold to the touch and free from damage. Frozen foods should be solid, with no evidence of thawing. Don't buy items that appear to have been left out of the cooler.
WS woman at checkout placing items on the conveyor MS items being bagged properly WS woman placing groceries in car MS woman at trunk placing cold items in cooler	(8) When you are finished shopping and reach the checkout counter, make sure that frozen and refrigerated foods are bagged together, and separate from other foods. When you leave the store drive directly home so you can store cold foods in the refrigerator or freezer. If your trip from the grocery store to home will exceed 30 minutes, remember to bring a cooler with ice to store the cold food.
Woman unloading groceries at home—opens fridge MS inside of fridge as woman stores milk and eggs Tilt down as fruits and veggies are placed in their proper spot	(9) (Proper Food Storage) When you arrive home from the grocery store, quickly place cold or frozen foods in the refrigerator or freezer. Products such as milk, eggs, and butter should be stored in their original package or tightly wrapped to prevent absorption of odors. Ripe fruits and vegetables should be stored unwashed in a separate area of the refrigerator because they may absorb the odors of other foods.

Placing fresh meat on the bottom shelf
Tilt up to see leftovers on shelf
Graphic screen slides in:
  Store in the freezer: *If not used within:*
  Ground meats/fish   *24 hours*
  Other meats   *3 days*
	(10)
	Fresh meat, poultry, and fish should be stored on the bottom shelf of the refrigerator, separate from fruits and vegetables. Also, make sure they're stored separately from leftovers to prevent possible contamination from raw meat juices. Bacteria can grow even in the refrigerator. To minimize bacterial growth, ground meats and fish should be stored in the freezer if they will not be used within 24 hours. Other meats should be stored in the freezer if they will not be used within 3 days.

MS inside of freezer. Woman places meat items. We see other items in plastic bags	(11) In the freezer, foods should be stored below 0 degrees Fahrenheit, as freezing inhibits the growth of bacteria. Store items in moisture-proof plastic or wrap to prevent freezer burn.
MS woman opening fridge—reaches in and pulls out thermometer CU thermometer above 40 degrees CU adjusting thermostat	(12) Keep a thermometer in your refrigerator . . . and check the temperature periodically, as it can change with the weather. The refrigerator should be set to stay below 40 degrees Fahrenheit. If it rises above that, adjust the control to bring the temperature down.

Script for Food Safety Video (continued)

Video	Audio
MS woman opening cabinets CU items being placed in the cabinets	(13) Finally, dry staple foods should be stored either in their original package or in tightly closed containers. Food storage cabinets should be clean and below 85 degrees Fahrenheit.
Pan of clean kitchen MS woman at sink—wets hands, lathers, rinses, and then dries with a paper towel	(14) (Handling and Preparing) Now that we've purchased and stored our food safely, let's prepare a dish such as meatloaf. Before preparing meatloaf or any dish, wash your hands with warm water and soap. Wet your hands . . . lather with soap for 20 seconds . . . rinse . . . and towel dry with a fresh towel. Now we are ready to prepare the meatloaf.

Graphic screen: *Listing of the ingredients*
    MS woman taking beef out of the fridge
    Slide transition to woman taking beef out of freezer
    Dissolve to meat in fridge, dissolve to meat under running water, dissolve to meat in microwave
    Transition to meat on counter—repeat the bacteria animation
	(15)
	Meatloaf can contain ground beef, bread crumbs, milk, egg, onion, celery, salt, spices, and seasonings. Use fresh ground beef that was recently purchased and stored in the refrigerator. If it comes from the freezer, it must first be thawed 24 hours in the refrigerator, under cold running water, or in the microwave. Never thaw frozen meat on the kitchen counter or in still water because bacteria will grow rapidly at room temperatures.

MS gathering items from fridge MS gathering items from cabinet MS woman rinsing the celery	(16) Gather the milk, egg, onion, and celery from the refrigerator, and the breadcrumbs, salt, spices, and seasonings from the kitchen cabinet. Prior to using, fruits and vegetables should be rinsed under cold running water to remove possible pesticide residues, soil, and/or bacteria.
MS mixing items together CU placing mix in clean pan MS placing in oven WS wiping counters MS woman washing hands	(17) Using clean, sanitized bowls and utensils, mix the fresh ground beef with the other ingredients. Place mixed ground beef and ingredients in a clean pan, and transfer to the oven. At this point, clean and sanitize all food contact surfaces, and wash your hands again with warm soapy water. It's important to always wash your hands after handling raw food products, before doing anything else. If not, you can easily transfer bacteria to other foods and surfaces.
CU oven. CG: *350 degrees for 1 hour and 30 minutes* MS woman opening oven and checking the temperature on a meat thermometer CU meat thermometer CG: *160 degrees* MS woman cutting and transferring meat to clean dishes Quick shot of woman serving food to people	(18) Most meatloaf recipes require you to cook the ingredients at 350 degrees Fahrenheit for 1 hour and 30 minutes. For doneness, the internal temperature of the meatloaf should reach 160 degrees Fahrenheit using a meat thermometer, and no pink should be visible inside the meat. Once cooked, portion and transfer the meatloaf to clean dishware for serving. Never place cooked food on dishware previously used for handling raw food.
MS woman placing meat back in oven and adjusting the temperature control CU cutting and placing portions in containers MS placing containers in fridge Danger Zone graphic	(19) If the mealtime is delayed, the meatloaf may be held in the oven above 140 degrees Fahrenheit for no longer than 4 hours, or portioned in clean, sanitized shallow containers and cooled in the refrigerator. Keep the temperature of the meatloaf out of the Danger Zone between 40 and 140 degrees Fahrenheit. Bacteria grow rapidly in the Danger Zone, especially at room temperature.

Script for Food Safety Video (continued)

Video	Audio
MS woman placing dirty dishes by sink and then filling sink with hot water, soap, and bleach Transition to MS woman placing leftovers in microwave for reheating CG: *165 degrees Fahrenheit*	(20) After the meal, clean and sanitize all food contact surfaces, dishware, and utensils with hot soapy water and a bleach solution containing 1 teaspoon of bleach per quart of water. Meatloaf leftovers may be reheated in the oven or in the microwave to an internal temperature of 165 degrees Fahrenheit.
MS fridge as woman checks the containers of food CG chart. Pop in each item as it is talked about: *Outdated food* *Immediately* *Leftovers* *3 days* *Poultry* *12 months* *Meat/fish* *6–9 months* *Ground meats* *4 months* *Outdated food* *Immediately* *Stale* *Immediately* *Show signs of spoilage* *Immediately* MS woman cleaning an empty fridge CU cleaning	(21) (Long-term Storage) Be sure to check your kitchen periodically for old or outdated foods that may pose a health risk. In the refrigerator, check for outdated food and discard leftovers after 3 days. After that, they are not safe to eat. In the freezer, poultry products may be frozen for 12 months, whole cuts of meat and fish for 6 to 9 months, and ground meats for only 4 months. Check your cabinets and make sure you discard foods that have exceeded their expiration date, become stale, or show signs of spoilage or contamination. It is not worth the risk of serious illness to keep outdated food around. In addition, it is important to defrost and clean your refrigerator on a regular basis, to prevent a buildup of mold and bacteria.
Back to the side-by-side shot idea from the beginning: Bacteria Beef/poultry Fruits/veggies Food handling Food preparing Shopping Storing food Closing shot of some sort—perhaps shot of serving food to family?	(22) Remember, the main causes of food-borne illness are improperly cooked beef and poultry, inadequately washed fruits and vegetables, and poor food-handling practices. Most food-borne illnesses occur from foods prepared and eaten in the home. This means that we all play an important role in helping to prevent these outbreaks. We've given you some guidelines for purchasing, storing, preparing, and handling food, and by following these steps, you can be assured that you are serving safe food for yourself and your family.
Credits	(23)

WS = Wide Shot

MS = Medium Shot

CU = Close-Up

Music will run throughout and consist of several different but related pieces.

| DESIGN AID |

Assigning Media Assets

Chunk/Outcome	Learning Event	Media Needed

Chapter 6
Evaluation

Chapter Overview

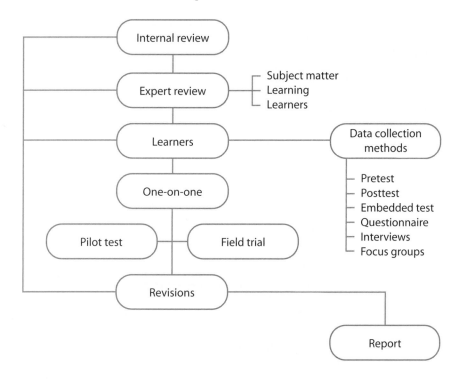

Internal review

Expert review
— Subject matter
— Learning
— Learners

Learners

Data collection methods

One-on-one

— Pretest
— Posttest
— Embedded test
— Questionnaire
— Interviews
— Focus groups

Pilot test

Field trial

Revisions

Report

Learning Outcomes

- Conduct expert reviews.

- Conduct one-on-one evaluations.

- Analyze the results of one-on-one evaluations.

- Conduct pilot tests and/or field trials.

- Analyze the results of pilot tests.

- Develop a revision table based on the results of formative evaluations.

- Define or explain summative evaluation.

- Justify evaluations to clients and employers.

Orientation within the Design Process

Recall that there are five phases in the instructional design process and that in each phase we visit each of the essential elements of instructional design, adding details and performing tasks as required by the deliverables of each phase. In this chapter, we examine the element of Evaluation. Evaluation examines the effectiveness of the instruction by considering how well the outcomes, assessments, and activities are aligned within the instruction and whether they are appropriate for the needs and characteristics of the learners (see Figure 6.1).

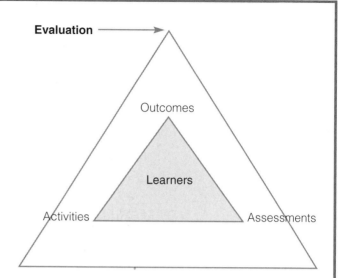

Figure 6.1 *Elements considered.* In this chapter, we examine Evaluation, the element that wraps around all the other elements.

Tasks at Each Phase

Table 6.1 summarizes the tasks of each phase as they relate to evaluation. In later chapters, you'll learn more about performing all of these tasks. For now, the table provides an overview of where evaluation tasks fit into the phases of design.

Table 6.1 Evaluation-related tasks at each phase

Define	• Determine plan for prototype development and learner tryouts. • Draft preliminary formative evaluation plan. Budget for it in proposal. • Educate client as to importance of this stage.
Design	• Prepare or modify formative evaluation plan. • Get suggestions for tryout learners. • Present evaluation plan to client for approval.
Demonstrate	• Gain access to learners for prototype testing. • Develop instruments and procedures needed for prototype testing. • Compile and analyze evaluation data. Develop proposed changes to product based on data.
Develop	• Gain access to learners for additional formative evaluations. • Schedule and conduct additional evaluations. • Analyze data and develop recommendations for modifications.
Deliver	• Conduct summative evaluation if requested.

Evaluation

As you will recall from Chapter 1, systematically designed instruction requires that we:

- Design instruction based on the needs and characteristics of the learners.

- Align the outcomes, assessments, and activities of instruction.
- Evaluate materials in order to improve their effectiveness prior to deployment or distribution.

In previous chapters, we considered the other four elements of instructional design. You learned to assess the needs and characteristics of learners, around which you create the outcomes, assessments, and activities of the instructional experience. You learned the need for the outcomes, assessments, and instructional activities to align. In this chapter, we consider the fifth element, Evaluation. Notice that evaluation "wraps around" the other elements in the essential triangle. Throughout the design process, you constantly monitor whether the instructional activities, outcomes, and assessments are in alignment and are appropriate to the needs and characteristics of the learners.

Formative and Summative Evaluation

As noted previously, evaluation may be formative and summative. **Formative evaluations** are conducted during the process of designing and developing the materials—while there's still time to make changes. **Summative evaluation** measures the effectiveness of instruction after it has been finalized. Companies often hire a third party to conduct an evaluation, especially summative evaluations on large projects. Some instructional designers specialize in evaluation.

Formative evaluation runs throughout each phase in the instructional design process. Designers build feedback loops into every deliverable, actively seeking comments, criticisms, and suggestions from clients, SMEs, colleagues, and, of course, learners. These review and revision cycles help them revise and refine the product incrementally, getting closer and closer to an effective final product with each evaluation cycle. For example, in writing this book, we prepared sample chapters (our prototype) and sent them out for review. In preparing the sample chapters, we had many discussions on the tone of the writing, style of the citations, order of the chapters, content of each chapter, kinds of graphics, and so on. We made a tentative decision on each of these factors based on our experiences teaching and training novice designers. We had informal conversations with a few potential learners, colleagues, employers, and faculty members. But at some point, we had to simply write the chapters. We had to prepare the instruction as best we could based on our knowledge of the needs and characteristics of our potential readers. When the sample chapters went out for review, we awaited the reviewers' comments with anticipation. After we received the comments, we pored through them, looking for clues that could help us strengthen our product incorporating the suggestions into the chapters.

As you go through the design process, make note of questions you may want to ask learners. Let's say your SME wanted to include content that you weren't sure belonged. Formative evaluation allows you to test your "best guesses," or tentative hypotheses, with learners and decide whether to include the extraneous information. You try out the materials or prototype with learners and collect data to determine which option is preferable. For another example, the reviewers of this textbook had differing opinions on the best way to cite sources. Some reviewers preferred an APA style, with sources cited in parentheses (like this); others preferred the MLA style with sources cited as endnotes.[1] Because there were differences in opinion, we decided to "let the users decide" and included a specific question asking about preferred citation style in a questionnaire to subsequent reviewers. Ultimately, we decided to place key source information in parentheses (last name(s), year, page numbers as appropriate), with full publication information at the end of each chapter. As we prepared the manuscript, we kept a file called "questions for reviewers" in which we made note of things that we wanted to let learners decide!

Traditionally, summative evaluation is conducted after the final product is in use in the field. Summative evaluation looks at how well the full product works in its intended environment. This evaluation shouldn't be done right after deployment but somewhat later, when the initial kinks are resolved and the program is fully implemented. At that point, there's enough of a track record to make the evaluation meaningful.

Don't be offended if you aren't asked to do the summative evaluation—it's good practice for someone completely removed from the development process to complete this task (see Figure 6.2). In fact, you may be asked to perform this service on projects you did not develop. You also may develop an evaluation plan that someone else actually implements. If you don't conduct the evaluation yourself, ask for a copy of the evaluation report so that you can learn how effective the program was and how well it was received. We won't describe the summative evaluation process here, but there are excellent references available including those listed in the Additional Readings section at the end of this textbook.

There's a fine line between formative and summative evaluation. It's actually more useful to think of evaluation as a continuous cycle (Smith & Ragan, 1999). Recall the collaborative ASC cycle:

- Assemble information and ask questions.
- Synthesize information and solve problems.
- Check and confirm your understanding.

The ASC cycle requires that you constantly seek information from a variety of stakeholders, those individuals who have an interest in the finished product. Learners are the most obvious stakeholders, but clients who fund the materials, SMEs who are associated with the project, production team members, instructors who may eventually use the materials, and many others may be stakeholders as well. Instructional design models frequently conclude with evaluation. Here, we encourage evaluation throughout the five phases of the design process. We also find it

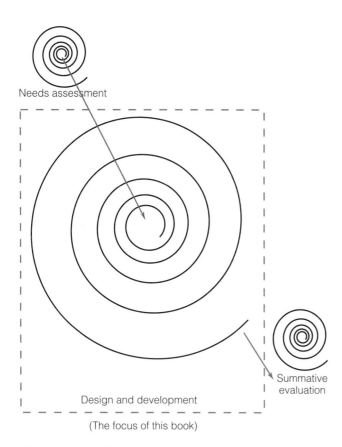

Figure 6.2 *Different processes.* In a full instructional development sequence, the process begins with needs assessment and concludes with summative evaluation. In this book, we focus on the design and development that occurs between those activities.

useful to define "evaluation" broadly to encompass all the feedback you receive throughout the project that helps you shape your product effectively.

1. *Define phase:* Assemble information and synthesize it into a project proposal. You check the proposal's validity when you present your ideas to the client. You modify your ideas based on your client's response until the proposal is acceptable to everyone.

2. *Design phase:* Assemble information from learners, SMEs, the client, and the design and development team, and synthesize it into a design document. You check the validity of the document with the client, SMEs, and project team members, and then modify it until it is approved by all parties.

3. *Demonstrate phase:* Assemble information from SMEs, the technical team, the client, and other interested parties, and synthesize it into content documents, templates, storyboards, and prototypes. In this stage, a variety of stakeholders experiment with a series of progressively more complete versions of the product. Early reviews may involve storyboards or paper mock-ups. Later, working prototypes can be used with learners for evaluation purposes. A prototype is only a small section of the total product, but it is usually sufficient to allow the client, SMEs, and learners to assess its effectiveness.

4. *Develop phase:* Assemble a final set of production specifications and synthesize them to generate the complete set of instructional materials. You check these materials with learners, the client, and other interested groups.

5. *Deliver phase:* Assemble recommendations for future versions, synthesize guidelines for use, and present the materials to the client for final approval. You conduct a summative evaluation if requested. You also engage in postproject debriefings to improve the ways in which team members work together in the future.

Table 6.2 illustrates the products reviewed in each phase, the purpose of the review, and the reviewers for the products.

Formative evaluation is a continual part of collaborative design. As you submit materials to a series of reviews and you collect data from more and more people, you progressively refine the materials. You start with internal reviews, move to external reviews by experts, conduct one-on-one reviews with learners, then do pilot tests with small-groups or field trials. As the materials become progressively more polished, the individuals reviewing them become farther removed from the project team. But evaluation isn't simply about collecting data. Instead, it's about using that data to make revisions that will improve the materials. After each review, use the findings to consider how to improve the product. It may take several cycles of evaluation to get it right, and you may need to test, revise, retest, and re-revise until learners are performing at the intended level.

As you proceed through the formative evaluation process, using the materials with more and more learners, you should find less and less need for revision. At some point, the materials are deemed acceptable. After that, the evaluation becomes "summative" in nature. Additional suggestions for improvement can be considered for future versions of the instruction. With continuous, ongoing monitoring of learners' responses to the instruction, evaluation results eventually become part of the needs assessment data for the next version of the instruction (Smith & Ragan, 1999). Instructional materials should be subjected to a cycle of continuous improvement.

Internal Reviews

Before materials are sent out for external review, the design team should perform an **internal review**. In the internal review, make sure that there are no obvious errors such as typos or misspellings; that the outcomes, assessments, and activities are in alignment; and that the

Table 6.2 Continuous evaluation by phase

	What	Why (Results)	Who
Define	Review project proposal (goals, activities, budget, schedule).	Modify project proposal (goals, activities, learner needs and characteristics, budget, schedule).	Clients
Design	Review design documents (strategy, outcomes, assessments).	Modify outcomes, strategy, assessments.	Clients, SMEs
Demonstrate	Review prototypes (storyboards, mock-ups, proof-of-concept).	Modify content presentation and assessments.	Clients, SMEs (content accuracy), learners
Develop	Review entire set of materials.	Identify effectiveness of materials, areas of weakness (tests, content presentation).	Clients, SMEs, learners
Deliver	Conduct product debriefing. Do summative evaluation of materials, if requested.	Improve future design and development efforts. Determine summative effectiveness of instruction.	Team, learners (for summative evaluation)

outcomes, assessments, and activities are appropriate for the needs and characteristics of the learners.

Identifying Errors

Your competence, and the competence of your organization, is being judged every time you send materials out for review. Examine the materials with the utmost care before submitting them to external reviewers. It's difficult to proofread your own work, so if possible, have someone else in your organization review the materials for errors. Your reputation is on the line.

Another type of evaluation is quality assurance (QA). This is the product testing that the team performs to find any errors or performance glitches prior to delivery. For print deliverables, the QA might include copyediting, fact checking, and rechecking such items as photo captions and credits. If possible, the people who develop the materials should not do their own QA testing. Have someone outside of the project team go through the materials and make detailed comments.

Aligning Components

Throughout the entire design and development process, your responsibility is to perform "quality control" on behalf of learners. You work to ensure that the outcomes, assessments, and activities are in alignment. Make sure that the students are taught what they are tested on. Make sure that the test items match the outcomes. Are all outcomes tested? If not, do you need to add more test items,

or eliminate outcomes? Do the activities prepare the learners for the test? If not, do you need to modify the test or the activities? It can be useful to prepare a table in which you check for alignment among components (see Example 6.1).

Thinking Like a Learner

When conducting internal reviews, you need to make sure the materials are appropriate for the needs and characteristics of the learners. Go through the materials from their perspective. Are the materials clear and logical? Do you know what to do at each point? Is there anything that may be offensive? Do the materials teach the skills needed by the learners? Of course, the learners are the only ones who can truly answer these questions. You simply want to identify, to the best of your ability, problems that may interfere with learners' ability to conduct a productive review.

External Reviews

When most people think of evaluation, they think of **external reviews**. Certainly, these reviews play a critical role in developing effective instructional materials. You work with experts, including content experts and learning experts, to get feedback on the materials. You also work with learners, starting with one-on-one reviews with a few learners and then moving to pilot tests involving small-group evaluations, followed by field trials.

The only way to determine the true effectiveness of the program is to try it out with real learners. Whether you are developing a product for pre-K, K-12, or college students, or for workers, you want to arrange to have representatives of the target audience participate in the evaluation. Just as it may have taken several iterations to get to the point of evaluating materials with learners, it may take several cycles of evaluation to perfect the instruction. Dick, Carey, and Carey (2001) provide excellent advice on data collection and analysis during one-on-one reviews, pilot tests, and field trials, so we base our discussion on their recommendations.

Expert Review

In designing instruction, you are likely to work with one or more experts. SMEs may contribute much of the factual content, but they also should evaluate your materials throughout the design and development process. SMEs can participate in design team meetings and respond to progressively more complete representations of the instructional materials. You may tap their expertise in developing visioning tools such as scenarios and get their feedback on low-fidelity prototypes such as storyboards. They also can try out materials, looking at the accuracy of the content, errors of omission, and problems with performance. Chapter 7 provides recommendations on conducting the expert reviews that should occur throughout the design and development process.

In addition to SMEs, you want evaluators who can view the materials through the learners' eyes. If you're working with adults or teenagers, the "learner experts" can be members of the target audience. Even when working with young children, it's often useful to work with members of the target audience, as well as their parents or teachers, as part of the project review team. Some organizations use a formal "pilot test group" or "focus group" program in order to conduct reviews quickly or gauge a market's reaction to a new learning product. In a focus group testing program, random representatives of the target audience review the materials to determine the appropriateness of the instruction for their peers. This strategy can be implemented in several ways. Different learners can attend each focus group test or a single group can return each time. The advantage of using different learners for each focus group test is that they lack preconceptions about the product and experience it fresh each time. The advantage of working with the same group is that members begin to understand how the product works, how it's being produced, and how it is improving. In either situation, you want to create an environment in which participants feel comfortable telling you their true feelings. As the participants experience the various deliverables, you gain their feedback on the product.

Other experts are knowledgeable in how people learn. This is often the instructional designer's role, but sometimes additional expertise is needed. This evaluator should review your instructional strategy and help you tailor the instruction to the needs of the audience (Dick, Carey, & Carey, 2001).

You're not obligated to use the suggestions of these specialists. They might not see the "big picture" as you do. For example, they may not understand the reasoning behind certain decisions. They might not understand the limitations of the budget, schedule, delivery environment, and other production factors. However, these specialists can alert you to issues that you might want to consider for subsequent evaluation cycles.

Example 6.1 Alignment among Design Components

This chart shows the alignment among outcomes, assessments, and activities for a first aid class. For the goal associated with controlling bleeding, learners need to recall the pressure points and respond appropriately depending on the location of the wound.

Outcome	Assessment	Activity
Recall pressure points that control bleeding.	State pressure points. Label pressure points on illustration.	List pressure points. Illustrate pressure points on diagram.
Identify correct pressure points to control bleeding at specific sites.	Identify correct pressure points when presented with information about wound.	Demonstration of correct pressure points in specific situations. Practice applying pressure in correct locations given examples.

One-on-One Reviews

One-on-one reviews are conducted with individual members of the target audience. Each learner works through the materials in the presence of the evaluator. The purpose of these evaluations is to catch errors that may have been missed in other reviews and to identify where learners may have problems in understanding the materials. You won't be able to draw conclusions about how effective the instruction will be when delivered in the actual instructional environment. Instead, think of the participants in these one-on-one sessions as "expert reviewers" or "learner experts."

When selecting participants for one-on-one reviews, you should include at least one representative from each of the subgroups in your population. For example, you may want one average learner, one who has a great deal of prior experience with the content, and one who may have trouble with the content. If your population represents a wide variety of age levels, you may want one learner from each of your major age groups. Select learners who differ on characteristics that may matter to the instruction. For example, if your materials are targeted to middle school girls, their teachers, and their parents, you probably should include at least one representative from each of those groups.

During these evaluations, you should watch learners work through the materials, taking notes of progress. Encourage learners to talk freely. You can answer questions and provide clarification where needed, but make note of areas where you need to provide additional clarification. To collect data, you might videotape the user progressing through the materials. A videotape provides you with a record of what was said at each point in the instructional material and what the learner was examining when a particular comment or question came up. If that's not possible, consider audiotaping learners' comments. In either case, be sure you gain their permission to record the session. Also be sure you take careful notes. One way to collect data during these evaluations is to make copies of the instruction and to record notes directly on the paper. If that's too unwieldy, an outline of the content is a good second choice (see Example 6.2).

In compiling data from the one-on-one evaluation, Dick, Carey, and Carey (2001) recommend that you:

- Describe the learners who participated.
- Indicate performance on pretest, posttest, and entry behaviors measures.
- Summarize comments and suggestions (see Example 6.3).
- Create a table comparing participants.

In addition, examining learners' mistakes and comments can give you clues as to areas of the instruction that may

---

Example 6.2 Sample Form for Recording Comments from One-on-One Evaluations

Best Practices in Distance Learning: Fundamentals for Teachers

Section	Comments
Overall comments	
Registration and log-in	
General navigation	
Look and feel	
Glossary	
Resources	
Help	
1. Welcome to Distance Learning!	
What is distance learning?	
Making the transition	
Being on camera	
Quiz 1	

(continued on page 130)

Example 6.2 *(continued)*

2. How Videoconferencing Works	
Classroom setup	
Connections	
Transmission	
Quiz 2	
3. Teaching Tools	
Instead of blackboard	
Using computers	
Simple steps to good design	
Quiz 3	
4. Teaching Strategies	
Preparing for class	
Assignments and assessment	
In classroom	
Quiz 4	
5. Engaging Students	
Getting to know students	
Pairs and groups	
Using the technology	
Quiz 5	
6. Contingencies	
Preventing cheating	
Emergencies	
Missing class	
Quiz 6	
Other Comments	

need improvement. If learners do poorly, determine if the assessment items, grading scale for the test items, or instruction itself are faulty. Although reviewers' likes and dislikes can alert you to important issues, don't make revisions based on the opinion of one or two learners. Instead, consider all data and suggestions in light of the responses of others. Keep asking questions until you see a clear trend developing.

You may want to use learners' suggestions to formulate the questions to ask during the next stage of review. For example, if two of your learners suggest that you restructure the navigation of your Web site, you may want to include items about the navigation in a questionnaire administered to a larger group of learners. You may have already given a great deal of thought to methods of navigation before settling on the current navigational scheme. The learners may simply be expressing a personal preference that would make no noticeable difference in the effectiveness of the materials. But don't ignore it, either. Try to achieve resolution by ensuring that it isn't a problem and needs no changes or getting corroboration that it needs to be fixed.

Example 6.3 One-on-One Evaluation Data

Four teachers participated in evaluating an instructional Web site. They were asked to comment on the tutorial and lesson plan—strong points, needed improvements, important considerations, anticipated usage, and so on. (Note: "SOLs" refer to state mandated "Standards of Learning.") The following table presents their comments.

Tutorial

Participant 1	• Use the table of contents or bullet formatting for all sections. Currently is a little too wordy. • When teaching how to pose questions, example questions would be useful. • Wanted a "home" button from within the tutorial. • Put something about SOLs in the planning stage of the tutorial (teachers are encouraged to reference SOLs in their lesson plans). • In the tutorial on designing a worksheet, it said how others had done it but not how to do it. If the link says "how to," then it should be procedural in nature. • No more information needed. • Confused by the use of the terms "assessment" and "evaluation."
Participant 2	• Need a button to get back to the start page. • Need a "next" button to progress to each stage serially (positioned at the bottom of each page).
Participant 3	• Navigation items neither clear nor consistent. • Would like to see pointers to other museum specimens.
Participant 4	• No comments.

Lesson Plan

Participant 1	• Connecting the lesson plans to the SOLs is important. • Structure the site in accordance with grade level, subject area, or SOL. • Don't see which SOLs the plans addressed at first. • Wasn't expecting a Word file when she clicked on the worksheet links for the first time. • The field trip worksheet is actually a plan for a lesson.
Participant 2	• Habitats worksheet link is broken. • Put grid lines in the worksheets.
Participant 3	• Label the numbered steps so that people know what they are. • Use icons to represent the different steps.
Participant 4	• Did not know what was happening when the Word documents took a long time to download. • In worksheets that do not allow for drawings, a section for drawings should be included.

Observations and Revisions

Following these one-on-one reviews, the designers concluded that the navigation was convoluted in nearly all sections. They recommended improving the navigation and correcting other errors to increase usability prior to pilot testing with a small group of teachers. Can you see how the designers drew these conclusions from the data? Would you have drawn similar conclusions?

As you compile your data, document the changes you plan to make and the data that support those changes. At this stage, revisions typically include clarification of ideas, layouts, usability issues, and the interface. If potential modifications are minor or if there is no clear pattern of suggestions, you might simply leave the instruction alone and make note of areas to pay attention to during the pilot tests.

Pilot Tests

After you've developed a sample of your instruction as a "proof of concept" prototype, you can do a pilot test evaluation. Like one-on-one reviews, pilot tests usually are conducted by the instructional designer or other members of the design team. During a pilot test, a small group of learners progress through the instructional materials with as little help from the designer as possible. The recommended size of a small group typically is 5–15 learners, but sometimes "small group" is relative. A group of 30 students can be a "small group" when testing a course support Web site for a class of 500 students. During small-group evaluation, learners use the materials independently, though it is helpful if you can bring them all to the same location so you can observe them as they progress through the instruction. You want to look for ease of use, the extent to which they achieve the desired outcomes, and their attitudes toward the instruction.

You can conduct a pilot test with learners in an existing setting, such as a course in which students are already enrolled. In some pilot tests, students use a completed curriculum product over the course of a semester while the instructor keeps careful notes about where problems occur. A different type of pilot test might involve a limited segment of the instruction used in a real classroom in lieu of other materials. For example, in a management training course, the instructor might substitute an online module on communication skills, part of a pilot test, in place of a classroom-based presentation. Based on these pilot tests, the instructional designer gets feedback on what changes to make in the product.

When conducting pilot tests, the most important data you can collect relates to the effectiveness of the material. Do the learners learn what the instruction is designed to teach? If not, what can you do to correct the problem? Do the learners need more practice? Better test items? Clearer examples? Learners may have difficulty learning the content for a multitude of reasons. You need to carefully structure your formative evaluation materials so that you can identify the probable causes of learning problems.

DESIGNER'S TOOLKIT

Attracting Participants

Many designers offer participants some type of gift or reward in appreciation for participating in an evaluation. Examples include payments, such as $25 for an hour or two and gift certificates to a store or restaurant or to an online vendor such as Amazon.com. In some cases, participants cannot accept any form of gratuity because of strict ethics rules and laws. But it still might be possible to provide the participating school or institution with some expression of appreciation, such as a complementary copy of the final product. For example, one publisher provided a middle school with a set of headphones for each computer in its computer lab in appreciation for allowing evaluators into the school.

If the group size is small enough, it's useful to conduct a debriefing session in which the participants make suggestions for improvements. Try to find out what they liked and what they want to see changed. You don't want to make changes that will reduce or eliminate features they perceived to be successful in attempting to improve areas they perceived as weak.

What kind of materials do you need for your pilot tests? You can conduct pilot tests with either your proof-of-concept prototype or a complete set of instructional materials. The materials need to have multiple data gathering points so you can identify where the materials are deficient. As you learned in Chapter 3, learners need to be tested on their knowledge of the content before, during, and after the instruction so that you can pinpoint where their comprehension falters. It's important to include a pretest item, embedded test item, and posttest item for *each* learning outcome so that you can identify where the materials fall short, even if these tests will be removed from the materials later.

Of course, this extensive testing may affect the tryout learners' attitudes toward the materials and extend the time required to complete the instruction, but that's understandable. If your learner analysis is correct, the learners shouldn't be able to answer many of the questions on the pretest successfully. To minimize their frustration, let them know that they aren't expected to know the answers to the pretest questions; you're merely trying to confirm what they may know about the content prior to the instruction. Attempt to cultivate an atmosphere in which participants feel as if they're helping you improve the materials. Stress that you're evaluating the materials, not the learners. Your job as instructional designers is to determine the cause of any difficulty and to correct it.

It's also useful to include an attitude questionnaire to collect qualitative data that may provide insight into factors that contributed to the learners' performance on the assessments (see Example 6.4). You may want to collect information on learners' likes and dislikes, and solicit suggestions for improvement. If the materials are self-instructional in nature, questioning learners on the ways in which they use the materials can provide information as to what aspects of the instruction they find most useful. For example, after analyzing the data from a pilot test of a Web-based course, the designers discovered that the students never used the discussion forum, preferring to communicate via e-mail. Thus, the discussion forum was eliminated from the final version of the course.

If you participate in administering the evaluation, remember that you aren't there to share your rationale for the program design. You're there to find out how the product really works and to hear what learners have to say about it. Try not to say anything about the design or the production. Listen politely, smile, take notes, and resist the temptation to defend your work. Also resist the temptation to help learners so they can perform better!

Example 6.4 Attitude Questionnaire

Posttest Survey

1. I was already familiar with this material.
   _____ No
   _____ Yes

2. If no, did the training help you understand the regulations?
   _____ No
   _____ Yes

3. Was the material at the right level for you?
   _____ Too difficult
   _____ Somewhat difficult
   _____ Somewhat easy
   _____ Too easy

4. How would you rate the computer program?
   _____ Easy to use
   _____ Somewhat easy to use
   _____ Somewhat difficult to use
   _____ Difficult to use

5. The best aspect of this program is:

6. This program could be improved by:

Field Trials

To better understand how well a learning product works in its intended delivery environment, you may want to set up a field trial. Field trials usually include more participants than do pilot tests, and the instruction is used in its intended setting—for example, in a classroom or online. There isn't a specific format to follow, but questions you want to answer include these:

- Does the instruction work? Do learners achieve the intended outcomes?
- Do learners like the program? What are their affective responses to it?
- Is the program easy to implement, deliver, and maintain?
- Will it be used again for this audience?
- What could be improved?

The data collection materials and methods for a field trial are almost identical to those for a pilot test. However, as the instructional designer, you usually are not involved in delivering the program for the field trial. Learners should complete a pretest, take the training, and then complete a posttest. Additionally, you might ask learners

Voice of Experience

Follow-Up Evaluations

A social services agency sent newly hired employees to an intensive six-week job skills training program at a central location. In addition to learning policies and procedures and technical skills, these employees learned interpersonal skills to help them work with clients. Their supervisors received training as well. The supervisors' training focused on how they should evaluate their new hires when they reported back to work following basic training. Training managers scheduled evaluation meetings with the supervisors six months after the basic skills training. The supervisors reported on how well the new hires were performing and identified areas in which they still needed training. This feedback was used to revise the basic skills training and to develop advanced skills training.

and instructors to respond to a questionnaire to determine their subjective attitudes toward the program. If there is an opportunity for a question-and-answer session, invite participants to share their thoughts and experiences. A field trial might include a preliminary interview with the teacher or trainer at the school or work site and a postevaluation debriefing. If the program is for job-related training, you may also want to survey the trainees' supervisors to find out how well the participants use the training skills on the job.

⟳ Interpreting Data from Pilot Tests and Field Trials

Reviewing the results from a formative evaluation can be a humbling experience! But the feedback allows you to spot problems and fix them before you spend all of the project's resources on a completed product—and then find yourself without the time, money, or energy to fix the problem. Initially, it may be crushing to hear harsh criticism of materials that you've poured your heart and soul into developing. As you become more comfortable with evaluations, however, you'll probably welcome the opportunity to improve your work based on data from a well-conducted evaluation.

You can analyze data from both pilot tests and field trials using simple descriptive statistics and data tables. You may want to prepare one or more of the following data tables:

- Individual student performance on items assessing prerequisite skills

- Individual performance on pretest for each objective
- Individual performance on embedded test items for each objective (see Example 6.5)
- Individual performance on posttest for each objective
- Performance on each test item by objective
- Summary of responses to an attitude questionnaire, surveys, and/or interviews

In addition, you may want to represent the results visually with:

- A graph of performance
- Insertion of the pretest and posttest performance on the instructional analysis chart (see Figure 6.3)

After you compile the evaluation results, examine the data to answer these questions:

- Are any of the students "outliers" in that they performed consistently better or worse than the rest? Is so, eliminate those scores from the rest of the analysis.
- Do students have the necessary prerequisite skills?
- Could they achieve any of the outcomes before the instruction?
- Do the pretest-to-posttest comparisons indicate that they learned from the instruction?
- Are any particular outcomes or assessment items problematic?

Example 6.5 ⟳ Students Mastering Objectives on Practice Items

Student	1	2	2.2.1.1	2.2.1	2.2	2.2.2.1	2.2.2	2.3.1	2.3	2.3.2.1	2.3.2.2	2.3.2.3	2.3.2	2.4	3.2	3	3.3	3.1	4	5.2.1	5.2.2	5	6
															Practice Performance by Objective								
A	1	1	0	1	1	1	1	0	1	1	1	1	1	1	1	1	1	1	1	1	1	0	0
B	1	1	1	1	1	1	1	1	1	1	1	1	1	1	1	1	1	1	1	1	1	1	1
C	1	1	1	1	1	1	1	1	1	1	1	1	1	1	0	0	1	0	1	0	0	0	1
D	1	0	1	1	1	0	1	1	1	1	1	1	1	1	1	0	0	0	0	1	1	0	0
E	1	1	1	1	1	1	1	1	1	1	1	1	1	1	1	1	1	1	0	1	1	0	0
F	1	1	1	1	1	1	1	1	0	1	1	1	0	1	1	1	1	1	1	1	1	1	1
G	1	1	1	1	1	1	1	1	1	1	1	1	1	1	1	1	1	1	1	1	1	0	0
H	1	1	1	1	1	1	1	1	1	1	1	1	1	1	1	0	1	1	1	1	1	0	0
% mastery	100	88	88	100	100	88	100	88	88	100	100	100	88	100	88	63	88	75	75	88	88	25	38

Key to coding: 0—less than 100% of questions correct for that objective
1—100% of questions correct for that objective

- Were there any unusual events that could account for the results?
- Do students like using the program?
- Do they have important concerns that need to be addressed?

Look for patterns in learners' responses. Consider whether an appropriate group was selected for the evaluation. Perhaps they already possessed many of the skills taught in the instruction or lacked the necessary prerequisite knowledge. Review the test item performance as mapped onto the subskills analysis for clues as to whether the instruction was sequenced and chunked properly. Consider whether particular learning outcomes and test items were difficult for the group.

If learners fail to obtain an outcome, what could have gone wrong? Various learning theories (see, for example, Driscoll, 2000) provide guidance on why learners might fail to perform successfully on an assessment. Typically, problems are due to either a failure to learn, or *encode,* information, or a failure to *recall* information on the assessments. Patterns of performance on the pretests, embedded tests, and posttests are likely to provide clues as to whether you need to improve the instruction or the assessments.

If students perform poorly on the embedded test items, they may never have encoded the information to begin with. If learners are unable to perform the task within the instruction, examine the instructional materials and outcomes to determine whether you:

- Adequately identified the necessary prerequisite skills.
- Cued the learners as to the prior knowledge upon which the new information builds.
- Established clear relationships among chunks of content.
- Correctly sequenced the information.
- Omitted a critical skill in the instruction.
- Provided sufficient practice.
- Provided opportunities to synthesize the information.

If students performed the task correctly on the embedded test administered during the instruction but failed to perform adequately on the posttest, it may be due to a failure in recall or to poor test items (Seels & Glasgow, 1998). Examine the instruction to determine if you need to:

- Make the differences between prior knowledge and new knowledge more explicit, to avoid interference effects that sometimes occur between new knowledge and related prior knowledge.

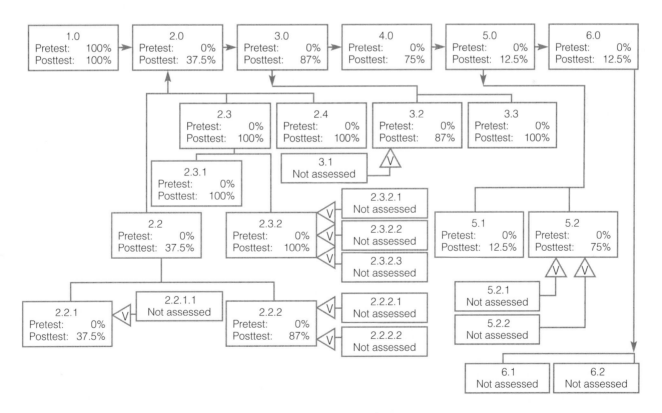

Figure 6.3 *Scores by subskill.* Group pretest and posttest scores on each outcome, mapped onto the instructional analysis.

Prerequisite Skills

A social services agency developed an online training program for its social workers. The trainees were all experienced employees who needed to learn to use a new online calculation tool. By entering information in the automated form, they could calculate a client's benefits. The training was developed and delivered in a computer-based training module. The module concluded with a multiple choice assessment. The course designers were stunned when assessments showed many failing and marginal scores. After investigating, they determined where they had made a faulty assumption. They had assumed that employees remembered how to perform arithmetic functions using fractions. In fact, like many adults, the trainees hadn't used these arithmetic skills in years, if not decades, and had forgotten the basic rules for fractions. The designers revised the course by creating a brief, optional module that reviewed the rules for fractions. With this additional content, employees quickly learned the content and performed well.

- Provide more opportunities to practice the skill within the instruction to increase retention.
- Provide a wide range of examples during the instruction so that students can determine the range of situations to which the knowledge should be applied.

Also, examine the test items to determine if you need to:

- Clarify test directions.
- Make the posttest items more closely parallel to the embedded test items.
- Ensure that the test items include adequate prompts as to what knowledge should be applied.

Now, consider the instruction and the assessments together:

- Did the materials contain adequate content to answer the questions correctly?

- Is the instruction too long or too short?
- Are the test items in alignment with the intended outcomes?
- Was the instructional strategy implemented as planned?

Reporting Results

Once you have analyzed the data and identified areas needing modification, organize the data and your conclusions into a report (see Example 6.6). It's often a good idea to review the evaluation results with your team and client. Guide SMEs, clients, and team members in responding to critical comments. They may not be used to having their ideas criticized, so handle feedback from the reviews diplomatically. You may need to summarize the comments and translate them into a form that is constructive rather than critical. Be tactful to ensure that

There isn't an exact correlation between evaluation in instructional design and in home construction, but there are similarities. Let's say you and your architect have devised a plan based on discussions about what kinds of spaces you require and for what kinds of uses. Your architect has drawn up blueprints. Your builder has developed a schedule and budget. Your architect may have even built a cardboard model or developed a 3-D model on the computer. As you review each of these documents and models, you consider how well the plan matches the requirements you developed initially. Will these plans yield the house you hoped for? It may be that in "walking" through the 3-D model, you realize that the sun will pour through west-facing windows in the afternoon. Perhaps creating an extension to the roofline will cut the afternoon glare, or reducing the size or changing the location of the windows may solve the problem. It's easier and less expensive to identify and correct potential problems during the planning and development process than after the home is built.

Example 6.6 Formative Evaluation Report

The following excerpt is from a report on the formative evaluation of a videotape (Mansfield, 1997). The instruction was designed to teach proper lighting techniques for video production. The program consisted of a humorous skit with poor lighting, a demonstration of techniques to improve the lighting, and the original skit with improved lighting. Data tables and explicit discussions of the data have been removed from the report to reduce its length.

The pilot test group involved 12 learners enrolled in a video production class. These students were graduate students with varying degrees of experience with video production. During the evaluation, the instructional design team administered a pretest, provided the instruction (videotape), administered a posttest, administered a questionnaire about the videotape itself, and conducted a small group verbal debriefing. Instruction, testing, and evaluation took approximately one and a half hours. Analysis of the evaluation data focused on areas of the instructional design that failed to provide appropriate levels of instruction to the learners.

The instruction, as measured by pretest/posttest performance scores and evaluation data, would have to be considered successful. All learners improved in performance from the pretest to the posttest. Percentage change ranged from 50% to 70%. Only one test question appeared problematic. Question 1 was answered incorrectly in the posttest by learner 10, who answered this question correctly in the pretest. After review of the distracters for this multiple-choice question and of the script it was found that this distracter was referred to during the video and should be changed to avoid confusion.

However, as was made evident by closer analysis of the evaluation data, the instructional materials can be improved. Revisions will be suggested that are within the realm of our performance objectives and instructional goals.

Clearly, the pacing of the instructional and review sections of the video need to be improved. The pacing in these sections needs to be slowed, with greater emphasis placed on reviewing lessons. Also, the graphical support for each section needs to enhanced. More still shots with text would be useful to help improve instruction on lighting placement. Additional instructional material should be included on how to use lighting accessories. Although not noted by the learners, instruction relating to safety should also be strengthened.

The most difficult question to answer concerning revision has to do with the skit. Although it was considered by many to be one of the strengths of the instruction, it was also noted for its possible offensive material and its likelihood of becoming dated. With regard to the nature of the material, consideration of the audience would have to be made before using this video for instruction. If everyone is too shocked or too offended to learn anything we fail before we begin the instruction. Conversely, some audiences will find the video's irreverence stimulating and make them more open to the instruction (I think we had both situations in the class). A more difficult potential problem is that the material will become dated or that the "in jokes" that make this video funny will be forgotten. This is not likely, at least for a while, but is a danger when using material based on current events. This video was made for a specific audience and the concept worked here. However, if this video were for wider dispersal another concept might be a safer and wiser choice.

Also, there were a number of comments requesting different placement of the skits to reinforce the lighting changes. The suggestions to change the placement of the skits resulted from the desire to see the lighting changes more clearly. If better examples of lighting changes are included in the body of the instruction I think we can avoid moving the skits. The skits work well where placed and most learners appreciated the structure of the video.

Example 6.7 Revision Table

The following excerpt is part of the revision table that resulted from a field trial of a Web-based course.

Component	Problem	Proposed Change	Evidence and Sources
Overall	Server would go down prior to quizzes because students were using Web to study.	Change quizzing system.	Student complaints. Documentation for quizzing database indicates it will support only 25 simultaneous hits.
Layout of main page	Students had trouble finding due dates, could see only part of screen at one time.	Make table narrower, make due dates clearer.	Student comments. Though only few students commented, a simple change.
Journal	Intent of journal was to provide place for students to take notes, but students never used this feature.	Because not used, eliminate.	Description of patterns of use and responses to direct question on attitude questionnaire.
Practice quizzes	Students really liked these and liked to print them out.	Make available as printable file.	Questionnaires.

you don't damage your working relationship with these important individuals. Help team members focus on looking for clear trends in the data. Examine outlier comments for elements of truth. Perhaps these individuals have identified something that others simply missed or something that you need to pay careful attention to in your next round of evaluations. Devise revisions when there is a consensus among responses. It is useful to compile a revision summary table that lists the components of instruction, any problems with each component, the evidence suggesting the problem, and proposed changes. For an example of a revision table, see Example 6.7.

If you choose to make a formal presentation, begin by outlining the project requirements, such as a summary of the learners, the goals and objectives, and the delivery environment. Briefly explain the evaluation methodology, highlight the results, and explain what the results mean and what you recommend. You might develop a handout to accompany your presentation that includes more detail. Use a limited number of detailed examples to illustrate points, but stick to an overview of the information.

Evaluation Issues

Not all clients will enthusiastically endorse the idea of learner testing. They may balk because of the additional time and resources required to conduct evaluations. They may believe that they can assess how well something is working without introducing another step in the process. Evaluations may be perceived as "nice" but not necessary. Part of the problem is that many people think of evaluation as something that occurs *after* development, as the final step at the *end* of the process. Unfortunately, by the end of the project, after so much time, money, and effort has gone into designing and developing a product, there may be few resources left for evaluation. Developers may be tired of the project and ready to move on. Unfortunately, all too often, materials are distributed with errors that could have been fixed with adequate evaluation.

If your clients are reluctant to support evaluations, you need to promote the evaluation process in terms of the benefits to your client. If your client values the reputation of the company, explain how formative evaluation data can be used in publicity materials to market the product. If your client values cost-effectiveness, explain how it is more cost-effective to test a prototype with a few learners and make revisions prior to full development than to develop the materials and then discover that they are not as effective as they should be.

As part of the process of educating your client, help him or her understand the benefits of continuous evaluations. Explain that evaluations are designed to yield meaningful information to guide the designer in making programs even more effective for learners. If your client resists all of your efforts to conduct an evaluation with learners, you can take comfort in the fact that the materials will have been reviewed by SMEs, clients, and, possibly, members of the target audience who serve as consultants to the design team, as part of the continuous improvement cycle of collaborative design.

Checklist for Data Analysis

Analyzing data from one-on-one evaluations:

- Describe the learners who participated
- Indicate performance on entry behaviors measures
- Summarize comments and suggestions
- Summarize posttest scores
- Create a table comparing participants

Analyzing data from pilot tests:

- Individual student performance on items assessing prerequisite skills
- Individual performance on pretest for each objective
- Individual performance on posttest for each objective
- Performance on each test item by objective
- Summary of responses to an attitude questionnaire

In addition, you may want to represent the results visually with a:

- Graph of performance
- Insertion of the pretest and posttest performance on the instructional analysis chart

Evaluation Report Checklist

- Executive summary (write last, and keep short: 1–2 pages)
- Project overview (summary of the learners, goals and objectives, and delivery environment)
- Methodology, including copies of any forms you develop
- Results (compiled data; you can include raw data in attachment)
- Analysis and recommendations

Summary

In each phase of the instructional design process, you evaluate your tentative understanding by presenting the deliverables to others for input as to whether your interpretation, as manifest in the deliverables, is on target for the client, SMEs, and learners. By continually "checking" your decisions by sharing documents and materials with others,

you confirm or modify your solutions. You evaluate your ideas when you present a project proposal for consideration. You evaluate your "best guess" solutions when you present design documents, storyboards, content outlines, and prototypes for discussion. You're involved in evaluation—in confirming or modifying—your design decisions, and the products of these decisions, throughout the Define, Design, Demonstrate, Develop, and Deliver phases.

In contrast to summative evaluation, which is conducted after the product is completed, formative evaluation refers to the fact that the product is still "in formation." In evaluating it at this point, you still have the opportunity to revise if necessary. Formative evaluation involves internal and external reviews. The purpose of internal reviews is always the same across all phases: to ensure alignment among outcomes, assessments, and activities; to ensure that outcomes, assessments, and activities are appropriate for the learners; and to make sure the content is accurate and free from errors. In external reviews, you get the feedback of clients and SMEs, and test the program with representatives of the target audience. Learner testing can involve one-on-one evaluations, pilot tests with small groups, or field trials. Each type yields important information on the program's effectiveness. Based on all of the reviews, you, your team, and your client can determine if changes need to be made.

Instructional design is an art and a science. There's the science built on research findings developed over years of trials and the experiences of hundreds of other designers. Once you take what you know from research, theory, and the experience of others, you can make a "best guess" of what will work for your situation and your learners—that's where the art comes in. To determine if you've "guessed" correctly, you need to test those assumptions through the process of evaluation. You're putting ingredients together in new ways every time you design instruction. Before it's served up to the masses, someone needs to taste the product!

Notes

[1]Like this.

[2]Based on an evaluation conducted by Inez Farrell, 1999. Used with permission.

[3]Documents prepared by David Halpin, Colleen Kerr, Peter Macedo, and Sandra Schneider, 1998. Used with permission.

References

Dick, W., Carey, L., & Carey, J. O. (2001). *The systematic design of instruction* (5th ed.). Needham Heights: MA: Allyn & Bacon.

Driscoll, M. P. (2000). *Psychology of learning for instruction* (2nd ed.). Boston: Allyn & Bacon.

Mansfield, M. (1997). *Formative evaluation of "taking the 'in' out of inappropriate lighting."* Unpublished report, Virginia Polytechnic Institute and State University.

Seels, B., & Glasgow, Z. (1998). *Making instructional design decisions* (2nd ed.). Upper Saddle River, NJ: Prentice-Hall.

Smith, P. L., & Ragan, T. J. (1999). *Instructional design* (2nd ed.). Upper Saddle River, NJ: Merrill/Prentice-Hall.

Application

1. The RealworldID Web site includes a case study of the formative evaluation of a workbook designed to supplement a course on Web site development. You are asked to examine the results of the evaluation to identify aspects of instruction that may need revision. Visit the RealWorldID Web site to analyze the case online or to print for use during class discussions.

2. In your reflective journal, summarize the key points of this chapter. How are the ideas presented consistent or inconsistent with your beliefs and prior knowledge? Compare your perceptions of the chapter with those of your classmates in group discussions.

3. As we've explored the essential elements of instructional design in Chapters 2–6, the entire class has been encouraged to function as an ID team to create the design specifications for an instructional module. In this chapter, your working group should develop a plan for formative evaluation. Consider:

   a. Who will conduct expert reviews?

   b. Who will you select for one-on-one evaluations? What steps will you take and what procedures will you use?

   c. How will you conduct a pilot test? What group will you use? What materials will you need?

4. Create a written justification for conducting an evaluation. Remember to keep the values of your clients in mind as you prepare your justification.

Ideas in Action

In Chapters 2–6, we follow the design of a videotape on food safety.[3] In this chapter, we include the plan for the pilot test that was presented to the client, the attitude questionnaire administerd to learners during the pilot test (along with the pre- and postquestionnaires presented in Chapter 3), and the list of revisions suggested by all of the evaluation data.

Handout for Food Safety Video Formative Evaluation Meeting

Project Goal
Viewers will choose safe shopping and cooking behaviors.

Purpose of Evaluation
Determine needed revisions, generate data for publications, and provide impact information for extensions promotionals.

Benefits of Evaluation

- Verifies prerequisite knowledge needs
- Determines general knowledge and behavioral changes and impacts
- Defines necessary revisions
- Identifies learners' general attitudes toward program

Design
Pretest, posttest, and attitude survey

Expert Review
Food safety expert, learner, and learning specialist

Audience
Ideal situation is to have representation of the entire potential audience.

Pilot Test Questions

1. How has this video influenced your views about safe food handling?
   - After viewing the video, do you believe your current food handling practices are safe?
   - What did you learn in the video that you did not already know?
   - How is this video likely to influence your future food handling practices?
   - Do you believe the video was effective?

2. What were your reactions to the video?
   - What did you like most about the video?
   - What did you like least about the video?
   - Were any parts of the video unclear? If so, which parts?
   - Did you find any of the material inappropriate?

3. Was the video relevant to you personally?
   - Is there anything that could be done to make the video more relevant (graphics, gender, review)?

Postvideo Attitude Survey

Please circle your answer to the following questions.

SA = Strongly Agree
A = Agree
D = Disagree
SD = Strongly Disagree

1. After viewing the video, I believe my current food handling practices are safe.   SA   A   D   SD

2. The video contained information about safe food handling that I did not already know.   SA   A   D   SD

3. This video has influenced my future food handling practices.   SA   A   D   SD

4. I will likely follow the safe food handling practices shown in the video.   SA   A   D   SD

5. The material in the video was appropriate to the subject.   SA   A   D   SD

6. The material in the video was relevant to me personally.   SA   A   D   SD

7. The video was easy to follow.   SA   A   D   SD

8. The messages in the video were clear.   SA   A   D   SD

9. I had a positive reaction to the video.   SA   A   D   SD

10. I enjoyed watching the video.   SA   A   D   SD

11. The video was effective at informing me of safe food handling practices.   SA   A   D   SD

Additional Comments (optional)

What did you like about the video?

What did you dislike about the video?

Any suggestions or additional comments for improving the video?

Requested Video Changes

Overall, the video received a positive response. The client mentioned that the video may be sold to other states and that they had two other video projects on the back burner that they may consider doing with us.

The following are the remaining changes, requests, and needs to finish this project:

1. The existing title should read only "Store to Fork."

2. The newspaper ADO spins are to be replaced with headline clippings that build to a collage on a stagnant background.

3. All bacteria animations must be one color, preferably green.

Changes Arising from the Pilot Test

Due to lack of time, the pilot test group consisted of a group of field specialists (these specialists actually interact with and instruct learners). Data will be collected from learners in the field, but it will not happen in time for us to incorporate their data in this version.

1. Food thermometer:
   - Larger type for degrees and "Danger Zone"
   - Mercury rising in thermometer not necessary

2. Extend shots of dry goods in grocery store or combine one shot into two.

3. Tone music down on level for older adults wearing hearing aids.

Comments:

Reinforces key safe food handling practices

Colorful

Flow of video excellent, except for dry good shots in grocery store

The food safety video will be useful for our program

| DESIGN AID |

Planning for Evaluation

Individuals Responsible for Following Internal Reviews

Free from obvious errors such as typos or misspellings	
Outcomes, assessments, and activities in alignment	
Outcomes, assessments, and activities appropriate for needs and characteristics of the learners	

Experts Who Will Review Materials

Subject matter experts	
Learner experts	
Learning experts	

Plan for One-on-One Evaluations

Who will participate as learners?	
What will they review?	
Who will conduct the evaluation?	
When is it scheduled?	
Where will it take place?	
Who will schedule learners and location?	

Pilot Test

What group will evaluate materials?	
What will they review?	
Who will conduct the evaluation?	
When is it scheduled?	
Where will it take place?	
Who will schedule learners and location?	

| DESIGN AID |

Key Formative Evaluation Questions

The following list includes several key questions that should be answered during the formative evaluation. The list is by no means comprehensive.

Learner Needs

- Do they like it? Is it readable, appealing, and so on?
- Does learning the materials solve the problem the materials were designed to solve?

Outcomes

- Do the learners achieve the intended outcomes?
- Were any critical skills overlooked?
- Are any outcomes too simple for the learners?
- Was any critical prerequisite overlooked?

Assessments

- Are the test items clear and understandable?
- Do they test the content?
- Do they measure the intended outcomes?

Activities/Strategy

- Is the instruction usable?
- Is it logical?
- Do learners understand it?
- Does it function well?
- Is it motivating?
- Are there adequate opportunities to practice the skills and receive feedback?
- Is it organized?
- Is there adequate learning guidance?
- Are there enough examples?
- Do learners recognize how they can apply the skills?

| DESIGN AID |

Revision Table

Component	Problem	Evidence	Proposed Change

Chapter 7
Collaboration and Communications

Learning Outcomes

- List the steps in the collaborative ASC cycle.
- Identify project team members.
- Outline a project communications plan.
- Select the best medium for communication.
- Conduct effective meetings.
- Use a variety of visioning tools including examples, scenarios, and prototypes.
- Manage the review and revision process.
- Solicit useful feedback on your work.
- Handle out-of-scope requests.
- Control project documents.
- Practice professional etiquette.

Chapter Overview

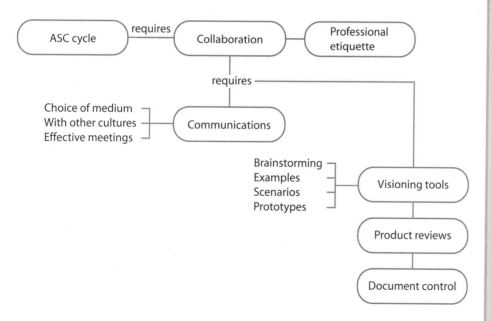

ASC cycle —requires— Collaboration — Professional etiquette

Collaboration —requires—

Choice of medium
With other cultures
Effective meetings — Communications

Brainstorming
Examples
Scenarios
Prototypes — Visioning tools

Product reviews

Document control

Orientation within the Design Process

Few people who practice instructional design can work independently. Teachers who know their content area well and who are competent in the delivery method may be able to design and develop instruction without collaborating with others. For most designers, however, instructional design is a collaborative enterprise, requiring frequent communication among many different kinds of people. Most designers produce their work for a client, rely on the expertise of subject matter experts (SMEs), develop products with a production team, and test materials with learners. They prepare documents, lead meetings, engage in dialogue, interview experts, evaluate learners, advise their colleagues, and give and receive feedback. Their communication and collaboration skills are critical to the success of every project. The topics covered in this chapter apply to *all phases* of the instructional design process.

Collaboration

Consider the case of Jack: When Jack was hired by e-learning developer T3L as an instructional designer, he came with glowing recommendations from his professors. His first assignment was to create Web-based instruction on quilting in cooperation with a nationally known quilting expert, Zelda Coleman. Jack prepared carefully for his first meeting with Zelda. He contacted her well in advance, offering to meet in her studio at her convenience. He wore his best suit and carried his new briefcase. When he arrived for his first meeting with Zelda, he was delighted to find that she already had developed a CD-ROM that provided instruction on quilting. It included high-quality video segments and step-by-step instruction on both the art and the mechanics of quilting. All he would have to do is to repurpose the material for the Web-based course. Jack left the meeting confident that his job was practically done. Zelda felt confident that her course materials were in great hands. However, Zelda's confidence diminished as she waited and waited to hear from Jack. Two months later, in mid-December, Jack finally called. He had a Web site ready for her to review. Although Zelda was a bit surprised that the Web site was finished after only one conversation with Jack, she had provided a very complete set of instructional materials.

She eagerly logged on to review the site. Her initial dismay at the cluttered look of the site grew deeper as she began to explore. The 150 pages of the site were arranged in a linear fashion with multiple choice test questions inserted periodically. The formatting was inconsistent from page to page. Zelda's conversational tone had been replaced with stiff academic prose, a problem compounded by numerous misspellings and typos. So many changes were needed, Zelda didn't know where to begin! But the online publisher had planned a launch for the first of the year, so she buckled down and worked nights and weekends to complete a detailed review. She carefully recorded each error and formatting change. After several weeks of intensive effort, she sent her comments to Jack.

Day after day, she waited to hear from Jack. After all, the Web site was scheduled for a January launch. Finally, she contacted him to ask if he had received her reviews. "Oh, sure," he said, "I knew there were lots of typos. I just wanted to know if I had correctly represented the content." In mid-March, Jack informed her that the site was ready for her review. They wanted to launch it in two weeks. Although Zelda had planned a vacation with her family, she postponed it for three days to review the site. She was pleased to see that the navigation had improved, the multiple choice quizzes had been replaced by activities and checklists, and the tone of the writing was more readable. However, the layout and type styles were still very inconsistent from page to page, and there were still lots of typos. Once again, she provided a detailed list of feedback, nine pages long, and sent it to Jack. Weeks went by with no comment. Finally, she could take it no longer; she contacted his supervisor to express her displeasure. Jack contacted her right away. "Oh sure, I received your feedback. But we have to change the entire layout to comply with new regulations anyway, so I didn't bother to get back to you." The site was finally finished in June. There were three complete versions, not counting the CD-ROM version that Zelda had originally given Jack. The project was extremely late and tremendously over budget. And Jack was in danger of losing his job.

What went wrong? What did Jack do right? What could have been done differently to minimize the unhappy outcome? Unfortunately, Jack's story is true. In this chapter, you'll learn how to avoid similar mistakes.

A crucial part of instructional design is having conversations, collecting information that can inform the development of the instructional materials, and translating that information into design specifications. In previous chapters, you learned about the essential elements of instructional design: learners, outcomes, assessments, activities, and evaluation. You consider each of these essential elements as you spiral through the phases of Define, Design, Demonstrate, Develop, and Deliver. In this chapter, we focus on a variety of tools and processes to gather information and convey it to other team members. We review the collaborative ASC cycle, introduce members of the project team, discuss the components of a communications plan, provide tips on managing meetings, describe some tools for establishing a shared vision among diverse team members, provide recommendations on conducting reviews and controlling documents, and give advice on professional etiquette.

The Collaboration Cycle

As you spiral through the phases of Define, Design, Demonstrate, Develop, and Deliver, you continually refine each of the essential elements of instructional design. But how do you move from one phase to another? How do you gain a progressively deeper understanding of each of the key elements of design? According to the ASC model, as you spiral outward through the phases, you:

- Assemble information and ask questions.
- Synthesize information and solve problems.
- Check and confirm your understanding. (See Figure 7.1.)

Each phase begins with your *asking* for certain information. You have many, many conversations with a variety of people. In those conversations, your role as instructional designer is to derive information that helps to answer the essential questions of design: Who are the learners? What are their needs and characteristics? What do they need to know? How can we tell if they know it? What activities can we provide to increase the probability of these learners gaining this knowledge? You *assemble* documents, observe processes, and use other means to gather the information you need to create tentative solutions.

After you collect information, you retreat to your "design shop," desk, or laptop and begin to make sense of

the information relative to the design process. You and your team attempt to generate tentative *solutions*. Under the best of circumstances, the ideas generated will be elevated to a level that you never could have achieved working in isolation. Through "synergy," the ideas produced by the group will be more than the sum of their parts. As you *synthesize* the information, you begin to create the deliverables of each phase in the design process: the project proposal at the Define phase, the design documents in the Design phase, the production documents and prototype in the Demonstrate phase, the instructional materials in the Develop phase, and the complete instructional package in the Deliver phase.

As you *confirm* your understanding by presenting materials to others for review, you gain additional information that helps move the project from one phase to the next. You negotiate a contract in the Define phase that leads to the Design phase. You gain approval of the Design document, which allows you to begin creating more detailed representations of the instruction in the Demonstrate phase. You review production documents and prototypes with clients, learners, and SMEs in the Demonstrate phase, which allows you to move into the Develop phase. And as you gain approval of the materials developed, you Deliver the materials to your clients and learners.

The Project Team

In your career, you're likely to collaborate with many different people on teams of many different configurations. The specific number and roles of the team members will vary depending on the content (adapted from current material, brand new material), the type of project (e-learning, video, classroom), the scale (one lesson or a full curriculum), and the media components (video, graphics, and so forth) among many other factors. At a minimum, most project teams are likely to include a client, instructional designer, SME, and production specialist (programmer, video producer, and so on) with expertise in the development of the delivery media.

Throughout the process, in your role as instructional designer, you work with each of these specialists. Of course, one person may play several roles. For example, a teacher can be an instructional designer, SME, and media developer for materials used in his class. A college professor may be both the client and the SME for an online course in her subject area. In smaller projects, you may fill all of the necessary roles; in large projects, you may work with an extensive team of experts.

Typically, larger teams are required when the project is extensive, its complexity requires specialized expertise, or the time frame is short. A large team may include numerous people for each major role in an instructional design project. Instructional design team members may include a project manager, researchers, writers, editors, and evaluators, in addition to instructional designers. Client teams may include a variety of people who have an

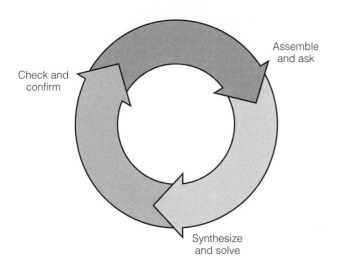

Figure 7.1 *Collaborative ASC cycle.* In the ASC cycle, you ask questions and assemble information, solve problems and synthesize material, and check and confirm your understanding.

interest in the project or who need to eventually accept or "buy into" the project. In addition, the client team should include anyone who has the authority to "sign off" on the project deliverables. SMEs may include one or more individuals who are experts in the content of the lesson. Teams also may include "learner experts" who are knowledgeable about the intended audience of the instruction and "learning experts" (Dick, Carey, & Carey, 2001) who are knowledgeable about instructional strategies and learning theories applicable to the project. Finally, production team members are charged with developing the instructional materials. Depending on the project, the team can include artists, video editors, programmers, and a variety of other production specialists.

Each of these specialists has important contributions to make to the product's success, but as an instructional designer, you're the cornerstone of an instructional design and development project team. You are the person responsible for developing the scope, sequence, content, activities, and assessment, as well as the team's advocate for learners. Your role is crucial to the Define and Design phases of the project, but it's also important during the Demonstrate, Develop, and Deliver phases. As you move past the Define and Design phases, more members of the team join you in working on the project. When there's a large instructional design and development team, the makeup of the team often changes during the project as different skills are needed. As the project evolves, some members leave or reduce their participation while new members join the team.

The Client

Clients come in many varieties! Your client may have initiated the project, or the project may have been assigned to him or her by upper management. She could be an expert in the topic or as unfamiliar with it as you are. Like you, he might also be an instructional designer, or he may have never heard of instructional design. The key factor is that your client is usually the person charged with signing off on the product—making sure it's completed on time, under budget, and at the expected quality level. Be sensitive to the fact that these projects are sometimes large and complex, and can advance or derail a client's career. In many e-learning projects, the budget may exceed six or even seven figures. When the stakes are this high, you have an opportunity to be the reassuring presence in your client's life! Regardless of how you feel about your client, your job is to make him or her happy with the outcome of the project.

The SME

Like clients, SMEs come in many varieties. In the corporate setting, the SME is seldom the client. The SME can be an employee of the client's organization or an independent consultant hired for the project. The client may hire the SME, or you may need to locate one yourself.

SMEs typically are professionals at the top of their fields. We can't emphasize enough: SMEs are busy people. Your project may be one of many for them, and even when they are well intentioned, SMEs can be completely unaware of how dependent you are on their assistance. As a designer, you rely on your SMEs both for content and for reviews of deliverables. The lack of content and timely reviews from an SME can seriously hinder a project. Without the SME's cooperation, the design team may find it difficult to complete their tasks on time and within budget.

The Production Team

Depending on the project, the production team might include a project manager, multimedia developers, graphic artists, art directors, video producers, audio engineers, programmers, writers, and a variety of other specialists. Some of these roles are unique to e-learning while others could be a part of any instructional project. Different companies and industries use different terms for each of these positions, and some individuals may perform several of the roles. For example, a video producer might also be the project manager. Each member of the production team has his or her own responsibilities, and as the instructional designer, it's your job to work with each of them to make sure the components they create reflect the product's instructional requirements.

Communications

You need techniques to communicate effectively with your clients, SMEs, learners, and other members of your project team. Given the pressures of working under deadlines, trying to understand a group of learners, and mastering the complexity of new content, not surprisingly, misunderstandings can occur within project teams. Each team should develop a communications plan that specifies when and how team members will communicate with each other. It doesn't need to be complicated or elaborate, but it needs to clarify how each team member will keep the others informed throughout the entire design and development process. At a minimum, a project communications plan should include the following tasks:

- Provide the project team with a list of contact information, including e-mail and phone numbers, for key staff that will be working on the project.
- Produce a weekly status report with a review of the past week's progress, the schedule for the upcoming week, and a list of any issues that need resolution (see Example 7.1).
- Hold a regularly scheduled conference call or meeting to review the project's progress, especially if clients and team members are in different locations.

Example 7.1 Status Report

Progress

- All tutorials from sections 1 through 38 are final. Yay!
- Revisions to sections 39 and 43 were posted for review on 4/29. Section 49 revisions were posted today.
- Activities 1 and 6 will be posted for review this afternoon. We'll send out an e-mail when this happens.
- Activity 7 revisions were posted yesterday, and we just received one small edit.
- Activity 5 revisions are in production with programming.

Pieces to Come from JTM

- Art credits due on Monday.
- ReadMe will contain JTM contact info.

Decisions

- Jared will get back to us next Wednesday with a decision on whether to license a browser and include it on the CD. We would download the specified browser for the burn.
- Erin is reviewing start.html. The QA team will also review the redirect function on multiple browsers and platforms.
- Erin or reviewers will let us know whether to create a CD disk image for review, and provide instructions in that event.

Tomorrow

- We will post a version containing all content except for activities 1 and 6. This version will not include the Credits pages or ReadMe.

- Build in one complete review and revision cycle for each deliverable.
- Conduct a conference call or meeting to "review the reviews" on each deliverable.
- Follow up each phone call with an e-mail or memo to participants summarizing decisions and action items. It's important to document all decisions with a paper trail.
- Report to your client every time you encounter a problem that you can't solve right away.
- Discuss sensitive issues privately. A large or "public" meeting is never an appropriate forum for a conversation that could embarrass an individual or jeopardize confidential information. If someone else brings up such information, gently but firmly explain that you will follow up with a private, or off-line, conversation.
- Celebrate every important accomplishment, recognizing the work of your peers by name and thanking your client's team when they've made important contributions.

Choice of Medium

As you implement your communication plan, you can modify it depending on your client and colleagues, and the nature of the project itself. You have a variety of communication options including e-mail, phone calls and conference calls, formal letters, and face-to-face meetings. Each form of communication has its advantages and limitations, and you will probably make use of all of them at different times. Communication may include these components:

Verbal cues: the words themselves

Auditory cues: the sound of the words, and voice inflections

Visual cues: nonverbal cues such as facial expressions, eye contact, body position, and hand movements

When fewer cues are available to you, there's a greater chance for misinterpretation. Face-to-face and two-way video conversations include all three sets of cues; phone conversations remove the visual cues; and e-mail and written communications contain only verbal cues. Think carefully about the visual and auditory cues that you want to send and receive. Do you need to demonstrate something? Would there be an advantage to seeing another person to determine how your ideas are being received? Face-to-face negotiations are more effective than phone conversations when you want to make an emotional appeal (Short, 1974). If the strength of your argument is in the facts, then phone calls may be an effective medium. Make sure to use the most appropriate medium, and use it to your best advantage.

E-Mail E-mail has dramatically changed instructional design practice. E-mail, and the ability to exchange documents electronically, has made it possible to work with distant clients and SMEs almost as easily as with people in the same city or even the same building. It's fast, efficient, and, mostly, effective. At one time, not too long ago, designers had to print out bundles of pages and send them by overnight delivery for client reviews. Now, materials can be e-mailed or posted on a secure Web site and downloaded within seconds. You can send and answer messages when it's convenient to do so. You never have to worry about contacting someone at an awkward time, and you can reach many people at once. The disadvantage is that the communication cues conveyed are restricted to the words themselves.

When using e-mail, use it to your advantage:

- Keep it brief. Most people expect e-mail messages to be short, and they expect to be able to respond quickly. When confronted with a long message, some people may postpone replying until later and then forget about it. Others may read only a portion of the message, missing critical information. Avoid this by using attachments when you have a long or formal text document that requires careful reading.

- If you have a number of issues to touch on, send several short messages rather than a longer message containing several ideas. That way, your recipient can respond to each one singly, and the issues won't become confused or overlooked.

- If questions can be responded to easily, use e-mail. If they require a long response, then call.

- Be careful when you have sensitive topics to discuss. If you expect a disagreement or the need for negotiation, pick up the phone or meet in person.

- Watch your language. Sometimes, people say things in e-mail that they would never say directly to another person. In some companies, e-mails are retained indefinitely, even when you think they've been deleted. So, if you are angry, wait until you calm down before you attempt to communicate with anyone.

- Compose your message with care. Copy edit your writing—read and reread your e-mail before you hit the send button to make sure you haven't been careless or said something that could be misinterpreted.

Phone Calls Use the phone when you want to minimize the chance of misunderstandings, deliver good or bad news, or strengthen a relationship. You can use your vocal tone to convey an emotion such as enthusiasm or excitement, and the vocal tones of others help you understand how well your message is being received. Phone calls may be warranted when you need to negotiate something; you can modify your delivery based on how your message is being received. When you need answers to several questions, it's much easier and often quicker for a busy person to answer your questions verbally than in writing. When a complete understanding is necessary, a phone conversation allows you to ask follow-up questions

and get clarification. Finally, some topics are sensitive, and some things should not be put in writing either because they are easier to discuss in a conversation or because they are confidential. If your phone call results in a decision or an action plan, it's a good idea to follow up with an e-mail documenting the conversation.

Formal Documents Although e-mail has become the preferred method of written communications on most projects, don't overlook the advantages of formal or hard-copy documents. These can include letters, proposals, reports, and production documents. Many legal documents, such as contracts, require a signature and need to be produced, and signed, in hard-copy form. Currently, formal documents are treated with more authority than e-mail. Unlike e-mail, a hard-copy signature can be attributed to the writer. Formal documents may be needed when there's a need for permanent records, as is often the case with letters of recommendation or appreciation. Hard copy also is useful when the document requires careful consideration on the part of readers, such as a memorandum used to introduce ideas that will be discussed later or a paper designed to persuade readers to adopt a viewpoint. Finally, when you want to control the presentation carefully, such as with a proposal, hard copies allow you to include special features such as binding, high-quality paper, and lamination.

Face-to-Face Communications Face-to-face communications provide us with a complete set of visual and verbal cues. When you can see the other person, you can judge his or her body language and facial expressions in addition to vocal inflections. You can share visual presentations and build rapport. In general, use face-to-face communications to:

- Build relationships among team members. Face-to-face meetings are especially valuable during the early stages of a project when team members are getting to know each other. If you can afford only one trip to visit with a distant client, do it early in the project. Also, don't overlook the advantages of periodic face-to-face meetings to celebrate achievements.

- Negotiate sensitive issues. The rich visual cues allow you to monitor your recipients' reactions and modify your presentation as needed.

- Present ideas, receive feedback, and discuss issues in depth. Face-to-face communications allow for both formal presentations and spontaneous interactions.

Personal Preferences Each of us has preferred modes of communication. Sometimes, this is due to a disability such as a hearing loss that might cause a person to prefer written communication; other times, it's simply a personal preference. Some people don't want to take the time to read a written document, especially if it's lengthy or complex. Others would much rather read a document than try to process the information aurally. Some people process new ideas by engaging in conversation—they do their thinking "out loud." Others show up at meetings having thoroughly considered an issue, ready to make a decision and move on.

Where feasible, try to work with each person according to her or his preference without sacrificing your productivity in the process. In particular, you should adapt to your client's preferences as much as possible. Take your cue from the manner in which your client contacts you. If the client typically sends e-mails, start using this channel to reach her. If the client often calls from his cell phone, it's probably his preferred channel of communication, so return calls to the cell phone instead of the office phone. Try to be as responsive as possible with your client, but don't allow your work to suffer from frequent interruptions unless you truly don't mind.

Communicating with Other Cultures

In many companies, international teams are part of the work environment. When team members are in different locations, and especially if the time differences are great, communications can be challenging. If you are in Boston and you have team members in London and Kuala Lumpur, e-mail and Web-based communications make the most sense. Scheduling a conference call with team members in all three locations means that someone's going to be participating at a very uncomfortable hour.

Learning to communicate with people from other countries and cultures is increasingly important. Sadly, many people who are native English speakers lack skills in second and third languages, a standard for professionals in most other parts of the world. As those for whom English is not their native language communicate with you in English, try to be sensitive to potential difficulties. Hopefully, they will be equally sensitive and encouraging if you make an effort to speak their language. If your team includes someone who speaks both English and the language of other team members, that person can serve as translator and provide critical support to your team. Sometimes, a tiny nuance in a language can make the entire content take on a completely different meaning. Work to avoid such mistakes by checking and rechecking everyone's intent.

If your work takes you to another country, try to prepare by learning some of its language, customs, and history. Show an interest in the country and its people, and you will likely be rewarded with a memorable experience. Offices and professional work environments around the world are often remarkably similar—there are cubicles everywhere! However, the importance of formalities, courtesies, and hierarchies can vary strikingly from one country to the next. Respect others traditions and values, and concentrate on doing your job well.

Effective Meetings

In your career as an instructional designer, you'll no doubt be involved in numerous meetings, including face-to-face, online, and phone meetings. As you collaborate with the many individuals involved in the design and development of instructional products, you'll initiate

---

Voice of Experience

Learning the Language

Jonathan, a training developer who worked for a global technology company, made frequent trips to a foreign country to deliver training programs. In that country, business hierarchies and protocols are more formal than in the United States. He found that, unlike in the United States, trainees did not participate by asking questions or offering comments in class, despite his concerted efforts to engage them. He was determined to find strategies that would help create a more comfortable environment for the trainees, leading to a more effective learning experience.

He began by asking his company to identify someone who could serve as his liaison. He worked to forge a personal relationship with this "insider." He relied on the insider to help him understand who was enrolled in the class and what the key relationships were, and to determine whether employees were enrolled along with their supervisor. He created activities that allowed groups to generate questions, instead of singling out individuals.

He also used strategies to break down the barrier between "teacher" and "student" by asking the class to teach him words in their language. The trainees became enthusiastic trainers, giving Jonathan feedback and encouragement whenever he'd use his new vocabulary words. Jonathan allowed himself to be seen both as vulnerable and as receptive to and respectful of the culture of the host country.

some meetings and be invited to others. Think for a minute about meetings you've attended in which everything seemed to click. What characteristics mark a successful meeting? The leader is prepared, there is an agenda, discussion is focused and constructive, and everyone participates in the decisions and action plans. The meeting starts and ends on time, and no one dominates the conversation. And the meeting is energizing—participants depart ready to tackle their assignments with enthusiasm and clear purpose. Regardless of who initiates the meeting and who attends, its effectiveness depends on what happens before, during, and after (Rothwell & Kazanas, 1998).

Who Should Attend If you are in a position to determine this, think carefully about whom to invite. Everyone who attends a meeting should be there because they have a contribution to make or because the meeting will affect them. Large meetings are best for disseminating information. For example, gathering everyone in one place for a project kickoff meeting or a weekly staff meeting enables you to distribute information efficiently and effectively. Small meetings create a comfortable environment for discussion, problem solving, and decision making. If there are many people at a meeting, strong personalities are likely to dominate the discussion. To foster effective problem solving in a large team, divide the group into subgroups or schedule several smaller meetings. For reviews or "roll-up-the-sleeves" work sessions, a handful of participants are likely to be more productive than a big crowd.

If you have sensitive information to discuss, restrict attendance to those people who are directly involved and must participate in the discussion. Sensitive topics include personnel issues, proprietary or confidential information, financial or legal issues, speculation about a customer or competitor, and any other information that potentially could harm the reputation of an individual, a company, or a project. Make it clear to the meeting's participants that the information must be kept confidential, and explain the ramifications if there is a breach. Don't make copies of any materials unless necessary, and clearly label all sensitive information as confidential.

Although it's popular to hold group meetings to gain "buy in" to action plans by all stakeholders, there's no point in soliciting opinions if the decision already has been made. Participants in such meetings are likely to feel demoralized and to believe that their contributions are not valued. It would be appropriate to hold a meeting to answer questions about the implications of a decision, but if you simply want to increase stakeholders' sense of ownership in the product, find other ways of gaining buy-in. For example, you can ask key individuals to provide examples to incorporate within the instruction or to use as illustrations of the content.

Before the Meeting When you arrive at a meeting prepared, you demonstrate competence. To establish your credibility, be prepared to say something about your skills and abilities. Some of the participants might not know about instructional design, so be ready to provide a brief description of the process along with an explanation of your role on the project. You might want to prepare a short biography that lists your skills, career highlights, and academic credentials (see Example 7.2).

To project an image of competence and authority during the meeting, you have to look and act the part. You also want to adhere to the "corporate culture" of your client's organization. Corporate culture can affect everything from the way you present your ideas to the way you dress for the meeting. Whether it's a formal or informal culture, you want to mirror your actions to their standards. By making this effort to "fit in," you are sending a signal to your clients that you are "like them." They'll feel more comfortable with you, and you'll be more effective in your work. The comfort of jeans and T-shirts is hard to relinquish, but when you are visiting clients and SMEs, running meetings, and giving presentations, you need to project a polished image and a professional appearance. You needn't don a pinstripe suit, but recognize that in your attire and behavior you can demonstrate respect for those with whom you're meeting and represent your own organization well.

If you need to make a formal presentation, determine the conditions under which you'll be meeting and the number of people who will be in attendance. A computer-based presentation can convey a professional image, but not if there's no power available, no Internet connection to

---

Example 7.2 Brief Bio

Janna Schendle is an instructional designer who oversees Linden's instructional design team, working with clients and the production team to keep everyone focused on developing effective instruction and delivering the right product on time and on budget. She brings 10 years of instructional product development experience including 4 years as director of new media at Sequoia Publishing, where she managed operations and the development of dozens of award-winning titles. She has also been a curriculum specialist and taught middle school history and government. She has a B.A. from Oregon State University and an M.A. in curriculum and instruction from the University of Washington.

a planned Web site link, or so much sunlight streaming in through the windows that no one can see your slides. It's up to you to anticipate and plan for such contingencies. If you're making a formal presentation, rehearse it until your delivery is smooth and effective. If it's a working session, make sure there are pads of paper, white marker boards, and flip charts available to record ideas and plans. It's never wise to rely on an Internet connection—copy the Web content to your hard drive or a CD-ROM.

When you are invited to a meeting, try to find out as much as you can about it: Who will be attending and what is up for discussion? Where will it be held? Get directions to the meeting location to ensure that you arrive on time. If it's a company you are unfamiliar with, research the company's products, its competitors, market trends, legal or political issues, and new technologies.

Suppose you've been selected to produce a videotape for restaurant employees on food safety. The first meeting will include the restaurant manager and a consultant who is an expert on food service safety procedures. To prepare for this meeting, you might check the Food and Drug Administration's Web site, research your local health inspector's regulations, and investigate other food safety programs. You might also conduct a Web search on the expert and review the publications accessible from his site. With this information, you'll be prepared to fully participate in the initial conversation with your client and the food safety expert.

If you are organizing the meeting, state the purpose for it in your initial contact with potential attendees. Be careful to follow the organization's protocol for contacting people. If you've never worked with the organization before, it's often helpful to have someone within it act as a liaison for you. That person can lay the groundwork for the meeting, invite participants, and orient you before it starts. You may want to offer to draft a memo or e-mail for your liaison to send out under his or her name.

If you're in charge of the meeting, prepare an agenda in advance (see Example 7.3). In setting the agenda, think about how long each item will take to cover. For example, you may have seven items on the agenda for a meeting scheduled to last for one hour. That's fine if each item can be covered in 5–10 minutes. However, if it's clear that the meeting will take two hours when only one hour has been allocated, notify participants either in advance or at the start of the meeting. Let the group decide if they want to extend the meeting time or schedule a second meeting. When people have to leave a meeting early, you lose their contributions, and they feel frustrated. Setting the agenda, like many other tasks in the instructional design process, requires thinking things through and planning carefully.

Send review materials a day or so ahead of the scheduled meeting to give participants a chance to examine the materials before getting together to discuss them. If you're requesting information from the participants, make sure

---

Example 7.3 Meeting Agenda

Meeting Agenda for Review Session

Participants: Steve, Robbie, Shania, Gary, Min, Zach

Location: Conference Room 203-B

10:30	Review goals: Final authorization of Module 2 storyboards, assignments, and schedule for Module 3, next meeting date
10:35	Review all comments and suggestions
10:55	Resolve any priority issues from Module 2
11:15	Assignments for Module 3
11:20	Schedule for Module 3
11:25	Next meeting date
11:30	End

---

you convey exactly what you want, why you want it, and how it will be used. Even when you send copies in advance, have handouts ready for participants during the meeting; inevitably, a few people will have forgotten theirs.

During the Meeting When you run the meeting, it's your job to ensure participation by everyone in attendance. Begin with a little small talk to set the participants at ease. Although a lengthy period of small talk is unnecessary, and may be counterproductive to establishing a professional, businesslike atmosphere, a brief exchange allows you to learn more about the values and interests of the participants. This information can be invaluable as you seek to establish rapport and maintain relationships throughout the project.

When you start the business portion of the meeting, state who you are, where you are from, and why you called the meeting. Then reiterate the purpose of the meeting and distribute the agenda. If the discussion strays, you need to determine if the off-task discussion will be beneficial to the group in the long run. Sometimes, deviations from the topic help build rapport in the group or provide insight into how a member feels about an issue. Remain considerate of others' viewpoints and feelings throughout. In some cultures, establishing rapport is the most important order of business in a meeting (Rothwell & Kazanas, 1998). When the discussion shifts to unproductive topics, restate the purpose of the meeting or review the agenda to gently steer people back to the topic at hand.

When speaking, check listeners' body language for cues that they are receiving your message and modify your delivery if reception seems to be faltering. As a speaker, try to vary your presentation to keep your listeners engaged and to prevent mental wandering. The average English-speaking adult can hear 500 words per minute but can utter only about 125 words per minute—so the listener has a lot of "mental spare time" when attending to the speaker's words (Adler & Elmhorst, 1996). The mind tends to wander simply because it "has the time."

Some people have dominant personalities and are comfortable taking the lead in expressing their views. However, if you are running the meeting, you may need to provide opportunities for everyone to express their views—if someone's at the meeting, it's because he or she has a view to contribute or a stake in the outcome. For example, you can go around the room and ask each person to comment, or you can ask each person to write his or her contribution to the discussion on an index card or a flip chart. Then review and refine the comments to arrive at consensus.

When a decision is made, acknowledge those who contributed ideas that were used, and also thank those who contributed ideas that were not used. Most importantly, provide a rationale for your decision. In doing so, you'll educate others as to what factors need to be considered under such circumstances and help them feel that their ideas were heard and considered. When the discussion draws to a close, be sure to thank the participants for attending and for contributing.

Of course, if the meeting has been initiated by another individual, you should let that person set the agenda. You need to listen carefully and determine what type of assistance is required of you. Ask questions as appropriate and take careful notes. The person who initiates the meeting should also decide when the meeting is over. When a meeting is drawing to a close, the initiator should summarize the discussion and clarify the next steps. If no one else summarizes the meeting, you might restate your understanding of the discussion and ask about the next steps.

After the Meeting Once the meeting is over, you should prepare a written summary and list the action items that need attention as a result of the meeting. If you called the meeting, send a copy of the summary to all participants. Even if you were only a participant, you may want to send a copy to the person who called the meeting if decisions were made that affect you.

Conference Calls and Web Meetings

If you're working with clients, SMEs, or team members in different locations, conference calls and Web-based conferencing tools provide an alternative to face-to-face meetings. There isn't a single right way to conduct a phone or Web-based conference, but participants need to agree as a team to follow a set protocol for it to work well. One of the main problems with conference calls is that it can be difficult to hear each person clearly, which makes it hard to concentrate. When participants at one location

Delivering Unpopular News

You may need to schedule a meeting to deliver bad news. For example, you may have to lay people off, make significant project or personnel changes, or inform the team about an unpopular decision. Do this as quickly as possible to prevent the rumors from poisoning the work environment. Wait until you have accurate information, but don't wait until you have every detail.

Be honest, clear, and brief. Acknowledge that this is not good news and that each individual will probably have strong feelings about the situation. After you deliver the news, give people an opportunity to vent their anger, frustration, or confusion. It's important to provide a safe outlet for them to express their emotions. Don't be defensive or reactive; merely listen and empathize with any difficulties they may be experiencing. Make sure you explain and adhere to ground rules such as keeping comments constructive. If the discussion becomes personal or is dominated by one individual, continue it in a one-on-one conversation with that person.

are gathered around a speaker phone in a conference room, the echo within the room can be disconcerting. When possible, use speaker phones specially designed for conference calls, or use directional microphones that minimize distortion. Some telephone companies offer conference services that allow each participant to dial into a central phone number. The auditory quality of these calls tends to be very good compared with other methods of connecting several phones at once.

To make sure the phone or Web conference is effective, follow these strategies:

- Agree on the time well in advance, and notify everyone via e-mail or a preliminary phone call.

- Send the agenda or other print materials in advance so that you don't waste time outlining them during the conference.

- If you are using a conference call service, have each participant announce him- or herself when they enter the call. If you are the moderator, welcome each participant and state the person's location so that each participant has a reference point for all the others.

- If you are not moderating, state your name when you speak—for example, "This is Joey in Orlando. I have a question about the timeline."

- If you are moderating, be aware that it's not over-doing it to restate Joey's question.
- Summarize ideas, decisions, and action items.
- Send a written summary to all participants following the conference.

Visioning Tools

To develop a sense of creativity, camaraderie, and synergy, each team needs to develop a shared vision that gets members working toward the same goal and working together to achieve it. Throughout the instructional design and development process, you reach for the appropriate "design conversation piece" (Tessmer, 1998) to start the visioning process. You may brainstorm ideas, demonstrate specific products to simulate the team's imagination, present or generate scenarios, or show a working prototype. The visioning process is likely to require more than one activity or session. As the team brainstorms ideas, examines products, considers scenarios, and reviews prototypes, you develop an increased understanding of the client's and learners' needs, goals,

and preferences. This refined vision should be incorporated into successive iterations of the product's design.

Brainstorming

When meeting with a group to creatively identify opportunities and solve problems, a structured **brainstorming** session can prove useful. The key is to design a process that allows people to contribute their best ideas. This takes careful planning. Think through what outcomes you expect from the brainstorming session. Your goal is to create an environment that encourages the best contributions from the group.

Schedule a time and location so that the group won't be interrupted. It might be best to hold the session away from the workplace to ensure that the group can work productively. A typical strategy is to devote the first part of the session to generating as many ideas as possible without applying any critical or subjective thinking about the suitability or feasibility of the contributions. In the second part, the group works collectively to begin organizing, analyzing, prioritizing, and discarding ideas. With good facilitation, the group should be able to identify the best ideas and devise an action plan to implement them.

Voice of Experience

Facilitating a Brainstorming Session

An instructional designer was asked to facilitate a strategic planning session for her team. She decided on a brainstorming session to help the group "think out of the box." She scheduled the session for a day when there would be few interruptions. Here is how she structured the half-day program.

When the group convened, she asked everyone to turn off their pagers, wireless e-mail devices, and cell phones, which was very difficult for some people! After a few minutes of introduction and small talk, she distributed pads of sticky notes to each participant. She asked them to take 2–3 minutes to write down every problem they could think of regarding the current situation—one issue per sticky note. Then she asked them to review their notes and give her the one with the single most critical problem.

Next, she read each note out loud, without revealing the name of the person who wrote it, and posted the notes on a flip chart. Once all of the notes were posted, she asked if the group detected themes. As they called out words or phrases that summarized the themes, she wrote the phrases at the top of flip

chart pages. The group collectively categorized the notes, putting each note under the appropriate heading.

Then she asked the group to hand in notes on the next problem. This time, as she read each note, she asked the group where to place it. If there was a new issue, they created a new flip chart page. They continued this process until they had reviewed all of the issues.

Next, they looked for opportunities to organize and collapse the categories, and to prioritize issues. They collapsed 12 categories into 5 and prioritized them based on the cost and immediacy of the issue.

Finally, they used a similar technique to focus on solutions for each of the problems. They tackled the issues one at a time—first writing their ideas on a sticky note, and then handing them in and reading them out loud.

This process elicited the group's best ideas by giving each participant a chance to contribute. Each of the participants left the meeting feeling valued for his or her contributions, both in identifying the problems and in finding appropriate solutions.

Example Products

Sometimes, a client's or SME's vision of instruction may be limited to traditional lectures and readings, simply because that's how they learned the content. Even when a client wants something different, he or she may be unable to imagine or articulate the possibilities due to a lack of familiarity with other modes of instructional delivery. When clients and SMEs lack the experience base or vocabulary to explain what they do and don't want, you can help alleviate this by reviewing examples of other projects with them.

If you already have a portfolio of projects to choose from, you may not need to look far to come up with a variety of examples. If you don't have good examples handy, you need to conduct a search. Ask the group if there are projects they admire that they could share with the group. Put together a wish list of the kinds of examples you're looking for, and circulate the list to colleagues and other production team members. Be specific about the purpose of your request and scrupulous in abiding by any terms required. For example, you might be able to access a Web-based product for a 14-day period, or you might be able to show a CD-ROM if everyone signs a nondisclosure agreement. If you still need more examples, check the Web sites of awards programs, which might give examples of or links to award-winning entries. Many e-learning companies also post demos of their products on their Web sites. A demo may present enough of the program to give the team an understanding of the program's functionality, look and feel, and special features.

Provide structure to the review process. You may want to prepare a handout that guides the team in reviewing and giving feedback on the kinds of products they like and don't like. Demonstrate both good and bad examples of what you hope to accomplish. To help your team understand the difference between a cluttered, confusing screen and a crisp, clear one, show examples of both. Think about the process of educating your team as an instructional design problem—you're helping a diverse group of people develop the critical evaluation skills they'll need to review the product you're developing together.

You may be surprised by what you learn from reviewing examples with your team. They may like things that you don't, or they may have very different ideas about what is most important. The team's comments are valuable, but your client's comments count most. If you and your client don't agree, try to identify why. Is the divergence due to aesthetics, or are there substantive differences in your views of the purpose or functionality of the product? If the disagreement is significant, find some mutually comfortable opportunities to discuss these issues. Explain your viewpoint in as straightforward a presentation as you can muster. Use objective language, focusing on the product and tasks, not the person or opinions. Listen to your client's views, and see if there's a way to compromise. If not, you'll probably have to adapt to your client's view. Above all, do not proceed until you and your client reach some kind of agreement.

Scenarios

One powerful means of moving your client, SME, and design team forward is through an imagined sequence of events, called a **scenario**. In this context, it's usually a story that describes a learner's experience with the instruction. The story might be about a learner who sits down at a computer and works through an online lesson. What does the learner do first? What does she or he see on the screen? How is the material presented? Is it inviting? Understandable? By using descriptive language to create an image of the instruction, scenarios can help the team coalesce around a common vision of the product.

Scenarios can be generated by designers, clients, SMEs, learners, programmers, or any other individual who has an interest in the project. SMEs can be asked to generate scenarios as a means of focusing on the content and the interactions necessary to teach the content. Learners can be asked to imagine an ideal learning situation and to describe the images, patterns of interaction, and anything else that they think might help them learn the content. For example, the learners may want to debate two sides of an issue to solidify the major points of a conflict in their minds; if such interactions are perceived as helpful, you can add similar activities to the instruction. You also might want to solicit scenarios from other team members and stakeholders. Each will have a unique perspective that reveals what he or she thinks is important. Conversely, it's often helpful for designers to create their own scenarios to convey the variety of instructional options to SMEs, clients, learners, and the technical team. Other team members may not be able to come up with a scenario on their own. However, when provided with one, no matter how incomplete or inaccurate, they often react to it in a way that contributes to your understanding of the content, organization, learners, activities, delivery methods, and other issues important to the design and development efforts. Scenarios allow you to describe the user's experience in a format that both inexperienced clients and highly technical team members can understand and find useful.

Throughout the process of designing instruction, you may find that a scenario evolves in a spiral fashion, as you and your client, SME, and project team develop ever greater clarity of vision. You may find it useful to develop progressively more detailed scenarios, with each iteration serving a unique function as you move through the stages of defining, designing, and demonstrating the project. Early in the design process, scenarios can help your client, SME, and design team clarify the goals of the instruction. These "**goal scenarios**" (Tessmer, 1998) are often the catalyst clients need to articulate their goals, expectations, and requirements. After the client and design team reach consensus on the overall approach to the learning environment,

Voice of Experience

Goal Scenarios

A designer was charged with redesigning a university course on child development. The design team met with the course professor several times, but no matter how many times they met, the professor seemed unable to move forward. Although she talked freely about her audience and course philosophy, the design team asked about her course objectives but got nowhere. Finally, in desperation, they proposed several possible scenarios for the course. After reading the options, the professor realized that she was comfortable with some but not others. As they discussed the various alternatives, they began to envision the activities of the class. As they discussed the activities, they began to identify possible outcomes and assessments. Once the professor had a concrete image of what they were all working toward in her mind, she was able to provide the design team with the details they needed to design the course. As they developed and pilot tested the course, it evolved beyond the original vision. But that original scenario gave them a place to start, a concrete image that the professor could both understand and imagine herself living with. The scenarios were the catalyst that enabled her to begin articulating expectations, requirements, desired learning outcomes, and the content for the course. The actual scenarios are included here.

Traditional Course with Support for Self-Regulation

It is commonly accepted that online courses require students to be self-directed in order to succeed in a less structured learning environment. This model will embed strategies to encourage learners to become self-regulated within the online course. Web materials will encourage students to follow a structured self-regulation protocol that includes goal setting and planning, monitoring their learning, and evaluating their progress.

Reflective Model

Due to the nature of adolescents and their focus on self-exploration, this approach will make extensive use of self-reflection and peer evaluation of other's reflections. Assignments for each chapter ask students to compare courses readings with their own experience. Students exchange reflections with a peer.

They read their peer's reflections and are asked to respond to the other's experience (How is it similar or different from yours? Do you know others who had similar experiences?).

Cases/Anchored Instruction Model

In this model, students will analyze the development of children in light of the theories and ideas presented in the course and textbook. Students will participate in activities authentic to the field of child development. Students will analyze video vignettes of child behavior in light of the theories and ideas presented in the textbook. For example, they will observe a child in the lab school and identify the stage of development according to Piaget. Test questions could be similar in format. This case-based model is consistent with anchored instruction, situated learning, cognitive apprenticeship models, and reflective practice.

Self-Study with Small-Group Meetings

This model is an attempt to use face-to-face lecture time for more meaningful interactions with small groups of students, rather than to relay course content that can be gained in some other way. Students say that they like to hear the professor give personal examples within lectures. This model proposes that the class be divided into small groups of 15 students who will meet with the professor four times a semester during "lecture time." The professor will continue to meet with the "class" three times a week as normally scheduled, but instead of meeting with the entire 300 students, will meet with rotating groups of 15 students. Sessions will be devoted to discussing key concepts and assignments. Students will be responsible for acquiring the course content through self-study. Course content will be available online, in computer-based lessons on lab machines, or through CDs purchased by the students.

Activity and Discussion Model

This format has four components: lecture sessions for the entire group of 300 students, "tutorial" sessions for groups of 50 students, small-group work for groups of 5 students, and individual

(continued on page 158)

(continued)

work. Ideas are introduced in the lecture sessions. Following each lecture, students do *individual activities,* discuss and synthesize the conclusions derived from individual work in *small-group sessions,* then meet in *"tutorials"* to share ideas synthesized from small-group work. Tutorials, small-group work, and individual activities cover a two-week span of class time. All students will attend one lecture session each week. Lectures will involve multimedia presentations incorporating video and audio. During each two-week block, students will have a choice of activities to do individually. Students will be randomly assigned to a small group of 5 students. Students will "meet" with their small group (online or in person) to perform and/or discuss individual activities. Small groups will compile insights gained from individual work. Each week, the course professor and teaching assistant will meet with three groups of 50 students. Each group of 50 students will consist of 10 "small groups" of 5 students. Tutorials will involve sharing the insights of the 10 groups of 5 students.

a "**user scenario**" provides elaboration on the ideas touched upon in the goal scenario. A user scenario is created to describe an individual learner's experience with the instruction (see Example 7.4).

The process of generating scenarios is very similar whether you're working with learners, SMEs, clients, or your project team. Using the following process, you can develop goal or user scenarios, depending on where you are in the evolution of the project.

- Present participants with the task that the system will be designed to help accomplish—for example, learning about mitosis (a cell division process).

- Have them imagine and describe the ideal method of performing this task. Encourage them to describe actual interactions and content in detail. For example, if a student says that she would like to watch an animation, ask for more detail. Explain that "watch an animation" doesn't provide much information. Ask, "What would you like to see in this animation? What images and sequence of information? What would you like to do with the information? Do you think practice activities would be useful?"

- Record each of the scenarios. After a sufficient number of scenarios have been generated—and sometimes one is enough—meet with the design team to determine which is the most viable option.

- Perhaps combine the ideas from these sessions into one master scenario that can guide your design work. Where users have competing ideas, you might generate multiple scenarios reflecting these different views and present them for review to your client, SMEs, and other decision makers.

Prototypes

If you've used scenarios and other visioning tools, the team should have arrived at a consensus on the learner's experience by the time you start to develop a prototype. A **prototype** is a "limited scale version" (Tessmer, 1998, p. 89) that explores what works and what doesn't—before you commit resources to full-scale development. The prototype is used to further refine the "instructional goals, learning strategies, and media features for the final product by using the initial prototype as a design conversation piece to stimulate ideas" (Tessmer, 1998, p. 88) for a later version.

Prototypes can take a variety of forms, from paper prototypes to fully functioning versions that represent a "slice" of the finished product. In a sense, when you create storyboards, site maps, and flowcharts, you're creating **paper prototypes.** You're developing enough of the product that a reviewer, or even a learner, can evaluate the product. Some clients, SMEs, and learners may be unable to interpret paper prototypes, and instead need a more concrete product. In these cases, it is useful to develop a mock-up or **rapid prototype** that includes primitive graphics and limited content. For example, you may want to create a rapid prototype using clip art and content placeholders such as "include text here" in order to demonstrate the functionality and interactivity of a Web site (see Figure 7.2). With some clients, it may be more efficient to gain their reactions to a rapid prototype or mock-up before committing time and resources to developing paper prototypes such as storyboards.

Sometimes, in designing a project, you and the team find two or more ideas equally viable. You might be able to create two or more rapid prototypes so that the team can consider the best options. It might be helpful to test both prototypes with learners to see which works best. Be aware that creating multiple prototypes adds time and cost to the project. Instead of building functioning prototypes, you might be able to use scenarios or paper prototypes, or show other products that display different aspects of the designs you're considering. Save multiple working prototypes for those situations in which they're truly necessary.

Once the design team has come to some agreement on the nature of the product, a common approach to

Example 7.4 User Scenario for a Multimedia Product

The learner (user) logs onto the registration screen, which brings up the main menu. It presents four modules. If the user has completed a section already, the section button is grayed out, but it can still be selected. A module is completed when the user has completed each section and the quiz.

The buttons that are available on the main menu, as well as every other screen, are Help, Contact, Quit, Glossary, and Resources. The help section explains how to use the program. Contact provides the vendor's e-mail, phone, and address information. Quit brings up a window asking the user if he or she wants to quit the program; the user has to click yes or no. The resources section lists other materials, Web sites, and organizations on the topic. In the glossary, the user can access 150 words and phrases, get the definitions, and hear the words pronounced in English and Spanish. To use the glossary, the user scrolls a list of the words and selects one from the list. There's also a search function so that the user can type in the first few letters of the word and bring up the definition.

The user selects a module that brings up a submenu screen listing the sections in each module. Most modules have four to six sections. Each module also contains a quiz covering the material in the module. The sections and the quiz are all available on the submenu screen. If the user has completed a section, it is grayed out but can still be selected.

When the user selects a section on the submenu screen, the first content screen comes up. Each section typically begins by presenting a game or puzzle that uses content from the section. The games might include a memory or concentration game, a matching exercise, or a puzzle.

This activity is designed to engage the learner and pique his or her interest in the material. Most sections have 10–15 screens. There is an interactive activity after each chunk of content. A chunk is usually 3–4 screens. The interactive activities are learning checks that pose questions, present checklists, or require writing in a journal (part of the online program) or other activity.

On a content screen, the learner has several navigation tools to determine where he or she is within the program. At the top of the screen is a "breadcrumb" that lists the name of the module, the section, and the title of the current chunk. There is a screen number that tells what screen the user is on and how many screens are in the sequence, such as "Screen 8 of 11." The user can click an arrow to go to the next screen or return to the previous screen. For the user's convenience, the direction buttons appear at both the top right and the lower right of the screen.

On a given content screen, the learner will see a title for the screen, and usually some text and a 2-D still image—either a photograph, diagram, chart, or other image. Some content screens present a short video clip or animation. The user has controls over these sequences and can start, stop, go forward, go back, or restart a clip. Note: Audio controls are set by the user's computer and speakers, not in the online course.

Quizzes are multiple choice in format, and there are 15 items in each module. The quiz items are generated randomly from a pool of items. There are two valid items for each of the 15 objectives. Although learners can start and stop the course at any time, when a learner starts a quiz, he or she must complete it. The quiz scores are stored in the system's database.

developing a prototype is to complete one section or "slice" of the instructional program that has the interface, content, look, and feel of the final program. If a product has 14 sections, the prototype might present one of those 14 sections. However, prototypes are part of the design process, not a complete and accurate representation of the final product. For example, it might be too early in the production cycle to include

a registration and tracking component, a functioning glossary, the search capability, or specific assets such as a graphic or video.

The point of the prototype—whether it takes the form of a rapid prototype mock-up, paper prototype, or working "slice" of the finished product—is to demonstrate enough of the learners' experience that the client, the team, and audience representatives can review it and

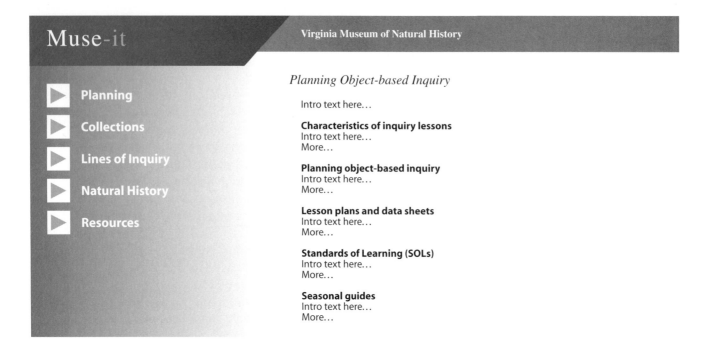

Figure 7.2 *Screen shot from a rapid prototype.* Although it lacks content and graphics, this rapid prototype was used to further discussions about the functionality of the program.

SOURCE: Created by Nathan Pienkowski, 1999. Used with permission.

provide meaningful feedback. Be sure to budget time for various stakeholders, to review the prototypes and for the design team to make the modifications suggested by the reviews. The more you can focus on refining and testing prototypes, the more likely you are to preempt lengthy, drawn-out reviews and revisions after the materials are completed.

Conducting Reviews

Instructional design is an intrinsically iterative process. During a project cycle, you communicate frequently with clients, SMEs, and learners to review and revise materials such as prototypes, storyboards, and design documents. You should build one complete review and revision cycle for each deliverable into your schedule and communications plan. Typically, this will correlate to a deliverable and review cycle in each phase of the design process. You can make the review process productive and efficient by carefully preparing your client and educating your reviewers.

Identifying Key Decision Makers

It's not unusual for your client to assign a team of experts to serve as reviewers. Typically, each person on the review team brings a unique perspective or different knowledge to the project. However, if there's more than one reviewer

for the same content, inevitably they will disagree on something, if not many things. If you try to mediate between these reviewers, you're likely to find yourself in a lose-lose situation. It's time consuming, tricky to negotiate, and a poor use of your time. Before beginning the project, have your client identify the reviewer with sign-off authority. One person on the client's team needs to be charged with making all final decisions. This means that your reviewers must work out any differences before their comments are returned to you.

A corollary of requiring your reviewers to arrive at a consensus is that you must also identify every person who has to approve the work and/or who could bring the project to a halt. You don't want to learn midway through the project that the person whom you understood to be the final authority is, in fact, not. Is someone who is on vacation or on a business trip going to join the team later and want to make changes? Is there a busy manager who could stop in one day to check on the team and wind up sending everyone back to the drawing board?

Talk with your client liaison to identify each person in his or her organization who needs to buy into the project. This information is sensitive, so this should be a private conversation between you and your client—it's not something to discuss in a large meeting. Then, for each person you identify, plan how to approach her or him. If some people can't join the review team because of time or other factors, you need to find a strategy that will satisfy them and still allow you to get your work done efficiently.

For example, if someone is an expert in specific content, find a way to have him review only that content. If a vice president or senior manager wants to check in from time to time, be sure to proactively keep her apprised of the project's progress.

Presenting Your Work to Others

Early in the design process, you should create a review schedule that indicates the dates for you to deliver your materials to the reviewers and for your reviewers to return materials to you (see Example 7.5). The first requirement for a review is to deliver your materials to the reviewers on time. It's hardly fair to expect other people to return reviews in a timely manner if you miss your deadlines! Your reviewers need adequate time to perform their tasks. In general, provide two or three days for minor components, such as several pages of material and five days for significant deliverables such as a complete set of storyboards or a prototype. If you provide too much time, the reviewer might get the impression that it's not a crucial task. When reviewers are tardy, the production team loses its rhythm.

Recognize that clients, learners, and SMEs have other responsibilities in addition to your project, so it's important to make the most effective use of everyone's valuable time. Review each deliverable internally before sending it to others for review. Don't send your client materials that have typos, are formatted poorly, or otherwise represent sloppy work. Each time you present a product to your clients or their representatives, your professionalism is being judged. Following each external review, incorporate changes into the product and, once again, review materials internally before sending them back to the client, SME, or other external decision makers for final approval.

Guiding Reviewers

Reviewers need guidance on how to perform their reviews. If there's no direction, the feedback you receive is likely to be hard to decipher. You'll be frustrated because the information is vague, and your reviewer will be irritated at having to do the task a second time. To prevent this, include a cover letter or explanatory e-mail each time you send work out for review. This document explains what needs to be reviewed and precisely how the reviewer should complete the task.

Your instructions should explain what to focus on, such as scope and sequencing, or content accuracy and completeness, or the creative treatment. Discourage your clients from engaging in word-smiting unless you are presenting text or script that learners will actually see or hear. For some projects, it's helpful to provide a checklist so that reviewers concentrate on everything you've listed and nothing else. It also helps them organize their

Example 7.5 Review Schedule

Deliverable	Design Team Delivers Product	Client and SME Delivers Reviews
Kickoff	March 5	March 5
Design document	March 20	March 27
Brainstorming	March 21	March 21
Content document	March 31	April 7
Prototype storyboard	April 14	April 17
Storyboard, Module 1	April 23	April 28
Storyboard, Module 2	April 30	May 5
Storyboard, Module 3	May 7	May 12
Storyboard, Module 4	May 14	May 19
Prototype	May 15	May 22
Prototype review	May 16	May 16
Storyboard, Module 5	May 21	May 26
Pilot testing	May 26–27	May 26–27
Test review meeting	May 30	May 30
Storyboard final review	June 3	June 3
Revised storyboards	June 13	

thoughts. You can use a two-column table format, with your checklist appearing on the left side and the right column left blank. Your reviewers can enter their comments into the second column (see Example 7.6). This simplifies their work and greatly improves efficiency in making revisions based on their comments.

With high-bandwidth connections, it's becoming standard practice to exchange documents through e-mail attachments or by posting the work on a Web site. For text documents, reviewers can make comments directly in the document. Many teams use the "Tracking" feature in Microsoft Word so that reviewers' comments appear in a distinct color and it's easy to see where changes need to be made. Be sure to label each incoming version so that you don't confuse document versions.

Getting Constructive Feedback

Instructional design requires feedback. In each phase of design, you need to get feedback from clients, SMEs, learners, and team members. However, it can be difficult to read or hear very direct feedback on your work, even

Example 7.6 Excerpt from a Completed Form

Program Review Instructions

Please review the program carefully. Note any items that need to be revised. Focus on text, graphics, and interactions. The structure and interface have been approved, so those are outside the scope of the current review. Comments due back April 7. Thank you for your feedback!

All Skills	Reviewer Comments
Look and feel Functionality Performance	Final screen—How does the learner know the section is done? There needs to be a cue here.
Section 1	
Content screens	No comments!
At-issue activity	Needs a period after last sentence.
Matching activity	If the student gets all the matches correct on the first try and clicks Submit, nothing happens. Could there be some feedback to let the student know he's answered correctly?
Try-it activity	"Try it" screen—Delete the comma in the last sentence.
Section 2	
Content screens	"Work carefully" screen—The instruction to "Do all problems first" doesn't make sense. Change to "Do all problems the first time through."
Try-it activity	Same as above.
Section 3	
Content screens	None!
Example	"Example" screen—The graphic showing "Example" being written out takes too long.
Matching screen	Same as above.

SOURCE: Based on an evaluation conducted by Inez Farrell, 1999. Used with permission.

though that's exactly what you need. Sometimes, the feedback will be highly critical. Don't take it personally when comments read like insults, and don't let them derail your project. Keep your eye on your goal, which is to produce a great product, and try to ignore irritations along the way. Over time, you will develop a thick skin.

Remind reviewers to use constructive words in their feedback, and give them feedback on their feedback. For example, "Wrong," "Not true," and "Sometimes" don't communicate much that's useful. Educate them to give you specific feedback. Ask them to restate incorrect information so it is accurate or to provide examples that they think are effective. Sometimes, asking reviewers to tell a story or provide an example can help them convey to you what's important about a situation, a process, or a concept.

Dealing with Difficult People

Friction among clients, SMEs, and other group members can crop up when individuals disagree about philosophy, values, goals, expectations, and desired results (Rothwell & Kazanas, 1998). A project team consists of people from various backgrounds, and each person has different skills, interests, and experiences. Given that you'll be working closely with each other, it's hardly surprising that disagreements may occur. However, if a reviewer consistently uses insulting or derogatory language, speak privately with your liaison or another person whom you trust, and ask for assistance. Under no circumstances should anyone have to listen to crude or demeaning language. In addition to being completely counterproductive to the project, it's unprofessional and

Winning Over a "Tough Customer"

A novice designer was assigned to work on a project that included highly technical content. The SME was an engineer with decades of experience. At the kickoff meeting, he made clear his skepticism about whether the designer, who was not an engineer, could produce a useful product. For her part, the designer was worried that the SME could undermine her work and, possibly, derail the project. The project required months of work resulting in an interactive program aimed at the client company's engineering customers. The designer was diligent about seeking the engineer's feedback on every deliverable and making sure his concerns were addressed promptly. Over the months of working together, they forged a successful working relationship. The engineer began to appreciate the designer's skills, and she began to feel more confident about her skills. When the production team debuted the completed program for the SME, he turned to the designer and said, "I'd be proud to show this to any of my colleagues."

uncivilized, and may be illegal. Rather than allowing a conflict to polarize and drain the group's energy, recognize differences when they occur and work to get the team back on track.

If you or another team member becomes angry, wait until tempers cool before attempting to communicate. No constructive communication can occur when tempers are flaring. When you have calmed down and believe you can listen to the other person, and when you have thought through what you want to say, make the call or compose the e-mail necessary to address the conflict. Remember, you have to continue working with this person to finish the project. Put aside your personal frustrations, and think in terms of getting the project completed successfully. The best way to prevent angry episodes is to keep everyone posted on all project issues.

Be aware that your presence as an instructional designer can be seen as a threat in some settings, especially if there are trainers or course developers who consider themselves capable of doing the work you've been hired to do. People who resort to insulting language or rude behavior may be masking their insecurity. Others may seem polite but act in a subtly arrogant or condescending man-

ner. Try to determine why a person may be acting in a confrontational or uncooperative manner, and see if there are actions you can take to alleviate the problem. It's often useful to think back to when the friction first appeared. Sometimes, merely being attentive to a difficult person, such as publically acknowledging his or her contribution to the project, will begin to win that individual over. You might also try to find significant tasks for this person to tackle so that he or she is busy contributing to the project. Difficult people are often skilled, knowledgeable individuals who have much to offer your project, and it's worth the effort to make them comfortable and productive.

Handling Irrelevant or Out-of-Scope Requests

Because designing and building a successful program is an iterative process, you can expect to make revisions at key stages of the project. However, requests for changes that aren't within the project scope can impact both the budget and the schedule. Changes made to the project after a deliverable phase, such as changing the look after it has been approved, or changing content after storyboards have been approved, should be considered **out-of-scope (OOS) changes**. In addition, clients sometimes want to add content or a feature that was not in the original plan or design document. This, too, is an OOS request and requires authorization for additional money and time.

Although no one is eager to confront issues such as these, they are not uncommon. To avoid surprises in a worse-case scenario, it's a good idea to include provisions for dealing with OOS requests in project proposals and contracts. (See Example 7.7 for a sample OOS clause.) If the client requests changes because of a mistake or miscommunication by you or your project team, you will probably need to make the changes and absorb the cost. But you can minimize the likelihood of this happening if you work diligently on communicating with your client all along.

As instructional designer, you have a responsibility to keep everyone focused on what is and is not subject to review and revision. Anything that was approved earlier is off limits; if reviewers want to change an approved item, let them know it will involve additional costs and will probably require more time. However, be careful in your language with your client. Don't put her or him off by saying, "No, you can't change that. You already signed off on it." Try saying, "Sure, I can change that. However, I need to point out that since it was approved earlier, any change will require a change order. I'll determine the cost of the change order, and you can decide if you want to authorize me to proceed with the changes." Help your client understand why the request is outside the scope of

Example 7.7 Out-of-Scope Clause for Project Proposal

We recognize that interactive course development is an intrinsically iterative process. To that end, Steppen Learning builds in one complete review and revision cycle for each deliverable phase. Changes made to the project after a deliverable phase (such as changing the look after the look has been approved, or changing content after storyboards have been approved) will be considered out-of-scope changes. We try to minimize these changes by communicating fully and frequently, providing clear directions and explanations of the process throughout the production cycle, and giving reviewers a heads-up prior to delivery of each phase. We know that some errors will escape our best efforts at detection and that some changes will creep into the project. We have accounted for this, though we will immediately contact you if we find there are revisions that cannot be handled within the scope. Please note that Steppen Learning will not initiate work on any OOS work without prior authorization from OakTek's project manager. We also recommend that OakTek escrow a contingency fund (10–15 percent of the total) that could be used to make any changes that would fall into the OOS category.

the project. If these changes will hurt the schedule, such as by throwing an important deadline off, remind the client about the deadline and, again, ask if you should proceed. Your client liaison may decide to fund the expansion or decide against it—the decision to move forward with an OOS or change order is completely up to the client.

Both change orders and OOS requests should be addressed on a case-by-case basis. Some teams use a project manager as the "bad cop" who delivers the difficult news to clients about time and money, allowing the instructional designer to focus on design and act as the "good cop." If you find yourself in an awkward situation between your client and your project manager, you have to support your project manager in getting the program produced within the scope—in the long run, that's the only way to truly serve the client. If you don't have the authority to approve cost or schedule overruns, you have to live within the project's means. Whether you are working with a project manager or not, you can minimize these OOS requests and change orders by communicating fully and frequently, and by providing clear directions and explanations of the process throughout the entire review, revision, and production cycle.

Document Management

Instructional design requires the creation, review, and revision of numerous documents. As you proceed through the review and revision cycle, you need to implement consistent procedures to manage your documents and to ensure the security of your client's information.

Version Control

Most documents initially are released as a first draft. Your reviewers provide feedback on the document, and you make revisions. There may be several more versions of that document, and this is likely to be true of all the documents and files you produce. There's nothing quite so discouraging as completing a great deal of work on a document only to realize it's the wrong version. It's a costly mistake but, fortunately, one that's completely avoidable. The key is to create a file naming convention to identify *each* version and include this identifier within the document, such as in the header or footer, as well as in the file name. Consult with your client and team members to devise a scheme that will work for everyone on the team. Some teams include the most recent date in the file name; others simply number the versions (see Example 7.8). There are software tools that track versions over networks, including the Web. Other procedures to protect against losing documents and confusing versions include creating folders for your project and consistently filing documents in those folders. Discuss the importance of file naming and version control at staff meetings to make sure everyone is aware of these procedures.

As you move through the review and revision cycle, it's critical to document, completely and accurately, all project elements. Maintain a log of when you sent versions out for review and when they were returned. To keep up with the flow of documents and versions, you may want to use a simple ruled pad, an electronic spreadsheet, or a database to track all files throughout the review, revision, and production process. No matter what system you use, your goal is to be able to track information on any specific file at any time.

Example 7.8 File Naming Convention

American Government Project

Anatomy of a production document file name:

s-xx-xx-xx = doc type–unit-section-version

Document types: s = storyboard, v = video script, a = audio script

File	Example
s-03-02-03	Storyboards for Unit 3, section 2, version 3
v-11-07-01	Video script, Unit 11, section 7, version 1
a-04-06-02	Audio script, Unit 4, section 6, version 2

Anatomy of a multimedia file name:

xx-xx-xx.xxx = unit-chapter-screen.file type

File	Example
00-00-00.jpg	Title graphic
01-03-12.txt	Unit 1, section 3, screen 12, text file
12-04-06.wav	Unit 12, section 4, screen 6, audio file

Backup Systems

Losing track of versions is a situation from which you can recover, but losing documents entirely could hurt your project and, in a worst-case scenario, even your career. Computers crash and hard drives fail—always, it seems at the worst possible time—so it's crucial to devise and implement a backup system for your work. You can simply post files to a location on a secure Internet server or e-mail files to a colleague after each major change. If you aren't on a network, you can copy all files and folders to an external hard drive that can be removed from the office each evening. You might want to enlist technical support to help you install and manage a backup program that automatically copies new work and saves these files to a hard drive, tape drive, or other storage device. There are new, relatively inexpensive memory products that can store many megabytes of data and yet fit easily in a pocket or purse. A good system shouldn't be burdensome, but it's critical that you use it consistently!

Computer Viruses

Your work will require sending files to and sharing files with clients and team members. An unfortunate reality of our connected world is that sometimes you'll receive or send computer viruses along with the documents. You must make every effort to maintain the safety and integrity of your work. You should install software to protect your computer from viruses and other breaches. If, despite your best efforts, you do acquire a virus, contact the virus protection software vendor and meticulously follow their recommended procedures for restoring your computer to health. You may need to enlist the services of an expert who repairs infected computers. You want to be sure there aren't other viruses lurking on your hard drive or somewhere on your network. Because you've implemented backup procedures, you shouldn't lose more than a few hours' or a day's worth of work. Notify everyone you have corresponded with, including clients and colleagues, if there is any possibility that you have sent them an infected document.

Confidential Information

It's not unusual to find yourself in a situation in which you need to handle confidential material. Perhaps your client's new product information must be kept under wraps or a defense contractor's content must be kept top secret. If you work with sensitive information, you must take appropriate steps to ensure that your files and documents remain confidential. You, and anyone you work with, can be held legally *and* financially liable for any breaches. Use your computer's security features, such as passwords, and keep hard copies of sensitive materials in locked file cabinets if your office is not secure. When out of the office, keep your laptop and files under your control at all times. When checking your bags and laptop through the security gate at the airport, keep your eyes on them. Don't jeopardize your career through careless behavior—at many companies, security lapses can be grounds for immediate dismissal.

Tracking Time

Most instructional design work is based on the cost of labor, so it's important to maintain a log of your project activities and the time you allocate to each task and each project—no matter how tedious you find it to do so. For projects with hourly billing, you track your hours in order to submit an invoice and be paid for the time you've worked. If you are working on a fixed-cost basis (either a specific amount for the whole project or certain amounts for each deliverable), you want to make sure your estimates are accurate. You can use this data to determine if you made or lost money on the final project, and you should consider this experience when estimating future projects. If you work for a company or institution and develop projects for internal customers, you still need to track your hours. Whether you're asked to or not, keep track of your hours for each project as a means of documenting your services and the value you provide to the organization.

Your company may have detailed procedures in place, or you may need to develop tools and strategies for documenting your work. You can keep a calendar on your desk and jot down the time you worked on a given project each day. If you have a PDA (personal digital assistant), you can make your notes there. Some people maintain a spreadsheet that can add the hours and also calculate other costs such as expenses. Network-based systems allow employees to track work on each project and project managers to view the status of each employee and each project; the data is automatically tied into the company's invoicing systems. No matter what type of system you prefer, find one that works for you, and use it.

In some companies, employees are asked to note project hours in 15-minute increments; in others, they may be rounded off to half or even full hours. Be sure to include the time you spend making phone calls, sending e-mails, attending meetings, and processing documents and materials. You can make your notes before you take lunch and before you leave at the end of the day in order to keep your records accurate. If you attempt to recall your workweek only once each week—say, on Friday afternoons—your records will not be very accurate. At regular intervals throughout the day, make note of what tasks you're work-

ing on and how much time you've allocated to each. The project log will help jog your memory of what you've accomplished when you prepare your weekly status report.

Professional Etiquette

Good communication techniques foster strong interpersonal relationships with your team members and clients. Professional etiquette strengthens your relationships with everyone around you. Successful instructional designers strive to project a friendly, service-oriented, can-do attitude toward customer care. Clients and their representatives should feel welcome to meet with you at any time. You can't overuse words like "please" and "thank you." Unfortunately, too many people have forgotten this childhood lesson. Some people confuse demanding behavior, which is always rude, with assertiveness, which can still be expressed in a polite manner. You may need to take a stand, but always remain respectful of other people and their opinions. Make an effort to be upbeat, friendly, helpful, and appreciative no matter whom you're working with. It's the

Analogy

House

Think for a minute about all the people involved in building a house. There's the architect, the architect's support staff, the builder, carpenters, plumbers, and electricians. There are the people who fill the orders for the building materials, the crew that digs the foundation, the ones who mix the paint colors, and on and on. Each person, at each point in the process, needs to correctly interpret your vision of a "house" in order for your dream home to become a reality. Throughout the home construction process, various tools are used to convey your vision to the many individuals who will make your dream home come true. The architect draws blueprints and constructs mock-ups. You examine paint chips and carpet samples. You talk about and around these concrete visioning tools before resources are committed to constructing your home. These concrete objects are used to convey your ideas to others who contribute to making your vision a reality. For example, paint samples are provided to the one who mixes the paint; the carpenters use the blueprint to frame the house.

Imagine what it would be like to have an initial meeting with an architect and builder and, months later, to receive a phone call informing you that your house is ready. What are the chances that the architect and builder would correctly interpret

your wishes from an initial conversation? How would you feel if you weren't consulted about building materials and color preferences? You would not stand for it. You want to be involved in continual communication with the architect and builder as the ideas progress from a vague vision to a completed structure. You want to be informed about the progress on your home, and you want to participate in decisions as issues arise. Similarly, when you produce an instructional product, your clients want to be kept informed and want to participate in important decisions.

Just as architects and builders use concrete objects to develop and clarify the vision and details for a structure, instructional designers use concrete objects to develop and clarify instructional products. Examples of similar or competing products, scenarios, and prototypes can help the clients, SMEs, and learners articulate their needs. These deliverables guide the production team in turning the instructional vision into a reality. Professional communication requires taking the time to keep others informed and to gather their input. Instructional design is an intrinsically interactive process; effective communication is the key to developing a successful product that meets the needs of learners in a way that is acceptable to clients and SMEs alike.

right way to act, and it also helps you get what you need from the people you work with—your co-workers and clients will notice your behavior and will respond in kind.

Establishing Trust

Your relationships with your clients and team members are built on trust—and trust building starts with the first conversation you have. If you don't know the answer, to something, don't guess or make something up. Explain that you need to check on the answer, and then make sure you get back to your client or team with the correct information. Don't promise anything you can't deliver, and don't agree to something that isn't reasonable or within the project's scope. It can be as simple as promising to phone your client at 10:00 A.M. on Friday and then doing exactly that. If you are late, or if you forget, your client may start to think of you as unreliable or untrustworthy. It can be very hard to rebuild trust when it's been eroded. If you know you're going to have trouble making a call on Friday at 10:00 A.M., tell your client upfront that you are not available. It's much easier for clients and team members to overcome a minor disappointment than broken promises. If you consistently deliver on your promises, your clients and team will view you as reliable and feel that you can be trusted in their projects.

Respecting Other People's Time

Clients, SMEs, and learners usually have other job responsibilities in addition to working on your project. They might have to squeeze project meetings and document reviews in around other pressing tasks. The following suggestions represent just a few of the many ways that you can demonstrate respect for their time; look for additional opportunities as you interact with clients, SMEs, learners, and other project team members.

- Notify them in advance when you expect to send any document or material that will take several hours to review. They may need to make room in their schedules for this task. Follow up on deliveries with a confirmation e-mail or phone call.
- Always acknowledge receipt of information from clients, SMEs, and learners with a note. Nothing is more disturbing than spending long nights reviewing a document, preparing detailed feedback, sending it off to the design team, and hearing nothing in return.

Showing Your Appreciation

You should always express your appreciation for the favors other people do for you. Every time your client fulfills a request, such as sending content or completing a review, be sure to acknowledge that action with a thank you. Anytime you meet with a SME or other expert, follow up with a thank-you note. If an administrative assistant or other support staff person helps you, such as by scheduling a meeting with a busy manager or booking your travel accommodations, take time to thank him or her personally.

Sometimes, an e-mail or phone call is sufficient; other times you need or want to do more to acknowledge someone's special effort or kindness. You can send a handwritten note, which signals that you've taken extra time to acknowledge the individual's contributions to your project. Choose your stationery carefully to project a professional image, or select a card you think the person would like to receive. For example, if your SME is an avid sailor, perhaps you can find a card with a sailing theme. When in doubt, stationary with your company's logo, your initials, or a simple "thank you" is always appropriate.

If someone has been particularly helpful to you, it may be appropriate to make a small gesture of appreciation in the form of a gift. Items that are appropriate in a business setting include a gift certificate, a box of mints, or a small

---

Voice of Experience

Thanking the Client

After completing a French language program for a college publisher, the development team wanted to show their client their appreciation. They donned berets, found little French flags, and gathered in front of images of Paris to take a team photo. When the photo was printed, they had it mounted and framed along with a copy of the CD-ROM package. They sent it to the client, the publisher's project manager, who was delighted with it. She put it up in a prominent position in her office.

Voice of Experience

Thanking the Team

Following completion of a CD-ROM project on criminal justice, the team celebrated with lunch at a favorite restaurant. The project manager recognized the contributions of each team member. Because the topic was criminal justice, she had fun with that theme. She printed certificates with fun citations (such as "handcuff specialist") for each team member. She also handed out tiny toy police figures that sported accessories such as handcuffs, pistols, caps, and billy clubs. The little police toys were a big hit.

DESIGNER'S TOOLKIT

Project Communications Checklist

Developing a Communications Plan

- ❏ List key addresses, phone numbers, e-mail addresses.
- ❏ Make weekly status report.
- ❏ Hold weekly meeting or conference call.
- ❏ Schedule review cycle for each deliverable.
- ❏ Determine best medium for various communications.
- ❏ Implement version control procedures:
  - Establish file naming convention.
  - Develop system for version tracking.
  - Provide dates associated with files.
  - Place files in correct folders.
- ❏ Develop plan for backing up files.
- ❏ Develop plan to safeguard sensitive information:
  - Create password protect files.
  - Use locked filing cabinets.
  - Watch bags while traveling.
- ❏ Have virus detection procedures in place.
- ❏ Implement procedures to report problems.
- ❏ Implement procedures to track time spent on project.

Using Visioning Tools

- ❏ Demonstrate examples of other products.
- ❏ Develop scenarios of use.
- ❏ Develop prototypes.
- ❏ Review prototypes with clients.
- ❏ Review prototypes with learners.

Conducting Reviews

- ❏ Identify key reviewers.
- ❏ Identify one reviewer with sign-off authority.
- ❏ Notify reviewers in advance of arrival of documents needing attention.
- ❏ Implement internal review process prior to external review.
- ❏ Check and double-check work prior to external review.
- ❏ Include header or footer with document title, date, page numbers.
- ❏ Include cover sheet or letter.
- ❏ Provide instructions on how to conduct review.
- ❏ Schedule conversation to review reviews.
- ❏ Acknowledge receipt of information with note.
- ❏ Keep project manager informed of project decisions, issues.
- ❏ Determine how to handle change orders and OOS requests.

Managing Meetings

- ❏ Research the meeting conditions:
  - What can you find out about the organization or in-house unit with which you will be meeting?
  - Who will be in attendance? What do you know about them?
  - Where will the meeting be held? What are the meeting conditions like?
  - What equipment is available? Internet access?
- ❏ Get directions to meeting location.
- ❏ Plan to leave early enough to get there on time.
- ❏ Dress appropriately.
- ❏ Be sensitive to corporate culture of the group with which you are meeting.
- ❏ If you called the meeting, be prepared with agenda. Otherwise, be prepared with questions for which you will seek answers.
- ❏ Have handouts ready for all participants. Where feasible, send electronic copies in advance.
- ❏ Send review materials a day or so ahead of scheduled meetings.
- ❏ Summarize decisions made during the meeting and outline next steps.
- ❏ Followup with memo summarizing decisions, next steps.

Professional Etiquette

- ❏ Adopt polite "can do" attitude.
- ❏ Establish trust.
- ❏ Respect others' time.
- ❏ Show appreciation.

bouquet of flowers. However, don't give a gift if there are any prohibitions designed to forestall even the hint of bribery. This often applies to government employees, who may be prevented from receiving any gifts, even something as small as a cup of coffee. Another simple and inexpensive way to recognize people is to print up certificates or make plaques acknowledging their contributions to the project. No matter how you choose to do so be sure to let people know you appreciate their efforts on your behalf.

Recognize your peers, too, when they've made significant contributions or achieved an important milestone, or at the conclusion of the project. Let each person know what you appreciate about him or her individually. For example, you might tell a graphics artist how pleased you are with illustrations that illuminate the content clearly and effectively. The best news you can give a programmer is that the product worked perfectly—and ran quickly. Don't say things that aren't true, but try to find ways to recognize your team members' contributions.

Summary

Remember Jack from he beginning of the chapter? What did he do wrong? In this chapter, you to learned about the many points at which you should communicate with others during the instructional design process. Jack neglected much of this advice. He didn't keep in touch with Zelda throughout the design and development cycle. There were no status reports, no weekly meetings, and no design documents or prototypes to review. When he presented the product, he gave her no guidance as to what to review. He didn't eliminate typos and formatting errors prior to sending it to her. When she submitted her comments to him, he failed to acknowledge her contributions. And he never met with her to "review the reviews." Although the list of errors goes on, he did a few things right. At the initial meeting, he met with her at her convenience, dressed in a professional manner, and made her feel comfortable with his skills. But after that, though he meant well, he consistently neglected some of the most critical aspects of being an instructional designer.

Instructional design is a collaborative endeavor. In all your interactions with clients, SMEs, team members, and so on, you want them to view you as trustworthy and knowledgeable. Projects can be stressful, so it's particularly important to have a strong rapport in place to get you over any bumps that occur.

References

Adler, R. B., & Elmhorst, J. M. (1996). *Communicating at work: Principles and practices for business and the professions* (5th ed.). New York: McGraw-Hill.

Dick, W., Carey, L., & Carey, J. O. (2001). *The systematic design of instruction* (5th ed.). Needham Heights: MA: Allyn & Bacon.

Rothwell, W., & Kazanas, H. C. (1998). *Mastering the instructional design process* (2nd ed.). San Francisco: Jossey-Bass.

Short, J. S. (1974). Effects of medium of communications on experimental negotiation. *Human Relations, 27*(3), 225–234.

Tessmer, M. (1998). Meeting with the SME to design multimedia exploration systems. *Educational Technology Research and Development, 46*(2), 79–95.

Application

1. The RealworldID Web site includes a case study involving a student of instructional design who has just landed her first contract creating a multimedia product. Due to her failure to gain control of the project, she quickly falls behind and misses her deadline, and the product is a dismal failure. You are asked to identify how the designer may have done things differently and to develop a plan to improve the situation. Visit the RealWorldID Web site to analyze the case online or to print for use during class discussions.

2. In your reflective journal, summarize the key points of this chapter. How are the ideas presented consistent or inconsistent with your beliefs and prior knowledge? Compare your perceptions of the chapter with those of your classmates in group discussions.

3. In Chapter 1, you were encouraged to develop instruction for an actual client. In subsequent chapters, you will be asked to complete the following tasks:

   a. Create a project proposal, present it to your client, and get sign-off (Chapter 8, "Define Phase").

   b. Prepare design documents, present them to your client, and get sign-off (Chapter 9, "Design Phase").

   c. Prepare additional design specifications and prototype instructional materials. Conduct formative evaluation of prototype, collect data on its effectiveness, and develop a report on the results of the prototype and suggested revisions. Review the prototype report and revisions with your client (Chapter 10, "Demonstrate Phase").

   d. Prepare a complete set of instructional materials that are acceptable to the client. Conduct formative evaluation of materials, collect data on their effectiveness, and prepare a report of the formative evaluation results and suggested revisions. Present the completed materials and results of formative evaluation to your client. (Chapter 11, "Develop and Deliver Phases").

   If you have not done so, select a client for whom to design instruction. You may want to consider a peer in the class. A peer will understand your time constraints and should be willing to provide you with the information you need when you need it.

a. Follow the suggestions in this chapter to prepare for your initial meeting with your client.

b. Determine a plan for communicating with your client. Use the Designer's Toolkit on page 168 as a guide to the things you should consider in your plan.

c. Begin to log your hours on this project. Create a weekly "status report" of your work for this class.

d. After meeting with your client, write about the meeting in your reflective journal. How did it go? What went well? What do you think you could have done differently?

4. Role-play a client meeting in your class.

Chapter 8
Define Phase

Chapter Overview

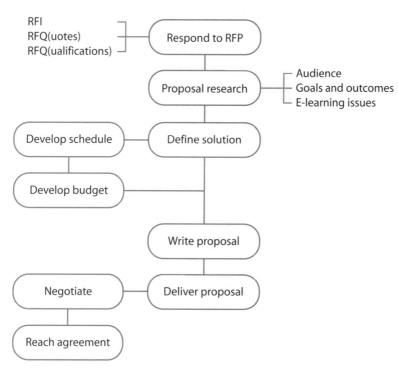

RFI
RFQ(uotes)
RFQ(ualifications)

Respond to RFP

Proposal research
— Audience
— Goals and outcomes
— E-learning issues

Define solution

Develop schedule

Develop budget

Write proposal

Negotiate

Deliver proposal

Reach agreement

Learning Outcomes

- Respond to a "Request for Proposals."

- Conduct research to define a project.

- Develop a project schedule and budget.

- Write a project proposal.

- Present a project proposal to client representatives for review and feedback.

Orientation within the Design Process

Recall that there are five phases in the instructional design process. In each phase, you should consider the five essential elements of learners, outcomes, assessments, activities, and evaluation, adding details and performing tasks as required by the products of each phase. In this chapter, we examine the Define phase of an instructional design project.

In the Define phase, the instructional designer is at the center of the spiral (see Figure 8.1). The designer is just starting to learn about the project in order to develop a proposal. The designer begins the process of describing the learners, outcomes, and assessments; starts thinking about activities and evaluation; and makes a first pass at identifying the production requirements. In each of the subsequent phases, the designer will learn more and more about each of these elements, circling out along the spiral path, until the product is completed.

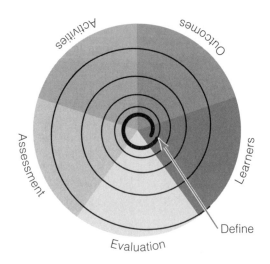

Figure 8.1 *Phases of instructional design.* In this spiral model, the designer begins in the center, the Define phase, and moves out through the phases, acquiring a deeper understanding of each element in each phase.

Tasks of This Phase

Table 8.1 lists the tasks of this phase related to learners, outcomes, assessments, activities, and evaluations.

Table 8.1 Define phase

Learners	• Determine needs that led to project. Gather informal data to confirm or alter needs statement as time allows. • Determine whom client perceives as learners. Gather informal data to confirm characteristics of learners as time allows. • Include statement of needs, as defined by client, in project proposal. • Describe audience and implications for instructional materials in project proposal.
Outcomes	• Determine client's perception of goals during initial correspondence (meetings, phone conversations, written correspondence). • Write preliminary goal statements. • Include goals in proposal document. Present to clients.
Activities	• Discuss content scope and possible instructional activities with client in initial correspondence. • Determine delivery environment and implications for activities. • Conduct limited initial brainstorming with team to develop ideas for activities to pitch to client. • Draft description of instructional activities and content. Present to client in proposal.
Assessments	• Determine what client would like learners to be able to do after this instruction. • Draft tentative ideas for assessments. Present to client in proposal.
Evaluation	• Determine plan for prototype development and learner tryouts. • Draft preliminary formative evaluation plan. Budget for it in proposal. • Educate client as to importance of this stage.

⟳ Define Phase

In this chapter, we begin examining the five phases of the instructional design process. In Chapters 2–6, we discussed the elements of instructional design—the individual components that need to be considered in designing and developing instruction. You learned about determining learner needs and characteristics, identifying instructional goals and outcomes, creating assessments and instructional activities, and planning and conducting evaluations. In Chapter 7, we introduced a variety of interpersonal tools for use in collaborative design efforts. You learned about project communications, visioning tools, the review and revision cycle, and other topics critical to smoothly navigating the real world of instructional design. In the next few chapters, we put it all together. We look at when and where to use the tools and methods you learned about in previous chapters.

We address the issue of designing instruction as a team because that is the most complex situation you'll encounter, but many designers work independently. For example, a teacher might create materials that he will deliver in the classroom. Or a designer might serve as a "one-person shop" in an organization that looks to her to handle all the tasks associated with development and delivery. Although these designers need to address each of the essential elements of instructional design in their work, they may not have to follow each of the steps in each of the phases. In other words, although they must consider learners, goals and outcomes, assessment, activities, and evaluation, they may not need to attend to each of the steps we outline in the phases. But all designers need to understand the instructional design process in order to determine which steps are necessary within the context in which they are working.

Every instructional design project starts with defining the project. Sometimes, you respond to a formal **Request for Proposal, (RFP)**; other times, you define the project through informal conversations with potential clients. In all cases, you develop an initial understanding of the project as you begin to explore the project goals, the audience, and the possible instructional activities that could help the learners and the client meet their instructional needs.

The Define phase cumulates with a project proposal in which you formally present your ideas to the client and establish the conditions under which you'll work together. In the project proposal, you address each of the elements of instructional design—to the extent that you understand them at this point in the project. You also describe the process you will use to communicate and collaborate with your client, subject matter experts (SMEs), and team members. The level of detail contained within the proposal differs depending on the client, but whether developed in response to an RFP or as a memorandum to your supervisor, the project proposal should reflect your understanding of the following topics:

Statement of the problem

Project goals

Audience description

Product description

Delivery environment

Steps you will follow to create the product

The product you will deliver

Project timeline

Costs

Assumptions about the project and potential threats to completion

The handling of out-of-scope requests

Qualifications of team members

The activities and deliverables typically associated with the Define phase are:

- Respond to an RFP.
- Define the project.
- Create a project proposal.
- Present your proposal for review.

⟳ Invitation to Submit a Proposal

Many companies routinely hire specialists to produce instructional projects—for example, to develop a series of workshops, produce an e-learning course, or conduct an evaluation of a training program. A small project might be successfully handled by an individual who works independently, known as a contractor or a freelancer. Large projects may require teams of people to complete them because of the scale of the product, such as writing a complete language arts curriculum for high schoolers. Or the project may require the contributions of various specialists, such as an instructional designer, graphic artist, programmer, and project manager. One of the client company's first tasks is to find a vendor to provide the instructional services. Many companies and organizations believe that they get the best product, price, and service if vendors are required to bid competitively for the work. The client company typically issues an RFP. In this book, **vendor** refers to anyone who provides instructional design and development services for a client, whether that client is another company, a school, a federal agency, an internal department, or a nonprofit group.

The ability to respond to RFPs is a skill that is applicable in many of the settings in which instructional designers find themselves. If you are a potential vendor,

Example 8.1 Memorandum of Understanding

Proposal for Food Safety Video

To:	Jacob Olan, Ph.D., R.D. Outreach Coordinator
Prepared by:	Instructional Design and Development Department
Project Manager:	Sandra LaCruz, Ph.D.

The goal of this project is to address the unique and specific issues of food preparation for the retirement-age individual. These issues deal with the purchasing, handling, storing, and cooking of foods chosen for preparation to prevent food-borne illness within the elderly community. Currently, most educational food preparation resources focus on the young with respect to child care, excluding the unique needs and perspective of this group.

This individual perspective of our 65-and-up community is influenced by financial constraints, age-specific issues and Depression-era experiences. The elderly are usually working within fixed or limited incomes, which may influence food purchases. Many individuals residing in retirement communities are dependent upon provided transportation to stores. Dependence upon transportation may influence decisions regarding food quality or choice of nonperishable over perishable goods. A great number of elderly are widowed, which may leave them with food preparation responsibilities requiring the development of new skills. This community's Depression-era sensibilities tend to influence retirement-age individuals to overstock or try to use food that may no longer be safe to eat.

The food safety video will educate the elderly community on food safety issues specific to their needs. This video will be shown in retirement communities, retiree functions, and groups such as the Kiwanis. The video will model safe food practices while offering consumer information to improve the retirement-age individual's choices regarding food selection and preparation. This information will be communicated by using models representa-tive of the average elderly person with scenarios set in the average kitchen or store. Overall, the video will follow a linear "store to fork" story line.

The ID&D team will contribute to the development of an 8- to 12-minute instructional video. These team contributions will include script development, shooting and editing of video, and evaluation of instructional effectiveness. In-kind donations include video and editing equipment, audio recording equipment, 250 hours of development time, and a VHS master. The client will provide talent, locations, and content.

The ID&D team requests additional funding from the client for:

1. (2) digital tapes @ $25.00 per tape—$50.00
2. Needle drop or music CD charge—$100.00

Project Team

The project team will be coordinated by Dr. Sandra La Cruz. Dr. La Cruz has over 20 years of experience designing and developing multimedia and video materials. She has assembled an excellent team to meet the needs of this project:

- David Carney has a master's degree in instructional technology and an undergraduate degree in film and video broadcasting. He joined the ID&D team 3 years ago with 5 years of prior experience as a video producer.

- Sandra Kerr has a degree in communications and worked for years as an instructional designer before joining the ID&D team as a scriptwriter and instructional designer. Sandra will be responsible for the script and project evaluation.

- Peter Larramore will serve as production assistant. In this role, he will assist in managing media assets, assist with video production, and conduct research as needed.

Please feel free to contact any of us throughout the project.

---

your first step is to convince a potential client that you can provide the needed instructional design and development services. If you are an instructional designer in a company that "outsources" instructional design and development projects, you may be called on to participate in selecting a vendor for the project. **Outsourcing** means hiring another company to provide a specific service to the client company. If your company's primary business is instructional development, such as a company that provides online training courses, the design teams may be organized in small groups or studios. In these companies, the studios might compete for projects just as if they were outside vendors.

In other organizations, instructional designers work with SMEs to compete for grant funding by submitting proposals to external funding agencies or to grant competitions within the organization. For example, academic institutions often have several groups of people competing for the same dollars and require proposals before funding particular projects. Nonprofit organizations sometimes fund instructional projects through grants and foundation support.

Usually, when companies seek vendors to provide services, they issue an RFP. Occasionally, companies issue requests for other preliminary documents such as a Request for Information (RFI), Request for Quote (RFQ), and/or vendor qualifications report. In general, companies that issue RFIs and RFPs tend to be large corporations with well-established procurement procedures, such as Fortune 500 companies.

Some organizations have internal instructional design groups that develop projects for internal clients. Sometimes, the instructional design group is "paid" for its services by charging the work to the client group's budget; this is called a charge-back. Other times, the instructional design and development group may receive organizational funding to create projects as requested by other units within the organization. For example, at some colleges, a faculty member simply requests the services of the institution's faculty support unit when he or she wants to create a Web site, produce a video, or convert a lecture course for distance delivery. The decision to support the project is determined by the unit's operating policies and procedures.

Even though there is no RFP for the internal group, it's still a good idea to prepare a "memorandum of understanding" (MOU) to define the proposed project clearly. In this document, you clarify the nature of the project, the goals, the expected outcomes, and the way in which the work will be completed. This protects both you, as the service provider, and the client from conflicts that can arise from the lack of agreement on key issues. (See Example 8.1 for an MOU for an internal client.)

Request for Proposals

When the client company sends an RFP to a group or individual whom they've identified as having the required skills, the vendor has to decide whether to respond. Why wouldn't a vendor want to respond? A number of factors influence a vendor's decision including the schedule, scope, and client, and the specific skills and experience of the vendor. A vendor may not have the right staff available, or the project too ambitious, or the deadline too soon, or the client difficult to work with, or the scope too small to be worthwhile. Sometimes, the vendor simply doesn't have the time to prepare a bid. Other times, even

DESIGNER'S TOOLKIT

Risk Assessment Considerations

- Is this an instructional problem? Can the product achieve the goals?
- Is the schedule realistic?
- Does the client have sufficient funding?
- Is the client's company stable? Do they pay their bills? Do they pay on time?
- Are SMEs available?
- Is the content collected in an organized form?
- Do we have the right team available?
- Do we have the resources to complete the project?
- Will we have access to actual learners?
- Are there unique hardware or software requirements?
- Will the client's reviewers be available to perform reviews when required?

when there are potential difficulties, a vendor will bid on a project to keep a customer happy or to gain experience with a client, an industry, or a type of project.

The proposal process can be highly time consuming, and, depending on the complexity of the project and the size of the contract, bidders sometimes divert significant resources to the effort. You might have to invest a considerable amount of time in defining a project without any guarantee that you'll be hired for the job. In rare cases, a client will pay a select group of vendors to prepare proposals and then will select the best one. However you develop your proposal, if you win the project your investment in the RFP process pays off because you've already accomplished a large chunk of the planning that will be required to complete the project.

As you can see in Example 8.2, in drafting the RFP, the issuing company has already started defining the project. An RFP might contain these sections:

- Overview—project goals and vendor expectations
- Product requirements—what the product must include
- Deliverables expected from the vendor—what the vendor will develop
- Funding cycle or product due date—the length of time that projects will be funded and/or date by which the funded project is due
- Information needed in the proposal—any specific organization or sections that must be addressed in the proposal
- Dates the proposal is due

Example 8.2 RFP

Request for Proposal to Produce New Lessons for the Online Course to Accompany Jasky's *Physics 2e*

Overview

To enhance and extend its textbooks, Jackson-Smith Publishers (JSP) is creating online lessons within the WebCT learning management system that correspond to textbook chapters. For the second edition of Jasky's *Physics,* JSP seeks a vendor to design and produce 55 interactive lessons, one for each chapter in the text. The vendor will be responsible for all design and production. The vendor will also need to secure the services of a subject matter expert (SME) to devise appropriate interactive lessons. JSP seeks lessons that are pedagogically effective and technically competent, and presentations that offer fresh, creative ideas that will appeal to this textbook's market.

Vendors are asked to review this RFP and notify JSP by July 31 if the company will be submitting a bid. Final proposals are due by close-of-business on August 31 and, due to the constraints of the schedule, there will be no exceptions.

Product Requirements

JSP anticipates that vendors will chose to use Flash for the animations. The minimum platform is Win 98, and the program must also perform well on Windows NT, 2000, and XP, using Microsoft Internet Explorer 5.x as the browser. The program must run over a 56K modem although JSP assumes most users will have broadband access.

Deliverables

JSP expects the vendor to deliver:

- Lesson outlines for each lesson
- Detailed storyboards
- Technical specifications document
- Sample screens presenting interface and look and feel
- Prototype presenting one complete lesson including all global functionality
- Each animation
- Beta version of entire product
- Final version of entire product
- Source code, documentation, and other files

Proposal

The vendor's proposal should include this information:

- Proposed development concepts
- Name and qualifications of SME
- Project team qualifications
- Estimated costs
- Project schedule

The final product must be completed by June 1.

Because the RFP is written from the issuing company's perspective, it usually will reflect the company's concerns about goals, deadlines, and resources. However, it might not reflect a deep understanding of the instructional design and development process or other issues critical to the vendor's instructional designer and project manager. The quality of RFPs varies greatly, which affects how well vendors can define projects. Each vendor who chooses to respond to the RFP becomes involved in the process of further refinement. As a vendor, you often need additional information on the scope of the project in order to develop a detailed proposal. As you submit questions and the client responds, you're collaborating on defining the project. The client's goal is to receive excellent proposals that allow an "apples to apples" comparison of the submissions. The goal for you, as a vendor, is to get a clear understanding of the project in order to submit a proposal that matches the client's needs within parameters that you can meet.

Some clients also provide copies of the criteria they will use to evaluate vendor proposals (see Example 8.3). This is an excellent tool for you to use in preparing a bid because it makes the client's goals and priorities very clear. However, don't let this type of instrument stop you from developing your own questions for the client and your own set of proposed solutions. Don't overlook any criterion that the client identifies as important, but don't limit your responses, either. Remember that the client team is probably not expert in developing this type of product. They may have provided a criteria checklist that doesn't adequately cover the project's requirements.

Request for Information

If a company believes that it doesn't have enough information internally to draft a strong RFP, it may first issue a **Request for Information (RFI)**. Vendors who respond to the RFI pro-

Example 8.3 Proposal Evaluation Form

This is an example of an evaluation tool used by an international company to evaluate proposals for development of an online training project.

Proposal Evaluation Form

	Maximum	Bidder 1	Bidder 2	Bidder 3
1. Business experience	10	09	08	04
2. User scope (functionality)	10	07	09	05
3. System/technical	10	06	09	03
4. Project management	10	09	08	06
5. General/overall	10	06	09	05
Score—Phase I	50	39	43	23
6. Innovation	15	11	13	09
7. Budget	15	09	03	12
8. Cost per module	20	15	08	18
Score—Phase II	50	35	24	39
Total score	100 (max)	74	67	62

vide the client company with the details it needs to prepare a good RFP. These details may include an analysis of the problem, ideas for the best solution, and delivery options, as well as a general estimate of the schedule, budget, and resources required for production. Usually, the vendors who receive an RFI also will receive the RFP. The downside of an RFI, for both parties, is that this adds time and extra work to the project definition process. However, if the RFI yields better proposals in the long run, then the step is certainly worthwhile. As a vendor, you have to balance competing concerns. On the one hand, you don't want to "give your work away" by providing a client with great ideas that the client doesn't pay for. On the other hand, responding to and RFI is an effective way of developing and solidifying a relationship with a client. RFIs typically are only a few pages long and usually do not require much time to prepare. They are equivalent to chatting over coffee to get information before launching a project. Think of the response to the RFI as a briefing paper.

Request for Quotes

A **Request for Quote** (sometimes called an RFQ, but not to be confused with the Request for Qualifications) is a request for a cost estimate for a project that is already defined and perhaps partly developed. Companies issue RFQs when they need to find contractors with specific skill sets or to quickly complete current projects. Because the company has already scoped the project to its satisfaction, it's merely seeking cost information and will make a

decision based on your qualifications and price. Sometimes, the quote will be based on your hourly rates or the rates for each person on your team.

Think carefully about whether you want to respond to an RFQ because the company has made it clear that its decision will be based solely on cost. When a competition is based solely on cost, individual vendors are not valued for their skills and experience. In the business world, this makes your services a "commodity" rather than a value-added service. Think of those products and services you wouldn't dream of paying more for because, in your view, all the offerings are the same. Perhaps you see all gasoline as essentially the same product, so you shop based on price. Now think of products and services you willingly pay more for because you believe that they deliver extra value. Perhaps you're willing to pay a premium price for a cup of coffee at an upscale coffeehouse because of taste, location, or ambience. As an instructional designer in the marketplace, you want your services to be perceived as "value added" rather than as a commodity.

Request for Qualifications

Companies rely on a number of strategies to identify a pool of vendors qualified to produce their projects—and vendors spend much time and energy trying to get the attention of prospective clients. One strategy that some companies use to identify and screen potential vendors is to issue a **Request for Qualifications** (sometimes called an RFQ, but not to be confused with a Request for

Example 8.4 Vendor Qualifications Request

Dear Sir or Madam:

In an effort to increase internal awareness of instructional and multimedia contracting options throughout the Capitol Museum Complex (CMC), we are inviting companies to submit information on their qualifications to be included in the centralized preferred vendor list database. In particular, we are seeking to identify small, disadvantaged, historically underutilized business (HUB) zone, and/or veteran-owned businesses specializing in Web design and multimedia services that have not done business with the CMC in the past two years.

In addition, small businesses that have worked with any CMC museum, gallery, or other institution in the past two years are encouraged to submit capabilities information about their firms, indicating projects completed during the last six months, for the purpose of updating their listing in the preferred list.

CMC reserves the right to employ a panel of experts to select vendors for the list and to identify and group participating vendors by category. To be considered for any of the Web/multimedia categories, vendors must provide no less than three (3) examples (URLs, electronic portfolio examples, etc.) of independent work created in each given category during the last 12-month period. Although each category asks that vendors identify no less than three samples for consideration, the same sample may be used as an example of work that meets the criteria for more than one category. A Web-design project, for instance, may involve database programming and a Flash-animation interaction qualifying in several categories. The next set of categories indicates small businesses as defined by the Small Business Administration (SBA).

Please indicate whether your firm can be designated in any of the following categories:

Web/Multimedia Categories

- Web Design—plumbing/back-end programming/CMS
- Web Design—GUI/front-end design
- Multimedia/CD/DVD kiosk (stand-alone)
- Animation
- Audio/video production
- Streaming media/audio/video
- E-commerce engines

Small-Business Categories

- Small business
- Small disadvantaged business
- Minority-owned business
- Woman-owned business
- Historically underutilized business (HUB) zone
- Veteran-owned business
- Service-disabled, veteran-owned small business

All information obtained for the list will become the property of the CMC. It will serve as a resource base for Web development and multimedia-based projects that may be implemented as funding becomes available. Firms interested in being considered for participation should respond no later than November 1. The CMC reserves the right not to consider late submissions. The CMC will make final selections on or before January 2. E-mail responses are preferred. We invite you to offer your firm for participation in the database, and look forward to increasing the opportunity for doing business with your firm as a result of this outreach initiative.

Sincerely,
The CMC Supplier Diversity Office

Quote). The qualifications document seeks to identify vendors with the skills, experience, and resources to perform the tasks required to produce a specific project or to serve the company in a particular service area, such as instructional design or e-learning development (see Example 8.4).

Of course, vendors don't have the luxury of waiting to be discovered or to receive invitations to submit their qualifications. They actively market their services by participating in trade shows, accepting speaking opportunities, getting involved in professional organizations, engaging in public service, and competing in awards programs. They employ marketing strategies such as mail campaigns, phone calls, e-mail, and press releases. An important emerging marketing tool is the Internet. Search engines make it possible for even very small vendors to get the attention of large corporations. As an instructional designer at a vendor's company, you may be asked to participate in some or all of these marketing activities to promote the capabilities of your organization.

Project Proposal Research

Whether you are responding to a formal RFP or an informal request for assistance in an instructional design and development effort, your first task is to gather as much information as you can about the project. Clients may not know what questions to ask designers and developers, and they might not be able to answer questions you have for them. You need to read and listen carefully and to extract from the documents and conversations information that will help you fill in gaps in your understanding. As an instructional designer, you can provide a critical skill in helping to educate the client about the design and development process and in eliciting the information needed to prepare a successful project proposal. You begin by reviewing relevant documents and talking with others. You want answers to these questions:

- Who will receive the instruction?
- Why does the client want to create this instruction in the first place?
- What goal or mission does the client want it to fulfill?
- When does the client need it?
- Who can help?
- What is the content?

In some cases, your client may have never considered what the learners will think or do after the program. He or she might not have considered how to measure changes in learners' thinking, skill levels, or behavior, or what activities might promote these changes. Your job is to work with your client to find these answers. In defining the project, your questions for your client will be different depending on the learner and the content. Here are questions for three projects: an antismoking program, a training program on pipeline repair for oilfield workers, and a module on Mayan archeological sites. These aren't exhaustive lists, but they suggest the kinds of questions that can help you and the client better define the project.

Antismoking Program

- What does the audience know about this?
- How do they feel about it?
- What are the health hazards this audience should know?
- What are some of the attitudes this audience has now?
- What attitudes should they have when they complete the program?
- What mistakes have other antismoking programs made?
- Have any programs had success in this area?

Pipeline Repair

- What are the specific tasks the learner needs to be able to demonstrate?
- What is the sequence of these tasks?
- Is there specific equipment and parts of equipment that the learner needs to know? Why does he or she need to know this? What does each piece of equipment do?
- Are there any common errors in this procedure? How would you explain this to someone to help that novice avoid making the error?
- Are there any potential hazards?

Mayan Sites

- What are the sites?
- What does the learner need to know about each site?
- What are the dates associated with each site?
- What are the characteristics associated with each time period?
- What do learners get confused about with this material?

Throughout the project, you revisit these same kinds of questions, each time acquiring more detail and a deeper understanding. Often, as a result of such questions, you learn that your prior understanding was incomplete or inaccurate. For example, it might turn out that the original goal, "Develop a course on pipeline repair," isn't quite right. After questioning, you might realize that the real goal is to "teach learners to develop a plan to repair a corroded pipeline." Your initial assumptions may prove to be incorrect, but the only way you can determine this is by starting somewhere. You begin with little information about and little understanding of the project. Slowly, you add to your understanding by gaining more information about the learners, the outcomes, the assessment, and the activities. As you gain additional information and do further research, you may need to make revisions. Nowhere in the instructional design process is the spiral model more evident than in the early stages of defining the project.

Some instructional designers develop a standard set of questions to ask clients, sometimes called a project planner or **project profile**. The project profile shown in the accompanying Designer's Toolkit box is a long document with many questions. Not all of the items will apply to every project, so be sure to modify a list like this so that it is tailored to the specific client and project. A client may feel overwhelmed by such a list—be sensitive to your client's tolerance for attention and detail. You need this information to respond to the RFP, but you also need to work with the client. You can ask these questions in a meeting or phone call, e-mail them, or simply use the profile as a checklist to make sure you haven't overlooked an important issue. The profile may alert the client to issues she hadn't considered or hadn't realized were important. Project profiles also can be useful in helping the client realize that his internal team members haven't

---

DESIGNER'S TOOLKIT

Sample Project Profile

General

- What is the project title?
- What is the purpose of this project?

Background and Market

- Why is this project important to the client company?
- Are there similar products? Are they successful?
- Are there companion products?
- What is the competitive environment? Are there competitive products?
- What are the company's goals for this product?
- Are these goals acceptable to those who must grant project approval?

Schedule

- What is start date for this project?
- What is the final due date for this project?
- Is the content collected in an organized form? If not, what is the content development schedule?
- Are there any obstacles to completion?

Reviews/Approvals

- Has the project team been identified?
- Who will have final approval over each deliverable?

Learners

- Describe the audience: age, occupation, location, language.
- Are they required to take the training?
- Are they motivated?
- Is this completely new material for this audience, or is it an update?
- What is their average level of education? Reading level?
- Have their needs been assessed?
- Are there any special considerations for this audience?

Outcomes and Assessments

- What will users be able to do after using this program?
- Under what conditions should the users be able to do these things?
- How can we determine if users have learned the content?
- Will this course need to satisfy certification or other requirements?
- Is there a pre- or postassessment available?
- Should there be performance tracking?

Content

- What information must be provided? What is the scope and sequence of the presentation?
- If content currently exists, what format is it in?
- What source documents or other materials are available?
- How stable is this content? Is it likely to change?
- Who will serve as the subject matter experts on the project?
- Who will copy edit or proofread the content?
- Are there any issues or obstacles to obtaining content?

Instructional Activities

- How much time will the average user spend with this program?
- Is this program being adapted from existing courseware or other material?
- Is this technical or complex content?
- What kinds of exercises might be included (for example, simple multiple choice, drag and drop, matching, labeling, text entry, simple games such as Hangman, crossword, or Concentration, or complex games)?
- Will there be simulations? If yes, how might they work?
- Should there be feedback on exercises? If yes, what kind?

(continued on page 181)

DESIGNER'S TOOLKIT

(continued)

Delivery Requirements

- How will the program be delivered? Classroom? Video? Via the Web? CD-ROM? Other?

Computer Requirements

- Will any materials be delivered via computer?
- What is the optimum platform for delivery? Minimum?
- What is the minimum connection speed for Web access?
- What platforms and browsers must it support?
- What features or functions must the program include:
  - Registration
  - Tracking
  - Bookmarking
  - Scoring (for tests)
  - Gradebook
  - Reporting functions
  - Glossary
  - Index
  - Documentation
  - PDF files
  - Links to other resources, other sites
- Will it run on a network? If yes, what type?

Visual and Interface Design

- What sort of "look and feel" should the program have (for example, hip, corporate, whimsical, sophisticated)?
- Does it need to coordinate with other products such as textbooks or marketing materials?
- Are there graphics standards such as corporate colors?
- What types of graphics might be included:
  - Simple animations
  - Complex animations
  - Line drawings
  - Graphs and charts
  - Illustrations
  - Schematics
- Who will provide graphics?
- Will images be licensed? If yes, who will handle?
- Will photos be included? If so, who will provide? Who will license?

Audio

- Is there audio? If yes, is there:
  - Narration
  - Music
  - Sound effects
- Who will provide:
  - Talent
  - Scripts
  - Recording
  - Audio editing and digital processing
- If narration needs to be produced, can you estimate how many minutes (for example, 30 seconds per screen, or five minutes for an introduction)?
- For the narrator, do you have a specific voice in mind? Should the talent be male or female?

Video

- Will there be video? If so, how much and for what purpose?
- If video needs to be produced, are there specific:
  - Locations
  - People (such as experts)
  - Events
- If existing footage will be used, what format is it in?
- Are there releases or licenses for existing footage?

---

reached a consensus on the project. If team members don't agree on any of the profile issues, it's critical that they work out a single solution before starting the project. The solution might be to give one person authority to make the final decision, or it may be that with more discussion all parties can come to a mutually agreeable decision.

It's often useful to schedule a visit or conference call in order to talk through some of the project issues or requirements. In addition to providing answers to your questions, a conversation can strengthen your relationship with the client and improve your chances of winning the project. Some companies gather the questions they receive from all vendors, group them, and provide both questions and answers to all interested parties. To streamline the process, some companies schedule a prebid conference in which they review the scope and answer questions from all vendors. At this type of meeting, vendors can see who the competition is—which can be both helpful and unnerving!

You don't want to rely solely on your client for information on the project. Depending on the project and the client, do your own research by searching the Web, reviewing books and periodicals, examining the client's products and marketing materials, interviewing customers, and using any other techniques you can think of to learn more about the company's structure, market, products, and needs. You may find it useful to look at competitor products and companies to better understand the market. You can learn a great deal about a competing company from its Web site, which may contain press releases, mission statements, customer lists, major products or services, and, if it's a publicly traded company, investor information such as the annual report.

Audience Description

A critical part of defining the project involves describing the learners. During this early stage in the instructional design process, you seldom have a chance to collect data from the learners themselves. At this stage, to develop a reasonable description of your audience, given your limited data, you have to listen carefully to your client. Clients often understand the learner well—perhaps not as a learner, but as an employee, or a sales rep, or a customer. Try to elicit from the client as much information about the learners as possible: What do they already know? Are they motivated? What is their average reading level? Will they be receptive to this program? All of this information tells you a great deal about the project and about the production task ahead. You'll spend more time learning about learners in the next phase, Design, but for now you merely want enough information to make good planning decisions about the project. Your goal in the proposal is to briefly describe the audience, relying on your personal knowledge, prior experience, research, and feedback from the client.

Goals and Outcomes

One strategy in working with clients to determine project goals and outcomes is simply to ask them to describe what they hope the final product will look like. Ask the client to describe potential benefits to the company and its customers. What if the client says the outcome of a training program is to "know about company's products"? That's a broad goal, but it doesn't give you enough information to develop a detailed proposal. You need to work with the client to turn that goal into something more specific. Suppose after more questioning you learn that the company expects the trainees to demonstrate 90 percent mastery on the posttest for product training. The content is fully contained in a 100-page manual. You also learn that everyone has had prior training but that

there are some important changes accounting for about 10 percent of the total material. With this additional information, you can have much more confidence in the efficacy of your proposed solution and in your production estimates for the schedule and budget.

Delivery Strategies

You'll have additional questions about the delivery mode, requirements for any media, technical specifications, and usability. The client may have a great deal of experience in producing this type of product and have many of the components in place. Or this may be the client's first project using the proposed delivery system, in which case you and your team will have more questions about the client's short- and long-term needs. Is this first effort going to be part of a series, or is it a sole effort? As the instructional designer on the team, you should take the lead in asking questions regarding the client's plans for developing instruction and meeting the needs of learners. It's important for instructional designers to be involved in defining elements such as interface, usability, and media requirements—too often they're left to graphic artists and programmers. Sometimes, these other team members are not sensitive to the needs of learners and make decisions that can interfere with learning effectiveness.

Perhaps the client needs you to produce computer courseware, or smaller units known as learning objects, that will run on the specific platform the company has invested in to support online course delivery to employees, customers, or students. If your client or organization uses a Learning Management System (LMS) or Learning Content Management System (LCMS), you need to design products that work with those systems. Your technical team can answer your questions about what you can and can't do in a given system. Each system has limitations and quirks, and you have to be aware of them.

When a course is delivered through an LMS, the actual instruction or content is delivered within a shell or window of the LMS. Some systems provide an array of built-in tools and resources that you can use in your instructional programs. Features often included in a basic LMS package are a journal or note-taking tool, online discussions and chat functions, and a variety of practice and feedback, and assessment options. Most LMS programs also collect data from the course on each learner, including performance on activities and tests. Most LCMS systems provide the course developer with relatively easy-to-use tools that allow for screen design, learner interactions, navigation functions, and other standard e-learning features. The benefit of using LCMS templates is that non-technical course developers, including SMEs, can put together effective online courses; the drawback is that the range of features might be limited. They make managing instructional delivery faster, cheaper, and easier. Their power as management tools comes partly at the expense of their utility in making instructional experiences effective for each learner.

⟳ Defining Your Solution

Once you have some answers, you can begin to develop a tentative plan to present to your client for approval, discussion, or modification. The proposal, like all documents you create, will serve to further the discussion and provide a means of clarifying the project goals and moving the group forward to the next stage in the design and development process. The most difficult task in any project is figuring out what it will be: What will it look like? How will it work? When you start the process of developing the solution, you typically are facing a blank sheet of paper or a blank computer screen. Almost everything after this point is an addition to, refinement of, or reaction to this original creation.

Depending on the size and complexity of the project, you may be working alone or with a team. As you learned in Chapter 7, the team might include instructional designers, SMEs, researchers, copy editors, graphic artists, and a project manager. Multimedia teams might include audio and video producers, e-learning teams also have usability specialists, media producers, programmers, and testers. If you are working with a team, you should engage it in brainstorming ideas for the proposal. Even if you are working as a solo practitioner, the brainstorming process can be productive. You may want to develop one or more goal scenarios, in which you present a narrative description of the users' experience with the finished product. As you brainstorm possible scenarios, on your own or with a team, try to develop your ideas in several areas:

- Think about your audience's needs and characteristics. How might their needs and characteristics affect the design of the instruction or their response to it? If it's possible to confirm your perceptions of the audience, even through informal means, you should do so. However, at this point in the process, you may need to make your "best guesses" due to a lack of time or availability of the audience.

- Attempt to clarify and refine the goals and outcomes of the instruction. What type of activities should be provided to enhance the probability of the audience learning these goals and objectives? How will you know they have learned?

There are likely to be easy solutions that you and any of your competitors can readily describe—and an obvious solution may actually be the best one. However, you owe it to yourself and your client to look for solutions that might require thinking "out of the box." You may identify some creative ideas to gain student attention or a clever

yet cost-effective solution to get the most out of a tight budget. Whatever ideas and solutions you generate, be sure to address every issue the client raises.

You might explore the possibility of discussing some ideas with your client before you complete the proposal. Of course, clients may refuse to discuss anything with you until they receive and evaluate all of the proposals. Some organizations, including many government agencies, have strict rules prohibiting reviewers from discussing any aspect of the project with bidders before making the final selection. These policies are designed to prevent unethical procurement practices—respect them, and do not put yourself, your company, or the reviewer at risk. However, if the client is receptive to discussing elements of the project before receiving your proposal, you can suggest an idea or two and gauge his or her reaction. This is an opportunity to identify any key issues you may have missed while you still have time to make changes.

As you develop tentative solutions, keep in mind the alignment among the project outcomes, assessments, and activities (see Example 8.5). Link the proposed activities to learners' needs and characteristics, and consider when and how you'll evaluate the effectiveness of the project. Although your ideas won't be fully developed yet, this level of detail is often what distinguishes you from the competition.

Schedule and Budget

Once you have a plan to address the instructional problem or opportunity, you can begin to develop a schedule and budget.

Schedule   To develop a project schedule or timeline, list the specific tasks and subtasks to be accomplished during the project, arrange them in a logical order, and determine who will be responsible for each. Project planning software can help you organize the project schedule, but you still need to estimate the time allocated to each task. Keep in mind that certain tasks can be performed simultaneously.

Estimating the amount of time to allocate to a particular task can be a very challenging process! As you acquire more experience, your estimates will become more accurate. Remember from Chapter 7 that it's a good idea to maintain a detailed log of project activities and the time you allocate to each task and each project. As you continue to log activities across projects, you'll begin to appreciate how much time each activity takes. And as you become more experienced, you'll become faster at producing each deliverable. In Example 8.6, the estimated hours reflect the time it probably will take for the instructional designer to complete each deliverable, and the dates show when these tasks will occur. The actual time required might be more or less than the estimate, but the estimate

---

Example 8.5 Matrix of Objectives, Activities, and Evaluation

This table is excerpted from a proposal to develop a Web site to promote gender-equitable science teaching. Notice how it identifies the alignment among the outcomes, activities, assessments, and evaluation data.

Outcomes	Web Site Activities	Assessments	Evaluation Data
1. Elementary teachers will demonstrate increased awareness of gender equity issues in science education.	• Provide background information on gender equity issues. • Provide specific gender-equity teaching strategies and instructional activities via Web. • Provide examples of materials—assignments, handouts, reading lists—via Web. • Provide chat room forum for ongoing discussion of gender equity issues via Web. • Provide links to other sites and e-mail contacts for specific info.	• Written assignments requiring classroom observations and reflection via Web • Baseline and follow-up data on teacher and student attitudes toward gender equity in science classrooms • Content analysis of chat room discussions • Content analysis of e-mail messages on issues of gender equity	• Data from assessments • Number of people contacted for additional information via e-mail links • Questionnaire on teachers perception of effectiveness of Web site

---

provides a place to start the budgeting and scheduling process.

The project timeline should include blocks of time for SMEs to perform their tasks and adequate time for the review and revision process. In Example 8.6, reviewers have one week to review and comment on each deliverable. For example, the review dates for the design document could be February 3–7, assuming a one-week review time. In this case, the designer would start work on the next deliverable while the previous one was under review. Some projects build in buffer time so that the designer doesn't spend time on elements that might change based on the review of the preceding deliverable. In other situations, the schedule is so tight that the designer or design team has to juggle several deliverables or phases simultaneously. Unfortunately, juggling is probably the norm on most projects. If you expect extensive revisions, you need to plan time in the schedule so that you can work on revisions without interruption. The project proposal provides an opportunity to educate your client on the tasks involved in the project and the time required for each task.

Many designers begin by simply looking at the time available and allocating that time to the necessary tasks. You may need to schedule tasks to take advantage of an SME's limited availability. Or you may want to have a prototype for an educational product ready to test with learners during the time when they will be studying the topic in class. In other cases, a product release date or the start

---

Example 8.6 Estimating a Project Timeline

Component Design	Hours	Production	Deliver	Review	Revisions
Design document	120	January 13–31	1/31	2/7	2/10
Content document	80	February 3–14	2/14	2/21	2/25
Storyboards	120	February 17–March 7	3/7	3/14	3/18
Prototype	80	March 10–21	3/21	3/28	4/1
Pilot test	40	March 24–28	3/24–3/28	na	na
Program Revisions	20	March 31–April 4	4/4	4/11	4/15

of a semester may be the incentive to complete a project by a certain date. Each project is unique and requires a schedule and review cycle that works for the client, the SMEs, and the designer, and that takes account of any scheduled events or learning requirements and the constraints of the schedule and budget.

Budget Once you have a detailed description of the tasks you plan to accomplish and the approximate time each task will take, you have enough information to begin developing a project budget. You may be working with a project manager or account executive who develops the budgets, or the task may fall to you. Using the project timeline as a basis for your budget, you need to estimate expenses for each phase in the project and the tasks for which your client should be billed. These expenses and tasks will vary depending on whether you are working for a company that is in the business of creating instructional solutions, for an internal client, or on a project with grant funding, and whether you are a freelancer or salaried employee.

For most instructional design projects, much of the cost is simply labor. Begin by listing the key tasks in the process and identifying who is needed to accomplish each task and how long it will take. This will enable you to esti-

mate the cost of personnel. For example, you may need a graphic artist to develop several animations that show the "lock and key" mechanism of neuroreceptors. You and the artist estimate that the job can be done in approximately 50 hours. If the graphic artist works for $30 an hour, you estimate a cost of $1500 for her or his services. And you repeat this process for each task.

Next, you identify the costs associated with each task, including software, supplies, equipment, long-distance phone calls, travel, and shipping. For example, you may need to buy specialized software for the graphic artist that will cost $500. And if your client is in another city or state, the shipping and phone costs can add up quickly. You don't need to be on-site at your client's facility to maintain strong communications. However, it's a good idea to budget for several trips to establish and maintain your working relationship with the client.

You also need to factor in the operating costs of performing the work, called "overhead." Ultimately, your winning bids cover all your expenses, or your company won't be in business for long. Regardless of whether you win or lose a bid, the cost of all bidding and marketing needs to be factored into overhead costs. However, you might not want to make this overhead cost a separate line item in your budget; instead, include it as a percentage of each of the other line items.

Another expense that often needs to be factored into the budget as a percentage of other line items is the project manager. Clients usually don't appreciate the value of strong project management and may object to the cost. But the reality is that good project management ensures that the project is delivered on time and budget to a satisfied client. It's not a place to cut corners.

After you've identified each of your projected expenses, you need to organize the costs in logical categories. Some budgets are organized according to task, such as costs for developing design documents, creating media, and so forth. Other budgets are presented according to accounting line items, such as salaries, office supplies, communications, and so forth. The budget presented in Example 8.7 is based on hourly labor costs. The $85 per hour charged for the instructional designer does not necessarily reflect what the instructional designer is paid. Rather, this is the cost of maintaining the instructional design function. The hourly rate includes not only salary but also benefits, taxes, overhead, hardware and software, training, and support. Many service companies figure that their actual costs are two to three times an employee's salary.

If possible, it is usually in your best interest to present the cost breakdown as a list of tasks or deliverables, not as labor costs. Whereas Example 8.7 presents the budget that was used to determine the costs, Example 8.8 shows the budget that was presented to the client. In this presentation of the budget, the cost for each deliverable is derived from the original budget estimate by adding

---

DESIGNER'S TOOLKIT

Developing a Schedule and Budget

To develop a timeline or schedule:

- List all of the tasks that must be done.
- Determine who will perform each task.
- Estimate approximately how long each task will take.
- Determine which tasks can be done simultaneously.
- Order the tasks in sequence.
- Assign deadlines to each task.

To develop a budget:

- List the key tasks in the process.
- Identify what personnel are needed for each task and how long each person is needed.
- Determine the cost of personnel.
- Identify the costs associated with each task (supplies, equipment, shipping, and so forth).
- Determine the percentage of overhead that will be charged to the project.
- Organize the costs in logical categories.

Example 8.7 Budget Estimate Based on Labor Costs

	Oct.	Nov.	Dec.	Jan.	Total Hours	Rate/Hour	Total
1. Project management	100	80	80	40	300	$100	$30,000
2. Instructional design	160	80	20	16	276	85	23,460
3. Graphics	8	160	20	16	204	75	15,300
4. Video production	0	16	40	6	62	75	4,650
5. Talent	0	0	4	0	4	250	1,000
6. Studio	0	0	5	0	5	125	625
7. Audio	0	0	40	4	44	75	3,300
8. Architecture	16	100	80	40	236	100	23,600
9. Authoring	0	80	160	160	400	75	30,000
10. QA	0	0	20	60	80	75	6,000
11. Total							$137,935

Notes for Budget Line Items

1. *Project management* provides a single point of responsibility and communication for the client, and a single point of leadership for the development team. At a minimum, the manager will provide a weekly status report and will be responsible for deliveries and reviews, and authorizing any changes.
2. *Instructional design* is the development of a high-level design document, storyboards, and the instructional strategies.
3. *Graphics* includes producing a visual design for the product that adheres to the appropriate usability and interactive standards; developing the "look and feel" of the overall design, any style guides, and navigation; and creating the production graphics used throughout the program to support instructional and navigational requirements.
4. *Video production* includes the costs of the video producer, production assistant, and equipment required for filming and postproduction editing.
5. *Talent* is the cost of the narrator for a half day of audio recording.
6. *Studio* is the cost of the recording engineer, facility, and director for the narration recording session.
7. *Audio* costs include the audio producer, editing and digitizing the audio files, and selecting and licensing sounds effects and music.
8. *Architecture* is the high-level programming task of designing, specifying, and developing the technical structure of the program, including building the interface and templates, and supervising the authoring and QA.
9. *Authoring* is the process of loading content and assets into the programmed templates.
10. *QA (quality assurance)* is the processes of testing the program on the delivery platform to ensure that it accurately reflects the specifications in the storyboards, functions correctly, and performs reliability.
11. *Total* is the cost for the delivered product.

together the relevant costs. For example, the Audio figure is the sum of the Talent, Studio, and Audio numbers from the earlier document and a percentage of the project management costs. In this example, the project manager estimated the time she'd need to spend on each deliverable and added those costs to each line item. Only the final column, Total, would be presented to the client. This approach allows the client to focus on the cost of the product and outcomes, not on the price of labor.

Be aware that companies may have specific requirements for how you should present your budget. If your client requires that you report the budget estimate in a

Example 8.8 Budget Based on Deliverables

Deliverable	Cost	Project Manager	Total
1. Design documents	$23,460	$6,316	$29,776
2. Production graphics	15,300	4,668	19,968
3. Video segments	4,650	1,419	6,069
4. Audio	4,925	1,213	6,138
5. Programming	49,600	14,554	64,154
6. QA	6,000	1,831	7,831
7. Total	103,935	30,001	133,936

Notes for Budget Line Items

1. *Design documents* include the instructional design document, content document, storyboards, treatments and scripts for video segments, usability testing, formative evaluation plan, and product training upon delivery.
2. *Production graphics* are the diagrams, photo preparations, illustrations, and 2-D animations required to support content in the program. We estimate there will be 30 diagrams and charts, 15 photographs, 15 illustrations, and 10 simple 2-D animations.
3. *Video* refers to segments shot on location at the client's site with employees of the company. Each of the five segments will include three to four shots and will run a total of 90–120 seconds. The video will be edited, digitized, and prepped for online delivery.
4. *Audio* includes the narration, music, and sounds effects for the audio track. There will be approximately 10 minutes of narration using professional voice talent recorded in a professional recording facility. The audio will be edited, digitized, and prepped for online delivery.
5. *Programming* includes the design and implementation of the product architecture, navigation and interface, administrative component, and content screen templates; the authoring process of loading content into the templates and compiling the program; and supervision of the testing.
6. *QA* (*quality assurance*) is the testing phase. The product is tested on all identified delivery platforms.
7. *Total* is the cost of the delivered product.

particular format, be sure to do exactly as requested. Your proposal could be disqualified if you fail to follow the procedures. As in estimating the project schedule, estimating the project budget becomes easier and more accurate with experience.

Even when you work with an account manager, project manager, or financial officer to develop the budget details, you may need to help your client understand the budget. Focus on the deliverables because they are the items that matter to the client. Provide detailed notes that explain what each line item means, such as what tasks are included. If the budget needs to be trimmed, think about what features or components could be reduced without affecting the instructional integrity of the product. Try to avoid cutting your rates, because you probably won't be able to raise them if you work with that client again.

Regardless of whether you are responsible for devising budgets, you should be familiar with the process. Your designs must adhere to the budget's constraints. For example, if the project budget has allocated $1500 for graphics work based on 50 hours of a graphic artist's time, you need to make sure your instructional strategies do not require 150 hours of graphics work. Because you won't always know the financial implications of your design recommendations, you need to meet regularly with your team to make sure you are keeping within the budget. The budget has implications for your design, and the reverse is true, too.

Example 8.9 Assumptions

Here is an example of assumptions included in a multimedia project proposal.

MediaPlus's production manager and IGF's liaison will:

1. Produce comprehensive functional and production specifications.
2. Develop a workable review process and schedule prior to beginning development.
3. Develop a final fixed-cost budget prior to beginning development, if applicable.
4. Agree on a payment plan based on milestones.

IGF will provide:

1. Clear objectives and expectations for product.
2. Timely delivery of all content, materials, and information.
3. Source content materials.
4. Images and other files as required.
5. Technical requirements and files as required.
6. Access to subject matter experts and reviewers.
7. Timely reviews.
8. A designated liaison or reviewer with final sign-off authorization in cases of conflicting requests.
9. A clear sign-off procedure for each deliverable phase.

Assumptions and Risks

When developing your timeline and budget, you do so under certain assumptions. Often, your schedule and budget may be based on all parties doing their tasks in a timely manner so that resources and personnel are used effectively. It's helpful to outline those assumptions in the project proposal and to address both the factors that pose risks to successful completion and suggested strategies for minimizing those risks (see Example 8.9).

The greatest risks to timely completion of a project are delays in receiving the content, review comments, and conflicting review comments. Thus, you need to reach agreement on a workable review process and schedule. If you openly communicate your assumptions and potential risk factors, you can work with clients to make the adjustments required to better meet their needs.

The Project Proposal

You've gathered all the information you can from your client and other resources. You've generated the best set of possible solutions with your design and development team. Now it's time to actually write the proposal and present it to the client in hopes that you will get the job. The proposal is your opportunity to make sure that your client won't be able to imagine hiring anyone else!

A proposal needs to be more than merely a price list and a few sentences about why the company should select you for the job. It's a sales tool, and, like everything you deliver to clients, it should be executed with great care. As an instructional designer, you're trained to put yourself in learners' shoes in order to create materials that will be effective for them. Think of the proposal in the same way—put yourself in your clients' shoes and try to imagine any concerns and questions they might have. In writing and presenting your proposal, use all of your communication and collaboration skills to convey your understanding of, and vision for, the project. Demonstrate to your clients how you can apply your specialized knowledge and skills to solve their problems in an effective and compelling manner. This is your chance to distinguish yourself from the competition.

Organizing the Proposal

The proposal is your first deliverable to the client. Structure and write it so that it makes sense to her or him. Although in this book we present instructional design as consisting of essential elements (Chapters 2–6) and phases (Chapters 8–11), your client probably won't think of the project in these terms. You simply incorporate information about the elements and design process into your proposal. There isn't a single formula for organizing proposals. If you are responding to an RFP, you often need to organize the proposal according to the sections identified in that document. But whether or not you are responding to an RFP, your proposal should always convey a clear message that you understand the client's needs and are equipped to provide an excellent product. In the proposal, you address each of the elements of the design process, to the extent that you understand them at this point in the project. You demonstrate your knowledge of the project's goals, market, learners, and delivery environment. You also describe the process you use to collaborate with your clients, SMEs, and team members. The sections of the proposal might include an introduction, the project definition, the budget and schedule, and your qualifications. (For examples of proposals, see "Ideas in Action" at the end of this chapter and the RealWorldID Web site.)

Introduction In the introduction, you state the need for the project as you understand it and give an overview of the structure of your proposal. This is your opportunity to show the client that you understand the problems that can be solved or the opportunities that can be gained with this project. Some proposals summarize the content in an executive summary that serves as the introductory section.

Project Definition In the project definition, you show how well you understand the project. This section typically includes a description of the project goals, learners, delivery strategies, content, and components. You may include technical specifications such as platform, compatibility, and screen resolution, and functional requirements such as data tracking features and overall navigation. If the RFP doesn't mandate a particular order, it's a good idea to present the topics in the way that is most effective for making your point. Remember, the purpose of the project proposal is to get the job, so you want to write persuasively.

As you describe the learners and their characteristics, discuss how this knowledge will inform the design of the product. And as you describe the delivery strategies, explain the implications for the instruction. State your initial understanding of the product and the overarching strategy of your program in a way that conveys your vision of and enthusiasm for how the materials will serve the needs of the client and learners.

Treat the proposal as an opportunity to educate your client about the instructional design and development process. Describe the specific strategies you'll use to produce the program, the steps involved in the design and production process, and the review and revision cycle. State exactly what you'll do and what's expected of the client at each step in the process.

Budget and Schedule In this section, you present a timeline of project milestones and the anticipated costs. Provide the dates associated with specific tasks, deliverables, and reviews, and outline a budget, giving a detailed description of each budget item. Because cost estimates and project timelines are based on certain assumptions, you should state those assumptions. You should also explain the factors that pose risks to potential completion of the project on time and under budget.

Clearly state the conditions under which tasks may be considered out of scope and your strategy for handling any OOS requests. You may want to suggest that your client establish a contingency for such requests. A **contingency** is a suggested amount (perhaps 10–15 percent of the total budget) that the client holds in escrow for use in making changes that are outside the scope of the project contract. A contingency represents a useful way to accommodate some of the changes that may occur after design approval.

Your Qualifications In this section, you can further demonstrate why you're the best choice for the job. Include the names of your team members, their biographies, and a brief description of what each team member will contribute to the project. Also list former and current clients, selected projects, and any honors or awards that you may have received. As you describe your qualifications, you want to emphasize your prior successes and potential for future success with this client. This section should appear at the end of the proposal unless the client specifies a different sequence.

Writing the Proposal

If you are writing a proposal with a team, make sure that a single individual has responsibility for crafting the final document. It should read with a single voice and tone. Whether formal or informal, the style should be consistent throughout the proposal and any supporting materials.

Pay rigorous attention to the proposal requirements, and follow the application directions meticulously. Have several people with good editing skills proofread the documents carefully to make sure there are no typos, omissions, factual errors, or odd phrases. Spell checkers are excellent tools, but they can overlook a correctly spelled word that is used incorrectly. For example, the word "timelines," can get turned into "timeliness," with very confusing results! Ensure that all ideas are fully developed and that the writing is persuasive. Check and recheck the schedule dates and the budget numbers to make sure you haven't made a mistake. And be sure you have spelled the client's name correctly!

Proposal Delivery

Once you've written your proposal, you want to present it in a professional manner. Many clients issue RFPs electronically and expect proposals to be delivered the same way. When you send a proposal electronically, make sure the electronic version is just as polished as a printed one.

DESIGNER'S TOOLKIT

Project Proposal Template

Introduction

- Statement of problem
- Overview of document

Project Definition

- Project goals
- Audience description
- Product description
- Delivery strategies
- Steps you will follow
- Product you will deliver

Schedule and Budget

- Project timeline
- Costs
- Descriptions of costs
- Assumptions and risks to completion
- The handling of out-of-scope requests

Qualifications

- Team overview
- Client list and selected projects
- Honors or awards

Include a brief memo in your e-mail thanking the client for the opportunity to submit the proposal, explain that the proposal is attached, and give information on whom to contact for answers to any questions. If you submit the proposal via e-mail, follow up with a phone call letting the client know that the e-mail has been sent. If you are required to deliver or send a hard copy of the proposal, print and bind the document carefully. Include a cover letter that summarizes your approach and provides a brief overview of the proposal contents. Send the package using a professional courier service that will guarantee on-time delivery. Many clients will not accept a proposal that is late. Even if the client will accept a late entry, your image will be clouded by your inability to meet the first project deadline.

If it's possible to deliver the proposal in person, do so. This gives you an opportunity to sit down with the client, present your ideas, and address any questions and concerns on the spot. You may be asked to make a presenta-tion, perhaps to a committee charged with selecting the vendor. Use PowerPoint slides or other visual aids to support your talk. Keep your presentation short and focused, quickly covering the project scope and goals, the production solution, highlights of any creative ideas, and a condensed version of your qualifications. Don't go into detail—instead, let the group ask questions on the details important to them.

Negotiating

Once you've turned in the proposal, the clients may have additional questions for you. This is not unusual, and, though it doesn't mean you have already gotten the proj-ect, it is a good sign. They'd be unlikely to ask questions if you were no longer being considered. If you are their top choice, they may need to engage you in negotiations on the price or schedule or some other factor. Negotiations are common for large or complex projects and often are necessary even for small projects. In these negotiations, you and the client can arrive at a contract that makes sense for both parties.

If you sense that the client wants to have conversa-tions on further defining the project, perhaps resulting in a second or third version of the proposal, you need to decide if it's worth it to continue to offer this service without charge. If your proposal failed to fully define the project scope or explain the rationale for your proposed solution, additional conversations may be needed. A second proposal and round of negotiations is not atypical, especially for a large project. However, if you are still competing against other vendors, and the client is looking for additional versions and concessions, you might want to reconsider pursuing the project. Although you need to provide a project definition within the proposal, asking you to provide additional consulting after you deliver the proposal is not fair, unless the client is willing to pay you for your services.

Reaching Agreement

Once your proposal has been accepted, you need to work with the client to produce a payment schedule, letter of agreement, or contract document detailing all project milestones and deliverables. Payment should be based on generating the mutually agreed-upon deliverables on time. It's not unusual to request a 10- to 20-percent down payment or initiation fee upon signing the contract. You may choose to list these conditions in the project proposal, but you will certainly need to discuss them once you've been awarded the contract.

When you are presented with a contract, read it carefully and don't sign anything you don't understand. Though there is a cost involved, it's usually worthwhile

Analogy

Let's go back to our home-building analogy: The Define phase in the instructional design process is equivalent to finding an architect and a contractor to build your house. What do you need to know about an architect before hiring her? You need to know her qualifications. You need to see her portfolio and some examples of her work. And you need to know what she will charge for designing your dream house. You will probably ask for references; when you talk to those individuals, you should ask about her ability to communicate and deliver on promises. You want to get a sense of how she'd handle your project if she was your architect of choice.

You should expect the architect to present her understanding of your house requirements, as well as her vision for the home and the specifics of how she will accomplish this. From your meetings, conversations with references, and her portfolio, you should be able to determine if this is the right architect for your project. You want to be sure that she shares your "big picture" goals, that she understands what is most

important to you, and that you can work with her. You want to feel reassured that she does what she says she will do, and that you will get the house you want.

As the instructional designer on a project, you are the architect. You consider the client's needs and determine if there is a good match between those needs and your skills and abilities. You ask questions and make sure that you fully understand both the vision (the big picture) and the specific requirements of the project (the details). You compile your ideas into a proposal that presents your understanding of the need and opportunity that this project will fill, your ideas for meeting those needs, and your qualifications. If you're successful, at the end of the Define phase, you'll have a contract to create the instructional product. You wouldn't want to engage an architect to build your house without a contract, would you? The design of an instructional product, like the design of a house, is too long and involved a process to be left to chance alone!

---

to have a lawyer review the contract and explain it to you before you sign it.

Clauses typically inserted in work-for-hire contracts, especially in the publishing and technology sectors, include nondisclosure and noncompete. **Nondisclosure (NDA)** is a standard requirement when working with technology companies; it means that you agree to not reveal any information about the company's products or business plans to any outsiders. Get clarification from your liaison as to what information is considered part of the NDA. The NDA provisions remain in effect regardless of your employment status. **Noncompete** usually is part of an employment agreement; it requires that you not work for a competitive company, or on a competitive product, for a specified length of time, usually for one year after leaving the original company. The noncompete clause does not apply if you are laid off. Contacts also specify strategies for resolving disputes. Often called "cures," these clauses spell out how the parties will resolve any disputes, such as first taking the issue to mediation before contemplating legal proceedings.

Especially when you are working with a client at a large corporation, the initial contract can be strongly one-sided in favor of the issuing party. It is not unusual for a large corporation to propose a contract that allows them to cancel at any time and not have to pay you, but not to afford you the same guarantees! It's worth asking for changes that either provide you with rights or at least minimize the force of the client's rights. For example, if there is an NDA clause, request that your client maintain nondisclosure about your business as well. Also ask that the noncompete clauses apply narrowly to the product and to the market for which you will be producing. If the terms are too broad, they could amount to a restraint of trade, limiting your ability to earn a living. Changes in the payment structure may be easy for the client to accept and ease the burden of up-front costs on the development company. In general, seek modifications that protect both parties.

Even when you're creating materials for a client who is part of your company, it's useful to draft a letter of agreement to be signed by all parties to minimize the potential for misunderstandings (see Example 8.10). The Define phase is merely the beginning of what should be a long and productive relationship among the participants in an instructional design and development project.

Example 8.10 Project Agreement

Food Safety for the Elderly

The attached timeline represents the instructional design and development team's best estimate of the time required to complete the project. Although the ID&D team will make every effort to complete the project by May 7, 1999, the team depends on the client for information and approval at various stages in the process; thus, the timely completion of the project may be jeopardized by:

- Delays in receiving information from the client by the dates indicated in the timeline.

- Changes in the project scope or indecision on project details by the client.

I have read and understand the conditions of this collaborative agreement.

_____   _____

[signature]   [date]

Outreach coordinator

_____   _____

[signature]   [date]

Project manager, Instructional Design and Development

Summary

All instructional design projects, whether initiated in response to an RFP or through other means, begin with a period of project definition. Whether responding to a formal RFP or an informal request for assistance in an instructional design and development effort, this phase should culminate with the development of a project proposal. In it, you describe your understanding of the project goals, audience, intended outcomes, and instructional activities. You outline a schedule that includes an evaluation plan, a budget, and the assumptions upon which the budget and schedule were based. Within the project proposal, you begin to educate the client by including a description of key tasks and project personnel. Finally, you develop a formal agreement with your client in which you outline the expectations of both parties.

The outcome of this phase is a coordinated idea for a project in which the goals, assessments, and activities of the instruction are in alignment and are appropriate for the learners. This idea may change as you build on it throughout the rest of the design and development process, and it definitely will become more fully developed. You refine the idea as you learn more about your audience and their needs. You elaborate on it as you develop storyboards and prototypes. You modify it as you collect data from learner tryouts of the product. But the initial idea originates in this critical Define phase.

On the instructional design process spiral, you're still at the very beginning, in the center of the circle. You have some understanding of the problem, and you're beginning to put together a solution. As you move from working on the proposal to working on the project, you "spiral out,"

building on your understanding of the big picture and your knowledge of the details of the project.

Application

1. The RealWorldID Web site includes a project proposal to develop online courses to provide customers with information on product installation. See if you can locate all of the recommended sections within the proposal. Visit the RealWorldID Web site to analyze the project proposal online or to print for use during class discussions.

2. In your reflective journal, summarize the key points of this chapter. How are the ideas presented consistent or inconsistent with your beliefs and prior knowledge? Compare your perceptions of the chapter with those of your classmates in a group discussion.

3. Identify a client for whom to design instruction. (Consider a classmate—this person will understand your time constraints and be more willing to provide you with the information you need when you need it.) In cooperation with the client, determine an information need or instructional problem. Create a project proposal that includes the following information *to the extent that it is understood.*

   I. Introduction

       A. Statement of the problem

       B. Overview of document

   II. Project definition

       C. Project goals

       D. Audience description

E. Product description

F. Delivery strategies

G. Steps you will follow

H. Product you will deliver

III. Schedule and budget

   I. Project timeline

   J. Costs

   K. Descriptions of costs

   L. Assumptions and risks to completion

   M. The handling of out-of-scope requests

IV. Qualifications

4. As you create your project proposal documents, make entries in your reflective journal. Explain why you made particular design decisions, how your ideas changed over time, and what you judge to be the next steps in the process.

5. Present your project proposal to your client for review and acceptance. Make note of requested modifications. Write about your meeting with the client in your reflective journal. How did it go? What went well? What do you think you could have done differently?

Ideas in Action

In Chapters 8–11, we follow the design of a computer-based training program on the Family and Medical Leave Act (FMLA). In this chapter, we include the project proposal.

Proposal to Produce Online FMLA Training

Introduction

NorLabs is growing and its training needs are increasing. To train all of its eligible employees about the Family and Medical Leave Act (FMLA), the company plans to produce a series of online courses. The first course will be targeted at all full-time employees in the United States, and the second course will be for supervisors.

MC Studio is pleased to present this proposal to produce the initial course for NorLabs. This proposal presents our understanding of the project, our proposed approach for developing it, our projections for the schedule and budget, and our qualifications.

Project Definition

The Family and Medical Leave Act (FMLA) allows eligible employees to take time off from work for their own health needs or to care for a child, spouse, or close family member. All full-time employees of NorLabs are eligible for FMLA, or will become eligible this year. In past years, NorLabs would have delivered this training to its employees in a traditional classroom course, but the company has grown dramatically in recent years, and its training needs are outpacing its ability to deliver classroom-based programs. With this FMLA training program, NorLabs will launch online training as an alternative to classroom- and videoconference-based delivery.

NorLabs envisions an attractive, easy-to-use online course that is engaging for learners and effective. The success of this inaugural online project will determine how the company decides to implement future online courseware. For this course, the company needs

to have all eligible employees trained in the first quarter. The registration and completion data for each employee who takes the course need to be sent to the Human Resources (HR) database.

NorLabs employees range from entry-level technicians to senior executives. Some have been with the company for decades while others have been hired this year. The course needs to be designed so that all employees will find the course interesting and worthwhile. All NorLabs employees have familiarity with computers as the company makes extensive use of computer applications in its internal management and communications systems.

The online training program will provide about 30 minutes of interactive curriculum including text, images, and exercises. A learning management system (LMS) will enroll employees and track performance, including sending completion data to the HR database. The program needs to run in Windows and use the Internet Explorer browser.

MC Studio's Approach

NorLabs is considering several LMS options and will make a selection by October 15. Because all of the systems under consideration are browser-based, we can begin designing the program using templates that will work with any of these systems. In this way, we can begin substantive work now so that NorLabs will not need to make a hasty decision on the LMS.

To guarantee the quality of our work and to deliver on time and on budget, we have developed procedures for producing online courseware. The following table shows the deliverables and tasks associated with producing each deliverable.

Review Process

At the kickoff meeting (which can be a conference call), everyone on the team will meet to introduce themselves and to review the objectives for the program. We'll review the production process, the schedule,

Table 8.2 MC Studio's approach

Deliverable	Tasks
Design document	Detailed description of: • Learning requirements • User requirements • Each group of users (clerks, technicians, sales reps, managers) and their unique user requirements • Definition of each component and function throughout the product and its purpose in the product • Specific instructional outcomes for each module • Description of the functionality required to accomplish specific instructional goals.
Preliminary site map/flowchart	Visual representation of the program's full structure including each function and component.
Technical specifications	Detailed description of: • Delivery platform • Development tools and strategies selected to accomplish the overall product architecture, as well as for each function or component • How the course will integrate with the LMS • File naming convention (coordinated with asset management, media, graphics, and instructional design)
Template guide	From the design document and the technical specs, we will develop: • Refined set of presentation screens and interactive sequences that accommodate the range of online and content requirements for each component • Screen shot (or shots) of the actual template with content • Detailed description of the template's functionality and requirements
Navigation wire frames	Visual representations of the functionality of the overall site, and the functionality and assets presented on each screen in a template and within each functional component.
Style guide for text	Set of conventions, with examples and nonexamples, for text presented anywhere in the product, including a checklist for writers, SMEs, and reviewers.
Style guide for media files	Set of conventions, with examples and nonexamples, for images and media assets presented anywhere in the product, including a checklist for producers and reviewers for each asset type (specifying fonts, headers, etc.).
Style guide for graphics	Set of conventions, with examples and nonexamples, for graphics presented anywhere in the product, including a checklist for artists (specifying palette, fonts, headers, line sizes, captioning, etc.).
Storyboards	Product's blueprint specifying what will appear on each screen and how the learner will interact with the program. This includes text, graphics, exercises, and navigation requirements.
Design comps	Cohesive visual design for a complex set of components, within the context of the Tab/Nav system that is currently being refined. These screens will be nonfunctional graphics that display the visual design for the overall site and for each component or template. We will produce and submit three to four comps for NorLabs to review.
Architecture	Programming required to build the shell and the templates as specified in the technical requirements and template guide.

(continued)

Table 8.2 *(continued)*

Deliverable	Tasks
Prototype	A complete section of a module including main menu, module and screen navigation, and a mock-up of the management system.
Formative evaluation	We will test the prototype with representatives of various NorLabs departments. We will use this feedback to revise the program prior to full production. We will also test for usability.
Production	This includes: • Completing all instructional design (storyboards) • Completing graphics and media selection • Loading content into templates
QA	Testing and refining the product's accuracy and performance on all delivery platforms.
Implement and deploy stages	MC Studio staff will be at NorLabs' facility during installation and deployment to ensure a smooth launch. We will also provide all source materials to NorLabs; conduct training as required; conduct a postmortem session to evaluate the production process.

the deliverables, and the review process. We recognize that you have other responsibilities in addition to this project, and we want to make the most effective use of everyone's limited time. We can provide most materials to you via e-mail, and you can provide specific feedback via e-mail to us. This works quite well in most cases. Design documents and text in general is easy to manage through e-mail, and your comments can be recorded using Word's "Track changes" selection under the Tools menu. Art and graphics files can be posted in a secure area of our Web site for you to access via a password. In addition to any planned meetings, you are welcome at MC Studio at any time. We will send review materials a day or so ahead of time (or whatever time frame you require) to give reviewers a chance to examine the material before conferencing to discuss it.

Standards

We will work with you to identify any standards that should be incorporated into the program. We will generate a standards list for all staff to follow including preferred nomenclature, file naming conventions, abbreviations, standards for numerical display, grammar, alphanumeric, and any other conventions specified by you and your reviewers and content experts.

Schedule and Budget

We project a 16- to 20-week project cycle for this first online course. We expect that we will be able to produce subsequent courses in 6–8 weeks. In order to have the course up and running in January, we propose this schedule:

Week	Date	Task/Deliverable
1	Aug 18	Kickoff meeting
2	Sept 8	Design document, site map, technical requirements
3	Sept 22	Storyboards for prototype, design comps
4	Oct 6	Prototype, formative evaluation
5	Oct 20	Templates completed
6	Oct 31	Storyboards completed
7	Nov 14	Graphics, media production completed
8	Dec 8	Beta testing and quality assurance (QA)
9	Dec 22	Delivery
10	Jan 2	Launch

This schedule is based on our understanding of the project requirements. It assumes that we'll receive content in a timely manner and that your reviewers will be available at key phases. Reviews will begin with the delivery of each item, and reviewers will have one week to complete and turn in their comments. There is one review cycle per deliverable. Additional changes will need to be authorized by NorLabs and will be billed separately.

Assumptions

MC Studio will:

1. Assemble a dedicated, experienced team that can produce within the deadlines you've specified.
2. Provide full and complete project status information on a regular and ongoing basis.
3. Maintain the security of project files and confidentiality of NorLabs intellectual property.
4. Notify you immediately of any issue that could threaten the schedule or budget.

NorLabs and MC Studio will:

1. At the outset, the MC Studios production manager and your liaison will produce comprehensive functional and production specifications.
2. Develop a workable review process and schedule prior to beginning development.
3. Agree on a payment plan based on milestones.

NorLabs will provide:

1. Clear expectations for product.
2. Timely delivery of all content, materials, and information.
3. Source content materials.
4. Photographs as required.
5. Technical requirements and files as required.
6. Access to subject matter experts and reviewers.
7. Timely reviews.
8. A designated liaison or reviewer with final sign-off authorization in cases of conflicting requests.
9. A clear sign-off process for each deliverable phase.

Based on the assumptions and schedule provided here, we estimate the following costs. However, this estimate is preliminary and will require further discussion once the LMS is selected and other deployment issues are settled.

Project management	$5,000
Instructional development	4,000
Graphics	6,500
Programming	8,000
QA	1,500
Total	$25,000

1. The project manager is the single point of contact for you and the person responsible for ensuring that your project is delivered on time, on budget, and to your satisfaction.
2. The instructional designer is responsible for producing the design document, flowchart, template guide, and storyboards.
3. Graphics includes the interface, look and feel, the design of each template, and the content-related graphics to support instruction.
4. Programming involves the architecture for the program, including the navigation and template functionality. The programmer is also responsible for building the prototype, coordinating work with the LMS, loading content, and supervising deployment.
5. QA is the process of testing the functionality and performance of the course on the delivery platform.
6. Total is the fixed price for development and delivery of the product as outlined in this proposal.

Risks to Completion

In our experience, the greatest risks to timely completion of a project are due to delays in receiving the content, delays in receiving review comments, or conflicting review requests. Our schedule and budget are based on adhering to timelines so that both our team and NorLabs' team can work most efficiently and effectively. To guard against problems that could adversely impact these estimates, we recommend that all key reviewers and anyone with ultimate sign-off authority attend the kickoff meeting. Having access to these key people early in the project saves time for everyone in the long term. It's also critical that a single person be identified as having final approval over specific deliverables to prevent consensus issues from slowing the work. Our project manager will notify your liaison immediately if anything jeopardizes the budget or schedule so that we can agree, together, on the appropriate action.

Out of Scope

We recognize that interactive development is an intrinsically creative and iterative process. To that end, MC Studio builds in one complete review and revision cycle for each deliverable phase. Changes made to the project after a deliverable phase (such as changing the look after the look has been approved, or changing content after storyboards have been approved) are considered out-of-scope changes. We work to minimize these changes by communicating fully and frequently, providing clear directions and explanations of the process throughout the production cycle, and giving reviewers a heads-up prior to delivery of each phase. We know that some errors will escape the best efforts at detection and that some changes may be required. We will immediately contact you if we find there are revisions that cannot be handled within the scope. Please note that MC Studio will not initiate or begin work on any OOS work without prior authorization from NorLabs project manager.

Modification Costs

Our goal is to develop long-term relationships with our clients, so providing ongoing services, such as modifications, is key to maintaining those relationships. If the changes are minor in scope, we can arrange an hourly charge. We would not begin the work without authorization from you.

Qualifications

MC Studio is well qualified to design and produce this training program. With a track record including three previous projects for NorLabs, we believe we understand your company. With the successful delivery of numerous online projects for other clients, we feel well equipped to provide NorLabs with the skills and guidance it needs in this inaugural effort.

Project manager for this assignment will be Carey Lansing, who has produced video- and classroom-based materials for NorLabs in the past. Jeremy Steiner, who will serve as instructional designer, has designed similar policy and procedures training for other clients. Lead programmer Terrell Macklin has extensive experience in developing online courseware for deployment in an LMS environment.

Chapter 9
Design Phase

Chapter Overview

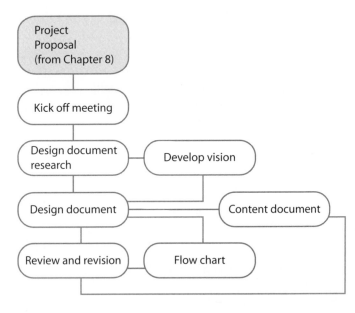

- Project Proposal (from Chapter 8)
- Kick off meeting
- Design document research
  - Develop vision
- Design document
  - Content document
- Review and revision
  - Flow chart

Learning Outcomes

- Conduct a project "kickoff" meeting.

- Write a design document.

- Present design documents to client representatives for review and feedback.

- Produce a flowchart of the product.

- Develop a content document.

Orientation within the Design Process

Recall that there are five phases to the instructional design process. In each phase, you should consider the five essential elements of learners, outcomes, assessments, activities, and evaluation. As you spiral through the five phases, considering each element in each phase, you add details and perform tasks required to create the products associated with each phase.

In this chapter, we examine the Design phase of an instructional design project (see Figure 9.1). As the name implies, the tasks of the Design phase are at the heart of the instructional design process. The design document and other products you produce in this phase are unique to instructional design.

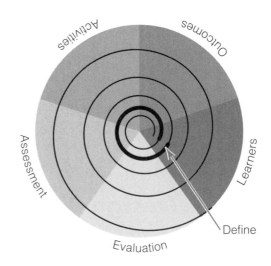

Figure 9.1 *Phases of instructional design.* In this second phase, you move out from the center of the spiral as you design the project.

Tasks of This Phase

The tasks of this phase related to learners, outcomes, assessments, activities, and evaluations are summarized in Table 9.1.

Table 9.1 Design phase

Learners	• Gain clarity on client's and SME's perception of needs.
	• Attempt to obtain permission to contact learners.
	• Fully define audience through conversations with client, learners, SME, learner expert, and project team. Conduct research and review of literature as needed.
	• Contact learners to confirm or modify statement of needs.
	• Present description of needs and learner characteristics as part of design documents. Gain approval or change as needed.
Outcomes	• Fully develop goals.
	• Discuss possible outcomes with client, SME, and learners.
	• Write and sequence high-level outcomes.
	• Determine prerequisite skills.
	• Present goals and outcomes to members of design team, client, and SME. Gain approval or change as needed.
Activities	• Work extensively with SME to define content.
	• Brainstorm potential instructional activities with project team.
	• Develop instructional strategy based on audience characteristics and needs, and instructional outcomes.

(continued)

Table 9.1 (*continued*)

	• Develop description of materials, including media and navigation, as needed.
	• Present instructional strategy and concrete description of materials to client for approval or suggested modifications.
Assessments	• Gather suggestions for assessments.
	• Develop concrete description of assessment instruments and/or specifications.
	• Present assessments ideas for client approval with design documents.
Evaluation	• Prepare or modify formative evaluation plan.
	• Get suggestions for tryout learners.
	• Present evaluation plan to client for approval.

Design Phase

In the Define phase, you scoped your project; tentatively identifying the need, audience, goals, delivery method, and projected costs and deadlines. Moving out to the next layer in our spiral, in the Design phase, you elaborate on the initial thinking and writing you began in the Define phase. At the conclusion of the Design phase, you should have a set of documents and files that start to build the blueprint for the product, whether it's an online course or a classroom-based workshop.

The Design phase is significant because it typically marks the start of the "clock," the moment when your client starts paying for your services or at least officially engages you to perform the work. The activities and deliverables typically associated with this phase are:

Kickoff meeting

Design document

Flowchart

Content document

You might wonder if it's really necessary to generate these documents—or your client might ask why you can't simply get on with actually making the product. It's helpful to use the home construction analogy, especially with your client. Just as you wouldn't build a house without a blueprint, you can't build an effective instructional product without the necessary documents. Early in the project, these documents are the primary means of communication among you, the project team, and the client.

The Kickoff Meeting

The kickoff meeting is designed to orient the team to the project. It sets the tone, introduces team members to each other, and ensures that everyone on the team understands the project and goals. It's usually not possible at the kickoff to accomplish significant work on content and design issues. However, properly run, this initial meeting enables you to begin functioning as a team more quickly and effectively. By taking the time to establish relationships, explain communication procedures, and review the project's goals and milestones during the kickoff, you save time in the long run.

In collaborative design, it's critical to involve everyone on the project team in the kickoff meeting. Invite all key reviewers and anyone with ultimate sign-off authority in order to gain their commitment. Gaining access to key people early in the project saves time for everyone over the long term. This first project meeting can accomplish several things:

- Forge the assembled individuals into a team.
- Orient everyone to the project's goals, schedule, and processes, including educating the client on the

DESIGNER'S TOOLKIT

Common Sequence of Events for Kickoff Meeting

- Lead ice breaker.
- Make introductions and assign roles and responsibilities.
- Articulate project vision and identify goals and expected outcomes.
- Give market overview.
- Define deliverables.
- Provide overview of schedule.
- Discuss review process.
- Set dates for next meetings.
- Make assignments.

design process, clarifying the purpose of the project, and reviewing the schedule and other constraints.

- Begin the process of gathering information for use in the design documents.

Team Development

The kickoff meeting, as well as all of the communications and meetings that follow, is important in forging personal relationships. Employ personal techniques to put the participants at ease and establish rapport in the first meeting. Learn the names of the attendees, avoid distractions like phone calls, exhibit a pleasant attitude and positive body language, attend to the body language and vocal inflections of others, and use active listening and careful questioning strategies.

Personal relationships help keep communications amicable and constructive when disputes occur—and disputes will occur! Instructional development projects can be complex, with many deliverables, components, team members, and deadlines. Each of these components can become the focus of a misunderstanding or a disagreement. If you start the project with strong personal relationships, those bonds help in resolving any conflicts that occur. One way to keep misunderstandings on a team to a minimum is through full, frequent, and accurate communications. Prior to the kickoff meeting, develop a communications plan in cooperation with your client, and review the plan with the rest of the team at the kickoff meeting.

Orientation to Project

In almost every instructional design project in which you are working with a client, one of your ongoing tasks is to educate your client about instructional design and your role in developing the curriculum. Some clients may question the need for instructional design, especially if they are trainers or teachers, or are working with a limited budget or schedule. Much of what we do in instructional design can seem abstract and remote to clients, and even to team members. Most clients haven't been trained to think about concepts like target populations, outcomes correlated to assessment, or content chunking. Think of educating your client as another one of your tasks. What does your client know already, and what are the gaps in his or her knowledge? The more your client understands what you are doing, the more responsive he or she will be, the more positive your interactions will be, and the better your work will be as a result.

In addition to educating clients, you may need to educate your team members. The proposal provides a good starting point for orienting clients and team members to the project. You may need to keep budget or other sensitive information confidential, but you can probably

review the key points of the proposal so that everyone starts with the same framework. Elaborate on the needs, goals, audience, and expected outcomes to the extent that you understand them. Define the project constraints including time, personnel, space, and budget limitations. Pay careful attention to the schedule, as cooperation from all parties will be necessary for the project's success.

Use the kickoff meeting as an opportunity to educate the client and team members on the processes and methods of instructional design. At this stage, you want to limit your presentation to a general overview, providing examples to illustrate the tasks and deliverables. Just as in our instructional design model, you'll find that your client's and team members' understanding grows in a spiral-like fashion. There is a tremendous difference between clients and team members who have participated in the instructional design process previously and those who are embarking on their maiden project.

When communicating with people who are not instructional designers, be careful to avoid jargon. Vocabulary that is meaningful to instructional designers can confuse your nondesign colleagues, clients, SMEs, and target audiences. Listen carefully to the words your client uses, and use them to describe what you mean. For example, if your client talks about the "purposes" of the program, use that word instead of "objectives." If you need to use a "jargon" word, immediately define it in context. For example, the term "SME" won't register until you explain that it is the person who will serve the project as the content, or subject matter, expert. When you begin to hear your client use these terms, you'll know they're no longer "vocabulary" words!

In educating your client and team members, you don't need to recount all of your training and experience—they aren't instructional designers and don't need to be. But you should be prepared to explain your role within the overall development process and to describe the specific contributions you are making to ensure the product's success. Without being strident or arrogant, emphasize that you serve as the advocate for learners throughout the

DESIGNER'S TOOLKIT

Professional Etiquette

If you call the meeting, it's a good idea to:

- Send a reminder just prior to the meeting day.
- Provide an agenda with estimated times for each activity. However, the client decides when the meeting is over.
- Include time for introductions, breaks, and reviews.
- Follow the meeting with a memo outlining key decisions and thanking the participants for attending.

Table 9.2 Kickoff and the elements of design

Learners	• Identify client's understanding of need.
	• Have client describe potential market for these materials.
	• Ask who potential learners are, what their characteristics are, and what implications of these characteristics are for instructional materials.
	• If appropriate, gain permission to contact potential audience members to learn more about needs and characteristics.
Outcomes	• Begin to discuss what kinds of changes in learner performance should occur following instruction.
Assessments	• During conversations about project outcomes, be alert to potential ideas for assessments.
	• Find out how you could determine when intended outcomes have been reached.
Activities	• Make note of client's and team members' suggestions regarding delivery platforms, activities they want to see in materials, sources of content, and available subject matter experts.
Evaluation	• Recognize that kickoff meetings seldom focus on evaluations! But think about what content to use for the prototype.

design and development process. Also explain that you are trained to produce effective instructional products using a systematic design process that has proved its effectiveness over decades of implementation. We often talk about the art and science of instructional design—in this conversation, you want to emphasize the science!

Design Issues

Although the primary purposes of the kickoff meeting are to establish collaborative relationships among the project team members and to orient everyone to the project, you might also begin to gather information applicable to the design and development of the product. Think of your project as a blank page—it's your job to fill in the blanks with descriptions of the audience, outcomes, activities, and delivery environment (see Table 9.2). Sometimes, you can gain insight on these issues simply by listening carefully. A casual brainstorming session on one or more of these topics may provide you with valuable information to further your progress toward defining the project. Remember, the kickoff session seldom yields definitive answers, but it may begin the process of narrowing the options. This will depend on the prior experiences of the client team, SME, and the time available. If you don't have time to brainstorm at the kickoff, it should be the next step.

One activity that can focus conversations and inform design is to explore market opportunities. If you are creating a product that your client will sell or that will help the client compete in the marketplace, it's especially helpful to have a market overview. A member of the client's team can make a presentation that includes a competitive analysis, the client's marketing goals, and a brief explanation of how the product you will develop fits into the company's overall product line.

Voice of Experience

Market Overview

A publisher developing a new middle school CD-ROM curriculum product scheduled a market review for the development team. The chief of marketing brought in competitive products and discussed the strengths and weaknesses of each. The designer and the rest of the production team had the opportunity to see, use, and compare each of these products. Some of the products were difficult to use and poorly executed, with sloppy graphics, awkward navigation, and instructional weaknesses. Other products, however, were highly appealing, with strong production values, effective instructional strategies, and good use of technology.

The designers began formulating strategies for creating a product that could gain a market share. Through this exploration, the team became aware of the particular niche that could be filled by the proposed project, accomplishing one of its goals.

On some projects, the kickoff can achieve other goals. If the client and team have experience with this type of work, and particularly if they've worked together before, you can move into complex tasks more quickly. For example, an experienced team on an e-learning curriculum project spent two days working through content and audience requirements in order to develop interactive templates. This jump-started the design process and probably shaved about a month off the 12-month schedule. In another example, a design team that was visiting the client's site for the kickoff was also able to tour the client's facilities to better understand the learning requirements. Although the tour came before the designer could fully appreciate all that he was seeing, it helped him and his client to begin working at a more sophisticated level.

The Design Document

Once the project is officially kicked off, your first task is usually to write a **design document**. This document articulates the "who, what, when, where, why, and how" of the project. As the conceptual blueprint for the project, it integrates all of the thinking that's taken place on the project with new research conducted during the Design phase.

You may wonder how the design document relates to the project proposal. They may share organization and information (or may not), but they are separate deliverables with distinctly different goals. The purpose of the proposal is to help you land the job. The purpose of the design document is to specify the requirements for developing an effective instructional product. Don't expect to reuse proposal material in your design document. If you can, that's great, but material from the proposal may not suffice for the design document. Remember that in the Define phase you were learning about the project. As you move into the Design phase, you will understand more and be able to produce a document of greater substance than you would have been able to do even a few weeks earlier.

Design Document Research

There's no single strategy for acquiring all the information you need to build your design document. Immediately after the project kickoff meeting, you should begin to record all you know about the learners and their needs, the project goals and outcomes, assessments, activities, and evaluation plans. As you collect information to build your design documents, think back to the chapters on the elements of instructional design. You need to define the learners (Chapter 2). You need to determine the goals and outcomes, as well as ways to deliver the assessment (Chapter 3); develop the instructional strategies and learning activities (Chapters 4 and 5); and evaluate the effectiveness of the materials (Chapter 6). You also need to work with the client and SME to develop the content (using the collaboration skills you learned in Chapter 7).

You can begin by reviewing any documents or materials your client or SME provides. Ask questions of your client and SME, and any other individuals whom they suggest you contact. You may want to survey or interview learners to confirm their needs and characteristics. You might also conduct research by conducting interviews, visiting job sites, observing employees on the job, attending classes, or reviewing instructional materials created for other courses. For example, if you're developing a course for sales staff about a new product, you should look at product brochures, marketing materials, technical documentation, and users' manuals. You might also speak with a marketing or product manager.

Working with SMEs   Although you should use anything and everything that proves useful in developing your content, most designers rely on an SME. But use your SME's time judiciously by first learning as much as you can on your own. It's not enough to ask your SME simply to give you the content—she won't understand what that means. It's also not the SME's job to generate objectives. He can help with this, but the primary role of the SME is to provide factually correct information. You need to find strategies that make it easy for the SME to provide you with information while recognizing that what works for one person will not necessarily work for another.

Although SMEs are usually flattered to be recognized as experts, remember that these typically are very busy people, so be respectful of their time. At the beginning of the project, meet with the SME and outline the time you estimate will be required at each stage of the project. Share this schedule with the SME early in the project. If one or more of the experts can't commit the time that's needed, you may want to find another SME. If that's not possible, you'll need to modify your design and development timeline to take the SME's availability into account.

In some situations, you should consider hiring your own SME. For example, if you are developing materials for a new software product, it might be advantageous to hire someone with advanced technical skills who really understands the product and can guide you in your learning—so you don't tie up the "official" SME's time. You do not need to understand the content as deeply as the SME—that is neither possible nor necessary. Sometimes, understanding the content itself is not your concern, but understanding the learners is. For example, if you are developing materials for early childhood education but have no experience in this field, you may want to work with an SME who understands these learners and knows how to teach them. Your approach will depend on the content, the learners, and the SMEs the client provides you. On projects for which you hire the SME, you need to develop an agreement or contract that specifies the work that the SME will produce, the schedule, and the compensation (see Example 9.1).

Recognize that, although SMEs are highly competent in their subject area (that's why they're experts), they may not know much about instructional design, or even about

Example 9.1 Expert Agreement

Expert Tasks

Review one module of the TenPro Repair course prepared by T3L Associates for Zeron, Inc. The review must follow guidelines provided by T3L Associates.

Participate in an audio conference focus group of approximately 2 hours in duration.

Provide written comments on the factual content of the module, suggestions for further improvement, and module organization.

Time commitment

An estimated 10 hours total commitment, which includes approximately:

- 6 hours for module review
- 2 hours for focus group audio conference
- 2 hours for preparing written comments

Compensation

T3L agrees to pay $75 per hour, not to exceed $750 total.

Milestones

- Receive signed agreement by July 1.
- Receive module by July 2.
- Review module July 3–July 10.
- Prepare written comments by July 14.
- Participate in audio conference on July 14.

- Receive compensation upon completion of audio conference focus group and submission of written comments.

Memorandum of Agreement

This agreement between T3L Associates and _____ (Contractor) outlines the agreed-upon responsibilities for participation in the expert review of the TenPro Repair module prepared by T3L Associates for Zeron, Inc.

T3L Associates will:

- Provide Contractor with the module of instruction.
- Provide Contractor with a written guide to the review process.
- Compensate the Contractor at the rate of $75 per hour, not to exceed $750 total, to be paid upon completion of the activities outlined herein.

Contractor Will:

- Review the module using the guide provided by T3L Associates by July 10.
- Participate in an audio conference focus group on July 14.
- Provide written reactions to the module using the guide provided by T3L Associates no latter than July 14.

Contractor	For T3L Associates
_____	_____
_____ (Date)	_____ (Date)

instruction. Often, SMEs don't understand why they are working with an instructional designer—after all, you know nothing about their area of expertise. They may have a difficult time accepting the fact that someone who is not knowledgeable in their content area can design instruction for that topic. In such a situation, you may need to educate your SME about the instructional design process and your role in it. Explain (gently!) that, just as he or she is expert in the content area, you are expert in developing instructional products.

You may wonder, too, if you really can produce effective materials in an area in which you have no content knowledge. As decades of practice have shown, well-trained instructional designers can develop excellent products even when they are not SMEs. Your contribution to a successful outcome is your knowledge and skill in developing effective instruction. You will probably never know all that your SMEs know, and you don't need to, but as you work on a project, you are likely to acquire a great deal of content knowledge. Ironically, you want to guard against becoming so familiar with the material that you lose the learner's perspective.

Refining the Content   As you develop an understanding of the content, you need to organize your thoughts in a way that will inform the design of the product. You may want to do a task analysis, instructional analysis, or content analysis to identify the subskills that contribute to learners' ability to obtain the desired outcomes. You don't need to identify specific learning

Hiring Your Own SME

A designer was hired to produce a series of online mathematics lessons to accompany a textbook for community college students. The designer, in turn, hired a community college algebra teacher who had used earlier editions of the same text in her classes. The teacher served as an SME to the instructional designer. Not only was the SME knowledgeable about mathematics and how to teach mathematics, but she was also able to help the designer identify concepts that students typically had a hard time mastering. If the SME had understood only algebra, or had taught at a high school level, she might not have had the same insights about this target audience.

Together, the SME and designer devised strategies for transferring classroom-based lesson ideas to the online lessons. The SME pinpointed where in a given lesson students typically have trouble and worked with the designer to develop content and exercises to counter those problems. Armed with this information, the designer developed online lessons that helped students learn these problematic topics.

---

outcomes until your client has approved the design document, but as you develop an understanding of the content, you should gain clarity on the desired outcomes and begin to see ways to assess learners' knowledge and skills.

It's not unusual for an SME to insist that certain content be included. If this content does not support, and perhaps even conflicts with, the instructional goals, you need to decide how to handle this. Clients and SMEs often misunderstand how instruction works. They may assume that everything is equally important and must be included in a course. If they work in the technology sector, they may be familiar with documentation or users' manuals that strive to be comprehensive. Instructional design, however, requires editing that comprehensive content and structuring it into a scope and sequence appropriate for a given group of learners.

If your SME insists on including extraneous material, think carefully about whether there will really be harm in including it. If you determine that including the content will confuse learners, make the instruction too long, or otherwise reduce the effectiveness of the instruction, summon up as much tact as you can and explain why the content isn't needed and may be counterproductive. If this doesn't work, or if it seems unwise even to try, appeal to your project manager. If he or she insists on including material you believe is detrimental, write a short, clear, and nonemotional memo outlining your concerns and give it to the manager. You want to go on record as advocating good instructional design, but you also need to accept the authority of clients and managers.

If the client or SME is committed to including a favorite idea in the instruction, another strategy is to let the learners decide. Fortunately, there's an opportunity built into the instructional design process to deal with such circumstances. You can test one or more alternatives with learners during formative evaluation of the prototype and determine how the learners respond to it. After all, you may be wrong, too. As you go through the design process, make note of questions and decisions on which there are opposing viewpoints, and structure your formative evaluation to seek clarity on these issues. When differences of opinion occur, you can avoid "us versus them" conflicts simply by letting the learners decide.

Developing a Vision

After you've identified the most important ideas, you need to determine the most viable way of presenting them to learners, considering both the delivery medium and the available budget. At this point, some designers like to develop a **goal scenario** to clarify the vision of the project team. As you will recall from Chapter 7, goal scenarios describe specific learner behaviors, images, animations, sounds, interactive sequences, and so on. Some designers develop goal scenarios on their own; others encourage the SME, client, and project team to imagine how learners will progress through a lesson on the topic.

If you choose to engage SMEs and clients in imagining the possibilities, you might show examples of other products that may contain something of value to your project. Perhaps you can locate a Web site with an interactive activity that works with the content under consideration. For example, the Web site might demonstrate how pH works in chemistry, while you are working on a botany project, but it doesn't matter for the purpose of visioning. You're simply demonstrating other projects that may or may not have elements of use to your project to get everyone's imagination rolling.

Suppose you are developing a CD-ROM program for middle school mathematics. Based on your understanding of these learners, you believe that they are likely to respond to stories and animated characters. You also need to develop an interactive exercise in which they put concepts into practice. You demonstrate a product you developed previously that includes animated characters and several interactive exercises to the client and SME. Based on this demonstration, you discuss the best use of animation and identify the type of interactive activity

Focusing Content

A designer working on a project for Space Center Houston, the visitors' center at NASA, collaborated with experts on various space shuttle systems. The resulting program was a computer-based simulation that allowed visitors to experience life onboard the shuttle. An SME who had devoted his working life to the shuttle's communication systems was dismayed to realize that the program would feature only the most basic information about how satellites relay communications from the shuttle to the command center in Houston. Not surprisingly, he considered this topic extremely important.

The designer helped him to understand that a casual visitor was likely to spend 10 minutes learning about the geosynchronous orbits that make satellite communications possible. The goal in this informal learning setting was for visitors to gain a high-level appreciation of the shuttle, not to delve deeply into the shuttle's complexity and sophistication. The designer explained that visitors who learn "just a few interesting things" about the communications systems might be intrigued enough to learn more. She pointed out that most of the engineers at NASA had become interested in working in the space program when, as children, they learned "just a few interesting things." Those interests sparked career decisions. The SME's attitude changed from disappointment to enthusiasm.

that may be most appropriate for the content and audience. Through this discussion, you create a description of the user's experience. For example, for a chunk of content introducing students to the concept of Xeno's Paradox, you might propose the following:

Present an animation of a student trying to finish her homework. She completes increasingly tiny fractions, and because it's Xeno's Paradox, she can never finish. Following the animation, you ask students to write their own stories illustrating Xeno's Paradox.

Of course, this is a description of only a small chunk of content, but it illustrates the narrative nature of the goal scenario.

Be aware that the decision to involve SMEs, clients, potential learners, or team members in developing goal scenarios is a personal one. Whereas some designers use these visioning tools early in the design process, others prefer to wait until later in the project to involve other individuals.

Writing a Design Document

There isn't a single "right" method for writing a design document, but one useful method is to start with an outline of the main sections. Armed with knowledge of the learners, their needs, and the content, you are ready to write down what you have learned. This document won't be complete or perfect, but it's a start. Write whatever you know at this point about the general goals, outcomes, and subskills. Think about what assessment methods will be effective for the goals, learners, and delivery environment, and include these initial ideas in the design document. Also think about what instructional strategies might be appropriate. Later in the instructional design process, you may conduct brainstorming sessions with the team, but for now, simply jot down your ideas about potential activities.

As you write these sections of the document, ensure that there is alignment among the goals and outcomes, instructional activities, and assessments. It's not unusual to begin with fragments in each section of the outline and to fill in additional material as you acquire and master it. Depending on your personal preferences and the project, client, team, SME, content, and any number of other factors, you can start with any section, knowing you'll be revisiting each section several times as you build your understanding.

Don't try to write a final draft of the design document the first time through. Expect your first draft to be just that—a draft. As you learn more about the content or the learners or the development tools, you can revise earlier ideas. This is expected and welcome. It doesn't mean that the design document should be sloppy or reflect lazy thinking or a lack of research. You should prepare it as carefully as possible, but with the understanding that it will undergo one or more revisions. You don't want to throw everything out with each new version, and you need to stay on schedule and within budget, but you should continually refine the product as you see opportunities to do so. This iterative process is repeated at every stage in instructional design and results in the strongest possible final product.

Chapters 2–6 presented some tools and methods that you, as the instructional designer, will use to design and develop the project. In Chapter 2, you learned to conduct an audience analysis and confirm needs, as well as outline the implications of the audience characteristics for the instructional materials. In Chapter 3, you learned to identify outcomes and goals, conduct subskill analyses, and develop assessment items. In Chapters 4 and 5, you learned to chunk and sequence content, create an instructional strategy, select a delivery mode, and assign media assets. During the Design phase, you create many of these documents as tools to clarify your thinking and communicate with the design team, but you won't necessarily present any of them to the client. The documents that are useful to you, as the designer, are often different from the ones that you will present to the client. You need to create documents that specifically communicate with clients in a way that is understandable to them.

The following sections outline elements you might include in your design document. Your company or your client may have a specific organization that they require for design documents, or they may divide the material to produce several documents instead of one comprehensive design document. There may also be other important material you want to include in your design document, such as information about previous training or the market opportunity. It's your job to craft the appropriate document for each client, project, and team. This means you may write very different-looking design documents for different projects and clients.

Executive Summary
Although this section is the first one in the document, you should write it last. In the executive summary, you sum up the key points, preferably in one or two pages. It may be distributed, as a stand-alone document, to other decision makers in your client's organization. It can be useful to think of your client's boss as your audience for this summary.

Learning Need/Market Opportunity
In this section, you briefly describe what is driving the decision to produce this instruction. What factors led to the conclusion that the situation required instruction? For example, a company may need to train its employees to use new equipment. Or perhaps a school has installed a new language lab and sees an opportunity to develop a course to help students learn foreign languages. If you or the company conducted a needs assessment and analysis, you can summarize the results here.

For some projects, especially those that will be sold as distinct products, it may be more appropriate to discuss the learning need in the context of the market. What about this product will be attractive to target customers? How will it meet customers' needs or appeal to their desires? How does it compare with the competition? Describe the competitive arena for this product, and explain how it will be differentiated from other products out there. Also address whether other market forces make the timing right for this product. For example, the product may be taking advantage of new technology, or better distribution, or new educational requirements.

Instructional Goal(s)
Next, you state what the instruction will accomplish. Why is this important? Is there a larger purpose? Goals are broad statements and can even be subjective. For example, a goal might be "Raise algebra comprehension," or "Discourage teen smoking," or "Reduce customer calls to the toll-free number."

Audience Definition
In this section, you describe the learners (also called the **target audience** or **population**) for this instruction (review the discussion of learners in Chapter 2). Are learners clustered at one location, or are they distributed? Is the audience diverse or homogenous? If the audience is diverse, can you define subgroups that have similar characteristics? For example, some children arrive at kindergarten already reading while others have not yet learned the alphabet.

You should focus on the audience's motivation, prior knowledge, and characteristics. When designing job skills training or materials for K-12 learners, pay particular attention to the audience's reading level, which may be considerably lower than college-educated instructional designers expect it to be. Many employees with a high school education or its equivalent (the GED) read comfortably at a sixth-grade level.

Motivation is another issue that requires careful consideration. For example, sales representatives tend to be "self-starters"—results- and action-oriented individuals eager to learn about new products so that they can be successful in selling them. At the other end of the spectrum might be adolescents who are more interested in extracurricular activities than class assignments. Some learners might be anxious about the learning experience, such as older women who have returned to the workforce after raising a family. Other learners are likely to be confident and comfortable learning new material, such as physicians enrolled in a workshop to learn about a new treatment protocol for heart bypass patients.

Delivery Environment
In this section, you describe the delivery model and context of the instruction. For example, will it be a classroom format, an online course, or some other venue? Will it be delivered synchronously (all students learning the same material at the same time) or asynchronously (students working independently)? You should also explain if it will be delivered to many learners in many locations or in a single session at a single location. If the instruction is to be delivered via computer, describe the platform as completely as possible because this can impact the design (see the section on online and computer-delivered instruction).

General Outcomes
Here, you identify what learners will be able to demonstrate that they couldn't have done prior to the learning. Recall from Chapter 3 that objectives or outcomes are tangible; they are something that an observer can see being done. So "Knowing the difference between longitude and latitude" is not an outcome, because we can't determine what is in the learner's mind. We can ask the learner to demonstrate her or his understanding of this principle, such as "Explain the difference between longitude and latitude." For the purposes of the design

document, keep the outcomes at a general level. When you actually begin working with the content, you can refine these general outcomes into the specific subskills that will guide development of each chunk of content.

Note that you might not be able to complete this section yet. You may need to finish the content document first (described later in this chapter) and then update the design document when you better understand the material. This can be true of other sections of this document, too. Complete what you can, and invite the client, SME, reviewers, and team members to supply you with additional information. Use their comments, and the knowledge you acquire as you progress through the spiral of instructional design, to update the design document.

Assessment Strategies
In this section, you address how learners will demonstrate their mastery of an outcome. Assessments can take a variety of forms, ranging from a 100-item multiple choice test, to a presentation, research paper, simulation, or demonstration. For example, learners in a first aid class might be asked to demonstrate correct procedures in treating a sprained ankle. Pilots are required to perform to certain standards in simulators that create unusual and dangerous conditions. Language students may be required to correctly pronounce vocabulary words. You may decide to assess learners using several assessment strategies because the outcomes include content from several domains of knowledge (for more on domains, see Chapters 3 and 4). A common example of this is the driver's license test. First, applicants must pass a written test that assesses their understanding of the rules and laws. Next, they must demonstrate that they can actually drive a car in the behind-the-wheel portion of the test.

Content Organization
Next, you explain what the content is for each outcome and how the content can be best organized for the audience, the delivery environment, and assessment. You might not have all the information you need yet, but exploring these ideas begins the process of determining how you'll present the content. You'll develop your ideas further as you create the content document, but you should include in the design document everything that you do understand at this point.

Content Sources
Yet another issue is where the content is coming from? Will you work with an SME, source materials, observations, or perhaps all of these? Will you need to conduct research? Identify where you'll be getting content for each of the general outcomes. This is another area in which you might not have all the information you need yet, but through this process, you can identify any gaps that you, and your client, need to fill.

Instructional Strategies
Given what you know about the audience, the outcomes, and the delivery environment, you should describe the instructional activities that will contribute to successful learning. Your planning is still highly preliminary at this point, but you should begin specifying the kinds of presentations and interactions you think will work. For example, will step-by-step demonstration, followed by practice and feedback, be effective? Or will a simulation work better? Should there be opportunities for online discussions to facilitate critical thinking skills and to process new ideas? How does the program guide learners? How will the assessments be structured? Can learners repeat tests? Some programs allow learners to repeat quizzes and practice exercises but not tests. Can they see their score, learn which items they missed, and view the correct answers? What domains of knowledge are represented by the content? A world languages course is likely to require procedural skills while a product training seminar may involve only intellectual skills. Think in terms of the motivation, prior learning, and preferences of the learners as you plan how you'll deliver the necessary learning events. If appropriate, describe how the program can provide remediation for learners who need help and provide enrichment for learners who need additional challenges.

For example, even at this early stage, you may already know that there are 12 units with four sections each. You may already have ideas for how to deliver specific lessons or how to handle certain types of content throughout the program. And you may have ideas for how to guide the target group of learners, engage them, provide feedback, and handle remediation and enrichment. Include this material in the design document and continue to review and refine this as you work through the phases of design.

Standards
In this section, you specify any standards that the design and production team need to adhere to in developing the material. For example, there may be certain standards for text, such as those in the *Chicago Manual of Style,* or there might be a graphics standard or an accessibility standard. Products developed for most public and academic institutions in the United States must comply with government standards requiring that instructional products be accessible to learners with physical disabilities. You may need to consult with an accessibility specialist to determine how to design features ensuring that your products will work with common adaptive devices. There also may be requirements for diversity to ensure that all learners relate to the material and feel included.

Media
Whether it's a classroom-based workshop or an online course, most instructional programs contain some type of media. You need to describe the types and extent of media you anticipate using in the program. If media elements are critical to the product, such as musical

recordings for a course on Mozart, explain how these elements will be used in the instructional activities and assessment. If you know the sources for any of the media, include this information here, too.

Evaluation and Testing Plans

The final issue involves pilot testing or other formative evaluation of the instructional material. The benefits of testing and evaluation can't be overstated. Although these activities add some cost and time, the feedback from testing can provide critical insight into what is and isn't working in the curriculum. Describe any plans for testing and evaluation, including who will conduct the test, what materials will be used, and where and when it will occur. Some companies prefer to use third-party evaluators to conduct testing.

Online and Computer-Delivered Programs

If your instruction will be delivered online or on a computer, you should include the following sections. You don't have to keep these sections in this sequence, and they don't have to follow the other sections. Rather, you should incorporate these sections into the design document where they make the most sense.

Overall Interface and Navigation

In this section, you describe the functionality that needs to be included in the interface and the way the navigation will work. This task requires the coordinated efforts of the production team including the graphic artist and the programmer. Your role is to advocate for learners' needs and to consider the outcomes, assessment, and instructional strategies.

Development Tools

The technical team may provide this information to you—a description or a list of the technical development tools necessary to produce the product. Development tools have implications for design including constraints and opportunities. For example, if animations will be developed in Flash, you won't be able to produce complex or dimensional images, but you will be able to deliver small files over the Internet quickly.

Delivery Platform

Like the development tools, the delivery platform description usually is determined by the technical team (or client) and has implications for design. If you are delivering on a single computer platform you can concentrate on exploiting the capabilities of that platform. If your product will be distributed for both Macintosh and Windows operating systems or for a variety of browsers, you have to be mindful of constraints on your production options. You need to ensure an equal experience on all platforms unless your client is able to allow one platform to be the primary delivery environment.

Usability

Here, you describe your plans for testing the program to ensure that it will be easy, and even effortless, for learners to use. Your team may include a usability specialist whom you work with to make the program usable. If a specialist isn't available, the task of ensuring usability is likely to fall to you.

Review and Revisions

The completion of a design document is a significant milestone in the instructional design process and should be treated as such. Before you release it to your client, review sections with the rest of your team to make sure that you haven't described a feature or strategy outside the project's scope and that the ideas are as robust as possible. For example, you may present some concepts for using video in the program to support certain instructional needs. After reading the sections on the video components, your video producer may have suggestions that are superior to the ones you devised. Get the team involved in the design solutions early so that they feel invested in the product and their expertise is reflected in the solutions.

The design document is a living document. This means, in most cases, that you write a first draft, review it, and make changes. Then you circulate it to your team, get feedback and revise it again, and present it to your client for review. Next, the client's team reviews it and requests changes. Just as the Design phase began with a formal kickoff meeting, it sometimes is useful to make a formal presentation of the design document so that you can answer any questions your client may have. If you send the design document, and any other deliverable, electronically, make sure you include a cover letter and detailed instructions to your reviewers on how to read and comment on it. After providing time for review, try to follow up with a meeting with your client. If you can't meet in person, schedule a conference call or online conference, and review each section together. The review of the design document offers a unique opportunity to further clarify and define concepts before committing the vision to paper or pixels.

It's likely that the document will continue to evolve even after this revision. As you continue to work with the content, as you learn more about the learners and the delivery requirements, and as your team and client come to understand more about the project, these new insights will lead to further refinements to the design document. It's a good practice to make those revisions available to everyone working on the project in a timely manner. Some teams keep the latest draft of documents posted on a project Web site so that it's available to any team member at any time.

The Trusting Client

A lead designer was working with a client who was always "too busy" to talk with her. Whenever she would try to talk with him, he would brush her off with "I trust you," or "I trust your team," or "I'm sure we'll be in perfect agreement." The designer would schedule meetings, but the client would fail to attend. She once ran into him at a local coffee bar and tried to have a quick conversation but he said, "I trust you! Anything you want to do will be fine with me." Well, that turned out to be a big problem!

Without any input from the client, the team had its work cut out for them. They did extensive research to see how other organizations had addressed the learning problem. They looked to the experimental and theoretical research in the field to determine the best way to address that particular type of learning outcome and content area. They searched demonstration Web sites funded by universities and government grants. After all this work, they came up with a plan of action that seemed innovative and effective.

As you may suspect, the client had absolutely no time to review the design documents. The designer finally convinced him to squeeze her into his busy schedule. Late one afternoon, just before he began his weekly staff meeting, they met. The designer simply needed approval of the key concept before committing resources to the development of the prototype. She quickly presented the design documents to the client as the rest of his staff waited around the table. The client looked at the design documents while the designer hurriedly reviewed the highlights of the product. To the designer's shock and dismay, the client hit the roof. He questioned their knowledge of the content and the approach. His staff jumped in with additional criticism. The designer reeled, fearing she was about to be fired! When she reported back to the development team, morale hit a new low. They had invested a lot in the design document. They had performed the research, given it their most creative push, and spent hours brainstorming—all without the client's guidance.

Amazingly, they salvaged the project. After that disastrous meeting, the client and design team began regular and consistent communications and held all the meetings they should have had weeks earlier. The project survived, and the materials were well received. Still, although the team performed their tasks professionally, they were hurt and discouraged by this experience.

What should have happened? The lead designer should have insisted that the client take the time to talk with them or delegate someone else to do this. She should have insisted on regular communications. She also should have insisted on making a formal presentation of the design document, carefully taking the client and his staff through the reasoning that brought the team to its conclusions. She should have explained the team's understanding of the need, the audience, and competing products. And she should have worked to bring the client to the point at which he could see that the proposed product was the very best option. There would have been some negotiations and revisions, but there would not have been the deflation of morale that occurred because they naively "trusted" each other!

Flowcharts

When designing programs that will be delivered via computers, a **flowchart** often is developed to illustrate the structure or organization of the content. The flowchart displays the program's hierarchy, similar to the table of contents in a book. Like the site map on a Web site, the flowchart should show the title of each main section and each subsection. The flowchart should also show any global functions that are accessible from anywhere in the program, such as a glossary or a resources section.

For anyone who thinks visually, flowcharts communicate the structure and strategy of an instructional product more powerfully than any of the many text-based documents produced in the instructional design process. For some designers, this is the tool that helps them solve problems; for others this is a difficult document to produce. The same is true for clients. Some clients will require that you include a flowchart with your design documents; others will not find the flowchart very helpful.

You might find it effective to develop the flowchart concurrently with writing the design document, or the flowchart might follow. There isn't a right or wrong time to create the flowchart. But you do need to spend some time thinking about how the content should flow and how users will navigate the program. If you did a task analysis, content analysis, or instructional analysis to identify the

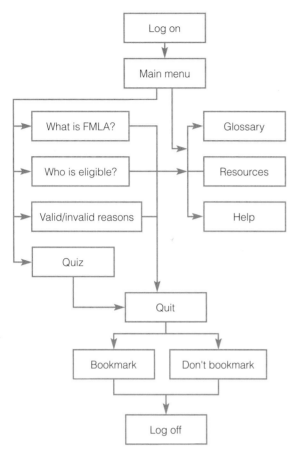

Figure 9.2 *Flowchart.* Notice the hierarchical arrangement of topics and subtopics.

subskills that contribute to the program outcomes, these hierarchies may be useful in developing the program's flowchart. However, it's important to recognize that the instructional flow may be different from the organization of the content. For example, a task analysis for a video production course might show that shooting scripts and storyboards should be created before filming begins. However, novices are unable to create such documents unless they know about common shot types and camera movements; thus, a program on video production should present information on the art of shooting video before information on planning techniques.

Through the process of creating a flowchart, you begin making decisions about the organization, chunking, activities, and practice and feedback for the product. As you develop a multimedia or online program, you need to work closely with the rest of your production team to create the flowchart. Many of the flowcharting decisions impact the work of team members and have implications for the budget, schedule, staffing, assets, and other resources. Expect the flowchart to evolve as you develop the program. As you gather content, you may find that you need more sub-sections; as you begin testing prototypes you may realize that you need to change the hierarchy. These adjustments are part of the process (see Figure 9.2).

 **Content Document**

Once the design documents have been approved, on many projects the next step is to accumulate and develop the content that will constitute the instruction, and then compile that content into a document. Not every project

DESIGNER'S TOOLKIT

Flowcharting

Several standard office supply products are invaluable in developing flowcharts. A white marker board allows you to draw and redraw a program's hierarchy as needed. You can use colors to represent different activities, concepts, or areas that need additional work. A marker board can help in communicating and collaborating with other team members, and is useful in brainstorming and other visioning exercises. The size of a marker board can also be helpful. A large board allows you to stand back and see the "big picture." "Memory boards" are marker boards that allow you to save an electronic copy or print out the material that's been drawn on the board.

"Sticky notes" are another useful tool in developing the structure and relationships between chunks of content in a program. You can position and reposition the individual notes until you are satisfied with the organization. Here, too, color is useful in capturing information on chunks of content. An advantage of sticky notes is that you can position them on large sheets of paper, such as flip chart paper, and fold or roll the paper up after the meeting. You'll have the materials available when you need to check or change something.

Flowcharting software, such as Microsoft's Visio program, provides sophisticated functionality for creating flowcharts. These tools allow you to create professional-looking flowcharts that you can save electronically and distribute to reviewers and team members. Visio, for example, can be distributed in a player format allowing viewers who do not have the software to view the document.

Content Document

A designer was working with a team of engineers to develop customer training on a new microprocessor chip set. The product was considered highly innovative and featured an approach to software development that was not standard at that time. The SMEs had not tried to explain the product to anyone outside their team. They had varying ideas of what should be included and what the structure should be.

After several meetings, the designer decided to begin compiling a content document. She met with each SME to gather content, organized and prioritized the material, and elaborated on the chunks to the degree she understood would be required to meet the goals.

When she distributed the content document to the SMEs, they were able to see what they still needed to explain and what needed to be added or deleted. Because the team hadn't articulated the full range of content issues among themselves, the content documents generated a great deal of discussion that was helpful to the overall project. With the designer's guidance, the team arrived at a consensus on what content to include, how to structure it, and how to prioritize it. With the revised and approved content document, the designer was able to move to the storyboard stage.

requires a content document, but if you're developing new material, you will find it helpful to write one prior to trying to develop the actual instruction. Consider writing one especially if the material has not been articulated or organized in a useful format. Unlike the design document, which describes the program in terms of the essential elements of instructional design, the **content document** focuses on the material itself. Here, it's appropriate to go into detail on the content, describing the information that learners will need to master this material. Without a content document, you have to juggle assembling and learning content simultaneously with developing effective instruction. Although the content document adds a step, it's likely to save time over the course of developing the project.

The benefit to writing a content document is that, once it's completed, you have everything you need, as you move into the Demonstrate and Develop phases, to create production documents such as storyboards. Although you begin assembling the content before you present your design documents for approval, you write the content document after the design document, because the process of developing the design document identifies the content you will need. If you assembled the content first, you might have too much or too little, or even the wrong content.

Assembling the Content

Depending on your client, project, and topic, you may gather content from a variety of sources including curriculum materials from related courses, product specifications, users' guides, marketing materials, interviews, surveys, books, journals, and Web sites. On most projects, you will also work with one or more SMEs. Regardless of where the content comes from, you should have an SME

review your content document to make sure the information is accurate and appropriate to the audience.

Educate yourself on the basics so that the SME's time is used most effectively in tackling the most complex information. For example, if your topic is the Bill of Rights, be sure to read it before talking to your expert! If the topic is the principles of flight, find an introductory book that explains and illustrates the concepts first. That way, when your SME refers to drag and lift, you will recognize these terms and not waste time with basic questions. Explain what you do understand so the SME doesn't need to repeat information. For some topics, however, you can't really learn anything on your own or ahead of time. This is particularly true for highly technical information and information on new products. In these situations, you have to rely on the client and SME to educate you on the topic.

It's your job to help your client and SME get you the information you need. If you merely write, "Need more content," you won't be successful. Exactly what content do you need? Be specific, clear, and brief. Provide the context for your question, and make it easy for your SME to get this information to you (see Example 9.2). For example, create a two-column table in your word processing program, list your topics or questions on the left side, and leave the right-hand column blank for the SME to enter responses. If your SME cites a reference, request a copy of the reference or clear bibliographical information so that you can locate the same source. Help your client and SME help you.

If you are repurposing content, such as developing an online version of a course that's previously been delivered in the classroom, the content is already assembled, so there's no need to start from scratch. Your task in this

---

Example 9.2 Request for Information from an SME

TO: SMEs

FROM: Terrell Jameson, instructional design team

RE: Sources for information

Here are the items I am still looking for. Please use the Source? column to indicate where I might be able to find this material. In order to incorporate this information into the design document, I'll need this by Friday, June 20. Thanks so much!

Product	Material	Source? Where can I find this information?
RL 394195	Marketing package	
RL 394828	Users' manual	
RL 398744	Users' manual	
RL 398744	Tech notes	

---

situation is to make the existing content effective in a new delivery environment. Sometimes, you are adding new sections or revising materials in an existing curriculum. Here, your task is to determine what content needs to be changed or replaced, assemble the new content, and ensure that the revisions are seamlessly integrated into the other material.

If you are revising or replacing a course, ask for copies of any materials that have been developed. Read through them and then list questions for the SME. Put your questions in a document that the SME can use to organize her responses. If the SME is also a trainer who has delivered this content, she will have insights into the way learners respond to the material and suggestions on how to strengthen the learning experience. If you can attend a class or workshop on the topic, pay attention to those moments during the class when you have trouble understanding the material—these are areas for which you may be able to develop strategies that are more effective in delivering the content. For example, if you're developing online tutorials for a professor, you should observe his class, study his handouts and assignments, and review the textbooks and workbooks used in the course.

It's sometimes possible to videotape an expert giving a presentation or conducting a workshop on the topic. But be sure to ask permission first. If there is any chance the video material might wind up in the product, arrange for the SME to sign a talent release. This agreement releases the client from any additional obligation to the "performer" and protects against any claims related to the product. Use the videotape of the expert to review the material. You can watch the tape as many times as you find useful, make a transcript of it, and formulate specific follow-up questions.

Use anything and everything that is useful to learn about the subject. You can quickly experience information overload, so be careful about how much you try to review at one time. Though the material might initially seem overwhelming, you'll soon find yourself becoming acclimated and realize that you understand the content, even in very technical areas. Be careful, too, not to overload your client, SME, and team members with information. Communicate quickly, concisely, and completely when you need to, but don't send off a flurry of e-mails or make a barrage of phone calls. Organize your questions so that your receivers can respond promptly and efficiently, without feeling as if they need to wait until they have a block of time to process reams of information.

Organizing a Content Document

There's no single best strategy for structuring a content document. One common technique is to create an outline using the goals and subskills from your design document as topic headings. Once you list the subskills, you can begin filling in the content that supports each outcome. Think of the content for each subskill as a chunk of information. You can also start with the flowchart and organize the content document using the structure from that document. Another strategy is to write each chunk of content on an index card, make stacks of cards on related topics, and then organize those stacks into a logical sequence.

Your content document is likely to require several iterations, because you won't initially understand things completely. Begin by developing a content outline, and even if you know it's imperfect, get feedback from the SME. Make the necessary revisions and then begin filling

Analogy

House

Builders use blueprints to perform every construction task on a home-building project. The blueprints contain specific instructions for almost every person working on the project. The framer sees where a load-bearing wall meets a non-load-bearing wall; the electrician learns that the recessed lights in the hall need to be on the same circuit as the outlet; the roofer sees how the roof tiles need to slightly overhang the gutters to prevent leaks. The architect, along with the structural engineer and builder, had to think through every element of the project in order to produce the blueprints. They had to solve big problems, such as how to place the building on a sloping lot, and small problems, such as where to place the thermostat to be convenient for the occupants. So the blueprints represent the final product of a design process, as well as a set of detailed instructions to the building team.

The design documents you produce in this phase, and the production documents you create in the Demonstrate phase, are equivalent to the blueprints that guide the construction of a building. Like the architect, you need to think through every aspect of the product and to solve problems, both big and small. The big problems are things like determining how to create a computer-based simulation, to replace a classroom-based role play, for a supervisor skills course. An example of a small, but important, decision involves providing context-sensitive feedback in the simulation.

As you solve problems and work with your client, SME, and production team to design the program, you document this information in the design document and flowchart. In this phase and the next, you create the documents that provide the production team with the instructions they need to produce the final, successful product.

in the outline, again getting feedback from the SME. Keep adding and revising as needed. By giving your SME materials to react to, you are structuring the SME's responses. This makes the process much more efficient and productive for both of you. Along the way, you acquire greater understanding of the material and have fewer "basic" questions.

If you are producing a large product, such as a semester-long course or a multicourse curriculum, you won't be able to compile all the information in one document. Several strategies work in this situation. You can coordinate with your design team to write individual content documents for each of the sections or chunks, as you assign them. You can compile source materials into file folders, electronic folders on a server, or three-ring binders—perhaps one for each section or chunk. The goal is to get all the information in one place and to become familiar with it, before you develop the content into instructional materials.

In some respects, the content document is for you. It helps you learn the material and assemble it in one place. At this stage, you dig into the material and begin learning it at a deeper level. You identify where you need to do more research or get assistance from an SME. You think about how the material can be chunked and presented to learners. You notice where you struggle to understand the material and think about how to create instructional experiences that overcome such obstacles. For many designers, this is when they start to really appreciate the implications of the content and where they begin to see logical ways of presenting it. Don't worry too much about getting it perfect at this point—remember, it's an iterative process, and you will be refining and revising all along.

You are moving out around the spiral and getting a clearer picture of the product as you develop each iteration of each deliverable.

Summary

In this chapter, you learned about the purpose and methods of creating a design document, flowchart, and content document. The design document sets the stage for the design and development activities that will occur in subsequent phases of the project. This document fully describes why there's a learning need, what the learning will accomplish, who the learners are, what the curriculum will include, how it will work, and how it will be delivered. It also identifies measures of success. The flowchart anticipates how the program will be chunked and structured. The content document combines all of the instructional content in one document.

The Design phase usually begins with a project kick-off meeting. The purpose of this meeting is to establish rapport among team members, orient them to the project, and begin to derive information that will inform the development of documents. As you create the design document, flowchart, and content document, you gather information from many sources including SMEs, documents, learners, and the Web. Your client SME, and team review these documents. Additional changes and suggestions from the client team may be incorporated into these documents before they gain approval. Consider these critical documents a means of creating dialog that will lead to greater clarity and product definition, and a superior end product.

Application

1. The RealWorldID Web site includes the design document for an e-learning course created for the aviation industry. See if you can locate all of the recommended sections within this document. Visit the RealWorldID Web site to analyze the design document online or to print for use during class discussions.

2. In your reflective journal, summarize the key points of this chapter. Are the ideas presented consistent or inconsistent with your beliefs and prior knowledge? Compare your perceptions of the chapter with those of your classmates in a group discussion.

3. Using the same design problem and client that you used in the previous phase, create a design document that considers each of the following:

    a. Executive summary

    b. Learning need/market opportunity

    c. Instructional goal(s)

    d. Audience definition

    e. Delivery environment

    f. General outcomes

    g. Assessment strategies

    h. Content organization

    i. Content sources

    j. Instructional strategies

    k. Standards

    l. Media

    m. Evaluation and testing plans

    For online and computer-delivered programs

    n. Overall interface and navigation

    o. Development tools

    p. Delivery platform

    q. Usability

4. As you create your design documents, continue to make entries in your reflective journal. Explain why you made particular design decisions, how your ideas changed over time, and what you judge to be the next steps in the process.

5. Present your design document to your client for review and acceptance. Make note of requested modifications. Write about your meeting with the client in your reflective journal. How did it go? What went well? What do you think you could have done differently?

Ideas in Action

In Chapters 8–11, we follow the design of a computer-based training program on the Family and Medical Leave Act (FMLA). In this chapter, we include the design document and content document. For the flowchart, see Figure 9.2.

FMLA Training Design Document

Executive Summary

This online course on the provisions of the Family and Medical Leave Act (FMLA) will be delivered to all employees in the first quarter. Another course will be developed for supervisors. Through a combination of content presentation and interactive exercises, employees will learn about FMLA. The program will use images and audio in addition to text. A scored quiz will verify that the employee understands the provisions of the law.

Learning Need

NorLabs is required to train all eligible employees on the provisions of FMLA. HR has set a requirement that training be ready by January 1 and that all eligible employees complete this training by March 31. FMLA provides eligible employees with up to 12 weeks of unpaid, job-protected leave per year. It also requires that group health benefits be maintained during the leave.

Instructional Goals

Employees who successfully complete the training will be able to identify four–five primary features of FMLA and will know where to go for additional information and clarification. NorLabs should experience an increase in the number of employees using FMLA to cover leave situations.

Audience Definition

All full-time employees in the United States will be required to complete the training, although the leave will not be available to employees until they have been employed one year. Employees range from entry-level clerks to senior managers. Because of the nature of the company's work, all employees use computers and have basic literacy skills. An eighth-grade reading level for text is preferred for this material. Most employees are expected to be interested in this course, with the youngest and newly hired employees expected to be least interested.

Delivery Environment

This course will be available at any Web-connected computer or terminal. Learners can use their employee ID to log on from home or any other location where the computer meets the minimum standards. Computers should also be fitted with speakers or headphones for audio. The delivery platform is the standard Windows XP platform distributed throughout the company. The program will run in the Internet Explorer browser. Users can download the course in situations where it isn't possible to work online. However, the quiz is only administered online.

HR will distribute logon information to each employee. The management system will track employees using the system and send information to the personnel database.

Employees will probably complete the training in 30–60 minutes.

Development Tools
Standard Web development tools will be used. The technical team is considering developing the program in XML to make future updates easier.

General Outcomes
- Identify who is eligible for FMLA coverage.
- Recognize situations that FMLA covers.
- Recognize situations that are not covered by FMLA.

Assessment Strategies
The lesson will conclude with a 10-item multiple choice quiz. Once the employee begins the quiz, he or she must complete it. Quiz scores are sent to the employee's personnel folder in the HR database.

The registration and tracking database will track learners who have completed the lesson, as determined by completion of the quiz. Additionally, the tracking database will provide bookmarking so that learners can pause a lesson and return to the same location later. This feature will allow NorLabs employees to complete portions of the lesson at their job station computer as time is available.

Content Organization
- What is FMLA?
- Who is eligible?
- Valid and invalid reasons for taking leave
- Quiz

Content Sources
NorLabs legal department; U.S. Department of Labor

Instructional Strategies
We will probably have 3 chunks of content and exercises. The typical sequence and strategies for presenting each lesson is:

- Introduce the lesson outcomes.
- Remind the learner of prior knowledge (where applicable).
- Introduce the factual information for each lesson.
- Present relevant examples.
- Present interactions (exercises) that require active processing ("checks for understanding") after each new concept or, at most, after 2–3 new concepts.

- Recap the key points after all new content is presented.

The lessons will be presented in a preferred order, although learners will have the option of completing them in any sequence. The concluding activity is the 10-item quiz.

Help   The Help function is globally available. From the Help menu, learners can select from a list of every function and feature in the program. The selection will display a screen grab of that feature and explain how to use the feature through a combination of text and audio.

Key Words/Glossary   Key words/glossary terms are indicated in a distinct color, such as blue. Acronyms and other jargon will be included in the Glossary. Learners can click a highlighted word to access the definition. The requested definition will pop up from the Glossary. Additionally, the Glossary will be available from anywhere in the program. Learners can access entries by scrolling alphabetically through the listing. Clicking on a specific entry brings up the definition. The directions for using the Glossary will be in the Help section, and help is available throughout the program.

Resources   A Resources feature will work like the Glossary. Resources will include publication numbers, Web addresses, contacts, and other information.

Exercises   After each concept is presented, or after several small concepts, there's a check for understanding requiring active processing of the new material. These exercises do not need to be relegated to the predictable true/false or abc style of multiple choice but could include a variety of objective activities: dragging and dropping entries onto a blank template, organizing steps in a timeline sequence, matching, or discriminating among similar examples (where only one is completely accurate).

Directions for exercises will appear onscreen and will provide clear, specific instructions for completing the work. Additionally, a Help option will be available from any screen in the program and will provide additional information on how to complete any interactive feature or exercise in the program.

After each exercise, learners get specific feedback. One possibility is for a window to pop up with the feedback. Correct answers are reinforced. Incorrect answers are given an explanation. Some answers may be very close to the correct answer, requiring careful discrimination. In these cases, learners should get strong reinforcement for approximating the correct answer, but point out why the other option is correct.

Interface
The course will be designed to run in a browser window and will take advantage of browser functionality (back,

next, print, refresh). Main menus will be available from any screen in the program. Once the user selects a main menu category, additional menu choices will become available for that section of the program. An outline of the navigation features follows:

Global Navigation , Available as Sidebar on Each Screen

> Lessons
> - What is FMLA?
> - Who is eligible?
> - Valid and invalid reasons for taking leave.
> - Quiz.
> Glossary (Access any glossed entry, click the entry to bring up the definition.)
> Resources (A list of sources for additional information.)
> Help (List of program instructions.)

Screen Navigation, Available at Top and Bottom of Each Screen

> Next (Highlights when learner has completed all interactions on screen.)
> Back (Return to previous screen where feasible in a lesson.)
> Location information (Lesson title, current screen number out of total in lesson.)
> Audio controls (Volume adjustment; replay option.)

Standards

The course will adhere to NorLabs standards for language, diversity, accessibility, graphics production, and online course delivery. The NorLab logo should appear on the opening screen of the course, and copyright information will appear at the bottom of every screen within the program.

Reading Level and Readability   The content will be written at an overall eighth-grade reading level as determined using the Flesch-Kincaid scale in Microsoft Word (located under "Check readability statistics" in the Spelling and Grammar option in the Tools menu).

The design will try to avoid relying on blocks of text to convey the content. Where possible, text will be kept to a minimum with an emphasis on bulleted text, lists that build, graphics with descriptive captions, and other uses.

Here are recommended strategies to ensure obtaining this reading level without resorting to choppy prose:

- Define new terms in context (they will also appear in the Glossary). Think of each of these new terms as words in a foreign language to the learner.
- Remove new terms from the reading scale evaluation (in other words, remove the new word or term from the paragraph, then check the reading level).

- Avoid using several new terms in one sentence where the impact may obscure meaning for learners. In other words, if you encounter one new word in a sentence, you can probably figure out the meaning by examining the context. If there are too many new words, there's not enough meaningful context.
- Avoid overly long or complex sentences—but be aware that too many very short sentences are frustrating and sound overly simplistic. Strive for balance.
- Choose simple, direct language—but not baby talk.
- Recognize that a given sentence or paragraph may run higher than the eighth-grade level. In such cases, look for other instructional devices to help convey the content, such as a graphic, explanatory narration, or activity. The reading level is measured over several paragraphs, not specific sentences.

Media

Images are important in this training as a means of providing a realistic context for the content information and of gaining and focusing attention. Photographs should accurately reflect NorLabs' work environment, including logos and uniforms, and represent NorLabs' commitment to ethnic and cultural diversity.

Audio narration should be used to introduce, reinforce, and extend the instruction, not to mirror the text word-for-word but to enhance the material. To provide auditory variety, the narration will use both male and female professional narrators.

Evaluation, Usability, and Testing

We will produce a rapid prototype and test with about 12 randomly selected employees. HR will handle the evaluation and report results back to us.

Because almost every NorLabs employee will take this course, we are concerned that it be very easy to use. As part of the prototype evaluation, we will look at the program's usability. Any identified problems will be corrected in the final version.

We are set up to perform QA testing on the prototype and final version of the course. We will test on both desktop and laptop computers.

FMLA Training

Content Document

Summary of Training Program

Online course for all employees on the Family and Medical Leave Act (FMLA), a federal law that applies to employees of NorLabs. Another course will be developed for supervisors.

Contact Time
Estimate one hour.

Source of Content
NorLabs legal department; U.S. Department of Labor

What Is It?
FMLA provides certain employees with up to 12 weeks of unpaid, job-protected leave per year. It also requires that group health benefits be maintained during the leave.

Who Is Eligible?
Eligible employees:

- Employed by NorLabs for at least 12 months. Any portion of a week that the employee is on the payroll counts as a full week. Employment does not have to have been continuous.

- Worked at least 1250 actual work hours during the 12-month period prior to the first day of the leave. Use only time actually worked in the calculations. Time paid but not worked (such as vacation, sick, etc.) does not count toward the 1250 hours.

- Not already used 12 weeks of FMLA entitlement in the current calendar year.

NorLabs employees are covered by FMLA because the company is engaged in commerce and has employed 50 or more employees for each working day in 20 or more workweeks in the current or preceding calendar year.

The Law
FMLA is designed to help employees balance their work and family responsibilities by taking reasonable unpaid leave for certain family and medical reasons. It also seeks to accommodate the legitimate interests of employers, and promotes equal employment opportunities for men and women.

For NorLabs employees, FMLA has these requirements:

- Affects only those employees eligible for the protections of the law.

- Involves entitlement to leave.
- Maintains health benefits during leave.
- Restores an employee's job after leave.
- Sets requirements for notice and certification of the need for leave.
- Protects employees who request or take leave.
- Includes certain employer record-keeping requirements.

Valid reasons for leave:

- Birth of a son or daughter to the employee and in order to care for such son or daughter.
- Placement of a son or daughter with the employee for adoption or foster care.
- Family leave in order to care for a spouse, son, daughter, or parent of the employee if such spouse, son, daughter, or parent has a serious health condition.
- Serious health condition that makes the employee unable to perform their job.

Special considerations:

- An employee taking FMLA leave due to a serious personal health condition must present a medical certification in order to go on leave.
- In order to return to work, an employee taking FMLA leave due to a serious personal health condition must present a medical certification of fitness to return to work.
- During an FMLA absence, all available leave accruals must be exhausted before the employee can be on absent-without-pay status. This includes leave that is accrued while the employee is on FMLA absence.
- Employees on FMLA must pay their health insurance premiums by the first of each month (they aren't being paid and there are no earnings from which to deduct the premium).

| DESIGN AID |

Design Document Template

Executive summary: What are the key points? Keep to one or two pages.

Learning need/market opportunity: What is driving the decision to produce this instruction? Briefly describe what factors led to the conclusion that the situation required instruction.

Instructional goal(s): What will the instruction accomplish? Why is that important? Is there a larger purpose?

Audience definition: Who is the audience? Can you define subgroups that have similar characteristics? Are learners clustered at one location, or are they distributed? Describe the audience's motivation, prior knowledge, and education level.

Delivery environment: Where will the instruction be delivered? How will the instruction be delivered? Will it be delivered to many learners in many locations or in a single session at a single location? Synchronous or asynchronous?

General outcomes: What will learners be able to demonstrate that they couldn't have done previously?

Assessment strategies: How will learners demonstrate the obtainment of learning outcomes?

Content organization: What is the content for each outcome, and how is the content best organized for the audience, the delivery environment, and assessment?

Content sources: Where is the content coming from? Will you work with an SME, review source materials, conduct research, or perhaps do all of these? Identify where you'll be getting content for each of the high-level outcomes.

Instructional strategies: What strategies will be effective for successful learning? Consider how you'll address each learning event.

Standards: What standards or requirements, such as a graphics standard, a style sheet, accessibility standards, or diversity requirements, apply?

Media: What media are required for the product? Also list sources if known.

Evaluation plans: What are the plans for testing and evaluation? List who will conduct the evaluation, what materials will be used, and where and when it will occur.

If your instruction will be delivered online, you'll also want to include the following sections.

Overall interface and navigation: What functionality needs to be included in the interface, and how the navigation will work?

Development tools: What software development languages or products will be used to produce this program? What are the implications for instructional design of the use of those tools?

Delivery platform: What will the delivery platform consist of? Like the development tools, the delivery platform has implications for design.

Usability: How will you or the project team will conduct testing on the product to ensure that users find it easy to use?

Chapter 10
Demonstrate Phase

Learning Outcomes

- Develop production documents including treatments, templates, storyboards, and scripts.

- Develop a prototype for client review and learner tryouts.

- Conduct and analyze results of the prototype evaluation.

Chapter Overview

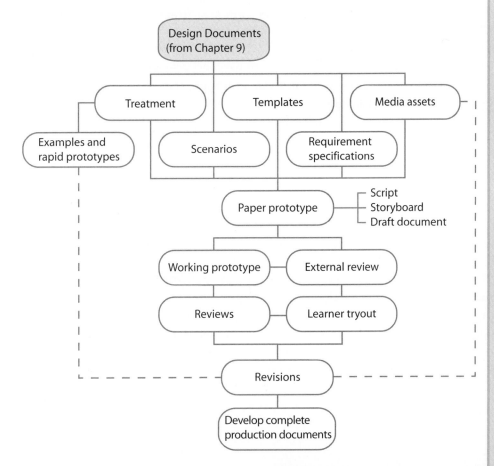

Orientation within the Design Process

Recall that there are five phases to the instructional design process. In each phase, you should consider the five essential elements of learners, outcomes, assessments, activities, and evaluation. As you spiral through the five phases, considering each element in each phase, you add details and perform tasks required to create the products associated with each phase.

In this chapter, we examine the Demonstrate phase of an instructional design project (see Figure 10.1). In the previous phases, your tasks focused on research and planning. In the Demonstrate phase, you begin to produce tangible instructional materials.

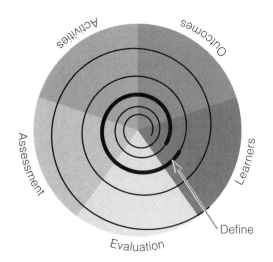

Figure 10.1 *Phases of instructional design.* In this third phase, you continue outward in the spiral path as you demonstrate the project.

Tasks of This Phase

The tasks of this phase related to learners, outcomes, assessments, activities, and evaluations are summarized in Table 10.1.

Table 10.1 Demonstrate phase

Learners	• Monitor development of production documents and prototype to ensure they are appropriate for audience.
	• Explain to client how materials will be appropriate for needs and characteristics of audience.
	• Monitor ability of materials to meet needs and characteristics of learners during prototype tryout.
Outcomes	• Monitor materials development to ensure consistency with outcomes and sequence.
	• Present prototype to client, explaining how developed to teach outcomes.
	• Monitor learners' obtainment of outcomes during prototype tryout.
Activities	• Develop production documents including page templates, storyboards, media requirements, and technical specifications. Gain approval and make suggested modifications.
	• Develop prototype of materials. Present to learners. Collect data on learners' response to prototype.
	• Present prototype and results of learner tryout to clients and SME. Present suggested modifications resulting from prototype testing.
Assessments	• Develop specifications for assessments.
	• Develop prototype assessment instruments. Administer assessment instruments during prototype testing. Alter assessments as indicated by prototype tryout.
	• Present assessment instruments and/or specifications to client for approval.
Evaluation	• Gain access to learners for prototype testing.
	• Develop instruments and procedures needed for prototype testing.
	• Compile and analyze evaluation data. Develop proposed changes to product based on data.

Demonstrate Phase

After you receive approval for your design documents, you can move on to the Demonstrate, or Demo, phase. This is a transitional stage between the design work you completed in the Define and Design phases and the production and deployment work to follow in the Develop and Deliver phases. The Demo phase is marked by high levels of interaction with your client and project team as you develop the production documents and turn your vision into reality. For a multimedia or online product, or for a large curriculum project, the Demo phase takes on particular importance because this is when you begin working extensively with the rest of the team. In this chapter, we devote significant attention to the tasks associated with multimedia projects. However, these interim documents are important for projects of all types and all sizes.

The Demo phase also includes the critical tasks of prototyping and evaluating and testing with learners. The goal of this phase is to help everyone "see" the project: See what it will look like, how it will work, and whether it will be effective. The more quickly you, the team, the client, and groups of learners start seeing real examples, the more quickly all of you can confirm whether you are on the right track and whether you need to revise or strengthen the material. You may try out these early, prototype materials with a pilot group to assess their success. And if you need to make changes, you still have time in the schedule to do so before you start the major production effort in the Develop phase. The best time and place to catch mistakes is early on and on paper rather than down the road or in pixels or programming. The materials developed at this stage further serve to guide the team through the development process. This phase can include the following steps and deliverables:

- Use the documents created in the Design phase to create a treatment.
- Write scenarios that describe users' experiences with each chunk of content.
- Develop reusable templates that illustrate reoccurring features such as activities, exercises, and assessments.
- Outline the requirements specifications for the instruction.
- Identify and describe needed media assets.
- Develop paper prototypes such as storyboards, scripts, and draft text.
- Develop a working prototype that includes the actual look, feel, and functionality.
- Test the prototype with learners.

These deliverables draw on the diverse media and disciplines that inform instructional design and instructional product development. In film and video production, the treatment is a narrative "sketch" that describes the scriptwriter's ideas for presenting the material. For instructional products, a treatment describes the designer's ideas for presenting the content to learners. Graphic artists use rough sketches, or **wireframes,** to work out the structure of their images, from screen designs to animations. In developing e-learning products, instructional designers can use their own version of wireframes to visually communicate with clients and team members about how screens should be arranged, how they should function, and what learners need in using the program. Programmers use rapid prototyping to quickly determine what works and what doesn't. In instructional design, rapid prototyping can be used to focus the team on the effectiveness of the product. Programmers also use templates to handle functional routines. Templates reduce programming time and costs, and provide better quality control. For instructional products, templates serve a similar function.

Not every project requires every one of these production documents, but you should always try to produce a prototype and test it with real learners. And these documents don't need to be developed in a set sequence. For example, you may develop a rapid prototype to explore treatment ideas. If an existing course needs updating or is being transferred to another medium, you probably don't need to write a scenario. If you're developing a small Web site or working with relatively simple material, you may be able to go straight to storyboards from the design document. Consider the other deliverables as part of your toolkit, and use the tool necessary to accomplish the task at hand.

You should share versions of these deliverables early and often with the client, SMEs, and project team. As you create each deliverable, you get progressively closer to the final product. It's important to maintain communication with your client during this phase. Because each deliverable builds on the prior one, you need to gain approval for each deliverable before committing resources to the next one.

In addition to being a transitional phase in the development of the product, this is a transitional phase for your role in the project, too. During the Design phase, much of the work on a complex project is the responsibility of the instructional designer. The production process waits on you, as designer, to define the audience outcomes, assessment, content, and instructional strategies. As you move into the Demo phase, the work on the project involves more team members. If you are both designing and developing the material, your role shifts from planning the work to beginning to turn each of the chunks into meaningful instruction.

As mentioned previously, the Demo phase is a transitional phase, and the documents and materials you create are transitional, too. As interim materials bridge the gap between design and production activities, they can help clarify information, develop ideas, and identify issues. In addition, on many projects and for many teams, they save time. They can make the difference between a perfectly acceptable final product and a spectacularly successful one.

Treatment

A **treatment** is a transitional document that outlines the instructional strategy. It details what the program will look like, how it will work, and what learners will see, hear, and do (see Example 10.1). In the treatment, you describe your production ideas, types of activities, and plans for assessing learning. One strategy for developing a treatment is to outline how you propose to present each chunk of content.

Recall that in Chapter 3 we discussed different types of learning outcomes (verbal, intellectual, motor, attitude, cognitive strategy) and that the type of learning outcome has implications for the activities and assessments. Recall from Chapter 4 that you should provide opportunities for learners to:

- Focus on the goals of instruction.
- Compare new knowledge with prior knowledge.
- Gain and integrate the content knowledge.
- Take action (practice) and monitor learning progress (through feedback).
- Synthesize and assess their mastery of the new knowledge.
- Extend and transfer the new knowledge to novel situations.

Example 10.1 Treatment

In this example, the designer was developing an online training program for an electronics company that needed to train field staff to use a new test component. The designer used the outline from the content document to create a table. The content outline is in the "Content Chunk" column, and the proposed corresponding treatment ideas appear in the right-hand column. When clients and team members reviewed the treatment, the designer created another column to the right of "Treatment Ideas." Reviewers entered their comments directly into the document, which made the job of compiling reviews easier for the designer.

#	Content Chunk	Treatment Ideas
1.	Introduction	Image of the Z-18, brief narrated introduction explaining the practice.
2.	Objectives	Objectives appear in a bulleted list while an image of the Z-18 displays alongside.
3.	Templates for Z-18: I/O Power Memory	Type a list—learner is prompted to key in the templates that he will need to work the Z-18. The instructions are presented in a bullet list, and a space is provided for the entry. Learner gets feedback on how his list compares to the standard approach.
4.	Explanation of each template and code	When learner clicks the scenario icon, a pop-up text box appears that contains the three Z-18 templates. Z-18 practice template menu: practice templates listed by code in the order they appear in the program. Each code has a rollover explanation. Note: This chart can be a PDF that the learner can print and have with him as he works the practice.
5.	Demonstrate and practice I/O template, Power template (PWR), and code entries	Learner types the ID and password, enters it. The I/O template displays. Narrator instructs learner to select the appropriate template for checking power (PWR) and to click the "Check Answer" button. All feedback in this program will work the same way. Correct answers get positive reinforcement. Incorrect answers get corrective feedback. Learner has a second chance to get the right answer.
6.	Memory template (MEM) and memory codes	The memory template displays on one side of the screen. Learner types the code, then enters. On the other side, text instructs him to key in the memory codes.
7.	Experienced user's perspective on Z-18 interface: easier to learn and use	"Ask the Expert" feature pops up. A seasoned employee explains how the power and memory information is used in the product. This could be a recurring feature showing employees who can provide additional background on a task. They can explain the importance of these functions from the customer's perspective.
8.	Review	Perhaps a drag-and-drop exercise to line up correct codes with screens?

Recall, too, that there are different learning theories (behavioral, cognitive, and constructivist) and that the theory on which the instruction is based has implications for the sequence and choice of learning events.

The treatment offers you an opportunity to try out various ideas as you seek the right combination of learning events and assessment for each learning outcome. You can start by roughing in the entire instructional experience or working on one chunk at a time. For example, you might pick a chunk of content that represents a single lesson and examine the goals and subskills. Consider the characteristics of the learners, the learning and application contexts, and the content as you plan the learning events for each chunk of content. You need to think about how to take advantage of the features the delivery mode offers. For example, if you're developing e-learning materials, it might be helpful to animate a process or allow learners to drag and drop components as they learn about certain equipment. If you are developing classroom-based materials, think about how the classroom can afford unique solutions to specific instructional problems. For example, if the course goal is to help supervisors develop interpersonal skills, you should consider group activities that give learners opportunities for practice and feedback from their peers.

Begin making notes about how you plan to develop each of the chunks of content. Determine how you will handle the events, or conditions, of learning for each chunk. Finally, design an assessment that is aligned with the outcomes and activities. Proceed through all of the chunks, reviewing and revising them to make sure they are consistent. After reviewing the treatment, you and your team may generate new and better ideas, fill in gaps, or correct errors. And making these changes won't cost you much time or money.

You might feel somewhat overwhelmed trying to ensure that you are applying the learning events appropriately and integrating them into a seamless lesson. Does a chunk of content require a constructivist approach? Is the material inherently procedural? Are learning events developed sufficiently? Keep going back through the material, making improvements iteratively. As you become more experienced, you'll internalize this knowledge, and developing the treatment for the instructional strategy won't be so time consuming.

A treatment is something to produce quickly both as a creative tool and as a means of communication. It gives you an opportunity to develop ideas and see how well they might work. It can help you identify strategies for organizing or presenting the content, and it gives your team and reviewers an opportunity to help you brainstorm solutions. The treatment also helps your client begin to visualize how the product will actually work and helps your colleagues understand what they need to do to make these ideas a reality. The design document and content document, the two major deliverables you have prepared at this stage, don't speak to your team members as directly as the treatment. It helps communicate the instructional strategy and production ideas to your client and team members.

Scenarios

The development of a user scenario gives you an opportunity to continue to refine your ideas and begin to explore how well they might work (see Chapter 7 for more on scenarios). A user **scenario** should describe what it feels like to progress through a lesson from the learner's perspective (see Example 10.2). It can be developed to explore ideas for the treatment or to communicate the treatment to the SME, client, and project team. A scenario also helps you describe an online program's navigation and functionality to the technical team. It should cover specific learner behaviors, images, animations, sounds, interactive sequences, and so on. For SMEs, clients, and team members who respond to narratives, this may be a preferred mode of communicating the project requirements to them.

Templates

Using the design document, content document, treatment, and scenario, you can work with your team to create a template for the recurring elements in your instruction. A **template** is a predesigned pattern of instructional events, screen displays, or set of functions used many times within a lesson or curriculum. With templates, your team can develop a set of ready-to-go "packets" that can handle almost all of the content. Because templates are the functional building blocks of your instruction program you want to have an appropriate range of templates to support the instructional strategies you require. For example, when writing this textbook, the template for our chapters consisted of the following categories:

Title

Overview

Graphic

Outcomes

Orientation within design process

Tasks at each phase

Content addressing topic of each chapter

Examples

Tables

Figures

Designer's toolkit

Voice of experience

House analogy

Summary

Example 10.2 Scenario for Computer-Based Lesson

Tyrone clicks the icon on his desktop, bringing up the log-on screen. He quickly logs onto the program, entering his user ID and password. The title screen for the course—"Environmental Studies: Water Quality"—launches. Beautiful photos stream across the screen: the oceans, lakes, rivers, creeks, waterfalls, rain, snow, and other images of water in nature. In addition to serving as an advanced organizer, these images convey some of the beauty and wonder of water's role in nature.

A text menu appears, and Tyrone chooses one of the 10 units. The units he has completed appear shaded. When he has completed part of a unit, an arrow appears to the left of the unit title. When he rolls over a unit title, the unit's submenu appears as a pop-up. The submenu shows the chapters in each unit. Chapters also are grayed out if they have been completed. However, there is no marker indicating if a learner has completed part of a chapter. The tracking system only records completed chapters. Each of the 10 units has 6–10 chapters, and there are a total of 82 chapters in the program. Tyrone has completed three units and is part of the way through a fourth. Each unit takes him about five hours of contact time (about 30 minutes per chapter), although the system doesn't actually track the time. He's working his way through the material in sequence although he could tackle units in any order if he chose to do so. He sometimes looks at other chapters to review or preview the content.

When he opens a chapter, Tyrone sees a main screen that gives an overview of the chapter and the objectives. He can move ahead through all of the chapter screens if he wants to, but he's focused on working through the material sequentially. Each screen of content presents some combination of text, photos, diagrams, tables, animations, and video or audio clips. On each screen, he can click to go to the next screen, go back, return to the main menu, log off, access the glossary or resources or his personal gradebook, or send an e-mail, such as to his instructor. Each screen also shows him how many screens are in the chapter and what screen he is currently looking at (such as 6 of 10). There are about 10 screens in each chapter.

Each chapter includes activities that help Tyrone check his understanding of the material. An activity might require placing the steps of a water quality testing procedure in the correct order along a timeline. Another activity might require classifying runoff particulate matter by dragging the name of each material to the correct column or box. After submitting his answers for an activity, Tyrone gets specific feedback on his answers. All activities are objective (can be scored by the computer) and interactive. There are two to three activities in each chapter.

Each chapter concludes with a 10-item quiz. When Tyrone completes a quiz and presses the Submit button, he gets specific feedback on his answers, but he can't repeat that quiz again. The record-keeping, gradebook program tracks Tyrone's performance on the quizzes. Completing a quiz also signals to the gradebook that he has completed the chapter, so that chapter will be grayed out next time he logs on. Tyrone completes a quiz and hits the Log Off button. A box pops up to ask if he wants to log off. He clicks "Yes," and the program closes.

Notes

References

Application activities

Ideas in action

Design aids

If you are designing a program to be delivered via computer or online, a template might be as simple as a screen with a header, a photo on the left, and bulleted text on the right. Every time you, as the designer, need to display a photo with bulleted text, you can select this template. In the example of a template shown in Example 10.3, the screen includes a header, up to four bullets in a list, and still images controlled with buttons that advance the image and let you go back. Of course, templates can be much more sophisticated than this example. Because each template can be reused many times, templates allow you to design programs with rich functionality and features while staying within the budget. A typical set of display screens (static screens) might include:

Image on left with text

Image on right with text

Example 10.3 Template

In this template for a multimedia product, the functions are listed in the left-hand column and the specifications on the right. The instructional designer can be involved in developing templates. Designers are often required to use templates when developing complex projects.

Still image template	Series of still images in viewer on left with bullet list
Header	Title up to 10 characters
Breadcrumbs	Main, menu, section
Screen sequence	Format: 4 of 7; minimum of 2, limit of 10
Screen controls	Back or next at top and bottom
Image viewer	Displays image on left of screen; square frame
Image controls	Play, pause, back
Caption	Optional; 100 character limit
Bullets	Up to four bullets in list, limit of 400 characters in all bullets
Audio	Optional; 30 seconds per frame
Global	Help, Quit

Large (horizontal) image with limited text below

Sequence of still images, video, or animation

Text only

Image only

You also need to create templates that deliver specific kinds of functionality. Interactions commonly used in computer-based learning programs include:

Forms for entering text

Multiple choice questions including true/false items

Drag-and-drop features such as a matching exercise

Fill-in-the-blank exercises

Checklists and timelines

Feedback following student responses

When creating templates for computer-based materials, you need to write **specifications** so that an artist can create the graphics and a programmer can write the code to support it. These template specifications often are included in a display specifications document (see Example 10.4).

In addition to the written specifications, you can create a wireframe, or sketch, of what you think the computer screen should look like (see Example 10.5). If you aren't an artist, don't despair! You can use a simple tool such as Microsoft's PowerPoint or the "draw tool" in Microsoft Word to create boxes illustrating the general layout and describing the functions of each screen. These planning tools can help you, the team, and your client get a sense of how various screens and screen events will look and work.

Explain to your client that the "art" in the wireframe isn't reflective of the art that will be in the final product. You can even label the screen "Draft" or something similar to make sure the message is clear. If you're working with an artist, she or he may be able to create wireframes that show how the screens will actually look in the final product. Make sure the artist's wireframe accurately reflects the functions and layout needed for instructional effectiveness. Although an artist's rendition is likely to be a polished creation, such proficiency isn't necessary at this point and may even be somewhat counterproductive. You want the team and your client to focus on what the screen does, not on details such as colors or fonts.

Most lessons include recurring patterns that provide a familiar structure for the instructional activities. For example, a trainer might begin by reviewing the agenda, proceed to define terms and concepts in a game format, and then have learners apply their skills in a role play before summarizing the lesson. Or each tape in a video series might begin with a montage, followed by an expert's presentation, examples of how the content is applied in context, and a summary. These patterns can be represented as "templates" to provide organization for each lesson in the curriculum.

Example 10.4 Display Template Specifications

This example was developed for a college-level multimedia science program that accompanied a textbook. The design team reviewed exercises in the textbook to begin designing templates for the online supplement. This example explains the functionality of the Animated Multiple Choice (AMC) template. The functionality involves both animations and interactions in the form of multiple choice questions. There are six templates in the program; this is the specification for one of them.

A. Elements

Goal Statement: to test knowledge acquisition relating to "Topic X"

Instructions/Prompts: (i.e., what does learner need to know to get activity started in terms of first interaction?)

Animation: referential animation key-framed into three–six segments

Stimulus (MC Question): two questions/items per key-framed segment; one answer right per item

Responses: five text responses per question/item

Feedback: textual feedback for right/wrong answers

Scoring: by item scoring/end-of-activity score (not saved); two tries before correct answer is given

Other: reset/play again button

B. General Remarks

This activity is especially useful when movement or "changing of state" (vs. "change of state") is critical to understanding biological concepts. Key is the notion of seeing change of position, scale, rotation, form, color, or opacity, *while it is happening.* In terms of "economy of production," it is critical that animations developed for the tutorial be "repurposed" as AMC activities.

C. Sample Content Delivery

General Description of animation with references to illustrations, models, etc. Key frames or "outcomes" should be storyboarded or thumb-nailed to the greatest extent possible. Each key frame should demonstrate a concept or topic that is critical to that particular stage.

Animation Description: From beginning to 1st key-frame (Note that this segment may inspire up to 2 questions)

Stimulus 1 (i.e., question): 1. What is the x, y, z of a, b, c?

Response 1: A. Hypothesis	**Feedback 1:** Sorry, incorrect.
Response 2: B. Theory	**Feedback 2:** You're wrong.
Response 3: C. Guess	**Feedback 3:** See page 12.
Response 4: D. Scientific Method	**Feedback 4:** Awesome!
Response 5: E. "A" and "C"	**Feedback 5.** Sorry, incorrect.

You might worry that templates impose limitations on your creativity. You want the freedom to create the perfect solution for each instructional episode. Actually, templates won't feel restrictive if you design them carefully. The key is to analyze the content, the learners, and the learning requirements carefully so that you can identify the kinds of displays and interactions you will need to deliver the instruction effectively. Once you begin designing with the templates, you may need to tweak a few things or even to add a template, but you'll probably

Example 10.5 Display Template Wireframe

In this example of a wireframe, the designer used PowerPoint to "rough out" the screen display and functions for each screen in the program. The designer explained to the reviewers that the design did not reflect the quality of the actual final graphics, but was meant to convey a sense of the layout and functionality. The wireframe communicated clearly to the client and team members. They brainstormed changes and refined some of the features. Then, using the wireframe as a guide, the artist created the actual graphics that were incorporated into the program.

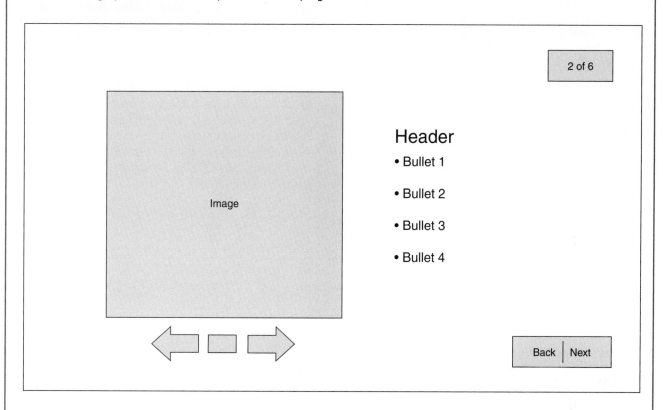

In this wireframe, the designer indicates that there should be a header and bulleted list for text, and images to one side.

also find that they free you to concentrate on developing the instruction without worrying about having to create a unique design for each screen, chapter, or lesson within your instruction.

Template Guide

It's a good idea to make a **template guide** that collects all of the templates and associated specifications in one location. You should provide a template guide to each member of the team and to each client and SME. If your team uses a secure Web location to manage project documents, you can post the latest version there. You can also print it out and collate the pages into a notebook or spiral binder to use as a reference. Some designers

laminate or use plastic sleeves for the pages, because the book can get rather ragged by the end of a project!

For many clients and SMEs, having all the templates in one place helps them start to really understand the scope of the product and the scale of the production process. If the technical specifications seem too complicated for these reviewers, consider writing simpler specifications for each template, perhaps just a brief description of its functionality and purpose. As you move from generating many design documents in the Define and Design phases to "making things" in the production phases, reviewers tend to have an easier time understanding each deliverable. They start to see the unique functions of different segments and screens, and how each of the activities will look and work. They also start to understand why it's important to create templates.

Requirements Specifications

Typically, the **requirements specifications** document identifies the software tools and strategies that will be used in producing the program, and defines the delivery format. For print-based products, the requirements specifications may include the font, margins, headings required, and other formatting details, as well as the computer software that should be used to develop the program. Requirements specifications for audio and video materials identify the file or tape format in which the program will be delivered. The requirement specifications for a computer-based program usually contain all of these details, including everything the program must do technically (see Example 10.6). You might think of them as "technical specs," but software developers call them requirements specifications (they also call themselves "developers"; in this book, to avoid confusion, we call them "programmers").

You also may be aware of the SCORM (Sharable Courseware Object Reference Model) standards for computer-delivered instructional products that have been adopted by many companies. In the online education business, one of the most-pursued goals is to devise a system that stores basic units of instruction so that these units can be assembled, on the fly, to meet the unique and immediate learning needs of each learner. These basic units of content are known as reusable learning objects (RLOs). The premise is that each granular piece of instruction is stored, tagged with keywords, and made available to other instructors and learners with access to the system. **SCORM** refers to a set of technical standards that enable organizations to continue to use and reuse courseware even when computer technologies and operating systems change. Learning Management System (LMS) products that adhere to SCORM standards are said to be SCORM-compliant. Using SCORM-compliant products can extend the useful life of electronic courseware and save organizations money.

Fortunately, SCORM's impact on instructional design is usually minimal. You may need to write a description of

---

Example 10.6 Requirements Specification

These are the specifications for a multimedia product for higher education.

Platform Specification

Windows	Macintosh
Pentium II CPU or higher	Power Macintosh or G3 system or higher
Memory (RAM): 32 MB minimum; 64–128 MB recommended	Memory: 64 MB RAM or higher
Free space on hard drive: 10 MB	Free space on hard drive 10 MB
Graphics adapter: SVGA or higher	
Monitor settings: 800 x 600, true color (24-bit or 32-bit) or high color (16-bit) modes	Monitor settings: 800 x 600; millions of colors (24-bit or 32-bit) or thousands of colors (16-bit) modes
SVGA color monitor	SVGA color monitor
CD-ROM speed: 2x or higher	CD-ROM speed: 2x or higher
Microsoft Windows OS: 98 and up	OS 8.1 and up

Functions

Browser	Netscape Navigator 4.7, Microsoft Internet Explorer 5.5 or higher
Required plug-ins	Shockwave, Flash, and QuickTime may be needed for certain activities
Screen resolution	min. 800 x 600
Screen size available for content	600 x 300 for nonscrolling

(continued on page 229)

Example 10.6 (continued)

Functions

Structure	Unit—8 Chapter—55 Page—to be determined
Global controls	Simulations Menu (Unit) Tutorials Menu (Chapter) Help Credits
Color, font, style for global headers	Black, Verdana, 10 bold
Screen-level functions	Next Previous Links (Glossary)
File naming convention	Associate with Unit/Chapter TOC
Color, font, style for screen-level headers	Black, verdana, 12, bold
Content text font, size, style	Verdana, 10
Text display requirements amount per screen	Around 80 characters per line (maximum) for body copy; text tables should be limited to 350 pixels wide
Captions standards	To be determined
Permission line credits	To be determined
Graphic/animation file formats	.jpg, .gif, .swf
Text file formats	.html, .txt, .doc, .pdf
Audio file formats	.wav, .aiff, .mp3
Audio file controls	Play Pause (QuickTime Player–based?)
Video file format	.mov
Abbreviations, grammar, spelling, punctuation standards	Chicago Manual of Style
Highlighting text standards	Maroon
Display of links standards	Blue

each chunk of content so that it can become an RLO. The description becomes part of the tag, or manifest, associated with that RLO. You may also be required to develop objective assessments, such as multiple choice items, so that the scoring can be reported to an LMS. Although these standards weren't developed to support instructional design, they usually don't get in the way.

The technical members of your team may be the ones charged with producing the requirement specifications document, but you will probably need to contribute to it, and you should certainly review it. Although a lead programmer often writes the specs for a computer-based program, you need to participate to make sure that they reflect the product's instructional requirements. This

typically requires several meetings and iterations of the document before arriving at a set of specifications that everyone can support. Make sure that the functionality, navigation, and delivery environment you require is included in the technical plan. If constraints require you to make changes, work with the technical team to explain what minimum requirements your learners must meet to master the material. There are likely to be alternative strategies that can deliver your requirements in a less expensive but equally effective manner. As with every document or deliverable, you have to make sure that the requirement specifications describe a product that will meet the needs of the learners. No one else on the team has this perspective, and it's a critical contribution. Your role is to ensure that all the work everyone invests in the project yields an instructionally effective result.

Communicating effectively with the technical team isn't always effortless. Just as you try to "get inside the head" of your learners in order to develop instruction for them, you need to use your communication skills to see what the tech team needs to produce the program. This often means drafting user scenarios that describe how learners actually use the program. Be detailed in your descriptions of the user experience, because each of these details may represent a specific type of functionality or navigation. Then meet with the technical team and talk through each of the user scenarios, even sketching out layouts, displays, navigation, or functions on a white marker board. This should give the tech team a much better understanding of the user requirements and should help you understand where your design might present problems for them. Enlist the team in finding solutions; once they understand why you want a certain feature, they can brainstorm to find alternatives. A side benefit is that, when you develop the program in concert with the team, everyone has a sense of ownership and feels invested in the project's success. Above all, work hard to prevent falling into an "us versus them" relationship that could derail the project.

Media Assets

When designing most types of instructional materials, you need to specify what media assets should be included. **Media assets** include photographs, illustrations, diagrams, animations, video, and audio—in other words, all the media that must be produced or acquired in order to deliver the instruction effectively. If you have media production experience, this probably won't be a difficult task. If you aren't familiar with producing media, work with your team members to determine what medium will work best, and what the budget will allow, for each instructional requirement. For example, if you are presenting content on bird migration, should you use video or an animation? Will a photograph work better than an illustration? Can a map be animated? Is narration helpful with a particular video, or should it contain only the audio of the action? For each project and each chunk of content, the answers will be different because the content, learners, and budget are always unique. (See Chapter 5 for information on selecting assets.)

When you develop the specifications for the media assets, you should sketch out your requirements for artwork and review these sketches with the artists and producers. Even if your skills are limited to producing stick figures, the drawings will be very helpful in guiding the artists and producers in their work. If the content for these images requires the use of certain colors, icons, or conventions, be sure to provide this information. For example, in the telecommunications industry, the connection between networks is always represented as a cloud—it's even called "the cloud." Be sure that your sketches contain all of the content that must be included, such as parts of a system, labels, the title, and relative sizes and relationships. And clearly label each item using the exact terminology needed in the image. Give the producers as much information as you can to help them create exactly the right asset.

Table 10.2 lists guidelines for communicating effectively with the media team.

Table 10.2 Assets and sources

Asset	Source	Provide producer with
Photograph	Photographer	Detailed description and/or stick figure drawing
Photo—existing	Photo archive	Specific image and archive
Illustration	Illustrator	Stick figure drawing
Diagram	Graphic artist	Pencil sketch, PowerPoint slide, Visio graphic; label all details
Video	Video producer	Video script
Video—existing	Archive	Specific clip and archive
Animation	Animator (usually Flash)	Stick figure sketches with labeled details, drawn as cartoon strip
3-D animation	Animator	Stick figure sketches with labeled details, drawn as cartoon strip
Narration	Audio producer	Narration script; discuss how to pronounce unusual words, abbreviations, or industry jargon
Sound effects	Audio producer	Description; provide examples if possible
Sounds—existing	Sound archive	Specific clip and archive
Music	Producer	Description; provide examples if possible

Voice of Experience

Finding the Copyright Holder

For a middle school American history program, the designer and client specified many source materials that would convey to students the look and feel of America's past. However, tracking down some of the copyright holders required some real detective work. In one case, the wife of a deceased artist was discovered living in a nursing home in Paris, and she spoke only French. The team obtained permission to use her husband's artwork by arranging to have a producer who was fluent in French call the widow at 3:00 A.M. Texas time, which was 10:00 A.M. in Paris.

DESIGNER'S TOOLKIT

Talent Release

Release of Rights

I, _____ ,

hereby assign and transfer to Casa Grande Learning Solutions ("Publisher"), its affiliates, subsidiaries, and successors, all rights to use, with or without copyright, my name, likeness, and/or voice, recorded on film, audio, or video recording device, or other media, for the purposes of producing *Language Arts Today* ("Product") for an unlimited time period beginning with the date of this agreement. No promises have been made to me to secure my signature to this release.

I warrant that my contribution is original with me and does not contain anything that violates any copyright or personal, proprietary, or other right. I acknowledge and agree that I have no right, title, or interest in the Product or the copyright therein, all of which shall be owned by the Publisher, free of any lien, encumbrance, or claim by me.

I release the Publisher, its affiliates, subsidiaries, and successors, from any and all claims for damages, libel, slander, invasion of the right of privacy, or any other claim based on the use of said material. I hereby warrant that I am of full age and have every right to contract in my own name in this regard.

Agreed and accepted:

_____   _____
Name   Date

To use existing assets such as photographs, video segments, audio clips, reproductions of artworks, or primary sources, you need to get permission from the copyright holder (see Chapter 5 for more information on permissions and licensing). This can be a costly and complex process depending on the asset, the copyright holder, and your project and its delivery environment. There are companies that specialize in licensing media assets and have fairly simple pricing and licensing agreements. There's usually room to negotiate, which is a job for a project manager or producer. Some assets, such as anything produced by the U.S. government, are free and readily available.

If you know what image or asset you want, specify it to the producer. Provide the source, if you know it, and any other relevant information that will help him or her find the asset. Also explain how critical it is to the success of the instruction. For example, you may want to use a few seconds of a CNN broadcast of a news program. This will need to be licensed and is likely to be expensive. However, if the content is about news delivery or a specific event, the cost of obtaining permission to use the clip may be worthwhile.

If you plan to photograph, videotape, or record voices or a musical performance, you need to obtain a talent release for each person who appears or is heard in the program. The responsibility for collecting signed releases may belong to the project manager or media producer, or it may fall to you. If you are involved in this work, check to see if your company or institution has a release form already prepared. If not, you can adapt the one presented here to meet your needs. Don't allow the project to be jeopardized by failing to secure releases.

Storyboards and Other Paper Prototypes

There you are at your desk, surrounded by piles of source materials, files stuffed full of reports, notes from meetings, interviews with experts, and your own design documents. How do you turn all of this into an effective instructional product? Where and how should you start? At some point, you have to simply start putting material on paper (or keyboarding it on your computer), knowing that it won't be perfect the first time. When creating computer-based programs, you begin by developing the storyboards. When creating video or audio files, you write the script. When creating text-based materials, you simply start drafting the content. For any of these products, it's best to put together a small section of the instruction and test it with learners before developing the complete set of storyboards, scripts, or text materials.

A common strategy is to develop a "slice" of the product that includes the basic global functionality and content for one complete section as a working prototype before completing the production documents for the entire project. For a multimedia or online project, the working prototype provides an opportunity to build a small section of the program with the actual look, feel, interface, and functionality. For classroom-based programs, the prototype might be a chunk of content that you can test with a group of learners. For video programs, you can create a "rough cut" and get feedback from learners. This slice of the program gives users a sense of what the learners experience when going through a complete chunk of content, from start to finish.

Let's say you're producing an online training program on first aid, and you've chosen the section on airway obstruction for the slice. This section will be one of 10 in the finished product. At the global level, this first aid prototype includes the title screen and main menu, along with functions such as the glossary, help screens, and resources. You begin with a "test your knowledge" activity to focus learners on the goals of the instruction and to remind them of their prior knowledge. You demonstrate the content on how to recognize airway obstruction and treat the victim through a sequence of photographs, followed by detailed procedures and illustrations for specific parts of the body. Additional detail might include how to handle unusual situations. You follow up with opportunities to apply this new knowledge using a timeline activity that reinforces the sequence of asking if the victim is choking, telling the victim you are going to try to expel the object, and performing the Heimlich maneuver. Another activity requires learners to identify items that often cause choking and to review the procedures for dislodging an obstruction in children and babies. Each activity provides specific feedback to learners. Next, you provide a review, and you conclude with a quiz. Using the prototype, you can demonstrate the pattern of activities planned for all 10 sections.

Prototyping doesn't need to "wait" until the production documents for the entire program are completed and approved. In fact, the sooner the production team begins mocking up the product, creating rapid prototypes that get team members thinking and brainstorming, the faster they will be able to arrive at a final plan for the product. If you are developing an online or multimedia product, it's important to look at real screens as soon as possible. One type of rapid prototype is a PowerPoint presentation of a sequence of the program, with static slides that illustrate the screens and the interactions. Reviewers spend so much time looking at paper documents that they can lose sight of the fact that the actual product won't be on paper. You can keep everyone mindful of the fact that the product is on-screen by developing real screens for review. The prototype conveys your ideas in a concrete way to your team, and to clients, SMEs, and learners so that you can refine those ideas before committing extensive time and resources to design and development.

Creating Paper Prototypes

When you begin writing the text, script, or storyboard for the instructional materials, you draw on all you've learned about the learners, content, instructional strategies, delivery environment, and media options to create an engaging and effective instructional experience. If you've written a treatment, you can use it as the starting point for developing your instruction. In fact, this is where a treatment saves you time in the long run. If you don't have a treatment, you need to determine how to structure the material. The structure might correspond to your content document, but your learners may need a different presentation. You need to chunk the content into digestible units and decide how to develop each chunk based on the learning outcome, learning theory, and events of learning (discussed in Chapters 3 and 4). Your design document, content document, and any visioning documents will all provide you with direction in developing the instruction.

If your team has developed templates, use your template guide to help you determine how to develop each section of the lesson. As the instructional designer, you are most concerned about the specifications for screen displays and interactions because these directly affect your design. For example, each template might contain a limit on the number of characters in the header and body text. For practice and assessment items, there might be requirements for the number of questions and possible answers, and the nature of feedback text. As you write the instruction, you'll start to memorize the specs for each template. You probably will still use the guide as a reference (or even an inspiration) when you're brainstorming ideas for making the content engaging.

Enlist your colleagues' aid in thinking about how to handle images, media, and interactions. Perhaps you can schedule meetings with the group or individuals to review sections of the instruction as you develop the paper prototypes. Tap them for ideas in developing certain chunks or in solving instructional problems. You also want their assistance in making sure that the ideas you have generated are feasible. They may advise you that an idea is too complicated to produce or suggest an even more effective way to present material. By actively seeking their participation, you help team members feel invested in the product. It also helps make it a better product—the contributions of a strong team are synergistic.

Writing the Text

At some point, you need to write the actual text for the instruction. Abbreviations, terms and words, and, especially, acronyms are common to various industries and subject areas. As you work with the content, you begin absorbing the jargon of that industry quickly, but be careful about how you use jargon in developing your instruction. When learners encounter lots of unfamiliar words in a sentence, they have to work too hard to derive meaning, and the instruction fails. A rule of thumb is to use no more than three new words (or acronyms) in a given sentence. Each time you introduce a new word, be sure to define it in context immediately. To make sure your learners understand new words, provide examples and, where appropriate, nonexamples. And give them opportunities to apply their learning quickly by providing exercises or activities that require using these words.

Reading Levels For sophisticated learners such as college students or college-educated professionals, you shouldn't be too concerned about the reading level. But for a general audience, try to keep the reading level at about that of sixth-graders. When readers encounter several new or difficult words in a sentence, it starts to interfere with reading comprehension. If you've struggled to translate a foreign language, you know how tedious and frustrating it can be to encounter strings of unfamiliar words. Some daily newspapers aim for a sixth-grade level, as do many government and public information documents. However, it can be difficult to write to this level, especially when the material includes technical or medical terms. For example, the Flesch-Kincaid Readability Index included with Microsoft Word ranks this paragraph at a twelfth-grade reading level. Many word processing programs allow you to check the reading level of a passage and provide guidance on language.

To achieve a lower reading level, keep sentences short, and use simple words. Communication experts caution that comprehension begins to decline when sentences run longer than 20 words. Take a cue from Abraham Lincoln. The Gettysburg Address is a mere 266 words in nine sentences, an average of 20.4 words per sentence. The reading level for one of the most celebrated speeches in history is grade 9.5.[1]

Translations In an increasingly interconnected world, educational materials often are developed for delivery in more than one language. Some products are created in two or more languages while others are fully developed in one language and then translated into others. If you are developing products that will contain more than one language, there are several factors to consider during both design and development. You will probably want to work with a translator and specialists in that language during the early phases of the project.

For products that will contain additional languages, consider how the languages will appear within the instruction. Suppose you are designing a middle school mathematics program on CD-ROM that will be produced in English and Spanish. Will learners be able to choose one language or the other, or will both languages be available at all times? If there is text, it will need to be available in both languages. Any labels, titles, credit lines, or other text that appears on graphics or in other areas of the program will also need to be available in both English and Spanish. When English text is translated into Spanish, the Spanish text usually requires as much as a third more space. So, if you have 100 words in English, it may require 133 words to say the same thing in Spanish. Leave room on the screen and on the graphics for these additional words.

If there is narration, it also needs to be written and recorded in both languages. Not surprisingly, Spanish also usually requires about a third more time to speak than English. If narration accompanies animation or a video, be sure to consider the timing in both languages when designing the material. It's important as well that your Spanish translator and narrator use the idioms, accent, and pronunciation appropriate to the target audience. For example, a Castilian Spanish accent might not be effective if the target learner has a Mexican or Puerto Rican background. Your client should be able to advise you on this.

English is read from left to right and from top to bottom, and that movement, from the top left of the page or screen to the lower right, is pervasive in Western countries. However, many other languages are read from right to left, or in columns from top to bottom. If you work with a translator early in the design process, you can ensure that the pages or screens will be easily adapted for all languages.

Voice of Experience

When Is a Word a Vocabulary Word?

Sometimes, simple words have complex meanings—and a computerized language checker won't catch this. For a high school economics program, the designer realized that many of the vocabulary words have other, simpler meanings. Every high school student understands the words "goods" and "services," and readability tools would not recognize them as difficult words. Yet, in the context of economics, they are complex concepts. The designer realized the need to treat these words carefully by defining them, using them in context, and providing examples.

Rules for Computer Display of Text

Text	If delivery includes narration, keep text to minimum, such as by using bullets.
Fonts	Use sans serif font on screen, such as Verdana, Helvetica, Tahoma, or Arial. For print, choose serif font for body text, such as Times Roman, Palatino, or Garamond.
Font size	Test font and size before selecting it. Usually, 12- or 14-point fonts display best on screen.
Font style	Keep styles to minimum! Use only one device to highlight (such as bold or italics), and highlight sparingly. Never display text in ALL CAPITALS—it's equivalent to shouting at readers. In addition, blocks of text in bold, italics, or all caps are hard to read.
Upper- and lowercase	Use upper- and lowercase, just as you would in print products. It's easier to read.
Contrast	Use dark letters on light background, and light letters on dark background. Check to make sure your selections will also work in black and white.
Colors	Use color for a reason, such as cuing or emphasizing. Bright colors work well on screen. Pastels are usually too subtle, but this depends on screen resolution.
Complementary colors	Avoid putting complementary colors next to each other—it creates high contrast and visual tension. Complements are color "opposites" such as yellow and purple, blue and orange, and red and green. Some color-blind users can't distinguish between red and green.
White space	Keep screens uncluttered, with plenty of space around each content element.
Scrolling	Try to limit scrolling, but don't hesitate to use it for short passages.

Instructional materials intended for delivery in multiple languages also need to be designed with consideration for other cultures. Phrases and examples that work well for an American audience might not make sense to learners from other cultures. Your client may be sensitive to these issues, or you may need to work with a cultural specialist to ensure that the materials will work for all learners.

Scripts

If your program will include original video or audio someone has to write a script. This might be assigned to a professional scriptwriter, or it might be your responsibility.

If you will be writing a script that will be produced by an audio or video producer, arrange to meet with that person before you start writing. Ask if he or she has a format for you to use in preparing your script. A document template might exist that should be used in writing a shooting script. Or the producer may prefer that you write a narrative treatment that the production team will convert to a script format.

If you haven't written a script before, look at models and ask the producer for guidance. One page of double-spaced, two-column text script usually translates to about one minute of video or audio recording. You can learn more about the process of script writing by reviewing one of many books or resources available online or in your community. You may be able to find an experienced scriptwriter who is willing to serve as your mentor or reviewer.

The most important consideration in writing a video script is to think visually. What will viewers see? The sound is very important in a video clip, but if you are merely presenting a shot of someone talking, why do you need video? If the "talking head" is an expert or has a compelling story, then the shot might be worth using. Use video when you really need it—for example, when you need to demonstrate a process (how to repair a bicycle tire), present historical content (President John F. Kennedy's inaugural speech), or show examples from nature (formations of birds in flight). Video production can be very expensive, so work closely with the producer or project manager to keep your ideas within budget.

The most important consideration in writing an audio script, such as for narration, is that it should be written to be heard. We don't speak in perfect sentences, and it's hard for listeners to make sense of long, complex sentences. Usually, contractions sound more natural than the alternative, such as "can't" instead of "cannot." And sometimes, sentence fragments sound better and make more sense than complete sentences. You don't need to use improper grammar, but you don't want the narration to sound as if someone is reading it. Arrange the script so that it's obvious how you want the words to be read. Note where pauses should occur, and provide direction on how to pronounce unusual words. Read your script out loud to see how it sounds. In the most effective narration, the narrator seems to be speaking his or her own words.

If your narration coordinates with on-screen text, try to avoid having the narrator read the text verbatim. Most

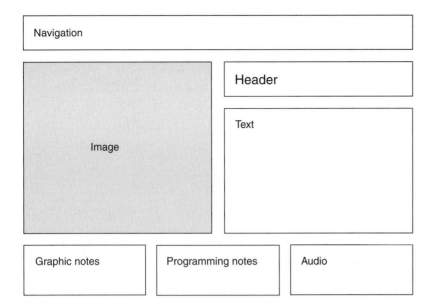

Figure 10.3 *Storyboard form.* In this storyboard form, each page corresponds to a screen or sequence in the program. There are sections for a sketch of the visual, the text, the audio, and notes for the programmer or producer.

readers can read faster than a narrator can say the words out loud. Even for slow readers, such narration can be tedious and can actually interfere with comprehension. If you plan to use narration with text in your program, shorten the text into bulleted lists, with each bulleted item a phrase or sentence fragment highlighting a key point. The one exception to this rule involves new readers. Children who are learning to read, and anyone learning a new language, will welcome having each word read to them. Because new readers read slowly, the narration is likely to dovetail with these users' relatively limited reading skills.

On some teams, script writing, either for narration or for video, is handled by specialists. If that's the case on your project, write the audio content so that the scriptwriter can convert this into the narration script. Also give the scriptwriter the design document and any other information that will help him or her understand the target audience. Ask to review the writer's work to make sure it's appropriate for the content, instructional strategy, and the audience. Provide constructive feedback to the writer when you review the script.

Storyboards

When you are developing computer-based and video materials, the creation of storyboards represents a significant milestone. They are the culmination of your instructional design work and usually the most visible deliverable you produce. From the moment you hand the storyboards off to the team, they direct all activities until the product is completed.

When you develop computer- and video-based instruction, storyboards are the blueprints for the production that follows. A **storyboard** is simply a set of specifications detailing what happens on each screen. The text, audio, video, graphics, animation, and interactions or exercises are all described in detail so that your reviewers and your team understand the program clearly. In fact, you should be able to perform QA (quality assurance) on the final program by testing it against the storyboards. If any program component doesn't match the storyboard, something wasn't produced according to specifications. Storyboards need a great deal of attention. If they are going to serve as a blueprint, they must be comprehensive and accurate.

There are many different formats for presenting storyboards, and what works for one project and one team might not work for another. One format presents one screen per page with notes explaining the interactions (see Figure 10.3). You'll notice that the storyboard form shown in Figure 10.3 includes space for a sketch of the visual, the text, the audio, and notes for the programmer or producer. Some designers use Microsoft's PowerPoint to develop storyboards using this strategy. They make the storyboard look roughly like the final product, with mocked-up visuals and interactions. This strategy works well for programs with many images and interactions, but not so well for programs with a great deal of text.

Another storyboard format is developed using a word processing program, spreadsheet, or database, and delivered in tabular form arrangement (see Example 10.7). Each row (across) represents a single screen. Each

Example 10.7 Storyboard Table

Screen	Title	Text	Production Notes
1Z000000	Vertel Online Training		Splash. Skip.
1Z000001	Vertel Online Training	Select a training path: Level I Level II Level III	User-level menu.
1T000000	Vertel Online Training for Level I	Getting started Desktop Presentations Assignments Reports Help — User level Index How to use this training program Quit	Overview.
1T100101	How to Use This Training Program	This program simulates the experience you'll have working with Vertel. Most sections guide you through the procedures for each function or feature. Usually, you'll see a Vertel screen along with text explaining how to perform the task.	Representative examples of program screens.
	Index	The Index allows you to access any training topic at any time. It presents a list of all of the topics covered in this training. When you click on a topic, the program goes to that training.	Index screen.
1T100102	Practice	Throughout this training program, you'll have opportunities to practice. Directions guiding you through the steps are in the box below the screen. You might be asked to click on a button or type in a name, simulating what happens in the live program. Once you've performed the step, click the Submit button to see the result. Try the example here to practice.	Representative Try It. Highlight the direction line window. Then highlight Submit button.
1T100103		Click on "Ronda I Green" in the list of Learners. The program will display Ronda's report.	Select learner.
1T100104	Feedback	The program won't save your entries, but it will allow you to compare your practice to the correct response. You can return to any screen for additional practice. You can also skip the practice if, for example, you just want to review a section.	Display Ronda's report.
1T110101	Quit	Are you sure you want to quit? Yes No	Yes, quit. No, return.

column (down) indicates the media or functions for that screen, such as text, graphic, audio, or exercise template. In this example, the columns represent the screen number (or file name), the title or header for each screen, the text that will appear on screen, and notes to the production team. In this storyboard, the "Notes" column includes directions about the images and interactions. These can also be listed in separate columns, as can video or audio, animations, and any other media.

Designers use a range of strategies to create storyboards. You might find it easier to divide the storyboard into separate documents corresponding to units or chunks or any other category that's useful to you. You can merge the documents later if needed. Some designers write a narrative in the text column and then go back through to select templates, specify visuals and media, and decide on interactions. Other designers think visually and prefer to sketch out their ideas first and then do the drafting. Still others think through every event on every screen first and then move on to the next screen. On some projects, a professional writer might write the on-screen text or develop the audio or video script. On other projects, a technical writer might be responsible for on-screen text, help, resources, or glossary files. There is no right or wrong way to prepare storyboards. Use the strategy that's best for you and your project.

Internal Reviews

As with each document you produce, you should prepare your paper prototypes carefully and be vigilant in searching for errors and correcting them before sending the materials out for review. The paper prototypes move the editing task to a new level because you don't want any errors in the delivered product. For example, the programmers can usually take the storyboard text directly from your document and convert it into the text that will appear in the final product. This includes any text that will appear on-screen, such as titles, body text, captions, or glossary definitions. It's much more expensive to fix errors once a product is produced, so it's critical to get the storyboards as close to flawless as is humanly possible. It's much easier, and cheaper, to fix a typo or other error by changing a word processing document than having to go into a programmed product and make the change there.

At the same time, it's hard to proofread your own work. As the writer, you are simply too close to your work to catch every typo or error. At the least, use the spell check feature in your word processing program (this is a good reason for using a word processing program instead of another storyboard development tool). Be aware, however, that the spell checker won't catch everything. If you are working on a team with other designers or if there's someone with good editing skills on the team, take advantage of those skills and have them review your work

Voice of Experience

Fact Checkers

In producing a middle school American history curriculum, the developer hired a team of fact checkers to verify every fact in the product. The publisher was adamant that each fact be supported by three recently published academic sources, such as peer-reviewed journals and scholarly texts. Even such obvious facts as "the Declaration of Independence was issued in 1776" required documentation. With this level of attention, a fact checker found a serious error that had escaped many levels of review by experienced editors. The sentence mentioned "President Alexander Haig." In fact, though he may have had presidential aspirations, Haig was secretary of state under Ronald Reagan. The credibility of the product would have been seriously undermined if this error hadn't been caught and corrected.

before sending it to clients and SMEs. If you have the budget for a copy editor, bring in someone with established skills.

External Reviews

Paper prototypes such as storyboards represent key documents that should be reviewed by the production team, client, and SMEs. Arrange a meeting with the production team when you complete a set of documents or storyboards, and perhaps when you complete each section. Distribute copies to all participants, and walk through the storyboards together, screen by screen or section by section. Encourage their feedback and suggestions—even call it a brainstorming session. This can be difficult, especially if you've been working alone up to this point, pouring your creativity and energy into crafting all of the materials. You're likely to feel a strong sense of ownership with this work, and it's not easy when new people come on board and start offering their ideas. Try to be receptive to other people's suggestions. When you work together creatively, the product benefits from the collective synergy of the team. Additionally, everyone feels more invested in the product's success.

Take time to train your client and SME reviewers so that they understand how to read storyboards, scripts and other draft documents. Walk through the documents with them, either in a meeting or a conference call, to make sure they understand what they are reading. If you delivered materials in a word processing format, the reviewers can make comments directly in the document. You can also create a new column for their corrections or additions. If reviewers comment in a separate document, provide them with a review guide that contains an outline of the program so they can organize their comments in roughly the same structure as the product.

Reviewers sometimes get hung up on "word-smithing" the text and narration. Although it's important that the words are "just right," you also want to be sure that reviewers are seeing the bigger picture—will this design be instructionally effective for the target learners? For example, let's say you've developed a unit on photosynthesis for a middle school science product. Ask your reviewers: Does the animation adequately convey the process of photosynthesis? Are there enough photographic examples? Does the narration achieve the right tone? Is the matching activity a good way of engaging 12-year-olds? Is the quiz too easy?

Working Prototypes

By now in the instructional design and development process, you've created many documents and been through many reviews and revisions. You might be wondering if the actual product will ever get made. Your client probably feels this way, too. This next step is the first milestone that starts to feel like production. The working prototype should contain enough of the program that stakeholders can properly evaluate the product. The team, clients, and SME can all see if it meets their expectations. For some reviewers, this will be the first time they "get it." These people may have trouble reading documents such as the storyboard and fully appreciating all the actual product will deliver. Another primary reason for producing a prototype is to try it out with real learners. You can set up pilot testing and other formative evaluations to help you identify problems that you can correct before investing in the complete production. They also serve to confirm what you are doing right.

Prototype Development

As the prototype is being developed, you should work closely with the rest of the production team to create each component. Meet with the artists and audiovisual producers to review the project's instructional requirements. Try to avoid instructional design jargon in explaining anything that isn't clear, and make note of, and get back to them on, any questions they have for which you don't have answers. If you've created a storyboard, review that document and see if the producers have any questions or better ideas for getting the content across. Because video can be expensive to produce, you and the producer may need to be creative in finding alternatives. Take time as well to read the technical team's documents, such as the requirements specifications, which detail the structure, functionality, performance requirements, and so on. Even

if this document is highly technical, it can help you understand the programming function of the team—and you might be alerted to a potential problem.

You should meet with each team member individually to review their work and provide constructive feedback where needed. Throughout this process, you constantly serve as an advocate for learners. This means monitoring the production to ensure that the materials are appropriate for the audience and that the outcomes, content, activities, and assessment items are all in alignment. Because your prototype may be used for testing with actual learners, consider if you have provided a complete and self-contained lesson. Think about the novice user. Is there enough of an introduction? Is there enough information, context, practice, feedback, guidance, review, and assessment so that he or she can complete the instruction successfully? You are the team member responsible for ensuring that the product meets learners' needs. No one else on the team has this perspective.

Review and Revisions

Once the prototype is completed, you and everyone involved in the project will review it. The prototype must be evaluated carefully, because once it's approved it will serve as the model from which all the rest of the program is developed. It is the last chance to make changes before going into full-scale production.

Initially, you want to demonstrate the prototype to the client, SMEs, and other experts who may be working on the project. With the production team, create a review form that your reviewers can use to record their comments about the prototype. The form can be adapted from the program's outline. Reviewers can follow the outline and enter their comments in the outline at the point corresponding to the program location (see Example 10.8). Some developers incorporate a handy notepad tool in computer-based prototypes so that reviewers can click a button and enter their comments in the notepad window. When printed, these notes retain information about which screen the reviewer was looking at when making the notes.

Always provide the reviewer with clear directions on how to review and what to review:

- Explain where the reviewer will find the prototype, such as a URL address or a CD-ROM that will arrive via overnight delivery service.

- Provide step-by-step instructions on the review process.

- Describe how to install or access the program.

- Provide a review log to capture comments—usually an outline of the program works well.

- Remind the client which items have already been approved (changing these items would result in new production charges). For example, perhaps the interface or the screen design has already been reviewed

Example 10.8 Reviewer Comments on a Prototype

When reviewing a prototype, reviewers wrote directly into a column created for their comments in the storyboard. Only a small excerpt from the review is included here.

Screen	Title	Text	Production Notes	Reviewer's Comments
1Z000000	Vertel Online Training		Splash Skip	I didn't understand the Skip feature— what is it for?
1Z000001	Vertel Online Training	Select a training path: Level I Level II Level III	User level menu	How does the learner know what to choose?
1T000000	Vertel Online Training for Level I	Getting started Desktop Presentations Assignments Reports Help — User level Index How to use this training program Quit	Overview	Didn't we talk about putting the Help in the same line at the top with the Quit button?
1T100101	How to Use This Training Program	This program simulates the experience you'll have working with Vertel. Most sections guide you through the procedures for each function or feature. Usually, you'll see a Vertel screen along with text explaining how to perform the task.	Representative examples of program screens	These examples are so small—I couldn't read the writing on the screens.
	Index	The Index allows you to access any training topic at any time. It presents a list of all of the topics covered in this training. When you click on a topic, the program goes to that training.	Index screen	We need to make this work perfectly because most tech types prefer to move around a program using the index.

and accepted, but the content and activities are new and need to be reviewed.

- Tell the reviewer when the review comments are due back to your team.

Learner Tryouts The only way to determine the effectiveness of a program is to try it out with actual learners. There are several ways you can use the prototype to do this. You can conduct one-on-one evaluations, small-group evaluations, or field trials (see Chapter 6 for more on evaluation). In addition to determining if the material is instruc-

tionally effective, you may have accumulated some questions you want answered in the evaluation. At various points in the instructional design process, you may have chosen to "let the learners decide" among competing options. You chose one of several options and made a note to pay careful attention to the learners' responses. Your prototype provides you with that chance.

Testing your prototype with real people is invariably an eye-opening experience! You may find that learners demonstrate mastery of one skill on the pretest but can't master another one after extensive instruction, practice, and feedback. By testing with learners, you gather data on how well the instruction works, whether learners liked the program, whether it's easy and inviting to use, and so on.

Even if your prototype is a paper-based document such as a storyboard or script, instead of a produced slice, you can still gather useful feedback from learners. You need to provide your learners with an understanding of what the materials represent so that they can evaluate them effectively. Prepare a brief explanation of what the materials are, how they will be developed into a product, and how to read them. When you collect feedback from these learners, try to determine which comments are really about the instructional materials, and discount ones about the prototype delivery.

Revisions

After all the time and energy you and the team have invested in the product thus far, you want everyone to be delighted with the product. The feedback from all of these sources may seem extensive and highly critical. It's easy to feel overwhelmed and discouraged. This doesn't mean you failed! Revisions are expected and are built into the process.

The next task is to assemble all of the comments from the prototype testing, organizing the data according to the evaluator (learners, SMEs, clients), product functions, and the content (organization). Collect the review comments into one document, and group similar comments together (see Example 10.9). For example, group all of the comments on each chunk of content together. Recognize, however, that not all requests carry the same weight. Some requests might seem silly or superficial, such as changing a color on a button in an e-learning project. Evaluate each comment, and determine if the change is appropriate and within the scope of the project. Because the scope is unique on each project, it's hard to generalize, but a rule of thumb is that any deliverable that's already been approved shouldn't be touched again without requiring additional charges.

Of course, as the instructional designer, you are always concerned with the product's instructional effectiveness for the target learners. For example, if the results from prototype testing indicate that the feedback wasn't helpful, you should recommend changing it even if it was approved earlier. If your SME finds a content error, you must correct it. If many of your evaluation participants failed to achieve an objective, you need to find out why and fix it. If you don't have the budget for such changes, determine what the costs will be and make a proposal to your client and project manager seeking authorization of the additional work.

After you develop a document that outlines reactions to the materials, potential revisions, and suggestions for improvements, present these materials to your client for approval. Although you want to invite a broad group of people to review the work, you should discuss the reviews with only your primary client, and perhaps your closest colleague. If everyone on the team attends, it's likely to be unproductive and could even be fractious. Your primary client should have the authority to make final decisions on all change requests.

Example 10.9 Revision Table

One strategy for compiling the suggestions for changes is to create a table with all of the change requests listed in a column. In the horizontal rows, indicate which changes are within scope, which are outside the scope, and which are worth doing even if outside the scope.

Changes Requested for History Project

Item	Change	In Scope	Out of Scope	Notes
1.	Global: change button to read "Glossary" instead of "Resources"		X	Easy to do and worth doing because this was confusing to students using prototype
2.	Section 1, screen 6: Feedback should read: Hamilton was Gen. Washington's *aide-de-camp*	X		
3.	Section 2, screen 1: Use photo of entire first page of Constitution		X	Wouldn't be able to read first line
4.	Section 4, screen 3: Add word: *President* Andrew Jackson, to differentiate from when he was general		X	Should have been noted at storyboard stage; however, easy to fix
5.	Section 7, screen 4: Correct date for Battle of Antietam—Sept. 17, 1862	X		

Client Requests

An instructional designer was developing an industrial training product. The client insisted on repeating a section on work hazards in each of 15 online modules. The content and assessment items on the hazards were to be identical in each section. The client's reasoning was that not every trainee would take every module, yet it was crucial to ensure that everyone knew this content. The way the product was built, it wasn't feasible to change the architecture so that the program could ensure that trainees took the hazard training one time. The designer felt strongly that all of the training would suffer if trainees had to endure the same material more than once (let alone the possibility of all 15 times!). Additionally, it meant that there was less capacity in the product to provide new and challenging content and assessment. The production team and the client brainstormed ways to satisfy both sides. They came up with a solution that provided some module-specific hazard content and assessment, and a limited amount of repeated content. It wasn't an ideal solution, but it was an improvement.

Sometimes, your client will overrule everyone on the production team and insist on a solution that you feel isn't instructionally effective. Even if you strongly disagree, try not to take this personally. If you are angry, don't talk with your client about it until you are positive that you can maintain a calm and professional demeanor. Then you can carefully broach the subject, explaining that in your professional opinion the selected strategy won't be effective and a different strategy would be beneficial to the learners. Be careful to avoid loaded words such as "stupid," "superficial," or "hollow" in describing the selected strategy. You can use phrases such as "instructionally weak" or "less likely to succeed." Provide the rationale for why your suggestion will yield better results. Recognize, however, that the client has the final say and that you, and everyone on the team, need to honor the client's decision.

Revised Production Documents

The purpose of developing a prototype is to solidify the design of the program. The results from prototype evaluations can point to needed changes in content, activities, features, functions, or any other component. Following prototype testing, you may have to make changes in the entire set of production documents. The treatment, templates, and storyboards may all need to be modified to reflect the changes indicated by your prototype testing. If the revisions are extensive, you may want to make the necessary modifications to the prototype

Consider our house analogy. After consulting with your architect, looking at various options, and answering numerous questions, you're eager to get a visual sense of what your house will be like. The blueprints provide you with a great deal of information about how the house will look and how the spaces will relate to each other. However, to really get a sense of what the space will feel like, you will probably want to see a model. A model might be a small cardboard mock-up of the home that you can view from all angles. Often, you can remove the roof to see how the rooms connect and flow—and even see how light streams through the windows. Architects also use 3-D modeling software that simulates the final construction so that you can do a virtual walk-through of the space. This can help you determine if the design is exactly what you had hoped for or if there are aspects that need to change. It's

much less expensive to change the placement of a wall when nothing has been built yet. These "prototypes" are tangible deliverables that you, as the homeowner, can experience and examine closely. You can make needed changes before committing to actual construction.

The Demonstrate phase aims to accomplish the same things for you, your team, and your client. You want to give your client an opportunity to experience a representation of the final product while there's still time to make changes cost-effectively. You want to give learners opportunities to interact with the product to determine where it works as expected and where it needs significant revisions, or perhaps just tweaking. Like the architect with the model, you invite and expect your client to find things that need to change. You want to identify the changes before launching the real construction.

and then conduct a second round of evaluations prior to moving into the Develop phase. Once you are satisfied that your design is appropriate to the needs and characteristics of learners, you can develop the production documents for the remaining sections of the instruction. Once these tasks are completed, the team can move into the Develop phase confident of the product's design and efficacy.

Revised production documents sometimes represent a final deliverable for the instructional designer. If you will be leaving the team at this juncture, be sure to thank each person with whom you've worked. If people have a good experience working with you, they'll ask for you in the future. Even junior members of the team deserve your attention—it's simply polite behavior—but also note that junior people don't stay that way. Over time, they move into positions of increased responsibility. Remember, too, that people move to new jobs at new companies, and you can increase your pool of potential clients simply by keeping in touch and on good terms with everyone with whom you've worked.

Summary

In this chapter, you learned about how to translate your design document into the actual product. The Demonstrate phase is a transitional phase—it's the bridge between instructional design and production. In this phase, you develop production documents including treatments, scenarios, templates, storyboards, and other paper prototypes. You also develop a working prototype for review and evaluation purposes. Finally, you present the prototype to clients, SMEs, and learners in order to solicit feedback and refine the plan for subsequent materials.

Notes

[1]This information was derived by downloading Lincoln's address from the Library of Congress Web site and analyzing the word count and readability using the tools available in Microsoft Word.

Application

1. In your reflective journal, summarize the key points of this chapter. How are the ideas presented consistent or inconsistent with your beliefs and prior knowledge? Compare your perceptions of the chapter with those of your classmates in group discussions.

2. Using the same design problem and client that you used in the previous phase:

   a. Prepare production documents that are acceptable to the client. They should include:
      - Treatment
      - User scenario
      - Templates
      - Requirement specifications
      - Descriptions of media assets needed
      - Paper prototype (draft document, script, or storyboards)
      - Prototype

   b. Present your production documents to your client for review and acceptance. Make note of requested modifications.

   c. Conduct formative evaluation of the prototype. Collect data on its effectiveness.

   d. Develop a report of the results of the prototype testing and suggested revisions.

   e. Review the prototype report and revisions with your client. Get sign-off.

3. As you create your production documents and prototype, continue to make entries in your reflective journal. Explain why you made particular design decisions, how your ideas changed over time, and what you judge to be the next steps in the process.

4. Reflect on your meetings with the client in your reflective journal. How did it go? What went well? What do you think you could have done differently?

Ideas in Action

In Chapters 8–11, we follow the design of a computer-based training program on the Family and Medical Leave Act (FMLA). In this chapter, we include a sample treatment, wireframe, and storyboard.

The following treatment presents the instructional strategy for the FMLA online training program. The outcomes of this lesson represent rule learning; thus, the lesson requires learners to recognize true statements and to identify instances where the rules apply. Only

the right-hand column, "Activity," would be presented to the clients. The left-hand column, "Learning Event," was used by the instructional designer to make sure he accounted for each of the learning events within the lesson.

Notice also that the chunking of content has changed somewhat from the way the information was chunked in the design document. As the instruction takes shape, minor modifications such as these are common.

FMLA Online Training Program
Treatment

Learning event	Activity
	Log on.
Focus on goals.	**Title.**
Recall prior knowledge.	**Intro sequence:** Series of photos of employees at their workstation with captions explaining situation that will require them to take FMLA leave.
Gain and integrate content information.	**What is FMLA?** Text and images in sequence of screens explain leave.
Gain and integrate content information.	**Who is eligible?** Image of FMLA (matrix) with photos of employees and families. Rollovers explain who is eligible.
Take action and monitor progress.	**Check your understanding:** Drag statements to folder graphic if true. Drag statements to trash can if untrue. Click Submit when ready. **Feedback:** Give specific feedback on responses.
Gain and integrate content information.	**Why is there an FMLA policy?** Explain law behind it.
Gain and integrate content information.	**Additional requirements:** Explain additional requirements using checklist graphic. As learner clicks on checklist, text with image appears. Learner clicks Done when ready for next item on list.
Take action, monitor progress.	**Check for understanding:** Click True or Untrue for series of statements on FMLA policy. **Feedback:** Give specific feedback on true/false items.
Gain and integrate content information.	**Valid reasons for leave:** Four quadrants representing each type of leave. Learner clicks on each quad for information on valid reasons for leave.
Take action, monitor progress.	**Check for understanding:** Match reason with type of leave. **Feedback:** Give specific feedback on responses.
Gain and integrate content information.	**Special considerations:** Additional issues presented with text and appropriate content graphics.
Take action, monitor progress.	**Check for understanding:** Present scenarios; learner has to match appropriate consideration. **Feedback:** Give specific feedback on responses.
Synthesize and evaluate knowledge.	**Quiz:** 10 items, pass/fail or true/false.
Extend and transfer.	For more information.
	Log off.

FMLA Online Training Program
Wireframe

Global navigation bar (GN)
Bar at top of screen
Bread crumbs: screens 1–17; Quiz is not included in this count.
Example:

| FMLA Training | 9 of 17 | | Help | Quit | < Back | Next > |

General template

Wireframe for FMLA training.

FMLA Online Training Program
Storyboard

	Text	Interaction/Description	Image
1.	The Family and Medical Leave Act	Auto play animation	Title and NorLabs logo
2.	What happens when you have a baby . . .	Intro sequence: Photos w/captions Auto	Pregnant woman
3.	Your elderly parents get sick . . .	Auto	Middle-aged man with elderly parent
4.	You adopt a child . . .	Auto	Parents with new born at hospital (adoption)
5.	Or you become ill or are seriously injured . . .	Auto	Young man with cast on leg, on crutches
6.	You may be eligible to take time off from work through the Family and Medical Leave Act (FMLA). This online training program is designed to help you understand your options. For more information, contact your HR representative.	Global navigation (GN): Next Back Help Quit	The four previous images in a montage

	Text	Interaction/Description	Image
7.	FMLA is designed to help employees balance their work and family responsibilities by allowing them reasonable unpaid leave for certain family and medical reasons. It tries to balance the needs of the workplace with employee concerns. It promotes equal opportunity for men and women.	GN	Photos of families
8.	FMLA provides certain employees with up to 12 weeks of unpaid, job-protected leave per year. It also requires that group health benefits be maintained during the leave.	GN	Collage of NorLabs employees (three–four representative individuals)
9.	What leave is covered? The birth of a son or daughter and the care of that child.	GN "Slide show " type sequence	Photo with text box Parent with newborn
10.	The placement of a son or daughter with the employee for adoption or foster care.	GN	Parent with child
11.	Medical care for a son, daughter, spouse, or parent if that person has a serious medical problem.	GN	Adult attending to elderly parent (pushing wheelchair?)
12.	A serious health problem that prevents the employee from doing his or her job.	GN	Adult in hospital bed
13.	Which of the following are valid reasons for FMLA leave? Check the boxes that are true.	GN Click to select. Click Check to see correct answers.	Graphic checklist
14.	A1: Provide care to father following heart surgery.		
15.	A2: Travel to another city to adopt a child.		
16.	A3: Recuperate at home from a broken collarbone.		
17.	A4: Provide care to teenaged daughter who is hospitalized.		
18.	Q1–4: All of these are correct. FMLA covers personal health problems, the birth or adoption of a child, and care for your children, parents, or spouse.	Feedback	
19.	Who is eligible? An employee who's been employed by NorLabs for at least 12 months. Any portion of a week that the employee is on the payroll counts as a full week. Employment does not have to have been continuous. An employee is anyone who's worked at least 1250 hours in the 12-month period prior to the first day of the leave. Only time actually worked can be used in this calculation. In other words, vacation or sick leave, does not count toward the 1250 hours. The employee may not have already used 12 weeks of FMLA entitlement in the current calendar year. Note that federal law requires NorLabs to provide FMLA to its employees. This is because NorLabs is a business that employs more than 50 people full-time.	GN Four rollovers explain who is eligible. Each text bullet is a rollover	Photo collage (matrix) with photos of employees and families
20.	Check your understanding. Drag each statement to the correct location. Drag it to the HR folder if the employee is eligible. Drag it to the wastebasket if the person is ineligible. Click Submit when you're ready to check your answers.	Check your understanding: Folder = eligible Trash = not eligible Display feedback after Submit clicked.	Three dragable statements Graphic of HR folder Graphic of wastebasket
21.	Q1: Geri is going to have a baby in four weeks. She has been at NorLabs for 10 months. She plans to take FMLA leave when she has her baby next month.	Not eligible	

	Text	Interaction/Description	Image
22.	A1: Geri will not qualify for FMLA leave because she will have only worked 11 months, not the required 12. She may have other leave available to her but not FMLA.	Feedback	
23.	Q2: Brandon injured his knee in a skiing accident over the winter holidays. He will need corrective surgery. He's planning to take FMLA leave in order to stay off his feet for six weeks. He has worked at NorLabs seven years. Last year he worked part time to complete graduate school. He clocked 1400 hours last year.	Eligible	
24.	A2: Brandon qualifies for FMLA. Although he didn't work full-time hours last year, he clocked more than the minimum 1250, and he worked in every month.	Feedback	
25.	Q3: Elosha had to take 12 weeks of FMLA two years ago to care for her husband, who had bypass surgery. He is going to have another operation, and Elosha hopes to take several weeks of FMLA leave.	Eligible	
26.	A3: If Elosha had taken the FMLA leave this year, she would not have been eligible again. But because she took the leave in a previous year, she is eligible.	Feedback	
27.	Continuing benefits: Employees on FMLA leave can continue their NorLabs benefits. However, the employee will need to pay NorLabs his or her portion of the benefit while on leave. Your HR representative can help you with this procedure.		Insurance carriers' logos?
28.	Requirements: An employee taking FMLA leave due to a serious personal health condition must present a medical certification in order to go on leave. In order to return to work, an employee taking FMLA leave due to a serious personal health condition must present a medical certification of fitness to return to work. During an FMLA absence, all available leave accruals must be exhausted before the employee can be on leave-without-pay (LWOP) status. This includes leave that is accrued while the employee is on FMLA absence.	GN Each text box scrolls onto screen. User clicks box to get next text box. Clicks Next to go to next screen.	Animated sequence
29.	Match the FMLA requirement to the correct situation.	User drags correct requirement to statement. Clicks Check for feedback.	Screen with statements and boxes of requirements
30.	Statements: S1: Jared has 96 hours of accrued leave that he must use before taking any LWOP.		
31.	S2: Nancy has obtained a letter from her doctor in order to return to work.		
32.	S3: Darrell needs a statement from his doctor before he can take FMLA leave.		
33.	Requirements: R1: During an FMLA absence, all available leave accruals must be exhausted before the employee can be on LWOP status. This includes leave that is accrued while the employee is on FMLA absence.		
34.	R2: In order to return to work, an employee taking FMLA leave due to a serious personal health condition must present a medical certification of fitness to return to work.		

	Text	Interaction/Description	Image
35.	R3: An employee taking FMLA leave due to a serious personal health condition must present a medical certification in order to go on leave.		
36.		GN Feedback—show correct answers.	
37.	Quiz: Click Submit when finished.	Quiz—T/F Only navigation is within quiz or Quit.	Quiz template
38.	Q1: A male employee may take FMLA to care for his child. T		
39.	Q2: A medical certification is required in order to go on FMLA but not to return to work. F		
40.	Q3: Employees on FMLA must pay their own portion of the company's health benefits. T		
41.	Q4: An employee is eligible to take FMLA even though she has 127 hours of accrued leave. F		
42.	Q5: Taking care of a foster child would not be covered under FMLA. F		
43.	Q6: FMLA is a federal law that applies to NorLabs because of the company's size. T		
44.	Q7: FMLA is available to employees who have worked for the company at least 1250 hours over the previous 12 months. T		
45.	Q8: An employee can arrange to take FMLA in order to care for a very close family friend. F		
46.	Q9: FMLA is available for taking care of family members, not for the employee's personal health problems. F		
47.	Q10: After taking 12 weeks of FMLA, an employee who needs to can take four more weeks in the same calendar year. F		
48.	Congratulations! You have successfully completed the online Family and Medical Leave Act training program. Your completion will be recorded in your HR file and reported to your supervisor. If you have additional questions, please contact your HR representative.	Score of 80% or higher	
49.	Thank you for taking time to complete the online Family and Medical Leave Act training program. Your results will be sent to your supervisor and HR representative. If you have additional questions, please contact your HR representative.	Score less than 80%	
50.		Log off	

| DESIGN AID |

Checklist of Activities in Demonstration Phase

Task	Description	Date Scheduled	Date Completed
Treatment	Outline of instructional strategy, identifying learning events and assessments for each chunk of content.		
Scenario	Narrative describing how users interact with program. These can describe segments of program or entire product.		
Template	Plan for each reccuring instructional event, screen design, and user interaction. Includes wireframe "sketches" of screen design, also providing mock-up of navigation.		
Requirements specifications	Comprehensive technical plan including description of each type of functionality, user interactions, delivery platform, and development tools.		
Media assets	Media assets that should be included, with details on specific content of each asset.		
Paper prototype	Script, storyboard, or draft text that serves as production "blueprint" for product. Specifies text, images, animations, audio, video, and interactions, and where each interaction leads users.		
Prototype	Complete "slice" of product providing all learning events for one complete content section.		
Expert reviews	Feedback on accuracy and completeness of content, ease of use, level of engagement.		
Learner testing	Test with representatives of target learning population, providing feedback on effectiveness of instruction, ease of use, receptiveness to this product.		

Chapter 11
Develop and Deliver Phases

Learning Outcomes

- Monitor materials production to ensure that design specifications are followed.

- Conduct continuous formative evaluations as allowed.

- Submit project materials to the client.

- Conduct a project debriefing meeting.

- Conclude project responsibilities by collecting feedback on performance, recording recommendations for future versions, conducting training on the product if requested, doing summative evaluation if requested, and summarizing project accomplishments.

- Calculate project costs and the instructional cost index.

Chapter Overview

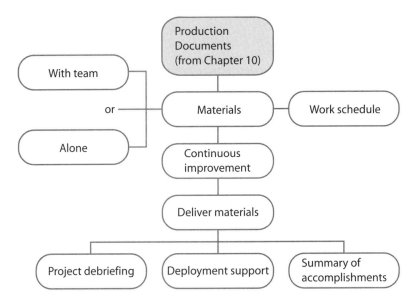

Orientation within the Design Process

Recall that there are five phases to the instructional design process. In each phase, you should consider the five essential elements of learners, outcomes, assessments, activities, and evaluation, adding details and performing tasks as required by the products of each phase. In this chapter, we examine the Develop and Deliver phases of an instructional design project. You are moving into the outer rings of the instructional design spiral (see Figure 11.1).

These two phases are distinct but can overlap. For example, you may complete sections of a large project and begin delivering those materials while continuing to work on other sections. Although these phases are important and can represent a major portion of the schedule and budget on a project, the instructional design role is less pronounced and more routine. Most of the significant instructional design work takes place in the Define, Design, and Demonstrate phases. We've grouped the Develop and Deliver phases together in one chapter for this reason.

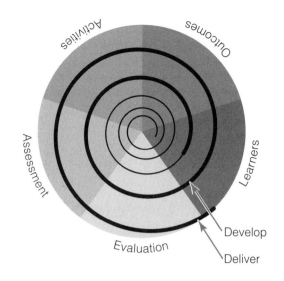

Figure 11.1 *Phases of instructional design.* In the Develop phase, the design work is largely completed and the focus is on producing the product. In the final phase, Deliver, the spiral reaches the outer perimeter of this version of the project. There may be additional work on subsequent versions.

Tasks of These Phases

The tasks of these phases related to learners, outcomes, assessments, activities, and evaluations are summarized in Tables 11.1 and 11.2.

Table 11.1 Develop phase

Learners	• Continue to monitor materials development to ensure that they are appropriate for audience.
	• Seek data on ability of materials to meet learners' needs during formative evaluation testing.
Outcomes	• Continue to monitor materials development to ensure consistency with goals and outcomes.
	• Seek data on learners' obtainment of outcomes during formative evaluation testing.
Activities	• Determine needed modifications to materials based on client's and learners' response to prototype.
	• Monitor materials development to ensure consistent with instructional strategy.
	• Create instructor's guide, training guide, and other supporting materials requested by client.
	• Use materials with learners during formative evaluation.

(continued)

Table 11.1 (*continued*)

Assessments	• Monitor development of assessment instruments to ensure consistency with specifications.
	• Use assessment instruments during formative evaluation. Seek information to determine clarity and usefulness of assessments.
Evaluation	• Gain access to learners for additional formative evaluations.
	• Schedule and conduct additional evaluation.
	• Analyze data and develop recommendations for modifications.

Table 11.2 Deliver phase

Learners	• Present learners' responses to evaluation.
	• Discuss suggested modifications. Determine whether modifications will occur during this development cycle or will form basis of recommendations for version 2.
Outcomes	• Present data on degree to which learners achieve outcomes during formative evaluation.
	• Discuss suggested modifications. Determine whether modifications will occur during this development cycle or will form basis of recommendations for version 2.
Activities	• Present materials to client.
	• Present results of formative evaluation. Discuss suggested revisions. Determine if changes will be made to current materials or future versions.
	• Compile project documentation.
	• Conduct training on use of materials if requested by client.
Assessments	• Discuss suggested modifications to assessment instruments resulting from formative evaluation. Determine whether modifications will occur during this development cycle or will form the basis of recommendations for version 2.
Evaluation	• Conduct summative evaluation if requested.

 # Develop Phase

In prior phases, most of the work on the project is either exclusively or primarily the responsibility of the instructional designer. In the Define and Design phases, the instructional designer is engaged in scoping the project, understanding the learners, determining goals and outcomes, developing the assessment, planning instructional strategies, and designing the evaluation. In the Demonstrate phase, the instructional designer plays a major role in developing the production documents and evaluating the prototype. In the Develop phase, however, in large-scale and e-learning projects, much of the work may shift to production team members. With all of the planning, testing, and reviewing that you and the rest of the design team have done, producing the final product should go smoothly. But this doesn't mean that your involvement ends. To the contrary, you don't stop communicating, reviewing, testing, and revising until the product is fully delivered.

Once materials have been defined, designed, demonstrated, and refined, it's time to crank out the rest of the product. It's not unusual for almost half the total project schedule to be given over to the Define, Design, and Demonstrate phases for only 10 percent or less of the total product to be generated. In those phases, you not only produced a small segment of the product but also planned what will become an "assembly line." And it's in the assembly line that the payoff occurs. The storyboards and other production documents that you created in the Demonstrate phase and modified based on the results of prototype testing are the blueprints that will be used to create the product.

If you've designed it right, working through all of the kinks and issues in the earlier phases, the actual development should go relatively smoothly. The goal is to

Voice of Experience

Time to Produce

A development company produced a language arts curriculum series for an educational publisher. The series included a separate CD-ROM for each of seven grade levels, from grades 6–12. Each level of the series featured about 60 grade-appropriate lessons on grammar. Each lesson was substantial enough to deliver a lesson lasting up to 40 minutes.

The instructional design team worked with language arts specialists and state standards experts to devise a scope and sequence, interactive templates, and diagnostic and guidance strategies for the series. They selected the eighth-grade program as a prototype and spent more than six months designing and refining it. They conducted pilot testing with a sample group of learners and teachers. They also arranged to conduct field testing in a middle school environment. They refined the design based on these evaluations.

Once the design for the eighth-grade program was finalized, they began work on the remaining six grade levels. These additional grade levels, representing 85 percent of the final product, were completed in less than a year. The production team became increasingly proficient at the task and was able to produce one final grade level program every two months.

get a production process in place so that the work "snaps together" like Lego™ blocks.

On large-scale projects, such as the development of a complete curriculum series, the Develop phase may actually be the most prominent phase of the process, involving the most people and absorbing most of the production costs.

Once the project goes into production, your responsibilities shift from creating materials to monitoring the production process, unless you're doing the production work yourself. On most projects, many other people start taking responsibility for creating the materials.

Working with a Team

The production team can include writers who create text, video and audio specialists, graphic artists, programmers who write code, authors who assemble programs using authoring software packages or load content into templates, and QA specialists who test software under various conditions and on target platforms. On a small project, one person might perform all of these tasks; on a large project, dozens of people may be involved.

On an e-learning project, depending on the scale, the technical team may devise the architecture (or infrastructure) on which the program is built. This is equivalent to the engineering design for a building. Authors who are proficient in using certain software packages, but who are not coders, build the lesson modules that attach to the infrastructure. There are programmers who specialize in different kinds of programming, such as XML or SQL. At the simplest skill level are technicians who load content into Web pages and do testing.

Audiovisual (AV) producers usually specialize in audio, video, or photography. Some generalists might be able to handle all of the AV tasks, but more typically, specialists with particular skill sets are involved. For example, on even a small video shoot, there might be a camera operator (called a videographer), a camera assistant (called a grip), a sound person, a director, a producer, and an assistant producer (called a PA). Once the video is shot, it's logged and edited during the postproduction process. You might need to communicate with all of these people, or your access might be limited to the producer or director. If you have the opportunity to visit the set or location during a video shoot, you will learn a great deal about this process.

Artists have much to contribute to the success of most instructional products. Imaginative and effective graphics can help learners master and retain content. E-learning products can require a "look and feel" interface design, and animations as well. Some versatile artists may be able to produce all of these pieces, but in most cases, artists with different specialties generate each type of graphic. On larger teams, the artists might report to an art director who develops and ensures a consistent visual standard across a project and within a company.

Managing the Production Process   Remember that, throughout the instructional design process, you serve as an advocate for learners. This means that you should review the design specifications with the production team, gather their creative input, and meet regularly with them. You need to ensure that the materials meet the needs of learners based on your design documents, storyboards, and feedback from formative evaluations. Check to make sure that the assessment items were developed as specified, the instructional strategy was followed, and the presentation remains true to the goals and outcomes of the instruction.

In the early stages of the design process, you depended on other people to review your work and provide you with timely feedback. Your ability to produce effective materials hinged on those reviewer comments. Now, it's time for

Working with Graphic Artists

Interface and Look and Feel

Some artists specialize in developing the interface for an e-learning product—the visual screen array that provides users with devices to navigate an online product. Other artists may be responsible for developing the program's look and feel—the color palette, textures, fonts, and other visual elements that give the program cohesion and consistency.

Regardless of who is responsible for the look and feel and the consistency of graphics, someone on the graphics team should be charged with developing a graphics standard. This standard should specify the colors, textures, and tone of all of the graphics produced for the program. You can help with this by reviewing the standard carefully and providing constructive feedback on any issues that could interfere with learning. For example, a young artist with keen eyesight might not realize that older learners, with declining eyesight, can't read small fonts.

If you are producing a Web-based product, it might require a style sheet to ensure a consistent look to all of the pages as they are generated. The interface artist is responsible for producing this style sheet.

Content Graphics

Content graphics can include diagrams, tables, charts, and other visuals that either support content or represent the primary means of delivering the content. You need to provide the artist with the content to be included in each of the images, but give the artist leeway in the arrangement—he or she might devise a superior visual solution.

Illustrations

It may seem somewhat counterintuitive, but not all graphic artists can draw. If you need an illustration, you can use an illustrator. If you have a particular illustration style in mind, provide the artist with examples. Some styles may not be appropriate for a particular audience, such as children, so help the illustrator select the style that will work for your learners.

Animations

The artists who fashion moving graphics work with different software packages to achieve different effects. The most complex and expensive graphics to produce are full 3-D animations, which require specialized training and software. These are the images that seem lifelike in terms of volume, shading and shadow, movement, and detail. Much simpler animations can be produced quickly using tools such as Macromedia's Flash. However, Flash does not show textures or details. In sketching out what you need in the animation, try drawing a cartoon strip showing the changes in each frame. This will help the animator understand what's important to demonstrate in the graphics.

---

you to return the favor. Be responsive to your colleagues when they need you to review their work. Recognize them for their accomplishments and be constructive in your feedback. The quality of their work now depends on you, as does the quality of the instructional materials for learners.

Reviewing Design and Production Documents In the design and production documents, you specified diagrams, animations, photographs, video clips, and audio that you determined were important in an instructionally effective product. In the Develop phase, these media assets will be generated, and you probably will be involved in this process.

To ensure that the instructional design is executed correctly, you should meet with the production team to review the design and production documents. You can meet with the entire team and work through each sequence together. Or you can meet with team members individually, reviewing only the components for which each is responsible. For example, you might meet with the graphic artists to review the graphic specifications and with the video producer to review the video requirements. Hopefully, you've prepared good storyboards, supplemental drawings, and other materials that document the instructional requirements clearly and completely. Work closely with these colleagues to ensure that the assets do just what you'd hoped they'd do. You may find it effective to have formal meetings with the entire group to review the production documents and then have informal meetings with individuals to monitor and review their work.

Gathering the Input of Others Regardless of whether you choose to meet with team members individually or as a group, your goals are to make sure team members understand what to produce *and* to elicit their production ideas. Some of your ideas and specifications are going to have to change. You may have specified a music clip that is unavailable or a photograph that is too expensive to license. Or the animator may have a more effective strategy for demonstrating a process that will also be faster to produce. Work with the producers to find alternatives. They may have ideas that will improve the presentation; be open to these ideas, but also make sure that the changes will enhance learning. Suppose you are producing a course on neuroscience and you specify a 3-D animation showing how endorphins work. In your view, a 3-D animation is called for because students need to see how the neurotransmitters fit in the neuroreceptors "just like a key in a lock." It's a visual that requires three dimensions, and it's a process that requires animation. Your producer might explain that this graphic would consume almost the entire animation budget. If this is the most important, and difficult, concept for students to learn, it might be instructionally appropriate to allot most of the budget to this one animation. But perhaps you can communicate just as effectively with a series of still images that students click through, as with a slide show, to understand the sequence. And perhaps a 3-D rendering isn't really necessary to show how the transmitter and receptor fit—it's possible that the artist can create an illustration that provides sufficient detail. You may need to work with the producer to find alternate strategies that are both instructionally effective and within budget.

What if a producer wants to change something you really want? There may be moments when you feel slighted, angry, or worse. Try to step back and look objec-

Getting Buy-In from the Team

Voice of Experience

An independent designer, working with a client's in-house production crew, met with team members to review the 15 storyboard sequences for an e-learning course they were developing. The internal trainers were initially cool to the designer's involvement; they felt they could do the work themselves although none were instructional designers. Sensing the problem, the designer made an extra effort to give each team member an opportunity to review the storyboards and to generate production ideas. She sought out skeptics to elicit their creative solutions to tough problems. As team members started to see their contributions reflected first in the storyboards and then in the final product, the initial tensions evaporated. The designer also made an effort to acknowledge the contributions of the in-house team to supervisors in the client organization.

The Right Media Assets

Voice of Experience

A designer was reviewing a video segment for a safety training program for employees in a construction company. The video clip was fast-paced and dramatic, showing a hazardous condition resulting from lax attention to safety. However, there was an extraneous scene from a local TV news program showing emergency vehicles. The producer defended these shots by saying that they gave the segment a sense of urgency and authenticity. The designer countered by saying that they made for a great video clip but weren't relevant to the training. He explained that the training objective was related to the safety procedures, not the impact of a tragedy on the local community. The news clip confused the issue of enforcing workplace safety. When provided with a valid reason, the producer agreed to delete the clip.

tively at the situation. Is the new idea better? Will learners benefit? If the new idea interferes with instructional effectiveness, you need to hold your ground. But the new idea may present the material not only more effectively but also less expensively or more creatively or closer to the product's technical parameters. Tap the creativity and production experiences of team members to come up with the very best solutions. In the long run, your product will benefit from the contributions of these capable people, and they will feel invested in the product's success.

You bring to the team an understanding of both learner and instructional requirements. When you review production work, your goal is make sure each piece works for the content, the delivery environment, and the learners. In evaluating each media asset, think of the learners. Will this asset help them master this content? Pay attention to how well the piece illustrates the specifications in the production documents. There are many reasons a specification may need to change. Perhaps it would be too dangerous to film a certain video shot or too expensive to produce a 3-D animation. But whereas an artist may be mostly concerned with the aesthetics of a graphic, and a video producer may be focused on the quality of a video clip, you are concerned that these media assets are what learners need. When an asset isn't appropriate, you need to speak up. And when the asset is right on target, don't forget to say so!

Sometimes, producers want to work directly with the client or SMEs in order to get direction on how to produce specific content. For example, an artist may have questions about how to depict a microprocessor: Is it acceptable to stylize the chip to show the different components, or should it reflect the actual proportional dimensions of the chip? A video producer may need to coordinate locations for a shoot, or an audio producer might want to confirm the correct pronunciation of technical terms or trade names. Depending on the parameters of your role, and those of the media producers, you may or may not want to participate in these sessions. If you can answer the questions without bothering a busy SME or client, that's an excellent use of your time. The producer may simply need additional clarification on what learners need from the program. You want to protect the SME from having to explain everything all over again to each team member. If you think it might be beneficial, schedule a meeting with the SME and all of the team members who may have questions for him or her. You can review the storyboards or prototype or look at specific design issues. This represents a more efficient use of the SME's time.

Meeting with the Team Regularly After your initial meeting with the production team, you should continue to meet regularly with individual team members, both formally and informally. Project schedules often include a regular weekly production meeting to review all deliverables, discuss current tasks and problems, and preview upcoming deadlines. If your company has regular staff meetings, the production meeting should be a separate event, focused solely on the project. A production meeting shouldn't dwell on what's not going well and who is not productive. The purpose of the meeting is to communicate clearly what each person is working on, how it fits into the whole, what is due when, who is reviewing each item, and what problems need to be solved.

Informal meetings are also important in establishing team camaraderie. Whether you are housed in an open work space or in cubicles, be sure to drop by regularly to see how each person is doing. Take breaks or go to lunch with team members to develop good relationships. At this point in the project, it's important to maintain a spirit of teamwork and cooperation. Everyone needs to feel they are working together to achieve the same goal: to produce the best product possible.

Managing Your Own Production Work

If you are working independently, producing the instruction in addition to designing it, you have some special considerations. Like the project team on bigger projects, you are moving into a new phase. You've prepared the design documents, production specifications, and prototype, and you've tested your prototype materials with a group of learners. Now, you produce the instructional material for each chunk of content and the activities that account for all the events of learning.

One of the most significant aspects of working independently is that you don't have to communicate com-

Voice of Experience

Developing Classroom Materials

For a training program on a new version of a software product, the instructional designer's deliverables included an instructor's guide, a student guide, and a set of PowerPoint slides. The training was going to be delivered by several different trainers in classroom settings. Because the instructor's guide needed to include all of the student material, as well as directions for the instructors, the instructional designer decided to produce this guide first. This made her task easier to manage and was also helpful to the reviewers. If she had created both guides at the same time, she would've had to incorporate any changes in the curriculum into both documents.

Once the instructor's guide was reviewed and revised, she developed the student guide. To prepare the student guide, she began by making a copy of the instructor's guide and removing content appropriate only for instructors. She then added material specifically for learners. She inserted introductions, summaries, resources, and other features so that learners could use the guide as a general reference following the class. After the student guide was reviewed and revised, she developed the PowerPoint presentation.

plex information to other production team members, although you may still need to communicate with your client. You can work productively by yourself, without interruptions. You manage your own work flow and schedule without anyone else directing your activities. If you work at home, you may find that you can accomplish more, in a shorter time, than your peers in organizations can.

The downside is that you won't have team members to turn to for ideas, support, or encouragement. There may be times when you appreciate the opportunity to bounce ideas off someone else or simply have another set of eyes review your work. One option is to enlist colleagues through a professional organization or an alumni association in forming a peer review group. If the instructional materials must be kept confidential, perhaps you can still obtain feedback on how to solve a general problem, whether it's on media selection, assessment, learning events, or any other instructional design topic.

One potential problem, particularly if you are working alone, is that you can lose sight of the "big picture." Perhaps you've developed each of the chunks and are satisfied that they are effective units of instruction. But you also need to see how they tie together. When you are developing instructional materials by yourself, it's more important than ever to test your materials with learners. Try to schedule a pilot test, do some field testing, and send the materials out to reviewers or peers for feedback. If you will be the instructor and will be delivering the material yourself, take good notes on what works and what needs to be revised. You can make revisions before delivering the material again.

Scheduling the Work

Whether you're working with a team or doing the production work yourself, you need to schedule the work flow to meet the project deadlines without exhausting anyone. Instructional design projects can be massive undertakings. During the Develop phase, you're on the home stretch. But the key to successful project completion is to set small, frequent goals and to monitor progress. Everyone needs to know who does what, and when. If you are working with a project manager, he or she will schedule and monitor the work of the production team. If not, the responsibility for pulling all of the components together to meet the project schedule often falls to you, the instructional designer.

If you are working alone, you need to manage your time and energy effectively. This means creating a schedule for deliverables that distributes the production tasks throughout the schedule. You will probably pick up speed as you get into the production "groove," but you should still leave some extra room at the end of the schedule to accommodate any last-minute changes. You want to arrange the schedule so that you will be fresh and productive all the way through all of the modules. You don't want to collapse in exhaustion early on, nor do you want to find yourself working day and night to complete the work by the final deadline.

If you are managing team members, you should schedule regular deliverables. Divide the larger job into subprojects, with specific deadlines for completing each component. Let's say you're producing an online learning project with six units. If you have 12 weeks to develop the materials, you need to complete one unit every 2 weeks. One way to ensure that the team meets the projected schedule is to encourage everyone to devise daily goals. How much will be completed on day 1? What will be completed on day 2? Encourage team members to write down their expectations for each day in the 2-week cycle. You may find that on some days more is accomplished than expected, and on other days things take longer. As long as the larger goals are met, that's fine.

If you have seven modules to produce and 10 weeks to complete them, a realistic schedule might look like this:

Week	Deliverable
1	Start module 4
2	Complete module 4
3	Module 1
4	Module 2
5	Module 3
6	Module 5
7	Module 6
8	Module 7
9	Revisions
10	Final delivery

In this example, you start with module 4 in order to work with the level of content and complexity that is representative of most of the product. You've scheduled 2 weeks to work through this initial effort. Then you start producing a module each week, leaving 2 weeks at the end of the schedule to accommodate revisions and any other issues that arise.

Minimizing Project Creep

Consider this scenario: Slowly, usually without anyone realizing it, there's an extra task here and a little feature there, adding to production time and cost. It's such a common problem that it has a name: **project creep.** Throughout the previous phases, you actively sought feedback and made revisions. But now, in the Develop phase, it's time to "freeze" content and other components that were approved long ago. It's not that potential changes aren't necessarily worthwhile, rather, managing project creep is essential to getting a product completed. If there are valid reasons for altering material, let your client know the arguments for and against the changes, and explain the schedule and budget implications. Then let your client make the decision.

If you discover that you've made an error after materials are in production, determine the ramifications of the error, and develop a proposal for a solution. It may be that when you actually see your product on the computer, in print, or on a video monitor, a defect jumps out at you. Admit to the error quickly, and consult with your client to devise a corrective strategy. If the error was due to carelessness or negligence, you should offer to perform the correction at no cost. Think about what happens when you take your car in for repairs: If your mechanic says the brakes are fixed, and you pay him and drive off only to discover there are still problems, you'll demand that they be fixed correctly, at no additional cost to you. Similarly, your client shouldn't have to pay an additional fee for your error. However, if you're diligent in your design work and later discover problems that are not due to negligence, then your client should pay for the necessary modifications.

Change Orders

For a sales training program delivered on video, the designer developed the content and wrote the shooting script. The client reviewed the scripts and, after making several changes, approved them. Several scenes were shot using professional actors portraying sales reps and potential customers. Additionally, a professional actor provided the voice-over narration. The client was on the set for some of the shoots and approved the narration.

As the client watched the final edited tape, he realized that the actors and the narrator had used the word "royalties." Unfortunately, in his company, the earnings that sales reps were paid based on sales were called a commission, not a royalty. Both the instructional designer and the client were shocked by this significant error at such a late date. But the designer had done everything he could to get feedback, and it was clearly the client who had let this error slip by. And the cost was significant. The narrator re-recorded the voice-over, and the scenes were reshot. This additional work also pushed back the deadline, which affected other elements in planning the rollout of the new product.

Continuous Improvement

Airlines develop and deliver an enormous amount of training ranging from maintaining pilot skills to training mechanics, reservations agents, and gate agents. They deliver training in classrooms, on simulators, online, and in blended formats.

One major airline developed online technical training courses for its employees worldwide. When each course was developed and delivered, they scheduled a post-mortem meeting for all team members, including outside instructional designers and producers. They flew everyone to a central location, usually the company's headquarters. The postmortem served as a "bookend" to the kickoff meeting, bringing the entire team together one last time to review the project and determine what worked and what could benefit from improvement.

A typical postmortem meeting was scheduled as a half-day session to allow for travel. At the meeting, the team reviewed the production process and generated a list of specific suggestions for improved communications, production, and delivery. At this company, continuous improvement was built into its business operations.

Making Continuous Improvement

After the complete set of instructional materials is produced, it should be subjected to a series of reviews. Many instructional design projects include Alpha and/or Beta versions of the final product. On an e-learning project, the Alpha version often represents a very sketchy approximation of the whole product. Some project teams include full functionality in an Alpha version in order to test the program's performance, but it may lack full content or assets. The Beta version typically includes full functionality and full content and assets so that reviewers and quality assurance testers can conduct a thorough analysis of the product before the final version. The Alpha and Beta formats aren't confined to e-learning programs. You and your client may choose to test a Beta version of instructional materials that are delivered in the classroom, through on-the-job training, or via other modes. The Beta stage is widely adopted in corporate and educational settings; the additional Alpha stage typically is associated with technology companies and information technology departments in large companies. In all settings and for all formats of instruction, the Alpha and Beta versions are preliminary versions of the product that are designed for purposes of review and testing to identify weaknesses in the instruction that require revisions. These products are subjected to internal review, and the Beta version often is used with learners in a one-on-one evaluation or pilot test in order to assess the need for any additional changes.

Whether these preliminary versions are included in the development process, what they need to accomplish, and what they are called depends on the company, the project, and the team. But before the materials are fully implemented, you or other members of the design and development team can review the materials to look for obvious errors and to determine if they work well as a unit. The SMEs can review the materials to determine if there are any factual errors. Eventually, members of the target audience need to review the materials from their unique perspective as learners. The effectiveness of the materials can be judged only by users actually attempting to learn from them.

Depending on the schedule and budget, you may be able to plan and implement a pilot test or field trial evaluation. Perhaps the opportunity to collect data that can be used to market the materials is the incentive that will convince your client to spend the additional time and resources for a group of learners to try out the materials. If you can get authorization to conduct an evaluation of the completed materials, you'll be able to collect data on pre- and posttest performance, attitudes toward the instruction, and anecdotal responses—all data that can be invaluable in developing effective marketing materials. Even if you can test the materials with only a few members of the target audience, these individuals can identify problems that those familiar with the materials may miss. Testing the materials at this stage allows you to correct errors before widespread distribution.

As you learned in Chapter 6, it is not unusual for you, as the instructional designer, to be involved in planning for evaluation but to turn the actual evaluation over to another person or entity.

🌀 Deliver Phase

Eventually, you reach the Deliver phase. Delivery is not so much a phase, however, as it is a destination. It's a time to celebrate your progress, even though there often isn't a neat and clean conclusion to your involvement. If you are teaching the materials yourself, such as serving as the instructor for a classroom or online course, you will still be actively engaged in the instruction. You can't shut off the part of you that is an instructional designer, but your role in delivering instruction is different from your role in designing it. Even when the instruction is developed for a client, the iterative nature of the design and development process doesn't end at delivery. At this stage, you submit all relevant materials to the client and conduct a project debriefing meeting. In addition, you may be asked to lend support during deployment by providing training to those who will deliver the instruction, correcting minor errors, or conducting summative evaluations. Finally, you need to document the project successes and consider future improvements to the process. Although the Deliver phase marks the end of one instructional design and development project, it can represent the beginning of a long and productive relationship with the client.

Submitting Materials

Delivery might be as simple as attaching a document to an e-mail and hitting the Send button or as elaborate as holding a ceremony akin to the changing of the guard. Sometimes, you simply hand deliver a three-ring binder filled with your work or notify the client that the final files have been posted to a server. Other times, you present the materials to your client in a formal meeting. If you're sending materials through the mail or via a delivery service, make sure the address is correct. Include a cover letter to your client listing the contents of the package. After you send the product, let your client know that it's on its way, and check back to make sure it's been

received. And don't forget to thank your client for the opportunity to work on the project and to express your wishes for the product to be a great success!

There are advantages to simply sending your materials to the client with a cover letter—it's quick and easy. But there are advantages as well to formal presentations. They convey a sense of finality and celebration that can serve as a fitting conclusion to a long and complex project. And when you feel as if you've been immersed in a project that seemingly would never end, a celebration is in order. The way in which materials are presented to the client varies from project to project and from individual to individual. Be sensitive to the dynamics of the project, the time commitments of team members and clients, and the personalities of those involved when choosing the method of material submission.

However you deliver the final product, make sure you provide the right materials! It's extremely embarrassing to have to acknowledge an error and then send the "real product." Although you want to be careful with all deliverables, you should take even more time to make sure your final product is as good as you can make it. Prepare high-quality printed copies on good paper, accurate file names, neat and professional labels, and fresh packaging material. If a client has spent a large sum on a project, it makes everyone feel it's money well spent when the final deliverable looks polished and professional.

If you are hired to prepare a custom-tailored e-learning solution, the source materials you create usually belong to your client. When outsourced projects are produced on a work-for-hire basis, the client typically owns all of the source components unless you've made other arrangements. Some software developers refuse to turn over source materials, including source code, in the belief that this will force the client to return to them for any necessary modifications. In fact, it's unethical, and perhaps illegal, to hold back source files if you have worked under a standard work-for-hire contract.

You don't need to release any trade secrets or unique work that you own, but your client should have all the components he or she will need to reproduce, modify, or create an updated version of the product. For example, if you interview a dozen experts and have audiotapes or transcripts, you should make copies for your client. Any original artwork, diagrams, maps, videotapes, audio, and programming source code are part of the source materials. It's possible that your client won't want these materials, but you should always offer. Sometimes, clients don't understand that a product can't be updated without going back to source materials; make these implications clear.

You should also copy everything prior to delivery. Label your copy carefully and store it in an accessible location. If your client needs changes at a later date, you'll be able to retrieve your version quickly. If your client wants you to maintain archives for future use, you should store the materials in a secure location, such as a bank lockbox. Your company could charge a modest storage fee but may prefer to absorb the costs to help secure future business. You should have an archival system in place for all your work so that you never have to face the daunting task of re-creating a file or an entire program. Make sure your labels and your file names are clear, comprehensive, and consistent so that you can find what you need later. A year from now, you won't remember that version 2C was the release version even though there was a version 2D—you almost can't go overboard in this task!

Final delivery also may include copies of any licenses used in the program, such as software licenses, and authorizations for use of copyrighted materials, such as permission to use a photograph. You also need to provide the talent releases for performances including photographs, video, or audio of a recognizable person. Check *everything* before submitting materials!

Project "Postmortem" Debriefing

It can be hard to get people excited about a postproject debriefing—they've worked long and hard, and want to move on. But this meeting can be invaluable to everyone who attends, including production team members, the client team, and SMEs. Sometimes called a **postmortem**, this meeting provides an opportunity to identify what worked and what needs to be improved on future projects. You want to gather the team to discuss project and production issues while the experience is still fresh. It's probably not a good idea, however, to combine the postmortem project debriefing with the submission of materials. Keep delivery celebratory; the nature of the postmortem is to be critical and analytical.

One strategy for conducting the postmortem is to retrace the production steps, beginning with the needs analysis and project definition, and moving through design, demonstration, development, quality assurance, and deployment. Guide the team in thinking through each step in the instructional design and development process. Ask if there are any ideas for improving the process. Was the right team in place? Did communication flow effectively? Were reviews efficient? Did the project deliver within the schedule and budget projections?

The postmortem meeting is not the appropriate forum for criticizing the work of individual team members. If the meeting veers in that direction, it's important for you or a manager to steer it back to constructive discussion. If someone wasn't an effective member of the team, and you feel that it interfered with your work or the quality of the program, take your concerns directly to that person's manager, and keep the conversation private. An even better strategy is to resolve staffing issues as soon as they arise rather than after the project concludes.

Deployment Support

The big day arrives, and the product is shipped or launched. After you've been immersed in the material for many weeks or months (or even years), deployment is usually completely out of your hands, unless you are teaching the material yourself. You probably will feel a sense of both pride and wistfulness about having to "let go," much the way a parent feels when a child starts school or leaves home. One of the great satisfactions in instructional design is observing learners using a program you designed, accomplishing the outcomes just as you intended. If you have a chance to observe learners using your product, take advantage of it. But you should be an unobtrusive observer, because if learners become of aware of your role, it may interfere with their performance.

As carefully as you prepared your materials, and as thoroughly as your client and reviewers examined them, problems may emerge once the program is deployed. Be prepared to field questions and address concerns even after you've delivered the last file. Sometimes, the problem can be fixed simply—for example by writing better instructions; other times, corrections may need to wait until subsequent versions.

Recommendations for the Next Version

During production, you and your team will inevitably generate ideas for the program that can't be implemented in the current version. On some projects, the refrain "V 2!" (version 2) becomes a frequent response to the many fine ideas that need to be put aside because of the realities of the schedule, budget, or other constraints. But keep track of these ideas! At the conclusion of the project, you can collect these thoughts from your own files, the team, the SMEs, and your client. Some of these good ideas may emerge from the postmortem meeting. You can prepare a document with these recommendations and deliver it to your client even if he or she hasn't asked for anything. And if you will be involved in planning the next version, you'll have an excellent framework for starting

Outline for Classroom-Based Training on New Instructional Product

Introductions	If you are delivering training in a classroom, first introduce yourself, review the agenda, and review the objectives for the session.
Icebreaker	If there are 25 or fewer participants, break the ice by asking each participant to introduce him- or herself. If there are more than 25 or so participants, ask general "getting to know you" questions that require them to raise their hands or call out answers. For example, ask where folks are from, if they have experience with this type of program, or if their customers are eager for the product.
Demonstration and interactions	Demo the product or highlights from the program. Then present an activity to get participants involved with the program. If you are training sales staff, you can role-play by pretending to be one of the sales reps, with one or more of the participants acting in the role of the customer. Learners learn by doing—so give these learners opportunities to do something active.
Hands-on practice	If you are training customer service or other product support staff, be sure each person gets hands-on opportunities to work with the product. Think about any issues that might be tricky for the customer or the trainees, and spend more time on those difficult topics.
Assessment	Most training sessions of this type are somewhat informal and do not include assessment. However, if assessment is required, devise a test on which learners can demonstrate the ability to perform these new skills on the job.
Job aid or handout	Develop a handout that participants can use both in the class session and after the class. Trainers often use Microsoft's PowerPoint to complement their presentation. A feature in PowerPoint allows you to create a handout of your screens with space for participants to take notes. Taking notes is a powerful learning strategy!
Follow-up questions	If appropriate, provide participants with your phone number and e-mail address, and encourage them to contact you with any questions. Often, participants will think of questions after they leave the classroom.
Evaluation	Be sure to ask participants to evaluate the class!

that work. This final deliverable is simply one more demonstration of the professionalism you've shown throughout the project.

Training When new instructional materials are implemented, users may require some sort of training on how to use them. You may have been asked to create an instructor's guide or tutorial as part of the instructional package. Perhaps you simply included a "how to use these materials" section in the software, on the Web site, or in the workbook you created. In other situations, clients may ask you to provide training on the program you produced. This is often the case when the product will be used by the sales or customer support staff. You also may need to train the person who will assume responsibility for managing the instructional program.

Designing the training is an instructional design project, so you need to consider your desired learning outcomes. What will success look like? What will this audience (not the audience for your product) need to be able to do following the training? If you have not delivered classroom training before, the strategies outlined in the Designer's Toolkit can help guarantee strong results.

Summative Evaluation You also may be asked to develop a summative evaluation plan. Where formative evaluation looked at how the product worked while it was still being developed, or in "formation," summative evaluation focuses on how well the final product works in its intended environment. Summative evaluations examine how effective the product is for a given audience, whether it is cost and time efficient, and whether it solved the problem that led to the instruction in the first place (Dick, Carey, & Carey, 2001). They often are used to determine if a program is of value in order to make a decision about its continued support. This evaluation shouldn't be done right after deployment but somewhat later, when the initial kinks have been ironed out and the program is fully implemented. At that point, there's enough of a track record to make the evaluation meaningful.

There isn't a specific format to follow, but the questions you want to investigate include:

- Does the instruction work? Do learners obtain the outcomes? Is it effective?

- Do learners like the program? What are their affective responses to the program?

- Is it easy to implement, deliver, and maintain? Is it efficient?
- Are the costs of implementation reasonable in relation to the benefits?
- Did the instruction solve the problem that led to instruction in the first place?

If you are responsible for developing a summative evaluation, begin by identifying the specific questions you want answered and those who can answer them. A summative evaluation might involve interviews with instructors, training managers, or administrators to assess the learning effectiveness and ease of delivery. They often include field trials with learners. Arrange to gather data by monitoring ongoing courses or by scheduling courses and making sure they are monitored. If the program is for job-related training, survey the trainees' supervisors to find out how well the participants are using the training skills on the job. Data from pre- and posttest-assessments, interviews, surveys, and other sources can be analyzed to draw conclusions about the effectiveness and efficiency of the instruction.

Don't be offended if you aren't asked to do the evaluation—it's good practice for someone completely removed from the development process to complete this task. In fact, you may be asked to perform this service on projects you didn't develop. If you don't conduct the evaluation yourself, ask for a copy of the summative evaluation report so that you can learn how effective the program was and how well it was received.

Summarizing Project Accomplishments

As the project nears completion, it's time to document your accomplishments. Remember the discussion of the need to promote the instructional design process in the Define and Design phases? You shouldn't be surprised by the fact that you've come full circle when you reach the Deliver phase. It's at this point in the design process that you collect data to help promote the instructional design process in the next project. To paraphrase an old saying, the project isn't complete until the paperwork is done!

Documenting Successes You should compile information on the project successes to use when you need to promote the systematic design of instruction. Nothing captures the flavor of an event like an anecdote, so reflect back on the project and jot down particular events that seem to illustrate the essence of the project. Contact clients and SMEs with whom you have developed a positive relationship, and ask if they would be willing to write a letter of support or appreciation for your contributions to the project. Collect data from learners as well (see Example 11.1). Do you have pre- and posttest achievement data that you can use to document the project's success? Do you have interview data on students' responses to the materials? What about responses to attitude questionnaires? You may want to ask instructors, learners, or clients to report successes they experienced as learners apply their new skills in the classroom or the workplace.

Getting Feedback from Clients Once the project is delivered, and perhaps after you've been paid the final installment, you can ask your client for feedback on your performance (see Example 11.2). Evaluation never ends! You can schedule a meeting or simply call. If you think your client will be more comfortable with a less direct approach, prepare an evaluation form, and send it to him or her with a stamped, self-addressed envelope. If a neutral third party is available, enlist this person or company to do the follow-up evaluation. The feedback you get from your client can be invaluable.

Example 11.1 Student Feedback

The following excerpt is from a report on a course Web site, with student comments included (Cennamo, Russ, & Roger, 2002).

The calendar-like GAME plan interface, with course materials organized in a table arranged by weeks, proved extremely popular with students. One student commented: "I like how the GAME plan is organized with the lecture routine and study guide and everything for the week you are on." Another student said: "I think that this Web site is very organized, and it's easy to understand what to do. I think that this is a great way for students to learn to manage their own time and work at their own pace." When asked how we could improve the Web site, one student responded: "I honestly cannot ask for anything more. I am so happy that I have been given the chance to work through a class the way this one is set up. It is so different from anything I have ever done in high school, and I absolutely love it!" Another student commented: "I can't think of anything more I would need that the Web site doesn't already have. The lecture online, the practice quizzes, and the outlines are all good means for preparing for a test or quiz."

Example 11.2 Postproject Client Evaluation Form

Circle one: 15 lowest rating, 10 5 highest rating

1. Overall, how would you rate our performance on this job?   1 2 3 4 5 6 7 8 9 10

2. Did we listen well? Were you able to communicate effectively with us, and did we communicate   1 2 3 4 5 6 7 8 9 10
effectively with you?

3. Did we meet deadlines? Do you feel we worked with you on any changes to the schedule?   1 2 3 4 5 6 7 8 9 10

4. Did we adhere to the project budget? Did we keep you informed about any changes in the budget,   1 2 3 4 5 6 7 8 9 10
including change orders?

5. Did we meet project goals and objectives? Was the project well received by the target audience?   1 2 3 4 5 6 7 8 9 10

6. Was our staff accessible?   1 2 3 4 5 6 7 8 9 10

7. Do you feel we were sensitive to your needs and project requirements?   1 2 3 4 5 6 7 8 9 10

8. Please rate the courteousness and professionalism of our staff.   1 2 3 4 5 6 7 8 9 10

9. Were revisions completed satisfactorily?   1 2 3 4 5 6 7 8 9 10

10. In what areas do you feel we need to improve?

11. What do you like *most* about working with us?

12. Least?

13. Additional comments:

Thank you for your feedback! And thank you for your business!

Calculating Project Costs There are many job aids that attempt to estimate the time required to develop instruction, but most designers find that there are too many variables for an all-purpose formula to be useful. The variables include the content, learners, client, delivery environment, experience of the staff, and complexity of the task. Regardless of whether you use an estimating tool, you need to develop your own understanding of your costs based on your own experiences. If you and your team members have tracked the amount of time they spent on each of the project activities, these data can be very helpful in estimating future assignments. Simply summarize the amount of time required for each task so that you can use this information when estimating time and cost requirements for future projects (see Example 11.3).

Calculating the Cost Index It's also useful to calculate the **instructional cost index**, or per student cost, of providing the instruction. To calculate the cost index, you simply divide the instructional costs by the number of students served. There are two kinds of instructional costs: development and operational. Development costs are the one-time costs of designing and developing the instruction; operational costs are the recurring costs associated with delivering the instruction.

The salary of a trainer, room rental, material duplication costs, and refreshments during the instruction are all examples of operational costs. For an online product, the costs of user support, the server, maintenance, and system upgrades are operational costs.

An awareness of the cost index can influence the way materials are designed and developed (see Example 11.4). If materials need to be used for several years to spread the cost of development over time, make sure the materials don't contain information that will become outdated quickly. Materials that need to be offered to large numbers of students in order to reduce the cost index should be designed for ease of administration and grading. For example, a CD-ROM course designed for hundreds of users can include a detailed rubric to be used to grade students' projects. Projected "cost per student" data often are useful in developing project proposals during the Define phase.

Celebrating

When the big day arrives and the product is shipped or launched, take the time to reflect on your achievement. If you've encountered problems, you've no doubt learned a great deal. As you've successfully overcome problems, you've improved your skills and competence. You may already be

Example 11.3 Comparing Projected with Actual Hours

For a multimedia instructional project, the projected and actual hours for each task were as follows:

Task	Projected Hours	Actual Hours
Project management	240	311
Instructional design	350	372
Graphic arts	275	255
Video/photo production	150	77
Audio production	100	134
Architecture	400	290
Content loading	100	93
QA	100	104
Total	1715	1636

The following table provides a detailed break down of the instructional design tasks:

Instructional design tasks	Projected Hours	Actual Hours
Design document	75	83
Content development	65	47
Storyboards	75	81
Other design docs	15	44
Prototype	50	34
Formative evaluation	40	57
Production consulting	25	23
Postproject	5	3
Total	350	372

In this project, the instructional designer developed templates, which took more time than the allocation for "other design docs" had projected, but ended up saving considerable time in production. With the approval of the project manager and client, the design overrun resulted in considerable savings in video and architecture costs as reflected in the project's total hours.

Example 11.4 Cost Index

This example involves a recertification course delivered through distance education. The course content was delivered on a CD-ROM that was mailed to the participants upon enrolling in the course. The costs were broken down as follows:

The development costs for CD-ROM are $46,000:

$10,000 designer

$21,000 video production and Web development

$5000 graphic artist

$10,000 overhead

The operational costs of the course include:

$3,000 course tutor (responsible for grading and responding to questions)

$3 per student for CD duplication and mailing

If the course is offered only once to 75 students, the cost per student is:

$$\frac{\$46,000 + \$3000 + (75 \times 3)}{75} = \$657 \text{ per student}$$

If, for this course, this cost is too high, the instructional cost index can be decreased by (1) decreasing the operational or development costs, or (2) spreading the costs over time. The operational

and development costs per student can be reduced by offering the instruction on the Web instead of through CD-ROM, though these savings will be minimal; reducing the costs to develop the materials, perhaps by eliminating the services of the graphic artist; or eliminating the need for a course tutor through assignments that are automatically graded. One of the easiest ways to reduce the instructional cost index is to create materials that can be used for several years. For example, if a CD-ROM course is used for five years, with 75 students per year, the price per student reduces to a little less than $166 per student:

$$\frac{(\$46,000/5) + \$3000 + (75 \times 3)}{75}$$

If the number of students is increased to 150 per year, the cost for the course tutor remains the same, and the costs for CD duplication and mailing increase due to the increased number of students, the price per student is less than $85 per student:

$$\frac{(\$46,000/5) + \$3000 + (150 \times 3)}{150}$$

Analogy

House

You can probably visualize this scene: The builder and several subcontractors are studying the blueprints, which are perched on a sawhorse. The blueprints continue to inform the team throughout the construction process. The builder and subcontractors meet regularly, if not daily or even several times each day. There are numerous small consultations to resolve issues, agree on the timing of work, or verify that an installation is correct. Projects are successful when there is a good design, a capable team that communicates effectively, and managers who can solve problems quickly.

Given all the planning that goes into earlier phases of a construction project, the development phase should proceed smoothly. Sometimes, however, unforeseen events occur that may require minor modifications of the original plan. Perhaps the builder discovers unstable ground while digging the foundation, requiring a modification of the original plans for a foundation. Some changes may be within the scope of the project—for example, simply moving the kitchen wall several feet into the next room may not affect the total costs for the project. Other changes, such as modifying the foundation, may involve additional costs and thus be considered out of scope.

Finally, the building is complete. There's the final walk-through to compile a list of items to repair, complete, or otherwise resolve. At the end of the construction phase, the owner is ready to take possession and move into the house of his or her dreams. But the story doesn't end there. The owner gets a copy of the blueprints and receives instruction on how to maintain the home. There are owner's manuals for each of the systems, such as the HVAC system, and appliances. The architect keeps in touch with the owner to make sure everything is fine. The owner may hold a housewarming party. The home may become part of the architect's and builders' portfolios. If the home has been designed well, its structure and features will enhance the owner's quality of life. Hopefully, it will exceed the owner's original dreams and expectations.

Like the architect, you want to make sure the product is delivered properly. You provide your client with the training and resources needed for successful deployment. You want to keep in touch with your client to see how well the program is working for the intended audience. Perhaps you design or participate in a summative evaluation. Your ultimate goal as an instructional designer is to realize the client's goals, and even to exceed them.

completely immersed in a new instructional design project. For now, take a few moments to recognize all of your efforts and the efforts of your team members. Get together with the project team, and celebrate your accomplishments!

Summary

The Develop phase marks the point in the process at which each chunk of content is produced in its final form. On a large-scale or multimedia project, your role in the Develop phase is to work closely with other team members in carrying out the specifications from your design and production documents. You review specifications with the production team and monitor the development of the materials to ensure that they are created as planned. You may also conduct formative evaluation of the instructional materials.

Finally, you deliver the materials to the client. The Deliver phase involves a variety of tasks that bring the project to a successful conclusion. There may be a project postmortem. Delivery may include training staff who will implement the instruction and designing and delivering summative evaluation. And you may be involved in determining and analyzing the costs of developing and delivering the instructional prod-

uct. Activities during this phase focus on the success of the product development process, as well as the product.

References

Cennamo, K. S., Ross, J. D., & Rogers, C. S. (2002). The Evolution of a Web-Enhanced Course Incorporating Strategies for Self Regulation, *Educause Quarterly*, *25*(1), 28–33.

Dick, W., Carey, L., & Carey, J. O. (2001). *The systematic design of instruction* (5th ed.). Needham Heights: MA: Allyn & Bacon.

Application

1. In your reflective journal, summarize the key points of this chapter. How are the ideas presented consistent or inconsistent with your beliefs and prior knowledge? Compare your perceptions of the chapter with those of your classmates in group discussions.

2. Using the same design problem and client that you used in the previous phase:

   a. Complete the development of the instructional materials.

b. Conduct a small-group test or field trial. Collect data on the effectiveness of the instruction.

c. Prepare a report of the formative evaluation results and suggested revisions.

d. Deliver instructional materials and results of the formative evaluation to your client.

e. Gather feedback on your performance throughout the design process in a postproject debriefing meeting.

f. Calculate a cost analysis and cost-per-student index for your materials.

g. Document the project successes by collecting student anecdotes and feedback from clients.

3. Continue to make entries in your reflective journal. Explain in why you make particular design decisions, how your ideas change over time, and what you judge to be the next steps in the process.

4. Reflect on the entire instructional design project. How did it go? What went well? What do you think you could have done differently?

Ideas in Action

In Chapters 8–11, we follow the design of a computer-based training program on the Family and Medical Leave Act (FMLA). In this chapter, we include a production timeline, project log kept by an instructional designer, evaluation plan for the field trial, field trial results, and the analysis of costs per learner.

Production Timeline

FMLA Online Training Program

Task/Deliverable	Delivered	Review/Comments
Kickoff	February 21	February 21
Design doc	March 1	March 5
Templates	March 5	March 12
Tech specs	March 5	n/a
Content doc	March 10	March 12
Storyboards	March 15	March 22
Look and feel	March 15	March 18
1st prototype	April 1	April 3
2nd prototype	April 5	April 10
All graphics	April 19	n/a
Beta	May 10	May 12
Field test	June 3–6	n/a
Revisions completed	August 1	n/a
Rollout	September 2	September 2

Time and Delivery Log

FMLA Online Training Program

These notes were kept by Sara Moore, instructional designer on the Family and Medical Leave Act online training program, produced for her employer, NorLabs, a diversified company in the health care and pharmaceutical industry.

Date	*Time*	*Task*
2-12	2.5	Staff mtg to plan FMLA training. Kickoff scheduled for 2/21
2-12	0.5	E-mail to HR reps to introduce project, timeline, etc.
2-14	1	Read background on FMLA
2-17	3	Develop kickoff presentation, agenda, packet
2-19	0.5	Prepare copies for kickoff
2-21	3	Kickoff
2-21	2	Write up notes from meeting: distribute
2-24	6	Begin design doc; questions for HR
2-25	1.5	Meet with HR team to answer questions
2-25	3	Production staff mtg
2-25	3	Design doc
2-27	2	Brainstorming mtg w/production staff
2-27	6	Design doc
2-28	2.5	Design doc; delivered
Feb	36.5	Total hours—Feb
3-3	3	Content doc
3-3	1.5	Template design
3-3	2	Production mtg; meet w/programmer
3-4	1	Mtg w/programmer
3-4	4	Content doc
3-4	2	Templates
3-5	0.5	Content doc
3-5	1	Review tech specs
3-5	1	Template design delivered
3-5	1	Review design doc comments
3-6	2	Mtg to review design doc changes
3-6	1	Mtg w/production team to review design doc changes
3-7	3.5	Content doc; delivered
3-10	4	Start storyboards
3-11	1	Production mtg
3-11	5.5	Storyboards
3-11	1	Prototype planning mtg
3-12	2	Review content doc and template comments
3-12	1	Mtg to plan revisions based on content doc, template changes
3-12	0.5	Review look and feel
3-12	7	Storyboards
3-13	11.5	Storyboards
3-14	6	Storyboards; delivered
3-17	7	Prototype planning w/production team
3-18	2	Mtg w/team; review look and feel comments
3-20	3.5	Planning for field tests
3-24	5	Storyboard review meeting w/team
3-25	4	Storyboard changes
3-26	2	Review prototype
3-26	2	Storyboard changes
3-31	1	Prototype 1 review; delivered
3-31	3	Review graphics w/team

(*continued on page 267*)

Date	Time	Task
Date	*Time*	*Task*
March	92.5	Total hours—March
4-1	3	Prototype review meeting w/team
4-1	1	Plan changes to prototype
4-2	1	Meeting w/artist
4-4	1	Meeting w/programmer
4-5	1	Review Prototype 2; delivered
4-10	2	Production meeting
4-10	1	Review Prototype 2 comments
4-11	1	Graphics review
4-11	3	Field test planning
4-18	2.5	Graphics review mtg; delivered
4-23	2	Production meeting
4-29	1	Review Alpha
4-29	2	Review Alpha w/team
April	21.5	Total hours—April
5-3	5	Review Beta w/team
5-4	2	Field test planning mtg w/HR team
5-4	1	Memo sent on field test
5-5	1	Review Beta; delivered
5-6	4.5	Develop field test docs
5-7	2	Review field test docs w/HR team
5-9	1.5	Revise field test docs
5-12	1	Mtg w/HR IT team on field test
5-12	5	Beta review mtg w/team
5-13	2	Production mtg
5-20	3	Mtg w/HR team on field test
5-21	3.5	Production mtg
5-26	1	Sent out letter to field test participants and supervisors
5-27	1.5	Meet w/HR IT on changes
5-27	1.5	Calls, emails on field test
5-30	2	Production mtg
May	37.5	Total hours—May
6-1	2.5	Module deployed on server
6-1	2	Contact nonrespondents
6-3	3.5	Field test begins
6-3	2	Troubleshooting test; contact nonrespondents
6-4	1	Troubleshooting
6-5	0.5	Troubleshooting
6-5	1	Contact nonrespondents
6-6	0.5	Monitor test
6-7	3	Review data
6-8	2.5	Review data w/team
6-9	4.5	Compile data
6-13	4	Write field test report
6-13	3	Production mtg w/team
6-24	2	Production mtg w/team; review changes
June	32	Total hours—June
7-24	2	Review changes
7-31	1	Mtg w/HR; product delivered
July	3	Total hours
8-15	3	Mtg w/team on rollout
8-31	1	Deployed
Aug	4	Total hours—Aug
Total	227	Total hours on project

FMLA Online Training Program Evaluation Plan for Field Test

TO:	FMLA training development team
CC:	HR reps
FROM:	Sara
DATE:	May 4
RE:	Plan for field trials for FMLA online training program

In anticipation of the rollout of the NorLabs Family and Medical Leave Act (FMLA) training in September, we are planning field trials next month. Since every Nor-Labs employee must complete the FMLA online training, we are scheduling this extra testing to ensure that the program is effective with a wide range of employee groups. These field trials will involve 50 randomly selected employees, and participation will require one hour or less of their time.

Time Frame
The trials are scheduled for June 3–6.

Participants
HR's IT group will generate the list of 50 randomly selected employees. HR will review the list to make sure none of the 50 are currently on leave, have leave requests submitted for those dates, are on assignment overseas, or are otherwise not available.

When they have the final list, they will notify each selected employee and his or her supervisor. The notification will include an explanation of the training, the trial, the training requirements, and timeframe to complete training. Participation in the trial will satisfy that employee's requirement to complete FMLA training.

Pretrial Package
Each participant will receive an e-mail in the week before the trial, which must be completed before June 3. It will link to a Web site with these items:

- An explanation of the trial
- A survey about computer use and online training experience
- A 10-item pretest on FMLA

Participants who do not respond by June 1 will be contacted by e-mail and phone. If there is no response by June 3, their supervisor will be contacted by e-mail and phone.

Trial Procedures
On June 3, we will send a link via e-mail to each participant. By clicking on the link, they will invoke the log-on screen for the FMLA online training program. They can complete the training anytime from June 3–6.

As an incentive to encourage participants to log on and complete the training, we have secured five $5 coupons good at any NorLabs food service operation. These will go to the first five employees to complete all of the training. We will publicize these awards to all 50 participants.

If a participant has not logged on by June 5, he or she will be contacted by e-mail and phone. If a participant has not completed the training by June 6, their supervisor will be contacted by e-mail and phone.

Posttrial
Following the training, we will send an e-mail to each participant who completes the training. The e-mail will link to a posttrial Web site with two surveys. The first will ask the participant's reactions to the online training program including ease of use, performance of the program on their computer, and online delivery of training. The second portion will ask their reactions to the FMLA training and if they feel they were able to master the content successfully. We will also encourage participants to send any additional comments.

Following training, we will send each participant and supervisor a personalized thank-you message acknowledging their contributions to this effort.

Compiling Results
We expect to compile data from the surveys and the pre- and posttests by June 15. We will report on the results with recommendations for changes by June 20.

FMLA Online Training Program Field Test Results

A total of 46 employees completed the field trial for FMLA online training.

Pretrial survey	Completed: 47 of 50
	7 participants (14%) had "extensive" computer and online training experience.
	12 participants (25%) had never used an online training program before.
	2 participants were "very concerned" that they would have problems using the computer program.
Pretest results	Completed: 47 of 50
	Range: 10–90
	Average score: 30
Posttest results	Completed: 46 of 47
	95% passing rate
	Range: 60–100
	Average: 90
	Failing scores (under 80): 2
	Failed to complete: 1
Posttrial survey	Completed: 46 of 47
	42 of 46 (91%) found the training easy to use and effective.
	39 (84%) would welcome additional online training.
	2 had trouble logging on and/or using the program.
	1 had trouble logging on and/or using the program but thought it was due to her computer, not the program.
FMLA training survey	78% thought the training was the right amount of information and practice.
	6% thought it was too easy.
	10% found it was somewhat difficult.

FMLA Online Training Program Cost Analysis

Number of employees	2014
Number completed FMLA training*	1877

Production costs	
Internal	$31,000
External	$7545
Total	$38,545
Cost per learner	$20.50

This does not include the cost of each employee's estimated hour of work time spent completing the training.

* As of October 1.

| DESIGN AID |

Checklist for Develop Phase

	Date Scheduled	Date Completed

Monitor production:

- Meet with production team to review project specifications
- Elicit creative input from production team
- Schedule regular meetings to review progress, problems, and upcoming deadlines
- Meet informally with production team members to establish rapport
- Create work schedule

Production personnel meetings needed (list):

_____

_____

_____

_____

_____

Conduct continuous evaluations as allowed:

- Expert reviews
- One-on-one evaluations
- Small-group evaluation
- Field trial

Experts to review materials (list names and contact information):

_____

_____

One-on-one evaluations:

Evaluator:

Participants:

_____

Small group evaluation:

Evaluator:

Participant group:

Field trial:

Evaluator:

Participant group:

| DESIGN AID |

Checklist for Deliver Phase

	Date Scheduled	Date Completed

Before submitting materials:

- Check everything!
- Make complete copies of everything you deliver.
- Label copy carefully and store in accessible location.

Final delivery should include:

- Final versions of all instructional materials.
- Professional presentation (high-quality printed copies on good paper, accurate file names, neat labels, and fresh packaging material, etc.).
- Copies of any licenses used in the program.
- Authorizations for use of copyright materials.
- Talent releases for photos, video, or audio of recognizable person.
- All source materials that are needed to update product.

When sending by mail, delivery service, or electronically:

- Include cover letter to your client listing contents.
- Thank client for opportunity to have worked on project.
- Make sure address is correct.
- Notify your client by phone or e-mail that materials have been sent.
- Check to make sure materials were received.

Project debriefing meeting:

- Discuss ongoing relationship.
- Review each phase in project.
- Gather suggestions for improvement.
- Submit ideas for Version 2.

Additional tasks:

- Collect feedback on your performance.
- Conduct training on product if requested.
- Conduct summative evaluation if requested.
- Plan celebration with project team.
- Calculate project costs.
- Calculate cost index of instructional materials
- Collect and summarize success stories.

Chapter 12
The Professional Designer

Learning Outcomes

- Identify common employment opportunities for instructional designers.

- Promote instructional design in a manner consistent with the values of the organization.

- List sources for continued professional development.

Chapter Overview

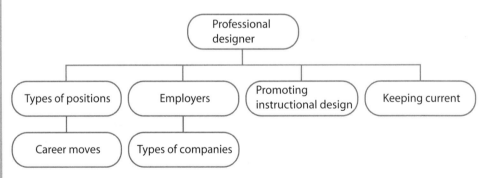

Orientation within the Design Process

Now that you've worked through the five elements and the five phases of instructional design, it's time to examine the instructional designer's role in a variety of institutions and settings. In this chapter, we look at the range of institutions and types of positions that designers hold, and the techniques to use to promote instructional design within an organization.

The Professional Instructional Designer

Fortunately for those of us in the field, instructional design is growing and maturing, and there is increasing demand for well-trained instructional designers (see also Chapter 1). This demand has been fueled by the growth of technology, a dramatic increase in distance learning, reliance on the Internet, and the prevalence of computers in general. All these factors have increased the need for people who have systematic skills and tools to understand learners, develop effective stand-alone instructional materials, and conduct evaluations—in other words, instructional designers. In fact, many Web development teams have come to value having an instructional designer on staff even if they aren't designing an instructional product; instructional designers bring skills that help ensure that a Web site is useful to and usable by its target audience.

Some people specialize in one of the elements or phases of instructional design; others are generalists and can do all of these things. For example, there are specialists who only conduct formative evaluations or write assessments. There are specialists in certain subject areas, such as mathematics or languages. And there are specialists who focus on a particular population, such as K-3, or college students, or corporate personnel. In your career, you may handle all the phases and elements of design, and you may have some jobs that focus on just one task or skill. You may be employed in a variety of positions, for various employers, both large and small, or you may move up the career ladder within a single company. A good instructional design education can prepare you for many different positions in the industry.

Types of Positions

Instructional designers come from many backgrounds and bring many interests to the field. That diversity continues to manifest itself as they move into the profession. Some common kinds of positions filled by instructional designers follow.

Staff Instructional Designer This is the "classic" instructional designer: the person who performs the work of the five elements and five phases of design. A designer might work with other team members, especially to produce technology-based products, or might work independently, such as to produce classroom-based instructional materials.

Project Coordinator At many companies, instructional design tasks are contracted out to freelance designers, but the person hiring and managing these freelancers is an internal employee, usually an instructional designer. This individual must be able to evaluate and guide the work of other designers.

Designer/Developer/Artist Designers who have a background in programming or other technical skills may be able to handle the technical aspects of a multimedia or e-learning project. Some designers perform all of the tasks associated with developing an e-learning product including graphics, media production, and programming. By using relatively easy-to-learn yet powerful tools such as Macromedia's Dreamweaver, a designer can serve as a "one person shop" and provide employers with a cost-effective, turnkey operation.

Increasingly, employers are expecting instructional designers to handle most of the tasks associated with developing e-learning programs. This works best in settings in which the work needs to be produced quickly, costs need to be controlled tightly, and the additional resources of specialized team members aren't necessary.

Career Moves

The instructional design team on a large project or in a corporate department often consists of a group of designers with varying levels of experience and education, and a manager who supervises the employees and the work. A typical career path for an instructional designer who moves up to the next level is to begin managing either the project or other instructional designers. Designers who successfully make this transition have good people skills, are organized, can manage time and money, and understand both the "big picture" and critical details. Because these management skills are also important instructional design skills, it's often a good fit.

Project Manager The person charged with delivering the right product on time and on budget is the project manager (PM), sometimes called the producer. An instructional designer often serves as the producer or project manager, especially if the designer has a background in media production or multimedia design work. The PM keeps the production team focused on the big picture by making it possible for them to attend to all the details in their respective jobs. The best PMs understand that they move projects along by supporting the team, not by barking orders. The PM is also responsible for making the client happy while staying within the scope of the project. The job requires the ability to impose structure and discipline but remain flexible and responsive; adhere to quality standards while meeting deadlines and staying within budget; keep everyone informed but not overwhelmed; and keep things moving. Recognize, however, that the decisions PMs make aren't always the same decisions instructional designers might make. It's important to realize there's a difference between the two roles, and sometimes a conflict.

The most effective PMs are personable, organized, energetic multitaskers who follow up on details and enjoy solving problems. Because it can be difficult to find people with all of these skills, some teams divide the role, with one person serving as the production manager who supervises the internal team and the other person serving as the liaison to the client. This strategy often is used on big projects that may take more than a year and involve dozens or even hundreds of staff positions. However, for this dual-manager system to function effectively, one of the individuals has to have final authority on all aspects of the project.

Instructional Design Manager On a large project, or in a company with several instructional designers, the manager is often an instructional designer. Managers can be involved in hiring and firing personnel, coaching designers, scheduling and budgeting projects, and reviewing work. Managers also establish standards for instructional design and train everyone on the design team to recognize and adhere to those standards. Good managers foster camaraderie among their instructional designers while recognizing that different designers have different working styles. New hires are likely to need a great deal of supervision and coaching, but as designers become more experienced, the manager's role diminishes. Helping to develop the skills of less experienced designers can be a satisfying learning experience for the manager—you learn a lot when you have to teach someone else!

Managers also must solve problems and deal with crises. The problems could involve other production staff or the client and SMEs. Regardless of who is involved, managers must take action as soon as they become aware of the problem. They need to research the problem and collect data from all appropriate sources before making any decisions. Sometimes, managers have to deliver bad news to a client or colleague. The individual might become angry about the news, but it's the manager's responsibility to address problems as soon as possible. One of a manager's hardest tasks is to stay calm and objective when emotions start to run high.

When an instructional designer just isn't a good fit for the company or the kinds of assignments available, the manager must make the difficult decision to let that person go in the most humane manner possible. Because of the nature of project-based work, many instructional designers will be laid off when projects conclude. This can happen many times over a career and in no way reflects the designer's skills and value to the projects. If you are a manager, you may have to make difficult decisions about whom to retain and whom to lay off. Work with your supervisors and personnel staff to follow the procedures your company has adopted.

Sales and Marketing Instructional design work is similar to the work marketers do in analyzing audiences and creating demand for products. This makes marketing a potential career move for instructional designers, especially if the market is instructional products. Although there are important differences between the two fields, instructional designers will find many similarities as well.

Sales is another area in which designers may find new career challenges. The earnings potential in a sales position may be significantly higher than in traditional instructional design positions. Opportunities exist for designers to sell instructional design services or educational products. As we've stressed in this book, good instructional designers need strong communication skills, which are also critical in sales and marketing.

Employers

Who hires instructional designers? Many companies and organizations produce materials and provide services that need the direction of an instructional designer. Here are some of the environments in which instructional designers work.

Corporate Professional Development Training departments typically are responsible for evaluating training needs in the organization, developing and delivering training, ensuring that training sequences support each career ladder, and managing any other training functions such as supporting employees in earning advanced degrees. In a training or staff development department, the instructional designer may develop curriculum for e-learning or for other trainers to deliver. Training is often part of the personnel or human resources (HR) department of the company, so the main career path for instructional designers is through the HR hierarchy.

Training departments often divide the training development and delivery functions into specific divisions within the organization. For example, manufacturers may employ trainers (and instructional designers) who specialize in developing training for particular manufacturing tasks or product lines. Some might specialize in training employees at partner companies such as suppliers or distributors. In many companies, separate training units support information technology, management, and sales. The instruction they develop can include orientation and basic skills for new employees, equipment and procedure-specific training, software applications, quality control, budgeting and financial concerns, and HR issues such as sexual harassment and hiring and firing, as well as other employment matters.

In his influential 1994 book *The Fifth Discipline: The Art and Practice of the Learning Organization,* Peter Senge argued that successful companies stay flexible and adapt to the rapid changes of the marketplace. They accomplish this by creating an environment in which employees learn at all times and at all levels. In other words, learning is integrated into the daily fabric of the organization—it isn't a special, occasional activity–and it's valued. He calls these companies "learning organizations." Even as business consultants like Senge have advocated that companies embrace a culture that adapts and grows, the need for ongoing training has grown, too. Companies are experimenting with how they develop and deliver this mission-critical training. Some have sought to promote the importance of training and increase its visibility within the company by elevating the training manager to a vice president level or changing the title to director of learning or chief learning officer. It might seem like mere semantics, but these efforts represent genuine attempts to send the message that learning is as important to the company's success as is finance and marketing. In this context, "learning" connotes a more proactive, flexible, and learner-centered approach to employee development than does "training."

Corporate Customer Support

Companies also offer a variety of courses to support their products. Particularly at technology companies, instructional designers may be involved in developing training for customers. This product training might be part of the company's marketing efforts, designed to help make the sale, or part of customer service after the sale. Programs can range from "how to" courses designed for novices to advanced courses leading to certification on a software product. Some courses provide customers with opportunities to enhance their skills in order to make better use of the company's products. For example, a manufacturer of color printers might offer courses on how to create effective newsletters or how to take better digital photos. Although these courses don't directly support the company's product, they do foster customer loyalty. Customer education courses may even be a profit center for the company, and the department might be fully funded by revenues from these sales.

Corporate Information Support

In many corporate training arenas, the line is blurring between purposeful instruction and information support. Corporate instructional designers traditionally have been a part of the training and staff development department to support employee training, or the marketing and customer service department to support customer training. Again, especially for technology companies, markets and products change so frequently that there isn't time to generate formal training. These companies adopted other strategies for meeting the information needs of employees and customers, such as online help, users' guides, specification sheets, job aids, and other resources.

Some companies call this "stealth" training or a variation on just-in-time training. John Coné, past president

Customer Education as Profit Center

A software company has three levels of customer education offerings, all designed to provide a return on investment so that the department is self-sufficient. The customer's lowest-cost option is a series of online course modules. The cost of individual modules is relatively low, but purchasing all of the modules would be pricey. This option works well for customers who use only a portion of the total software product or who need to stretch the costs of training out over time. The next level up is also a computer-delivered version, but it includes Flash animations and voice-over narration to guide learners through the software's functionality. The most expensive option is a one-week classroom-based training program. Although these courses are conducted at locations throughout the world, the costs of the class, of travel, and time away from work can be significant. This tiered approach has been popular with customers and generates revenue for the company.

of the American Society for Training and Development (ASTD) was formerly vice president for learning at Dell Computer, where he promoted "on-demand learning." He explained: "The ideal 'learning event' at Dell has a class size of one, lasts 5 to 10 minutes, and takes place within 10 minutes of when someone recognizes that he or she needs to know something. Our challenge is to reduce learning to its smallest, most-useful increments and to put the learner in charge of the entire process" (Dahle, 1998, p. 178).

Publishers Educational publishers offer resources to supplement or replace textbook offerings. Some online products replace the workbooks that once accompanied textbooks. There are supplemental products that serve niche markets such as ESL, literacy, developmental math, and enrichment programs. Some publishers specialize in training programs for corporate functions—for example, sales training, management training, or communication skills. A growing market is the homeschool sector, which includes parents who choose to provide their children with home-based instruction. All of these programs require instructional design and production, just as with any online or multimedia product.

Health Care Industries Like other industries with rapidly changing technology, the health care sector has many training requirements. Physicians, nurses, and other practitioners have to maintain their licensing by completing continuing education programs each year. Pharmaceutical companies need to develop training for their sales staff, providers, and customers. Hospitals and other institutions must provide training to their staffs and education for their patients. Educational materials for patients and their families include information on preparing for a surgical procedure, taking care of ill or disabled family members, and maintaining good health. Some hospitals provide ongoing patient education via internal cable channels available to patients in their hospital rooms. All of these health care instructional programs can be delivered in classroom settings, online in an e-learning environment, through videotapes or DVDs, or via blended learning.

K-12 Education Some schools and many school districts have curriculum specialists who are responsible for developing instructional materials, devising and implementing scope and sequence programs at each grade level and across grade levels, and ensuring that schools implement state standards appropriately. As schools bring more technology into the classroom, there's a growing need for school-based specialists who understand both learning and technology. This specialist might be responsible for helping teachers develop and deliver lessons using technology or for devising technology-based projects for students. She or he is also likely to be involved in planning and budgeting for instructional technology at the institution.

Another path for instructional designers is in developing and delivering professional training to teachers and other staff. For example, most school districts provide opportunities for professional development to teachers during the school year, and most states require teachers to attend a certain number of continuing education programs each year. Instructional designers may find themselves in demand to deliver workshops on topics such as curriculum development, educational technology, and project management. State agencies have many of these same needs, as do their local administrative units. This can be a rewarding and challenging job, especially for the instructional designer with prior classroom teaching experience. In fact, classroom experience is often a criterion for employment in these positions. Even when not required, experience in the classroom greatly enhances designers' credibility when working with this group of clients.

Many countries understand that education represents a critical investment in their competiveness in the global economy. They are investing heavily in instructional development and technology to boost their students' knowledge and skills. Even countries that have lagged in educational investment in the past are looking to standards-based and technology-based delivery to achieve rapid gains. With centralized planning and development, they can deploy these programs nationally. And they rely on instructional designers to develop and implement these programs.

Higher Education In recent decades, institutions of higher learning have gone from having mainframe computers with "dumb terminals" available only to computer science students to being among the most wired institutions anywhere. Higher education settings include community colleges, small colleges, state universities, major research institutions, and online degree providers. A new type of institution of higher education has emerged in recent years, catering to busy adults seeking undergraduate and graduate degrees. These colleges do not have physical plants but instead have invested in the electronic resources necessary to provide a full, online instructional experience.

Online degree programs are offered by "brick and mortar" colleges and universities, as well as through new institutions founded specifically to serve distance learners. Some are linking students at different campuses, and even in different countries, through Web-based initiatives designed to foster the kinds of collaborative skills needed in the global economy. Many professors also use the Internet in traditional classes, posting assignments and readings online, and using tools such as chat software and discussion boards.

With this remarkable transformation of higher education has come increasing demand for specialists to produce effective computer-delivered instructional materials. Each of these institutions hires specialists to design and develop materials to support or supplant classroom teaching. An instructional designer might develop materials to support lectures, produce ancillary materials, maintain Web sites, and teach faculty to use technology effectively. At the largest institutions, groups of instructional designers might support individual schools or departments.

Extension Services Universities have offered extension services for many years. Originally seeking to reach rural learners, many now offer online courses and even complete degree programs. The extension courses are not always the same as those offered by the primary institution. For example, the primary institution may require that students be admitted to the university whereas extension courses typically are available to anyone who enrolls. Extension offerings can include courses for college credit, noncredit courses for professional or personal enhancement, and high school courses.

Virtual Schools Another development in online learning involves virtual schools, usually high schools that serve students who are homeschooled or have special requirements. These students may include rural students, elite athletes, students with medical problems that prevent attendance at a regular school, and young people who are confined to juvenile detention centers. These virtual schools offer diplomas and have academic requirements similar to those at a regular school. They are administered by both established educational institutions and organizations founded specifically to provide online instruction.

Nonprofit Associations To meet the needs of members who must satisfy annual continuing education requirements, some nonprofit associations have found that they can offer these courses and bring in needed revenue at the same time. These offerings are tailored to the specific needs of the association's members. Members who complete the training programs earn credits, which may be required for continuing certification or licensing. One popular online option is for a for-profit company to develop and deliver the courses to association members at no cost to the association. The company then uses a revenue sharing formula to provide the association with a percentage of the receipts. Many associations offer Continuing Education Unit (CEU) workshops through videoconferencing sessions featuring one-way video and two-way audio hookups.

Museums and Parks Public institutions such as art museums, historical sites, special collections, zoos, aquariums, botanical gardens, science centers, parks, and nature preserves typically have an educational purpose as part of the institution's mission. However, many also have other goals such as entertaining visitors, collecting artwork, or preserving natural environments. Because public institutions compete with myriad other leisure activities, they may have a market-driven orientation to developing the educational aspects of their presentations and user activities (Savenye, 2003).

E-Learning Developer Whether delivered over the Web, or from a CD-ROM, hard drive, or a network, computer-based training, or e-learning, is capturing a rapidly growing share of corporate higher education and workforce development education. Companies that specialize in producing these courses are e-learning developers. They might develop and sell proprietary training products or provide customized development services to other companies. Some developers specialize in serving niche markets while others are generalists. An e-learning developer might only serve the educational publishing industry or only produce management training. Some companies develop training only for certain platforms while others support all major systems.

Other Settings Instruction is a significant component of the work of many other organizations such as religious institutions, the military, and government agencies. The success of these institutions depends on designing and deploying effective instructional materials to target audiences. There are instructional design opportunities in all of these environments.

Types of Companies

Regardless of where you start your career, you are likely to work at several different jobs along the way, perhaps even as an independent contractor. Instructional designers are employed by a variety of companies, both large and small. Although each employment option has its advantages and limitations, an awareness of them can help you select the option that is right for your skills and interests.

Large Companies Some companies employ entire departments of instructional designers; others might have one person who does instructional design among other tasks. At large, established companies, this work can be very steady and predictable. But this doesn't necessarily mean the work is repetitive. On the contrary, when you work for an established company with a strong hierarchy, finely tuned procedures, and ample tools and resources, you are free to concentrate on the job of instructional design. You aren't scrambling to obtain materials or spending time establishing how things get done. Instead, you are getting training on new software, receiving your

A Personal Journey

by Debby Kalk

In this chapter, we describe the great range of employment directions in which your instructional design career can take you. You might find just the right place early on and stay there for your entire career, or you may work in a variety of environments. My career is an example of the latter. I don't remember what I expected when I decided to become an instructional designer, but I'm certain that my experiences have exceeded my expectations. I like to say that I have the perfect career for someone with an attention span that lasts six months, which is about how long I'm typically engaged in a project. So, a couple times each year, I learn about a new industry and new content; meet new clients, SMEs, and learners; and grapple with new technology and new delivery requirements. I don't think I've ever been bored.

I have worked in companies of all sizes and types: in a training department for a large corporation with 16,000 employees, for a small multimedia developer with a few dozen employees, and in a media support position at a college. I've owned a company with as many as 70 employees, and I've been a freelancer. I've worked on teams with a hundred people, and I've been the entire team, serving as instructional designer, SME, and producer.

My clients have included Fortune 500 companies, educational publishers, universities, nonprofits, and individuals.

They've hired me to write instructor's manuals for classroom delivery, produce educational videos, and create online courseware. I've produced training programs on mission-critical software for engineers and developed a program that aimed to change middle school students' attitudes about drug use. There have been stints immersed in learning about the electric utility industry, the oil business, airlines, banking, health care, technology, social work, business development, the space program, and teacher training. For educational applications, I've developed programs on world languages, math study skills, economics, English grammar, history, film appreciation, and criminal justice, for secondary and higher education. I've worked with tremendously talented artists, programmers, and producers; trained novice instructional designers; and learned much from colleagues, clients, SMEs, and learners.

As you will discover, it's deeply satisfying when the feedback from evaluations indicates that your learners have really learned something. It's exciting when a project you've designed wins an award. And when clients return for repeat business, you know you are doing something right. In this field, you meet many interesting people, some of whom become close personal friends. There just aren't many occupations that can deliver so much variety, so many challenges, and so many rewards.

---

paycheck on time, attending conferences, and participating in professional organizations. There are also likely to be mentors in the organization who can help you with your career. One disadvantage of working in a big company is that you might not get noticed and might not attain a decision-making position for several years or more.

Another issue is that your skill set—instructional design—might not reflect the company's core product. For example, if you work for a company that manages health care billing services, your instructional design skills may be important to the company but not critical. If you were an accountant or a registered nurse, your skills might be useful in moving into leadership positions. As a specialist who doesn't contribute to a company's mission, you may need to change jobs to move up the career ladder. By moving to a larger company, you may be able to fill a series of positions with increasing levels of responsibility. Of course, if you work for a company that produces instructional products, there probably will be strong career opportunities within that company.

Small Companies   Sometimes, small companies can provide instructional designers with more opportunities than can larger companies. Designers may participate in a wide variety of projects, take on more and more responsibility, and become increasingly important to the company. These companies usually are flexible and, in turn, allow you to be flexible in designing and delivering training. There are fewer procedures but more opportunities to try new strategies and set policies for the training function. A disadvantage of working for small companies is that they might not be as financially solid as bigger companies. You may not enjoy perks such as paid membership in professional organizations, trips to conferences, or reimbursement for graduate school tuition. If the company has no history of working with instructional designers and no department in place, you might have to work hard to educate and gain the respect of your co-workers. However, in a small company, you will probably have more interactions with managers and more opportunities to demonstrate your value. In fact, instructional designers who work with many different kinds of internal and external clients have ample opportunities to fully understand the business. You are likely to develop strong communication and management skills, which will be in demand in many leadership positions.

Independent Contractors

It's not unusual for an instructional designer to spend at least part of her or his career as an independent contractor. Some designers find this to be a very satisfying work arrangement because it offers opportunities to work in a variety of industries, on different kinds of projects, and with different teams. As a contractor, you usually have control over your hours and working conditions. The disadvantages are that you have to market yourself, you have no employee benefits, and the work can be "feast or famine"—too much to do or too little. You also have to manage your finances and time well. Despite these drawbacks, in the current era of corporate cutbacks, it's reassuring to have a skill set that lends itself to the opportunities of the freelance market.

Most independent contractors or freelancers offer their services to companies and institutions on a project-by-project basis, such as to produce a specific course. For example, a pharmaceutical company may need to train its sales reps on new applications and dosages for a popular drug. The company has an in-house staff, but they don't have time to do the project, so a freelance instructional designer is hired to create the design document, treatment, and storyboards for an e-learning program.

Other companies may hire contractors to work in-house for a set amount of time—say, 10 weeks—either to assist other staff or to produce one or more deliverables. For example, a start-up company readying its product for a pilot test might bring in an instructional designer to develop the materials for the test (akin to a formative evaluation). Because there will be many deliverables and the designer will need to work with a variety of staff members to develop different components, it makes sense for that individual to work on-site, billing at a full-time rate.

As an independent contractor, you may have some ability to negotiate your compensation. You can work on a fixed-payment contract or on a flexible basis, such as by the hour or deliverable. If you can complete the task quickly, it's probably in your best interest to negotiate a fixed price. You can shoot for an hourly-based compensation if you are concerned about the scope of work or if you are worried that the schedule will slip. For example, charge by the hour if you think that the client won't deliver the content on time or your reviewers might be slow in supplying their comments. If clients have to pay for their own delays, they tend also to pay more attention to the schedule.

Promoting Instructional Design

Just because an organization has hired you doesn't mean that everyone will value or understand your role as the designer. The field is still relatively young and still must prove itself in many settings, so consider yourself an ambassador for instructional design. Some people confuse the discipline of instructional design with the implementation of educational technology. Others may have had experiences with designers who lacked strong communication or collaboration skills, hurting the project and team. Regardless of the attitudes your colleagues bring to a project team, you can demonstrate your value.

Whenever you interact with others in an instructional design project, you want to promote your role in a manner consistent with the values of the organization. But you also want your colleagues to understand what you bring to the team. For example, engineers are systems oriented, so they usually will respond to the systems approach in instructional design. If the person you want to influence values organizational effectiveness, explain what you do in terms of increasing organizational effectiveness. If she values the reputation of the organization, present your work in terms of enhancing the company's reputation.

Rothwell and Kazansas (1998) outlined a structured approach to the process of educating others. They observed that in every organization there are individuals with social power—others look up to them and seek their opinions. Rothwell and Kazansas (p. 356) suggested that

---

Voice of Experience

Who Are You, and What Do You Do?

A video production company was branching out into the new world of interactive media. They started by hiring a team of instructional designers. One of the video producers sent the designers a memo addressed to "The Industrial Design Dept." Another staff member appeared at the design department's door one day and peered in quizzically. The designers sat at their computers, conducted long telephone conference calls, and pored through thick reference volumes. The walls were covered with flip chart pages full of flowcharts. She asked, "What exactly do you guys do in here?" Clearly, the work the designers were doing was not obvious to their colleagues.

you identify these opinion leaders and seek answers to three questions:

- What special interests exist in this group that might lead its members to explore—and perhaps support—a rigorous, professional approach to instructional design?
- How might the members of this group benefit from a rigorous approach to instructional design?
- What would opinion leaders in this group need to know to be persuaded to support such an approach?

After you have answered these questions, you can develop a plan to promote professional instructional design within the organization. Your strategies may include routing articles about instructional design to opinion leaders, bringing in outside speakers, developing cost-benefit reports, and gathering testimonials from satisfied clients, SMEs, and learners (Rothwell & Kazanas, 1998).

If you have the time and authorization to do so, schedule a one- or two-hour workshop on instructional design for the team including your clients and SMEs. You might devise a simple, even obvious, instructional design problem that could reasonably be completed in a brief time. Choose something that everyone in the group knows something about, such as "how to use an ATM machine," "recycling in your neighborhood," or "sections of the newspaper." Develop a handout or packet of forms for participants to use during the workshop.

At the event, have participants work, individually or in pairs, through each phase of the instructional design process. This experience will not only enlighten the team but help them make better contributions to your work.

Although this book presents an instructional design model with five elements and five phases, as you work on various projects in different environments, you are likely to encounter many other models (also discussed in Chapter 1). You may be employed by a company that follows another instructional design model, perhaps one that the company has developed specifically for its learners and content. Most of these instructional design models follow the same general principles presented in this book but emphasize different strategies or steps. The spiral model was designed to reflect the way many designers actually perform their work, considering each of the essential elements in each phase of the design cycle, and building on their understanding as the spiral loops out from the center. If you use other models, be aware of how they address the five essential elements and the five phases of design. Above all, use the terminology and model that is most appropriate for the setting in which you are employed.

If you are among the first instructional designers at your company, you may be able to develop and implement design standards and procedures. You can develop a proposal for your supervisors that spells out what will be involved in developing standards and how the

---

Other Models

A short bit of library investigation on the topic of instructional design will yield many, many design models.[1] Below, four of the many alternatives to the spiral model presented in this text are briefly discussed.[2]

Dick, Carey, and Carey Model

Walt Dick and Lou Carey began teaching their model in 1968 at Florida State University (Dick, Carey, & Carey, 2001). Their textbook *The Systematic Design of Instruction* has introduced thousands of students to the field of instructional design. Although their model is usually thought of as a linear sequence, Dick, Carey, and Carey emphasize that instructional design is a system with a built-in feedback loop. They stress the need to obtain feedback and to revise deliverables based on that feedback throughout the process. Notice how

all the components of the Dick, Carey, and Carey sequence model are addressed in the spiral model presented in this text (see figure).

Willis's R2D2 Model

Jerry Willis (1995) developed his R2D2 (recursive, reflective design and development) model at the University of Houston and NASA's Johnson Space Center. Willis wanted to counter the linear limitations of other models with a process that is recursive, reflective, and participatory. Willis's model identifies the three focal points of Define, Design and Develop, and Disseminate (see figure). An instructional designer should work on all three areas in an iterative fashion. Willis's focal points align with the five phases—Define, Design, Demonstrate, Develop, and

(continued on page 281)

DESIGNER'S TOOLKIT

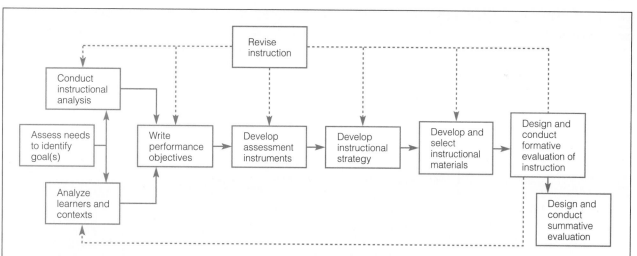

The Dick, Carey, and Carey model is a classic model of instructional systems design.

SOURCE: From Walter Dick, Lou Carey, James O. Carey, *The Systematic Design of Education,* 5th ed. (Boston, MA: Allyn and Bacon, 2001). Copyright © 2001 by Pearson Education. Adapted by permission of the publisher.

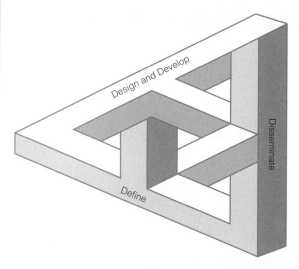

The R2D2 model emphasizes a nonlinear, iterative process.

SOURCE: From Jerry Willis, "A Recursive, Reflective Instructional Design Model Based on Constructivist-Interpretivist Theory," *Educational Technology,* Nov./Dec. 1995: 5–23. Reprinted with permission.

Deliver—used in this textbook. He also addresses the collaborative and iterative nature of instructional design as it is presented in this book, and he uses the concept of a spiral to describe the process of design.

Tessmer and Wedman's Layers-of-Necessity Model

Martin Tessmer and John Wedman (1990) developed the "layers-of-necessity" model to counter the inflexibility they saw in other instructional design models and reflect the realities of working in "the real world." They see instructional design as consisting of layers of interrelated tasks, with each layer representing increased complexity (see figure). Tasks of a layer may include situational assessment, goal analysis, instructional strategy development, materials development, and evaluation and revision. Although they are careful not to prescribe specific activities for each layer, they emphasize that the output of the tasks at each layer should be consistent with each other. In other words, if the designer performs the tasks mentioned above, the materials should be consistent with the instructional goals and strategy, appropriate to the situation, and evaluated and revised. Above all, designers should allocate their time to the tasks that have the greatest instructional benefits. As time and resources allow, additional "layers" of design and development tasks can be added.

Tripp and Bichelmeyer's Rapid Prototyping Model

Acknowledging the efficiency with which modern software allows designers to create and modify prototypes, S. Tripp and B. Bichelmeyer (1990) proposed using rapid prototyping as an instructional design model, especially when creating computer-based materials. According to this model, learners' needs, the content, and objectives are determined as the prototype is

(continued on page 282)

DESIGNER'S TOOLKIT

(continued)

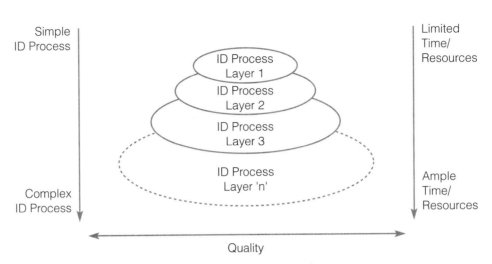

The layers-of-necessity model illustrates that designers perform tasks as resources and time permit.

SOURCE: **From Martin Tessmer and John F. Wedman, "A Layers-of-Necessity Instructional Development Model,"** *Educational Technology Research and Development,* **Spring 1990: 77–85. Reprinted with permission.**

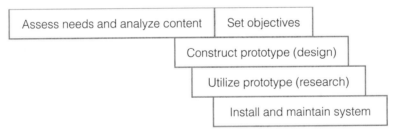

The Rapid prototyping model, emphasizes feedback from learners early in the design process.

SOURCE: **From S. Tripp and B. Bichelmeyer, "Rapid Prototyping: An Alternative Instructional Design Strategy,"** *Educational Technology Research and Development,* **Spring 1990: 31–44. Reprinted with permission.**

constructed and utilized rather than prior to development (see figure). Rapid prototyping is based on the philosophy that instructional situations are complex and that spending a great deal of time on front-end analysis without consulting learners lengthens the time required for a design project without necessarily creating a better product. Tripp and Bichelmeyer emphasize that testing instructional materials that are near completion, as in formative evaluation, is not as efficient as rapid prototyping.

company will benefit. Try to state the benefits in terms that your managers will appreciate—in other words, how will it improve the bottom line? The most significant benefit is likely to be faster development of effective instructional materials and systematic design standards and procedures that allow the design team to be more productive and ensure that trainees will be better prepared in transferring their new skills to the workplace.

In addition to promoting the practice and value of instructional design within your organization, you want to find ways to promote recognition of your contributions. You need to exercise some caution here—you don't want to become so associated with self-promotion that your message is dismissed as mere aggrandizement. Be sure to always deliver substantive and effective work products, to recognize the contributions of colleagues and peers, and to restrict your self-promotion to appropriate venues. That said, don't hesitate to build your name recognition. Consider these opportunities:

- Write a monthly, or perhaps quarterly, e-mail newsletter on instructional design news and tips and circulate to decision makers and colleagues.
- Write articles on instructional design for publications or forums such as your company's internal newsletters and Web sites, local newspapers, and professional journals.
- Offer to give lunch-hour talks and workshops.
- Speak at meetings of local professional organizations.
- Submit proposals to speak at conferences.
- Mentor students at nearby colleges and sponsor interns at your company.

Ultimately, what wins adherents to instructional design is the quality of your work. Your professionalism, communication and collaboration skills, problem solving, and proactive approach, as well as the products you develop, are what convince colleagues that instructional design is valuable. There is no substitute for substance.

Keeping Up with the Field

Those of us who work in technology-dependent areas have to try especially hard to keep up with technical innovations and developments in our field. When we began working in instructional design, there were few personal computers and no public Internet. In less than 20 years, the field has changed dramatically. How to cope? There are many ways to work at this, but no single method can keep you completely current.

Numerous professional organizations hold conferences and provide publications and online resources. The largest organizations are the Association for Educational Communications and Technology (AECT), the primary academic association serving the instructional design field; the American Society for Training and Development (ASTD), the largest professional association serving the training community; the International Society for Performance and Instruction (ISPI) serving professionals interested in workplace performance, which can include instruction; and the International Society for Technology in Education (ISTI), which focuses on the effective use of technology in K-12 education. Your community may have local professional organizations that sponsor presentations, online forums, workshops, or networking meetings. Get involved by offering to serve on a board, organize a program or workshop, or give a presentation. You might also write articles for association newsletters, journals, or other publications. Many associations, both locally and nationally, invite designers to apply to become judges for instructional product awards programs. Judging is difficult work, but the experience can be highly rewarding.

As you consider where you want to go in your career, you might identify people you admire and try to arrange an informational interview. Call and ask if you can spend 20 or so minutes talking about instructional design practice. Even busy people often will grant this request, which gives you an opportunity to ask questions about the industry. It also allows you to introduce yourself to a

---

Voice of Experience

A Personal Journey

by Katherine Cennamo

I began my career as an elementary school teacher, moved on to directing the media support services at a small college, and eventually ended up as a university professor. Along the way, I've designed and developed classroom instruction, videotapes, multimedia products, and online courses for groups as diverse as automotive manufacturers, elderly patients, and university students.

I've found that instructional design is the perfect profession for those who enjoy learning. As I've designed instruction for various clients, I've learned about child development, water treatment plants, signs of child abuse, and a wide variety of other topics. Designers also must have excellent problem-solving skills.

When software is unstable, SMEs are reluctant, and deadlines are looming, designers must be able to reconsider options and find a way to move the project forward despite the obstacles. They must be comfortable with some ambiguity and enjoy creating order out of the initial chaos. Instructional design requires the ability to look at situations as though through a zoom lens—to zoom out and see the big picture, and them to zoom in and attend to all the details required to design and develop a successful product. There is a sense of accomplishment when one project draws to an end and a sense of excitement when another one begins. It's always challenging, sometimes frustrating, but consistently rewarding. May you find it as enjoyable as I have!

Analogy

House

Just as some instructional designers specialize in certain kinds of projects or types of design, architects usually specialize in types of buildings and styles of architecture. An architect might focus on designing restaurants or hospitals, or renovating historic homes, just as an instructional designer might focus on technical training, or workforce development, or programs for early learners. Architects work in many types of offices ranging from large construction companies, to design studios, to solo practices. In your instructional design career, you might work for a large consulting firm, an academic institution, or a multimedia developer, or as an independent contractor. You might find a company that's a perfect fit for your skills and goals, and spend a rewarding career there. Or you might find that different employers meet your career needs at different points in your development.

Just as an architect may need to promote the benefits of a custom-designed house, you may need to promote the benefits of systematically designed instruction to employers and clients. Methods of home design and construction have changed over the years, and methods of designing, developing, and delivering instructional materials have changed as well. Throughout it all, you need to find ways to keep your skills current in a rapidly changing field.

---

possible mentor, employer, or other decision maker. You should be sure to arrive on time, dressed professionally, and to adhere strictly to the agreed upon-format and time frame. And follow up with a thank-you note.

The forms in which learning is supported continue to change and evolve, and designers need to apply their skills in new ways, and in new contexts, and using new means of delivery. Throughout it all, the premises of systematic instructional design hold true. You seek information from a variety of resources to develop a product that's focused on the needs and characteristics of learners. You engage in a cycle of review and refinement that brings you from a vague vision to a complete product. You make sure the goals, assessments, and activities of the product are in alignment. And you test the product with learners throughout the design and development cycle in order to deliver an end product of proven effectiveness.

Summary

In this chapter, we discussed issues of importance to your career as a professional instructional designer. We looked at the range of institutions and types of positions that designers hold. We examined the benefits and drawbacks of different settings and types of employment options. And we provided advice on promoting the instructional design process and keeping current in a rapidly changing field. As you work in the profession, you'll adopt instructional design methods and techniques that are effective for you. You'll probably reach a point at which you have internalized the instructional design process and rarely think about the individual steps. At this point, you'll be an expert! We wish you the best of luck as you embark on your professional career!

Notes

[1] Summaries of instructional design models were contributed by Charles B. Hodges.

[2] For an excellent overview of a variety of instructional design models, see Kent L. Gustafson and Robert Branch, *Survey of Instructional Development Models,* 4th ed. (Syracuse, NY: ERIC Clearinghouse on Information and Technology, 2002).

References

Dahle, C. (1998). Learning—John Cone. *Fast Company,* 178.

Dick, W., Carey, L., & Carey, J. O. (2001). *The systematic design of instruction* (5th ed). Needham Heights: MA: Allyn & Bacon.

Rothwell, W. J., & Kazanas, H. C. (1998). *Mastering the instructional design process: A systematic approach* (2nd ed.). San Francisco: Jossey-Bass.

Savenye, W. (2003, October). Really open learning environments: Conducting needs assessments and formative evaluations in informal settings. Paper presented at the meeting of the Association for Educational Communications and Technology, Anaheim, CA.

Senge, P. (1994). *The fifth discipline: The art and practice of the learning organization.* New York: Currency/Doubleday.

Tessmer, M., & Wedman, J. F. (1990). A layers-of-necessity instructional development model. *Educational Technology Research and Development, 38*(2), 77–85.

Tripp, S., & Bichelmeyer, B. (1990). Rapid prototyping: An alternative instructional design strategy. *Educational Technology Research and Development, 31*(1), 31–44.

Willis, J. (1995). A recursive, reflective instructional design model based on constructivist-interpretivist theory. *Educational Technology, 35,* 5–23.

Application

1. In your reflective journal, summarize the key points of this chapter. How are the ideas presented consistent or inconsistent with your beliefs and prior knowledge? Compare your perceptions of the chapter with those of your classmates in group discussions.

2. Interview several instructional designers who work in different environments. Consider how their jobs are similar and how they are different.

3. Investigate career opportunities for instructional designers by examining Web sites or reading journal articles. What particular skills are needed for each career?

4. In Chapter 1, we asked you to describe what instructional designers do, what their day-to-day work involves, and what skills might be most beneficial. Reread your reflections from Chapter 1. How have your ideas changed throughout the course?

5. Locate several instructional design models. Identify how each model addresses each of the five elements of instructional design discussed in this book.

Additional Readings

The following resources provide additional information about the topics addressed in this book. For further information, please use your passcode to access the expanded list of readings and Web links available on the RealWorldID Web site.

Assessment

Bloom, B. S., Hastings, J. T., & Madaus, G. F. (Eds.). (1971). *Handbook on formative and summative evaluation of student learning.* New York: McGraw-Hill.

Forte, I., & Schurr, S. (1995). *Making portfolios, products, and performances meaningful and manageable for students and teachers: Instructional strategies and thematic activities.* Nashville, TN: Incentive.

Hudspeth, DeLayne. (1997). *Testing learner outcomes in Web-based instruction.* In B. Khan (Ed.), *Web-based instruction.* (pp. 353–356). Englewood Cliffs: Educational Technology.

Mager, R. F. (2000). *Measuring instructional results.* Atlanta: Center for Effective Performance.

Pellegrino, J. W., Chudowsky, N., & Glaser, R. (Eds.). (2001). *Knowing what students know: The science and design of educational assessment.* Washington, DC: National Academy Press.

Popham, W. J. (1978). *Criterion-referenced assessment.* Englewood Cliffs, NJ: Prentice-Hall.

Audience/Learner Analysis

Gagne, R. M. (1985). *The conditions of learning* (4th ed.). New York: Holt, Rinehart & Winston.

Hallahan, D. P., & Kauffmann, J. (2001). *Teaching exceptional children, cases for reflection and analysis for exceptional learners: Introduction to special education* (7th ed.). Boston: Allyn & Bacon.

Jonassen, D. H., & Grabowski, B. L. (1993). *Handbook of individual differences, learning, and instruction.* Hillsdale, NJ: Lawrence Erlbaum.

Taylor, R. L. (2002). *Assessment of exceptional students: Educational and psychological procedures* (6th ed.). Boston: Allyn & Bacon.

Careers in Instructional Design

Andrews, D. H., Moses, F. L., & Duke, D. S. (2002). Current trends in military instructional design and technology. In R. A. Reiser & J. V. Dempsey (Eds.), *Trends and issues in instructional design and technology* (pp. 211–224). Upper Saddle River, NJ: Merrill/Prentice-Hall.

Carr-Chellman, A. A. (2002). Whistling in the dark? Instructional design and technology in the schools. In R. A. Reiser & J. V. Dempsey (Eds.), *Trends and issues in instructional design and technology* (pp. 239–255). Upper Saddle River, NJ: Merrill/Prentice-Hall.

Davidson-Shivers, G. A. (2002). Instructional technology in higher education. In R. A. Reiser, & J. V. Dempsey (Eds.), *Trends and issues in instructional design and technology* (pp. 256–268). Upper Saddle River, NJ: Merrill/Prentice-Hall.

Mager, R. F. (1996). Morphing into a 21st century trainer. *Training Magazine, 33*(6), 47–54.

McCabe, L. L., & McCabe, E. R. B. (2000). *How to succeed in academics.* San Diego: Academic Press.

Pershing, J. A., & Lee, S. H. (1999). Employment profiles and compensation for educational technologists. *TechTrends, 43*(6), 7–14.

Reiser, R. A.., (2002). What field did you say you were in? Defining and naming our field. In R. A. Reiser & J. V. Dempsey (Eds.), *Trends and issues in instructional design and technology.* Upper Saddle River, NJ: Merrill/Prentice-Hall.

Richey, R. C., & Morrison, G. R. (2002). Instructional design in business and industry.In R. A. Reiser, & J. V. Dempsey (Eds.), *Trends and issues in instructional design and technology,* (pp. 197–210). Upper Saddle River, NJ: Merrill/Prentice-Hall.

Rossett, A. (2000). What's academia got to do with it? An informal tour of what managers are seeking from entry-level instructional technologists. *TechTrends, 44*(5), 32–35.

Surrey, D. W., & Robinson, M. A. (2001). A taxonomy of instructional technology service positions in higher education. *Innovations in Education and Teaching International, 38*(3), 231–238.

Collaboration and Project Management

Barbazette, J. (2001). *The trainer's support handbook: A practical guide to managing the administrative details of training.* New York: McGraw-Hill.

Beach, M., & Kenly, E. (1999). *Getting it printed: How to work with printers and graphic imaging services to assure quality, stay on schedule and control costs* (3rd ed.). Cincinnati, OH: North Light Books.

Duncan, W. R. (1996). *A guide to the project management body of knowledge.* Newtown Square, PA: Project Management Institute.

Eyres, P. S. (1998). *The legal handbook of trainers, speakers, consultants: The essential guide to keeping your company and clients out of court.* New York: McGraw-Hill.

Fuller, J. (1997). *Managing performance improvement projects: Preparing, planning, implementing.* San Francisco: Jossey-Bass/Pfeiffer.

Garstang, M. (1994). Checklist for training project management: The team's perspective. *Journal of Instruction Delivery Systems, 8*(1), 29–33.

Greer, M. (2001). *The project manager's partner: A step-by-step guide to project management.* Amherst, MA: HRD Press.

Hackos, J. T. (1994). *Managing your documentation projects.* New York: John Wiley.

Hargrove, R. (1995). *Masterful coaching.* San Francisco: Jossey-Bass/Pfeiffer.

Smallen, D., & Leach, K. (1999). Making a NICER transition to the millennium: Five keys to successful collaboration. *Educom Review, 34*(4), 20.

Tessmer, M. (1998). Meeting with the SME to design multimedia exploration systems. *Educational Technology Research and Development, 46*(2), 79-95.

Wellins, R. (1991). *Empowered teams: Creating self-directed work groups that improve quality, productivity, and participation.* San Francisco: Jossey-Bass.

Communication Challenges

Allred, K. G. (1997). Conflict management. In L. J. Bassi & D. Russ-Eft (Eds.), *What works: Training and development practices* (pp. 27–50). Alexandria, VA: American Society for Training and Development.

Baker, H., & Morgan, P. (1989). Building a professional image: Handling conflict. In F. Stone (Ed.), *The American Management Association handbook of supervisory management.* New York: AMACOM.

Constantino, C. A., & Merchant, C. S. (1996). *Designing conflict management systems.* San Francisco: Jossey-Bass.

Hiam, A. (1999). *Dealing with conflict.* (A self-assessment instrument.) Amherst, MA: HRD Press.

Communication Modes, Media, and Cues

Bolton, R., & Bolton, D. G. (1996). *People styles at work.* New York: American Management Association.

Khan. B. H. (1998). *Web-based Instruction.* Englewood Cliffs, NJ: Educational Technology.

Mayer, R. E. (2003). The promise of multimedia learning: Using the same instructional design methods across different media. *Learning and Instruction, 13*(2), 125–139.

Shepard, R., Fasko, D., Jr., & Osborne, F. H. (1999). Intrapersonal intelligence: Affective factors in thinking. *Education, 119*(4), 633–642.

VNU Business Media. (2002). Choose wisely: Communication modes and their uses. *Sales and Marketing Management, 154*(11), 25.

Communication Plans

Daniels, A. C. (1999). *Bringing out the best in people* (2nd ed.). New York: McGraw-Hill.

Swenson, J. (1999). Communication. In D. G. Langdon, K. S. Whiteside, & M. M. McKenna (Eds.), *Intervention resource guide: 50 performance improvement tools* (pp. 91–97). San Francisco: Jossey-Bass/Pfeiffer.

Content Analysis

Merrill, M. D., & Tennyson, R. D. (1977). *Teaching concepts: An instructional design guide.* Englewood Cliffs, NJ: Educational Technology.

Neuendorf, K. A. (2001). *The content analysis guidebook.* London: Sage.

Sink, D. (2002). ISD — Faster, better, easier. *Performance Improvement, 41*(7), 16–22.

Reigeluth, C. M., et al. (1978). The structure of subject matter content and its instructional design implications. *Instructional Science, 7*(2), 107–26.

Wedman, J. F. (1987). Conceptualizing unfamiliar content. *Journal of Instructional Development, 10*(3), 16–21.

Contextual Analysis

Richey, R. C., & Tessmer, M. (1995). Enhancing instructional systems design through contextual analysis. In B. Seels (Ed.), *Instructional design fundamentals: A reconsideration* (pp. 189–199). Englewood Cliffs, NJ: Educational Technology.

Tessmer, M., & Richey, R. C. (1997). The role of context in learning and instructional design. *Educational Technology Research and Development, 45*(2), 85–115.

Tessmer, M., & Wedman, J. (1995) Context-sensitive instructional design models: A response to design research, studies and criticism. *Performance Improvement Quarterly, 8*(3), p.38–54.

Cross-Cultural and Cross-Discipline Communication

Brake, T., Walker, D., & Walker, T. (1995). *Doing business internationally: The guide to cross-cultural success.* Burr Ridge, IL: Irwin.

Gundling, E. (1999). How to communicate globally. *Training and Development, 53*(6), 28–31.

Murrell, A. J., Crosby, F. J., & Ely, R. J. (1999). *Mentoring dilemmas: Developmental relationships within multi-cultural organizations.* Mahwah, NJ: Lawrence Erlbaum.

Sanchez, C. M. (2000). Performance improvement in international environments: Designing individual performance interventions to fit national cultures. *Performance Improvement Quarterly, 13*(2).

Effective Meetings, Presentations, and Written Communication

Anderson, D., Benjamin, B., & Paredes-Holt, B. (1998) *Connections: A guide to on-line writing.* Boston: Allyn & Bacon.

Coe, M. (1996). *Human factors for technical communicators.* New York: John Wiley.

Peoples, D. (1992) *Presentations plus: David Peoples' proven techniques* (2nd ed.) New York: John Wiley, 1992.

Formative and Summative Evaluation

Carey, L. M., & Dick. W. (1991). Summative evaluation. In L. J. Briggs, K. L. Gustafson, & M. H. Tillman (Eds.), *Instructional design: Principles and applications* (2nd ed., pp. 269-314). Englewood Cliffs, NJ: Educational Technology.

Cronbach, L. J. (1963). Course improvement through evaluation. In D. Ely & T. Plomp (Eds.) (2001), *Classic writings on instructional technology* (Vol. 2, pp. 123–134). Englewood, CO: Libraries Unlimited.

Kirkpatrick, D. (1996). Great ideas revisited. Techniques for evaluating training programs: Revisiting Kirkpatrick's four-level model. *Training and Development, 50*(1), 54–59.

Marelli, A. (1993). Ten evaluation instruments for technical training. *Technical and Skills Training, 4*(5), 7–14.

Nichols, G. W. (1997). Formative evaluation of Web-based instruction. In B. H. Khan (Ed.), *Web-based instruction.* Englewood Cliffs, NJ: Educational Technology.

Popham, W. J. (1993). *Educational evaluation* (3rd ed.). Boston: Allyn & Bacon.

Rossi, P. H., Freeman, H. E., & Lipsey, M. W. (1999). *Evaluation: A systematic approach.* Thousand Oaks, CA: Sage.

Sanders, J. R. (1992). *Evaluating school programs.* Thousand Oaks, CA: Sage.

Scriven, M. (1972). Pros and cons about goal-free evaluation. *Evaluation Comment, 3*(4), 1–4.

Stake, R. (1967). The countenance of educational evaluation. *Teachers College Record, 68,* 523–540.

Stufflebeam, D. L. (1971). *Educational evaluation and decision making.* Itasca, IL: F. E. Peacock.

Tessmer, M. (1993). *Planning and conducting formative evaluations: Improving the quality of education and training.* London: Kogan Page.

History of Instructional Design

Association for Educational Communication and Technology. (1977). *The definition of educational technology.* Washington, DC: AECT.

Eraut, M. (1989). Educational technology: Conceptual frameworks and historical development. In M.R. Eraut (Ed.), *The international encyclopedia of educational technology* (pp. 11–21). Oxford: Pergamon Press.

Morgan, R. M. (1978). Educational technology—Adolescence to adulthood. In D. Ely & T. Plomp (Eds.) (2001), *Classic writings on instructional technology,* (Vol. 2, pp. 257–264). Englewood, CO: Libraries Unlimited.

Reiser, R. A. (1987). Instructional technology: A history. In R. M. Gagne (Ed.), *Instructional technology: Foundations.* (pp. 11–48). Hillsdale, N.J.: Lawrence Erlbaum.

Saettler, L. P. (1968). *A history of instructional technology.* New York: McGraw-Hill.

Saettler, L. P. (1992). *The evolution of American educational technology.* Englewood, CO: Libraries Unlimited.

ID Competencies

American Association of School Librarians (AASL) and Association for Educational Communications and Technology (AECT). (1998). *Information power: Building partnerships for learning.* Chicago: American Library Association.

American Society for Training and Development (ASTD). (1983). *Models for excellence.* Washington, DC: Author.

Association for Educational Communications and Technology. (2000). *NCATE program standards for initial and advanced educational communications and technology programs.* Washington, DC: Author.

Berge, Z., de Verneil, M., Berge, N., Davis, L., & Smith, D. (2002). The increasing scope of training and development competency. *Benchmarking: An International Journal, 9*(1), 43–61.

International Society for Technology in Education (ISTE). (2001). *Educational computing and technology literacy: Initial endorsement guidelines.* Available: *http://cnets.iste.org/ncate/*

International Technology Education Association (ITEA). (2003). *Advancing excellence in technological literacy: Student assessment, professional development, and program standards.* Reston, VA: Author.

Piskurich, G. M., & Sanders, E. S. (1998). *ASTD models for learning technologies: Roles, competencies, and outputs.* Alexandria, VA: American Society for Training and Development.

Rasmussen, K. L. (2002) Competence at a glance: Professional knowledge, skills, and abilities in the field of instructional design and technology. In R. A. Reiser & J. V. Dempsey (Eds.), *Trends and issues in instructional design and technology* (pp. 375–386). Upper Saddle River, NJ: Merrill/Prentice-Hall.

Richey, R. C., (Ed.), Fields, D. C., & Foxon, M. (2001). (With R. C. Roberts, T. Spannaus, & J. M. Spector.) *Instructional design competencies: The standards* (3rd ed.). Syracuse, NY: ERIC Clearinghouse on Information and Technology, International Board of Standards for Training and Performance Improvement (IBSTPI).

Stolovitch, H. D., Keeps, E. J., & Rodrigue, D. (1999). Skill sets, characteristics, and values for the human performance technologist. In H. D. Stolovitch & E. J. Keeps (Eds.), *Handbook of human performance technology: Improving individual and organizational performance worldwide* (2nd ed., pp. 651–697). San Francisco: Jossey-Bass/Pfeiffer.

ID Models—Old and New

Gustafson, K. L., & Branch, R. (2002). *Survey of instructional design models* (4th ed.). Syracuse, N.Y.: ERIC Clearinghouse on Information and Technology.

Ragan, T. J., & Smith, P. L. (2004). Conditions theory and models for designing instruction. In D. H. Jonassen (Ed.), *Handbook of research for educational communications and technology* (2nd ed.) (pp. 541–569). Mahwah, NJ: Lawrence Erlbaum.

Reigeluth, C. M. (Ed.). (1999). *Instructional design theories and models: A new paradigm of instructional theory,* (Vol. 2). Hillsdale, NJ: Lawrence Erlbaum.

Implementation Training/Train-the-Trainer/Innovation Adoption

Christensen, C. M. (2003). *The innovator's dilemma.* Boston: HarperBusiness.

Hall, G., Loucks, S., et al., (2001). Levels of user of the innovation: A framework for analyzing innovation adoption. In D. Ely & T. Plomp, (Eds.), *Classic writings on instructional technology* (Vol. 2, pp. 113–121). Englewood, CO: Libraries Unlimited.

Havelock, R. J. (1995). *The change agent's guide* (2nd ed.) Englewood Cliffs, NJ: Educational Technology.

Rogers, E. M. (2003). *Diffusion of innovations* (5th ed.). New York: Free Press.

Incorporating Revisions

Hackos, J. T. (1994). *Managing your documentation projects.* New York: John Wiley.

Information Gathering/Data Collection Techniques

Argyrous, G. (2000). *Statistics for social and health research, with a guide to SPSS.* London: Sage.

Creswell, J. W. (1998). *Qualitative inquiry and research design: Choosing among five traditions.* Thousand Oaks, CA: Sage.

Creswell, J. W. (2003). *Research design: Qualitative, quantitative, and mixed methods approaches.* Thousand Oaks, CA: Sage.

Krueger, R. (1988). *Focus groups: A practical guide for applied research.* Thousand Oaks, CA: Sage.

Salkind, N. (2000). *Statistics for people who (think they) hate statistics.* London: Sage.

Instructional Analysis

Gagne, R. M. (1964). Learning hierarchies. *Educational Psychologist, 6,* 1–9.

Rossett, A. (1999). *First things fast: A handbook for performance analysis.* San Francisco: Jossey-Bass/Pfeiffer.

Instructional Design Considerations

Dick, W., & Carey, L. (1978). The systematic design of instruction: Origins of systematically designed instruction. In D. Ely & T. Plomp (Eds.) (2001), *Classic writings on instructional technology,* (Vol. 2, pp. 71–80). Englewood, CO: Libraries Unlimited.

Dick, W., Carey, L., & Carey, J. O. (2001). *The systematic design of instruction* (5th ed). New York: Longman.

Hannafin, M. J., & Hill, J. R. (2002). Epistemology and the design of learning environments. In R. A. Reiser & J. V. Dempsey (Eds.), *Trends and issues in instructional design and technology* (pp. 70–82). Upper Saddle River, NJ: Merrill/Prentice-Hall.

Hodell, C. (2000). *ISD from the ground up.* Alexandria, VA: American Society for Training and Development.

Kristof, R., & Satran, A. (1995). *Interactivity by design.* San Jose, CA: Adobe Press.

Rosenfeld, L., & Morville, P. (1998). *Information architecture for the World Wide Web: Designing large-scale Web sites.* Sebastopol, CA: O'Reilly.

Instructional Design Elements

Briggs, L. J. (Ed.). (1977). *Instructional design: Principles and applications.* Englewood Cliffs, NJ: Educational Technology.

Briggs, L. J., & Wager, W. W. (1981). *Handbook of procedures for the design of instruction* (2nd ed.). Englewood Cliffs, NJ: Educational Technology.

Gustafson, K. L., & Branch, R. M. (2002). *Survey of instructional development models* (4th ed.). Syracuse, NY: ERIC.

Heinich, R. (1984). The proper study of instructional technology. *Educational Communication and Technology, 32,* 67–88.

Jonassen, D. H. (Ed.) (2004). *Handbook of research for educational communications and technology* (2nd ed.). Mahwah, NJ: Lawrence Erlbaum.

Morrison, G. R., Ross, S. M., & Kemp, J. E. (2003). *Designing effective instruction* (4th ed.). New York: John Wiley.

Rothwell, W. J., & Kazanas, H. C. (1998). *Mastering the instructional design process: A systematic approach* (2nd ed.). San Francisco: Jossey-Bass.

Seels, B. B. & Richey, R. C. (1994). *Instructional technology: The definition and domains of the field.* Washington, DC: Association for Educational Communications and Technology.

Tyler, R. (1949). *Basic principles of curriculum and instruction.* Chicago: University of Chicago Press.

Instructional Devices

Ertmer, P. A., & Quinn, J. (2003). *The ID casebook: Case studies in instructional design* (2nd ed.). Upper Saddle River, N.J.: Merrill/Prentice-Hall.

Harless, J. (1986). Guiding performance with job aids. In M. Smith (Ed.), *Introduction to performance technology.* Washington, DC: National Society for Performance and Instruction.

Newstrom, J., & Scannell, E. (1980). *Games trainers play: Experiential learning exercises.* New York: McGraw-Hill.

Rossett, A., & Gautier-Downes, J. (1991). *A handbook of job aids.* San Diego: Pfeiffer.

Instructional Purpose/Organizational Goals

Mager, R. (1972). *Goal analysis.* Belmont, CA: Fearon-Pitman.

Popham, W. J. (1970) *Establishing instructional goals.* Upper Saddle River, NJ: Prentice-Hall.

Instructional Strategies

Ausubel, D. (1960). The use of advance organizers in the learning and retention of meaningful verbal material. *Journal of Educational Psychology, 51,* 267–272.

Briggs, L. (1977). Designing the strategy of instruction. In L. Briggs (Ed.), *Instructional design: Principles and applications.* Englewood Cliffs, NJ: Educational Technology.

Gagne, R., & Driscoll, M. (1988). *Essentials of learning for instruction* (2nd ed.). Englewood Cliffs, NJ: Prentice-Hall.

Jonassen, D. H., Grabinger, S., & Harris, N. (1990). Analyzing and selecting instructional strategies and tactics. *Performance Improvement Quarterly, 3*(2), 29–47.

Miller, G. A. (1956). The magical number seven, plus or minus two: Some limits on our capacity for processing information. *Psychological Review, 63,* 81–97.

Silberman, M., & Silberman, M. L. (1996). *Active learning: 101 strategies to teach any subject.* Boston: Allyn & Bacon.

Willis, B. D. (Ed.). (1994). *Distance education: Strategies and tools.* Englewood Cliffs, NJ: Educational Technology.

Interpersonal Relationships and Skills

Beck, C. E. (1999). *Managerial communication: Bridging theory and practice.* Upper Saddle River, NJ: Prentice-Hall.

Carnegie, D. (1937). *How to win friends and influence people.* New York: Holiday House.

Cennamo, K. S., & Holmes, G. (2001). Developing awareness of client relations through immersion in practice. *Educational Technology 41*(6), 44–49.

Hargrove, R. (1995). *Masterful coaching.* San Francisco: Jossey-Bass/Pfeiffer.

Ingram, A. L., et al. (1994). Working with subject matter experts. *Performance and Instruction, 33*(8), 17–22.

Kouzes, J. M., & Posner, B. Z. (1999). *Encouraging the heart: A leader's guide to rewarding and recognizing others.* San Francisco: Jossey-Bass.

Moller, L. (1995). Working with subject matter experts. *TechTrends 40*(6), 226–27.

Learning Styles and Modalities

Gagne, R. M. (1985). *The conditions of learning* (4th ed.). New York: Holt Rinehart, & Winston.

Sprenger, M. (2003). *Differentiation through learning styles and memory.* Thousand Oaks: Corwin Press.

Tobias, C. U. (1998). *The way they learn.* Colorado Springs, CO: Focus on the Family.

Tobias, C. U. (1998). *The way we work: What you know about working styles can increase your efficiency, productivity, and job satisfaction.* Nashville, TN: Broadman & Holman.

Vernon, M. D. (1971). *The psychology of perception* (2nd ed.). Baltimore: Penguin.

Witkin, H. A., Moore, C. A., Goodenough, D. R., & Cox, P. W. (1977). Field-dependent and field-independent cognitive styles and their educational implications. *Review of Educational Research, 47*(1), 1–64.

Learning Theories

Bandura, A. (1986). *Social foundations of thought and action.* Engelwood Cliffs, NJ: Prentice-Hall.

Brown, J. S., Collins, A., & Duguid, P. (1989). Situated cognition and the culture of learning. *Educational Researcher, 18*(1), 32–42.

Bruner, J. (1966). *Toward a theory of instruction.* Cambridge, MA: Harvard University Press.

Burton, J., Moore, D., & Magliaro, S. (2004). Behaviorism and instructional technology. In D. H. Jonassen (Ed.), *Handbook of research for educational communications and technology (*2nd ed, pp. 3–36). Mahwah, NJ: Lawrence Erlbaum.

Cognition and Technology Group at Vanderbilt. (1990). Anchored instruction and its relationship to situated cognition. *Educational Researcher, 19*(6), 2–10.

Dewey, J. (1933). *How we think.* Boston: Heath.

Driscoll, M. P. (2000). *Psychology of learning for instruction* (2nd ed.). Boston: Allyn & Bacon.

Ertmer, P. A., & Newby, T. J. (1993). Behaviorism, cognitivism, constructivism: Comparing critical features from an instructional design perspective. *Performance Improvement Quarterly,* 6 (4), 50–71.

Gagne, R., Briggs, L., & Wager, W. (1992). *Principles of instructional design* (4th ed.). Fort Worth, TX: HBJ College.

Gardner, H. (1993). *Multiple intelligences: The theory in practice.* New York: Basic Books.

Hlynka, D. (2004). Postmodernism in educational technology: Update: 1996–2002. In D. H. Jonassen (Ed.), *Handbook of research for educational communications and technology* (2nd ed, pp. 243–246). Mahwah, NJ: Lawrence Erlbaum.

Jonassen, D. H. (1991). Objectivism versus constructivism: Do we need a new philosophical paradigm? *Educational Technology Research and Development, 39*(3), 5–14.

Knowles, M. (1998). *The adult learner: The definitive classic in adult education and human resource development.* San Diego: Gulf Professional.

Lave, J., & Wenger, E. (1990). *Situated learning: legitimate peripheral participation.* Cambridge, UK: Cambridge University Press.

Mager, R. (1988). *Making instruction work.* Belmont, CA: Lake.

Pavlov, I. P. (1927). *Conditioned reflexes.* (G.V. Anrep, Trans.). London: Oxford University Press.

Piaget, J., & Inhelder, B. (1969). *The psychology of the child.* New York: Basic Books.

Postlethwait, S. N., Novak, J., & Murray, H. (1972). *The audio-tutorial approach to learning.* Minneapolis: Burgess.

Reigeluth, C., & Stein, F. (1983). The elaboration theory of instruction. In C. Reigeluth (Ed.), *Instructional design theories and models.* Hillsdale, NJ: Lawrence Erlbaum.

Schon, D. A. (1987). *Educating the reflective practitioner: Toward a new design for teaching and learning in the professions.* San Francisco: Jossey-Bass.

Skinner, B. F. (1968). *The technology of teaching.* New York: Appleton-Century-Crofts.

Skinner, B. F. (1974). *About behaviorism.* New York: Vintage Books.

Slavin, R. E. (1995). *Cooperative learning: Theory, research, and practice.* Englewood Cliffs, NJ: Prentice-Hall.

Vygotsky, L. (1978). *Mind and society: The development of higher psychological processes.* Cambridge, MA: Harvard University Press.

Watson, J. B. (1913). Psychology as the behaviorist views it. *Psychological Review, 20,* 158–177.

Media Assets and Attributes

Barron, A. E. (2004). Auditory instruction. In D. H. Jonassen (Ed.), *Handbook of research for educational communications and technology* (2nd ed, pp. 949–978). Mahwah, NJ: Lawrence Erlbaum.

Clark, R. E. (1983). Reconsidering research on learning from media. In D. Ely & T. Plomp (Eds.) (2001), *Classic writings on instructional technology* (Vol. 2, pp. 139–153). Englewood, CO: Libraries Unlimited.

Cronbach, L. J., & Snow, R. E. (1977). *Aptitudes and instructional methods: A handbook for research on interactions.* New York: Irvington.

Dale, E. (1946). The cone of experience. In *Audio-visual methods in teaching* (pp. 37–51). New York: Dryden Press.

Hartley, J. (1996). Text design. In D. H. Jonassen (Ed.), *Handbook of research for educational communications and technology* (pp. 795–820). New York: Simon & Schuster/Macmillan.

Hawkridge, D. (1990). Who needs computers in schools, and why? In D. Ely & T. Plomp (Eds.) (2001), *Classic writings on instructional technology* (Vol. 2, pp. 189–196). Englewood, CO: Libraries Unlimited.

Horton, W. (2000). *Designing Web-based training: How to teach anyone anything anywhere anytime.* New York: John Wiley.

Jonassen, D. H. (1996). *Computers in the classroom: Mindtools for critical thinking.* Englewood Cliff, NJ: Prentice-Hall.

Kozma, R. B. (1991). Learning with media. In D. Ely & T. Plomp (Eds.) (2001), Classic writings on instructional technology (Vol. 2, pp. 155–188). Englewood, CO: Libraries Unlimited.

Lee, W. W., & Owens, D. L. (2000). *Multimedia-based instructional design: Computer-based training, Web-based training, and distance learning.* San Francisco: Jossey-Bass/Pfeiffer.

McAlpine, L., & Weston, C. (1994). The attributes of instructional materials. *Performance Improvement Quarterly, 7*(1), 19–30.

Pett, D., & Wilson, T. (1996). Color research and its application to the design of instructional materials. *Educational Technology Research and Development, 44*(3), 19–35.

Reiser, R. A., & Gagne, R. M. (1983). *Selecting media for instruction.* Englewood Cliffs, NJ: Educational Technology.

Salomon, G. (1994). *Interaction of media, cognition, and learning: An exploration of how symbolic forms cultivate mental skills and affect knowledge acquisition.* (2nd ed.). Hillsdale, NJ: Lawrence Erlbaum.

Message Design

Anglin, G. J., Vaez, H., & Cunningham, K. L. (2004). Visual representations and learning: The role of static and animated graphics. In D. H. Jonassen (Ed.), *Handbook of research for educational communications and technology* (2nd ed., pp. 865–916). Mahwah, NJ: Lawrence Erlbaum.

Aspillaga, M. (1991). Screen design: Location of information and its effects on learning. *Journal of Computer-Based Instruction, 18*(3), 89-92.

Cooper, A. (1995). *About face: Essentials of user interface design.* Foster City, CA: IDG Books Worldwide.

Dwyer, F. M. (1972). *A guide to improving visualized instruction.* State College: Pennsylvania State University, Learning Service Division.

Fleming, M., & Levie, W. H. (1993). *Instructional message design: Principles from the behavioral and cognitive sciences.* Englewood Cliffs, N.J.: Educational Technology.

Horton, W. (1994). *The icon book: Visual symbols for computer systems and documentation.* New York: John Wiley.

Lohr, L. L. (2003). *Creating graphics for learning and performance.* Upper Saddle River: NJ: Merrill/Prentice-Hall.

Moore, D., & Dwyer, F. (Eds.). (1994). *Visual literacy: A spectrum of visual learning.* Englewood Cliffs, NJ: Educational Technology.

Tufte, E. R. (1990). *Envisioning information.* Cheshire, CT: Graphics Press.

Tufte, E. R. (1997). *Visual explanations: Images and quantities, evidence and narrative.* Cheshire, CT: Graphics Press.

Williams, R., & Tollett, J. (2000). *The non-designer's Web book* (2nd ed.). Berkeley, CA: Peachpit Press.

Metacognition

Brown, A. L. (1978). Knowing when, where, and how to remember: A problem of metacognition. In R. Glaser (Ed.), *Advances in instructional psychology* (Vol. 1, pp. 77–165). Hillsdale, NJ: Lawrence Erlbaum.

Brown, A. L. (1987). Metacognition, executive control, self-regulation, and other more mysterious mechanisms. In F. E. Weinert & R. H. Kluwe (Eds.), *Metacognition, motivation, and understanding* (pp. 65-116). Hillsdale, NJ: Lawrence Erlbaum.

Brown, A. L., Bransford, J. D., Ferrara, R. A., & Campione, J. C. (1983). Learning, remembering, and understanding. In J. H. Flavell & E. M. Markman (Eds.), *Handbook of child psychology: Cognitive development* (Vol. 3, pp. 77–166). New York: John Wiley.

Ertmer, P. A., & Newby, T. J. (1996). The expert learner: Strategic, self-regulated, and reflective. *Instructional Science, 24*(1), 1–24.

Flavell, J. H. (1979). Metacognition and cognitive monitoring: A new area of cognitive-developmental inquiry. *American Psychologist, 34*(10), 906–911.

Flavell, J. H. (1987). Speculations about the nature and development of metacognition. In F. E. Weiner & R. H. Kluwe (Eds.), *Metacognition, motivation, and understanding* (pp. 21–29). Hillsdale, NJ: Lawrence Erlbaum.

Hacker, D. J., Dunlosky, J. & Graesser, A. C. (1998). *Metacognition in educational theory and practice.* Hillsdale, NJ: Lawrence Erlbaum.

Kluwe, R. H. (1987). Executive decisions and regulation of problem solving behavior. In F. E. Weinert & R. H. Kluwe (Eds.), *Metacognition, motivation, and understanding* (pp. 31–64). Hillsdale, NJ: Lawrence Erlbaum.

Lin, X. (2001). Designing metacognitive activities. *Educational Technology Research and Development, 49*(2), 23–40.

Lin, X., Hmelo, C., Kinzer, C. K., & Secules, T. J. (1999). Designing technology to support reflection. *Educational Technology Research and Development, 47*(3), 43–62.

Osman, M. E., & Hannafin, M. J. (1992). Metacognition research and theory: Analysis and implications for instructional design. *Educational Technology, Research and Development, 40*(2), 83–99.

Rosenshine, B., Meister, C., & Chapman, S. (1996). Teaching students to generate questions: A review of the intervention studies. *Review of Educational Research, 66*(2), 181–221.

Schmitt, M. C., & Newby, T. J. (1986). Metacognition: Relevance to instructional design. *Journal of Instructional Development, 9*(4), 27–33.

Motivation

Bandura, A., & Schunk, D. H. (1977). Cultivating competence, self-efficacy, and intrinsic interest through proximal self-motivation. *Journal of Personality and Social Psychology, 41*(3), 586–598.

Green, T. (2000). *Motivation management: Fueling performance by discovering what people believe about themselves and their organizations.* Palo Alto, CA: Davies-Black.

Keller, J. M. (1987). Development and use of the ARCS model of motivational design. In D. Ely & T. *Plomp* (Eds.) (2001), *Classic writings on instructional technology* (Vol. 2, pp. 223–238). Englewood, CO: Libraries Unlimited.

Keller, J. M. (1999). Motivational systems. In H. D. Stolovitch & E.J. Keeps (Eds.), *Handbook of human performance technology: Improving individual and organizational performance worldwide* (2nd ed., pp. 373–394). San Francisco: Jossey-Bass/Pfeiffer.

Maslow, A. H. (1970). *Motivation and personality* (2nd ed.). New York: Harper & Row.

Needs Analysis/Assessment

Kaufman, R., & English, F. W. (1979). *Needs assessment: Concept and application.* Englewood Cliffs, NJ: Educational Technology.

Rossett, A. (1987). *Training needs assessment.* Englewood Cliffs, NJ: Educational Technology.

Rossett, A. (1999). *First things fast: A handbook for performance analysis.* San Francisco: Jossey-Bass/Pfeiffer.

Triner, D., Greenberry, A., & Watkins, R. (1996). Training needs assessment: A contradiction in terms? *Educational Technology, 36*, 51–55.

Zemke, R., & Kramlinger, T. (1982). *Figuring things out: A trainer's guide to needs and task analysis.* Reading, MA: Addison-Wesley.

New Developments/Trends in IDT

Duderstadt, J. J. (2000). *A university for the 21stcentury.* Ann Arbor: University of Michigan Press.

Goleman, D. (1998). *Working with emotional intelligence.* New York: Bantam Books.

Moore, M. G., & Anderson, W. G. (Eds.) (2003). *Handbook of distance education.* Mahwah, NJ: Lawrence Erlbaum.

Reiser, R. A., & Dempsey, J. V. (Eds.)(2002). *Trends and issues in instructional design and technology.* Upper Saddle River, NJ: Merrill/Prentice-Hall.

Senge, P. M. (1994). *The fifth discipline.* New York: Doubleday.

Outsourcing—Development, Production, Distribution

Bratton, B. (1979-1980). The instructional development specialist as consultant. *Journal of Instructional Development, 3*(2), 2–8.

Leitzman, D. F., Walter, S., Earle, R. S., & Myers, C. (1979). Contracting for instructional development. *Journal of Instructional Development, 3*(2), 23–28.

Rogers, M. A., & Volpe, S. (1984). Evaluation of vendor courses: A common-sense guide. *Performance and Instruction, 23*(10), 18–22.

Weiss, A. (2000). *Getting started in consulting.* New York: John Wiley.

Performance Improvement

Argyris, C. (1970). *Intervention theory and method: A behavioral science view.* Upper Saddle River, NJ: Pearson/Addison-Wesley.

Langdon, D. G., Whiteside, K. S., & McKenna, M. M. (Eds.). (1999). *Intervention resource guide: 50 performance improvement tools.* San Francisco: Jossey-Bass/Pfeiffer.

Pipe, P., & Mager, R. F. (1999). *Analyzing performance problems: Or you really oughta wanna.* Atlanta: Center for Effective Performance.

Robinson, D. G., & Robinson, J. C. (Eds.). (1998). *Moving from training to performance: A practical guidebook.* San Francisco: Berrett-Koehler.

Rossett, A. (1999). *First things fast: A handbook for performance analysis.* San Francisco: Jossey-Bass/Pfeiffer.

Stolovitch, H. D., & Keeps, E. J. (Eds.). (1999). *Handbook of human performance technology: Improving individual and organizational performance worldwide* (2nd ed.). San Francisco: Jossey-Bass/Pfeiffer.

Van Tiem, D. M., Moseley, J. L., & Dessinger, J. C. (2000). *Fundamentals of performance technology: A guide to improving people, process, and performance.* Washington, DC: ISPI.

Performance Objectives

Bloom, B. S., Mesia, B. B., & Krathwohl, D. R. (1964). *Taxonomy of educational objectives* (2 vols: *The Affective Domain* and *The Cognitive Domain*). New York. David McKay.

Gagne, R. (1977). Analysis of objectives. In L. Briggs (Ed.), *Instructional design: Principles and applications.* Englewood Cliffs, NJ: Educational Technology.

Gagne, R., Briggs, L. & Wager, W. (1992). *Principles of instructional design* (4th ed.). Fort Worth, TX: HBJ College.

Gronlund, N. E. (1999). *How to write and use instructional objectives* (6th ed.). Upper Saddle River, NJ: Prentice-Hall.

Mager, R. F. (1997). *Preparing instructional objectives: A critical tool in the development of effective instruction* (3rd ed.). Atlanta: Center for Effective Performance.

Yelon, S. L. (1991). Writing and using instructional objectives. In L. J. Briggs, K. L. Gustafson, & M. H. Tillman, (Eds.), *Instructional design: Principles and applications.* Englewood Cliffs, NJ: Educational Technology.

Planning the Production Process

Emmott, L. C. (1998). Automating the production of interactive technical documentation and EPSS. *Journal of Interactive Instruction Development, 11*(1), 25–34.

Hackos, J. T. (1994). *Managing your documentation projects.* New York: John Wiley.

Yang, C., et al., (1995). Managing courseware production: An instructional design model with a software engineering approach. *Educational Technology Research and Development, 43*(4), 60–70.

Problem Analysis

Curcio, F. R. (1987). *Teaching and learning: A problem-solving focus*. Reston, VA: National Council of Teachers of Mathematics.

Mager, R. F., & Pipe, P. (1999). *Analyzing performance problems, or you really oughta wanna* (3rd ed.). Atlanta: Center for Effective Performance.

Problem- and Project-Centered Instruction

Curcio, F. R. (1987). *Teaching and learning: A problem-solving focus*. Reston, VA: National Council of Teachers of Mathematics.

Dewey, J. (1933). *How we think: A restatement of the relation of reflective thinking to the educative process*. Boston: Heath.

Dewey, J. (1938). *Experience and education*. New York: Macmillan.

Eggen, P. D., & Kauchak, D. P. (2001). *Strategies for teachers: Teaching content and thinking skills*. Boston: Allyn & Bacon.

Lave, J., & Wenger, E. (1991). *Situated learning: Legitimate peripheral participation*. New York: Cambridge University Press.

Scandura, J. M. (1977). *Problem solving: A structural/process approach with instructional applications*. New York: Academic Press.

Production, Content and Production Documents

Alten, S. R. (2001). *Audio in media with InfoTrac* (6th ed.) Belmont, CA: Wadsworth.

Beach, M., & Kenly, E. (1999). *Getting it printed: How to work with printers and graphic imaging services to assure quality, stay on schedule and control costs* (3rd ed.). Cincinnati, OH: North Light Books.

Cartwright, S. R. (1996). *Pre-production planning for video, film, and multimedia*. Burlington, MA: Focal Press.

Parker, R. C. (2003). *Looking good in print* (5th ed.). Phoenix: Paraglyph Press.

Zettl, H. (1998). *Sight, sound, motion: Applied media aesthetics* (3rd ed). Belmont, CA: Wadsworth.

Zettl, H. (2003). *Video basics 4 with InfoTrac*. Belmont, CA: Wadsworth.

Zettl, H. (2003). *Television production handbook with InfoTrac* (8th ed.). Belmont, CA: Wadsworth.

Professional Development Plans — Publications, Organizations, Conferences, and Education

Bassi, L. J., & Van Buren, M. E. (1999). Sharpening the leading edge. *Training and Development, 53*(1), 23–33.

Bowsher, J. E. (1997). *Revolutionizing workforce performance: A systems approach to mastery*. San Francisco: Jossey-Bass/Pfeiffer.

Industry Report, 2003. (2003, October). *Training, 40*(10).

Klein, J. D. (2002). Professional organizations and publications in instructional design and technology. In R. A. Reiser & J. V. Dempsey (Eds.), *Trends and issues in instructional design and technology* (pp. 367–374). Upper Saddle River, NJ: Merrill/Prentice-Hall.

Reiser, R. A. (2002). Getting an instructional design position: Lessons from a personal history. In R. A. Reiser & J. V. Dempsey (Eds.), *Trends and issues in instructional design and technology* (pp. 347–356). Upper Saddle River, NJ: Merrill/Prentice-Hall.

Project Budgets

Barbazette, J. (2001). *The trainer's support handbook: A practical guide to managing the administrative details of training*. New York: McGraw-Hill.

Graphic Artists Guild. (2004). *Graphic artists guild handbook: Pricing and ethical guidelines* (11th ed.). New York: Graphic Artists Guild.

Waagen, A. K. (2000). How to budget training. *InfoLine, 7*.

Project Proposal and Contracts

Cohen, H. (1989). *You can negotiate anything*. New York: Bantam Books.

Porter-Roth, B. (2001). *Request for proposal: A guide to effective RFP development*. Reading, MA: Addison-Wesley Professional.

White, R. M. (1999). A modest proposal for course design and delivery. *Organization of American Historians Magazine of History, 14*(1), 57–60.

Project Schedules

Beach, M., & Kenly, E. (1999). *Getting it printed: How to work with printers and graphic imaging services to assure quality, stay on schedule and control costs* (3rd ed.). Cincinnati, OH: North Light Books.

Bennatan, E. M. (1992). *On time, within budget*. New York: John Wiley.

Promoting ID

Cohen, S. L. (1993). The art, science, and business of program development. *Training and Development, 47*(5), 49–55.

Gilley, J., & Eggland, S. (1992). *Marketing HRD within organizations: Enhancing the visibility, effectiveness and credibility of programs*. San Francisco: Jossey-Bass.

Matthes, K. (1992). Ways you can market and integrate training programs. *HR Focus, 69*(9), 18.

Training. (1989). Everything you wanted to know from Malcolm Knowles (and weren't afraid to ask). *Training: The Magazine of Human Resources Development, 26*(8), 45–50.

Prototype Development

Piskurich, G. M., (2000). *Rapid instructional design: Learning ID fast and right*. San Francisco: Jossey-Bass/Pfeiffer.

Quality Assurance/Quality Control

Beach, M., & Kenly, E. (1999). *Getting it printed: How to work with printers and graphic imaging services to assure quality, stay on schedule and control costs* (3rd ed.). Cincinnati, OH: North Light Books.

Goetsch, D. L., & Davis, L. (2002). *Quality management: Introduction to total quality management for production, processing, and services* (4th ed.). Upper Saddle River, NJ: Prentice-Hall.

Senge, P. M., et. al. (Eds.) (1994). *Fifth discipline fieldbook: Strategies and tools for building a learning organization.* New York: Currency.

Quality Control

Bonstingl, J. J. (1992*). Schools of quality: An introduction to total quality management in education.* Alexandria, VA: Association for Supervision and Curriculum Development.

Deming, W. E. (1982). *Quality, productivity, and competitive positions.* Cambridge, MA: MIT Press.

Sherry, A. C. (2003). Quality and its measurement in distance education. In M. G. Moore & W. G. Anderson (Eds.), *Handbook of distance education* (pp. 435–460). Mahwah, NJ: Lawrence Erlbaum.

Return on Investment (ROI) and Risk

Davidove, E. (2002). Maximizing training investments by measuring human performance. In R. A. Reiser, & J. V. Dempsey (Eds.), *Trends and issues in instructional design and technology.* Upper Saddle River, NJ: Merrill/Prentice-Hall.

Fitz-Enz, J. (2000). *The ROI of human capital: Measuring the economic value of employee performance.* New York: AMACOM.

Phillips, P. P. (2002). *The bottom line on ROI: Basics, benefits, and barriers measuring training and performance improvement.* Atlanta: Center for Effective Performance.

Waldman, D. P. (1997). Interactive multimedia: Measuring the ROI. *Journal of Instruction Delivery Systems, 11*(1), 21–23.

Review Cycle

Thiagarajan, S. (1999). How to design and guide debriefing. In E. Biech (Ed.), *The 1999 annual: Volume 1, training* (pp. 247–257). San Francisco: Jossey-Bass/Pfeiffer.

Task Analysis

Gagne, R. M. (1985). *The conditions of learning* (4th ed.). New York: Holt, Rinehart, & Winston.

Hackos, J., & Redish, J. (1998). *User and task analysis for interface design.* New York: John Wiley.

Jonassen, D. H., Tessmer, M., & Hannum, W. H. (1999). *Task analysis methods for instructional design.* Hillsdale, NJ: Lawrence Erlbaum.

Merrill, P. F. (1987). Job and task analysis. In R. M. Gagne (Ed.), *Instructional technology: Foundations* (pp. 143–174). Hillsdale, NJ: Lawrence Erlbaum.

Zemke, R., & Kramlinger, T. (1982). *Figuring things out: A trainer's guide to needs and task analysis.* Reading, MA: Addison-Wesley.

Teaching Strategies, Learning Procedures

Ebert-May, D., Brewer, C., & Allred, S. (1997). Innovation in large lecture—Teaching for active learning. *Bioscience, 47*(9), 601–607.

Gagne, R., & Medsker, K. (1996). *The conditions of learning: Training applications.* Fort Worth, TX: Harcourt Brace.

Joyce, B., & Weil, M., & Calhoun, E. (2000). *Models of teaching* (6th ed.). Boston: Allyn & Bacon.

Orlich, D. C., Harder, R. J., Callahan, R. C., & Gibson, H. W. (2001). *Teaching strategies: A guide to better instruction.* Boston: Houghton Mifflin.

Rowland, G. (1994). Educating instructional designers: Different methods for different outcomes. *Educational Technology, 34*(6), 5–11.

Skinner, B. F. (1954). The science of learning and the art of teaching. *Harvard Education Review, 24,* 86–97.

Suchman, R. J. (1964). Studies in inquiry training. In R. Ripple & V. Bookcastle (Eds.), *Piaget reconsidered.* Ithaca, NY: Cornell University Press.

Testing: Pilot, Usability, Field, and Prototype

Barnum, C. M., & Dragga, S. (2001). *Usability testing and research.* Upper Saddle River, NJ: Longman/Pearson.

Dumas, J. S., & Redish, J. C. (1999). *A practical guide to usability testing.* Bristol, England: Intellect.

Dustin, E., Rashka, J., McDiarmid, D., & Nielson, J. (2001). *Quality Web systems: Performance, security and usability.* Reading, MA: Addison-Wesley.

Forte, I., & Schurr, S. (1995). *Making portfolios, products, and performances meaningful and manageable for students and teachers: Instructional strategies and thematic activities.* Nashville, TN: Incentive.

Rubin, J. (1994). *Handbook of usability testing: How to plan, design and conduct effective tests.* New York: John Wiley.

Schriver, K. A. (1996). *Dynamics in document design: Creating text for readers.* New York: John Wiley.

Usability Testing/Prototype Evaluation

Mayhew, D. J. (1999). *The usability engineering lifecycle.* San Diego: Morgan Kaufmann.

Nielsen, J. (1994). *Usability engineering.* San Diego: Academic Press.

Schriver, K. A. (1996). *Dynamics in document design: Creating text for readers.* New York: John Wiley.

Visioning Tools, Brainstorming, Scenarios

Carroll, J. M. (1995). *Scenario-based design.* New York: John Wiley.

Clark, C. (1989). *Brainstorming: How to create successful ideas.* Hollywood, CA: Wilshire Book.

Cooper, A., & Saffo, P. (1999). *The inmates are running the asylum: Why high tech products drive us crazy and how to restore the sanity.* Indianapolis, IN: Sams.

Kelley, T., Littman, J., & Peters, T. (2001). *The art of innovation: Lessons in creativity from IDEO, America's leading design firm.* New York: Doubleday.

Latham, J. R. (1995). Visioning: The concept, trilogy, and process. *Quality Progress, 28*(4), 65–68.

Warmke, C., & Buchanan, L. (2003). *Idea revolution: Guidelines and prompts for brainstorming alone, in groups or with clients.* Cincinnati, OH: How Design Books.

Writing and Readability

Gunning, R. (1952). *The technique of clear writing.* New York: McGraw-Hill.

Kellogg, R. T. (1994). *Psychology of writing.* Oxford, England: Oxford University Press.

Sharples, M. (1999). *How we write: Writing as creative design.* New York: Routledge.

Strunk, W., Jr., & White, E. (2000). *The elements of style* (4th ed.). Boston: Allyn & Bacon.

Index